CELEBRATING CHRISTIAN
MARRIAGE

CELEBRATING CHRISTIAN MARRIAGE

Edited by

ADRIAN THATCHER

T&T CLARK
EDINBURGH & NEW YORK

T&T CLARK LTD

A Continuum imprint

59 George Street
Edinburgh EH2 2LQ
Scotland
www.tandtclark.co.uk

370 Lexington Avenue
New York 10017–6503
USA
www.continuumbooks.com

First published 2001

ISBN 0 567 08820 0

British Library Cataloguing-in-Publication Data
A catalogue record for this book is available from the British Library

Typeset by Fakenham Photosetting Ltd, Fakenham, Norfolk NR21 8NN
Printed and bound in Great Britain by MPG Books, Bodmin

Contents

Introduction

Adrian Thatcher

How is the good news of Jesus Christ to be spoken, heard and lived in the area of sexuality and marriage? Amid the bad news of the global marriage crisis, what is the good news? What signs of hope are to be discerned in the gloom of marital breakdown and avoidance? *Celebrating Christian Marriage* is a source book of hope. It is offered to all Christian people who are interested in marriage or whose ministry touches marriage, marriage preparation and marriage enrichment. It is a *theological* book which, borrowing biblical language, breathes new life into marital theology and makes it serviceable to the churches and their ministers. It is for bishops and clergy, for clerical and lay people, and particularly for students and researchers in Christian theology, Christian ethics and Christian marriage.

No one will deny that marriage at the beginning of the new millennium is in a world-wide crisis. The crisis is economic (because of the cost of family breakdown), social (because of the consequences for schooling, housing, welfare support, etc.), political (because governments face increasing pressure from alarmed groups to discriminate positively in favour of marriage), personal (because the death of a partnership is likely to cause hurt, sometimes far beyond the partners themselves), moral (because a society in which marriages come apart becomes incapable of providing support for marriage as an institution), and spiritual (not least because the rise of marital breakdown may be linked to the rise of increasing individualism, or, more familiarly, selfishness).

The contours of the crisis are, by now, well known. The average age of first marriage is now in the late 20s: not surprisingly couples live together before marriage (at least 70% of them), and, more often, with no thought of marriage at all. The rising number of births outside of marriage (currently a third in the United Kingdom) indicates the severing of the age-old connection of marriage with parenthood. There is growing evidence that, generally speaking, divorce damages children and that father absence is a burden for them, especially for boys. Short-term cohabitations often end up as single-parent families. These changes are themselves to be understood within broader global trends and demographic shifts (which are analysed in Part 1). The sheer number of people living together prior to marriage, and marrying again after divorce, has placed traditional Christian teaching under enormous pressure and caused seismic disagreement within the churches.

In June 2000 an international four-day conference to discuss these matters was held at the College of St Mark and St John, Plymouth, UK – a Higher Education College of Anglican foundation. This book is based on the best of the papers presented at the conference, all of them revised for inclusion within it. The conference had very specific aims. It sought to stimulate fresh interdisciplinary scholarship and research in the area of Christian marriage; to promote dialogue between different theological, ecclesial and religious traditions; to provide new thinking for the churches in coping with the theological and pastoral problems associated with marriage and marital breakdown; to deepen Christian understanding of all aspects of marriage in rapidly changing social settings, and to learn from the experience of single, divorced and remarried people, and from Christians who are lesbian or gay.

A team of world leaders in the field was invited, and then a further call for papers was issued. The conference attracted a unique blend of researchers and practitioners. There were leading theologians and ethicists. They represented all the major areas of Christendom – Roman Catholic, Orthodox, Anglican, Lutheran, Reformed, and other Protestant denominations. The ecumenical dialogue was rich, but was supplemented by another dialogue, between theologians on the one hand, and historians, canon lawyers, demographers and psychotherapists on the other. Then, in the best traditions of *applied* theology, representatives from various marriage ministries and marriage charities, eager to draw from theology and quick to detect when theological teaching is unserviceable in the context of marriage ministry, further enriched the conference dialogue.

This then was no ordinary academic conference, but one which was unusually ecumenical, interdisciplinary, practical and highly focused, all at the same time. One hundred and thirty people from eleven countries came together. It has not been possible to find room for every paper, and several of them have been reduced in order to increase the range of topics available within the covers of a single book. Forty papers were presented. All but one of the twenty-seven published in this volume are published for the first time. The papers are arranged in eight parts. Each has a short introduction which is intended to make the book easier to use. Part 1 examines the changing global context for marriage; Part 2 examines the beginning of marriage, attending to the recovery of the theology and practice of betrothal, and to the practicalities of marriage preparation as a vital Christian ministry. Part 3 contains contemporary Orthodox and Roman Catholic treatments of marriage, especially the place of love within it, and a sociological account of love, which is likely to be useful to theologians for many years.

Part 4 concentrates on the marriage relationship. There are chapters on the need to complement skills training with theological understanding, on recognising (and avoiding) the causes of marriage breakdown, on coping pastorally with the male 'mid-life' crisis, on the positive incorporation of the ageing process into shared marital experience, and on the 'hell' of violent, patriarchal marriages. The shorter Part 5 raises crucial questions about children: whether the intention to have children is fundamental to marriage, and whether many contemporary social attitudes to children, including the intention to avoid having them, are evidence of a serious social malaise. Part 6 contains two highly original contributions to the growing body of literature on single-sex marriages. These two chapters both introduce readers to some of this literature while contributing uniquely to it.

Parts 7 and 8 provide a range of Roman Catholic (Part 7) and Anglican (Part 8) perspectives on annulment, divorce and remarriage. The four Roman Catholic papers severally explain and defend, and critique and reconstruct, Catholic teaching, especially on indissolubility (and its pastoral consequences). Part 8 includes a highly qualified episcopal view of recent Church of England publications on marriage and divorce, and highly illuminating contributions from historians and canon lawyers on the development of Anglican attitudes over several centuries.

Chapters in every part are capable of provoking further reflection, dialogue and research. They provide a rich digest of ecumenical and interdisciplinary materials from scholars and practitioners at the cutting edge of their respective disciplines. The book itself is striking evidence of a resilience of positive, international marital theology that will encourage new hopes and agendas for years to come.

Contributors

Alan Bray is an historian and Honorary Research Fellow of Birkbeck College, University of London. He is author of the pioneering *Homosexuality in Renaissance England* (London: GMP, 1982; Tokyo: Sairyusha, 1993; New York: Columbia University Press, 1995). His forthcoming book *The Friend* is a history of friendship in traditional European society.

Aldegonde Brenninkmeijer-Werhahn is Director of the International Academy for Marital Spirituality (INTAMS). Her recent publications include 'An Interview with Cardinal C. M. Martini' (*INTAMS Review*, 1999), 'The Year of the Lord in Married Life' (*INTAMS Review*, 2000) and *Se former toute au long de la vie: authenticité et développement: Se préparer à vieillir ensemble* (forthcoming 2001). Current projects include *Tussen Man en Vrouw (For Better and for Worse)*, a television broadcast, and the INTAMS Summer Course 2001, *For Love's Sake? Rethinking the Basis of Marriage.*

Don Browning is Alexander Campbell Professor of Religious Ethics and the Social Sciences at the Divinity School, University of Chicago. He is Director of the Lilly Endowment funded Religion, Culture, and Family Project. He is co-author of the summary book of the project titled *From Culture Wars to Common Ground: Religion and the American Family Debate* (Westminster John Knox, 1997). He is the author of seven other books, including *Religious Thought and the Modern Psychologies* (Fortress Press, 1987) and *A Fundamental Practical Theology* (Fortress Press, 1991).

Timothy J. Buckley is a Redemptorist priest, ordained in 1970, who has had a variety of pastoral experiences. These include the preaching of missions and retreats, being parish priest of two large parishes, and working in the formation of future priests at the Franciscan Study Centre in Canterbury. In 1990 he undertook a research project on the pastoral care of the separated and divorced for the Catholic bishops in England and Wales. They received their report in 1994 and his doctoral thesis on the same subject was published under the title *What binds Marriage?* (Geoffrey Chapman, 1997).

Jon Davies was until recently Senior Lecturer and Head of the Religious Studies Department at the University of Newcastle upon Tyne. He is now retired. He is married with three children and two grandchildren. He has written on urban politics and town planning, the family and sexual behaviour, war, war memorials and war remembrance. His most recent book is *Death, Burial and Rebirth in the Religions of Antiquity* (Routledge, 1999). He is a contributor to Digby Anderson's *A Dictionary of Dangerous Words* (The Social Affairs Unit, 2000). He is joint editor of *The Lance*, the parish magazine of St George's Church, Newcastle.

Jack Dominian is now a retired psychiatrist. He is chairman of the marital research organisation One Plus One. In 1994 he was awarded the MBE for his work on marriage. He is author of several books on marriage and sexuality, including *Passionate and Compassionate Love* (Darton, Longman & Todd, 1991). His latest book, *Let's Make Love* (Darton, Longman & Todd, 2001), is a Christian study of sexual intercourse. There is a forth-coming book called *The Church: A Community of Love.*

Duncan Dormor has been Chaplain of St John's College in Cambridge since 1998. In addition to his liturgical and pastoral duties he teaches sociological and anthropological approaches to religion in the University. He holds degrees in Human Sciences and Theology from Oxford as well as a Masters in Demography from London. Before ordination into the Church of England, he worked for the charity One Plus One, Marriage and Partnership Research and has published in the area of marriage, cohabitation and divorce including *The Relationship Revolution* (One Plus One, 1992), and on the ethics of genetic research.

Margaret A. Farley is the Gilbert L. Stark Professor of Christian Ethics at Yale University Divinity School. She is the author or editor of five books, including *Personal Commitments: Beginning, Keeping, Changing* (San Francisco: Harper, 1986). Her numerous published essays include 'The Role of Experience in Moral Discernment' in *Christian Ethics: Problems and Prospects* (eds. J. Childress and L. Cahill, Cleveland, OH: Pilgrim Press, 1996). She is currently working on a book entitled *Just Love: A Framework for Christian Sexual Ethics.* She is past president of the

Society of Christian Ethics and of the Catholic Theological Society of America.

Greg Forster has been Rector of Northenden, in S. Manchester, since 1979. Until recently he was co-ordinator of the editorial panel for Grove Ethical Studies, and is currently preparing a study on the ethics of the Epistles of James and John for that series. A parallel project (reflected in this collection) is a study of Jesus' ethical teaching methods in their historical context. His critique of the Anglican bishops' *Marriage in Church after Divorce* appeared in *Anvil* (17:3) in 2000. He is the author of *Healing Love's Wounds, a pastoral approach to divorce and remarriage* (MarshallPickering, 1995).

Stavros S. Fotiou, BEd (Pedagogical Academy of Cyprus), BTh (University of Athens), ThD (University of Athens), is Assistant Professor of Christian Education in the Department of Education at the University of Cyprus. His latest books are *Freedom and Love* and *Sexuality, Eros and Love*. He has recently published articles in *Theology Today*, *Phronema* and *Greek Orthodox Theological Review*.

Reg Harcus, BD, MPhil, is Vicar of St Mary Magdalene, Bolney, in Chichester Diocese and Area Adult Education Officer in the diocese. He is on the staff of the Centre for Continuing Education, University of Sussex, currently researching a PhD thesis on Clement of Alexandria. He is Canon of St Peter's Cathedral, Koforidua, Ghana. He is author of articles on Clement of Alexandria, Cyprian and the early history of marriage.

Jacqueline Humphreys is a barrister practising from St John's Chambers in Bristol. She specialises in family and matrimonial law and is a regional and national committee member of the Family Law Bar Association. She is also undertaking an LLM in Canon Law at Cardiff University and is a lay representative on the General Synod of the Church of England.

Lisa Isherwood is Senior Lecturer at the College of St Mark and St John, Plymouth. She is executive editor of the journal *Feminist Theology* (Sheffield Academic Press) and a founder member of the Britain and Ireland School of Feminist Theology. Her publications include *The Good News of the Body*

(Sheffield Academic Press, 2000), *Liberating Christ* (Pilgrim Press, 1999) and *Introducing Body Theology* (with Elizabeth Stuart, Sheffield Academic Press, 1998).

Thomas Knieps-Port le Roi has a PhD in theology from the University of Bonn, Germany, and is academic collaborator of the International Academy for Marital Spirituality (INTAMS) and co-editor of *INTAMS Review*. His doctoral thesis was published as *Die Unvertretbarkeit von Individualität: Der wissenschafts-philosophische Ort der Theologie nach Karl Rahners 'Hörer des Wortes'* (Würzburg: Echter, 1995). He is currently working in the field of the sacramental and ecumenical theology of marriage. He is married to Annette Port le Roi and living in Leuven, Belgium.

George Lotter is Associate Professor in Practical Theology and Director of the Pastoral Counselling Centre, Potchefstroom University, South Africa. His recent publications include *The Great God with Small Groups* (1999 – co-author), *Pastoral Care of Ministers' Wives* (1999 – co-author) and *Reconciliation and Possible Symbols of Reconciliation in Contemporary South Africa* (*Koers – Bulletin for Christian Scholarship*, 2000). His current projects include 'The Bible and Human Rights' and 'Women in Church and Society' (with special focus on compassion and South African women).

Philip A. Mellor is Senior Lecturer in Sociology of Religion in the Department of Theology and Religious Studies at the University of Leeds. He is the author, with Chris Shilling, of *Re-forming the Body: Religion, Community and Modernity* (Sage, 1997), the forthcoming *The Elementary Forms of Social Life* (Sage, 2001), and numerous articles dealing with religion, identity and society.

Cathy Molloy received her Licentiate in Theology from the Milltown Institute of Theology and Philosophy in Dublin where, until recently, she was an Associate Lecturer, specialising in the theology of marriage. She is author of *Marriage: Theology and Reality* (Dublin: Columba Novalis, 1996). She has worked with groups in Dublin and Belfast and as a member of the Cherry Orchard Faith and Justice Group she is co-author of *One City Two Tiers: A Theological Reflection on Life in a Divided Society* (Dublin: Jesuit Centre for Faith and Justice, 1996).

Cordelia Moyse is a twentieth-century historian who is writing a history of the Mothers' Union while acting as that organisation's consultant archivist. Her research has taken her to Ghana and South Africa. She is a fellow of the George Bell Institute, a supranational fellowship of writers, scholars and artists. Recent publications include 'Déjà vu – Marriage, Divorce and the Church of England in the Twentieth Century', *International Family Law* (May 2000); 'The Novels of Sushaku Endo', *Humanitas* (Sept. 1999). She was a contributor to BBC Radio 4's 'Divorce – Right or Privilege?' (Summer 2000).

Philip Newman was born in Melbourne in 1940, where he attended an Anglican school. He trained for the ordained ministry through King's College, London. He married an American in 1965 and they had three children, one of whom died in his twenties. Ordained in Melbourne in 1967, he has served mainly in parishes there. An archdeacon for seventeen years and Vicar of St John's, Toorak, for twelve, his main interests are parish ministry, social justice, ecumenism and human relations.

Augur Pearce is a solicitor and ecclesiastical notary, now pursuing research into church legal history at Magdalene College, Cambridge, where he holds the Kingsley Bye-Fellowship. His principal area of interest is the development of church-legal institutions and the understanding of the church-nation relationship to which these testify; and his doctoral thesis will compare nineteenth-century Prussia in this respect with twentieth-century England. Among his articles recently published or accepted for publication are 'Denomination or Public Religion? The Law's Recent Attitude to the Church of England', 'Sacred Time – An Historical Perspective' and 'Public Religion in the English Colonies'.

Paul Robbins is a judge of the Metropolitan Tribunal of Liverpool with the title Assistant to the Judicial Vicar. He is in full-time employment with the Archdiocese of Liverpool processing applications for marriage nullity. He is a regular contributor to the Newsletter of the Canon Law Society of Great Britain and Ireland. He has published a book, *What God has NOT United* (Minerva Press, 1996), which explains for lay people the theory and practice of marriage nullity within the Catholic Church.

Michael Scott-Joynt has been the (Church of England) Bishop of Winchester since 1995. He serves as the Archbishops' Liaison with Broken Rites, the self-help organisation for deserted clergy wives. Since its inception in 1994 he has been a member of the House of Bishops' Working Group on Issues in Human Sexuality. He chaired the House of Bishops' Working Party which produced the Discussion Paper *Marriage in Church After Divorce* (January 2000). He and his wife have been married for thirty-five years, and have three adult children.

Helen Stanton studied theology at the Universities of Birmingham and Manchester. An Anglican lay woman, she has worked in a variety of church contexts, including Christian Aid, and as Anglican Chaplain to the University of Sheffield. Currently she is Social Responsibility Officer for the Diocese of Bath and Wells. She teaches and writes mainly about liberation theologies, including feminist theology. She has published several articles in the *British Journal of Theological Education*. She is author of *Christian Feminism: An Introduction* (Darton, Longman & Todd/Affirming Catholicism) and editor of Tissa Balasuriya's *Mary and Human Liberation* (Mowbray, 1997).

Elizabeth Stuart holds the Chair in Christian Theology at King Alfred's College, Winchester. She is executive editor of the academic journal *Theology and Sexuality* and executive general editor of the book series *Studies in Theology and Sexuality* published by Sheffield Academic Press. She has published several books on theology and sexuality including *Just Good Friends* (Mowbray, 1995) and (with others) *Religion is a Queer Thing* (Cassell, 1997). She is currently working on a critical history of lesbian and gay theology.

Simon J. Taylor is an ordinand at St Michael's College, Llandaff, and an Associate Research Fellow of the Lincoln Theological Institute, University of Sheffield. He is currently engaged in research in two areas: the ethics of the global economy; and the ecclesiological implications of the establishment of the Church of England.

Adrian Thatcher has taught at the College of St Mark and St John, Plymouth, since 1977, and became Professor of Applied Theology there in 1995. He was the organiser of the International Marriage Conference. After writing *The Ontology* of *Paul Tillich* (Oxford University Press, 1978) and *Truly a Person, Truly God* (SPCK, 1990), he turned to questions of Christian sexual ethics. *Liberating Sex* (SPCK, 1993) and *Marriage after Modernity* (Sheffield Academic Press and New York University Press, 1999) are among his best-known writings. He is married to Grace, and is an Anglican.

John Wall, PhD (The University of Chicago Divinity School), is Assistant Professor of Religion at Rutgers University in Camden, NJ, USA. He is co-editor of the forthcoming *Marriage, Health, and the Professions: The Implications of the Health Benefits of Marriage for the Professions of Law, Medicine, Ministry, Therapy, and Business* (Eerdmans, 2001). He is author of several articles on the moral thought of French philosopher Paul Ricoeur, and on various issues in family ethics. He is currently finishing a book on Ricoeur's ethics and starting a new book on the meaning and purpose of child-rearing in the Christian traditions.

Timothy J. Woods is Director for Church and Society in the Anglican Diocese of Salisbury, having previously served in parish ministry in Devon. His paper entitled 'A Tendency to Unaffected Cheerfulness: Some Theological Reflections on Downs Syndrome' was published in *Contact – the Interdisciplinary Journal of Pastoral Studies*, 127 (1998), and his essay entitled 'Remarriage and the Church of England' appeared in *INTAMS Review* 6 (Autumn 2000). He is married to Philippa, and they have four children.

Acknowledgements

The book could not have been written without help from many people. Thanks are due to the Principal of the College of St Mark and St John, Dr John Rea, and the Dean of Social Sciences and Humanities, Dr Geoff Stoakes, for their unfailing encouragement and support for the conference as a big idea that was allowed to happen. I thank the conference attenders (getting to Plymouth from anywhere is no easy matter) as well as the invited speakers and distinguished readers of papers. Their interaction was a sign of hope for the future of marriage and an indicator of how marriage research must proceed. Caroline Major has been indefatigable in her support for the conference and for this book, from beginning to end. She helped to plan the conference, then organised it, and then acted as research assistant in compiling the final manuscript for publication and dealing with queries to and from authors. Her flair was a major reason for the success of the overall project. Most of all, support from Grace Thatcher for her husband, during the hours of planning and preparing, delivering and editing, enabled the project to happen.

Marriage at the Start of the New Millennium

Introduction

Part 1 grounds the changes happening to marriage in broader social perspectives. Don Browning provides a description of 'the world situation of families'; Duncan Dormor confines himself to Europe. Both authors use social theory and empirical observation in order to explain some of the sociological and demographic shifts which are shaping present and future attitudes to marriage, and which are 'pre-theological', so to speak, in that they provide the very earth in which any seeds of Christian hope might be sown. Browning borrows from social theory the concepts of modernisation and globalisation and notes the evaporation of earlier optimism about each in the 1990s.

Dormor describes and analyses the 'second demographic transition', i.e., how the evolution of the social system in Europe is connected by demographers with profound changes in marital and reproductive behaviour. This transition generally assumes the power of contraception to alter sexual and 'relationship formation behaviour'. It assumes a 'path of innovation' which diffuses unconventional behaviour and over a short time renders it conventional. The processes involved are generally thought to be inevitable (and convergent), and something called 'individualism' or 'individualisation' is thought to be heavily implicated in what is going on. Dormor assesses these assumptions. He accepts the first, but shows how diversity of behaviour in the different parts of the continent of Europe (e.g., in premarital cohabitation and recourse to divorce) does not justify uniform or predictable trends. And he holds that a certain kind of individualism is actually compatible with positive support for marriage and family.

The lack of inevitability about the direction and force of the social changes accompanying the experience of marriage reverberates loudly in Browning's essay, for he firmly believes that the forces of modernisation are yet able to be controlled and harnessed in support of human good. The 'reformation' of marriage is achievable in the USA, and everywhere else. This is the 'cultural work' he advocates. Such work requires the critical reformulation of Christian theological traditions, and a coalition of interests in which the churches play a part and seek to influence public life. Browning's description of the elements of such a coalition deserves to become a theological and ecclesial agenda which will preoccupy theologians and religious leaders for many years.

1

The World Situation of Families: Marriage Reformation as a Cultural Work

Don Browning

Over the last twenty years, there has been a momentous debate in the United States over the present and future well-being of the American family. The United States is not alone in these disputes; other societies, especially among the so-called modernised countries, have analogous controversies. During recent trips to Australia, South Korea, England, and South Africa, I learned that these countries also have conflicts over the family and that the disputing parties and contentious issues are analogous to those in the United States. In each country there are progressive and conservative voices of both a religious and secular kind, various brands of feminism, and Catholics, Protestants, Jews and other religions that are divided between liberal and orthodox wings.

These debates are about real issues. There are powerful new trends sweeping through both advanced and underdeveloped countries that are changing families and undermining their ability to perform their customary tasks. These forces are often called the forces of modernisation. Modernisation and its effects on families will be a central concern of this chapter. But theories of modernisation are now being extended by theories of globalisation.[1] Whether one refers to these forces with the terms modernisation or globalisation, these processes are having disruptive consequences on families in all corners of the

---

[1] Roland Robertson, *Globalization: Social Theory and Global Culture* (London: Sage, 1992).

earth. Older industrial countries have the wealth to cushion the blows of this disruption, but poorer countries may be wounded beyond recovery.

Most social scientists are now ready to acknowledge that these forces are disruptive to families and costly to society. These scientists feel there is very little that can be done to alter their inevitable consequences. I do not share this view. I argue that much can be done, but only if we understand the task as a complex cultural work. By a cultural work, I have in mind something like weaving together a richly designed tapestry containing many different threads. The threads needed for this cultural task are religious, political, legal, economic and psychological. No one strategy alone can accomplish what needs to be done. In addition, this cultural work must be world-wide in scope.

Not all changes wrought by modernity are negative to families. New educational and economic possibilities for women in many countries are promising, but they may not always convert into realities. Furthermore, they may go hand in hand with other trends that could undermine these advances, such as the mounting impoverishment of millions of women and children due to family disruption, the increased violence of many young people, and the growing absence of huge numbers of fathers from their children. Education and jobs will not by themselves cure world family disruption. These worthwhile strategies must be supplemented by the world-wide revival and reconstruction of the institution of marriage.

Modernisation and the World Situation of Families

The world is large, and contemporary transformations of family life are quite complex. For that reason, we should avoid becoming lost in the details of what is happening in specific countries. Permit me, therefore, to begin with some grand theories of family change. There are a small number of outstanding sociologists who are attempting to describe and explain the world-wide metamorphoses of family life. I will review the writings of William Goode, David Popenoe and Alan Wolfe as examples of such efforts. Although social scientists by profession aspire for objectivity, what distinguishes these three has more to do with their wider philosophical and ethical assumptions than their methodologies or empirical facts.

William Goode

William Goode is the father of the sociology of world family transformations. In two massive books, written thirty years apart, he collected huge quantities of data and developed a commanding theoretical framework to account for what is happening to families throughout the world. He moved fearlessly over the face of the earth – Western Europe, the United States, Asia (India, China, Japan and Malaysia), and sub-Saharan Africa. In 1964 he published *World Revolution and Family Patterns* which demonstrated the global movement away from extended-family patterns to the convenient fit between industrialisation and what he called the 'conjugal' and 'companionate' family pattern.[2] This early book had an optimistic, if not triumphalist, tone to it. He thought that the West, more specifically England and Northern Europe, had exported to the world a modernising trend which joined a conjugal family pattern to a wealth-producing industrialisation process. This conjugal family had helped both to create and then to serve the emerging industrial order. He admitted that we may never know whether this new family brings more happiness than older, extended and patriarchal patterns. However, he did say,

> I welcome the great changes now taking place, and not because it might be a more efficient instrument of industrialization, for that is irrelevant in my personal scheme. Rather, I see in it and in the industrial system that accompanies it the hope of a greater freedom: from the domination of elders, from caste and racial restrictions, from class rigidities. Freedom is *for* something as well: the unleashing of personal potentials, the right to love, to equality within the family, to the establishment of a new marriage when the old has failed. I see the world revolution in family patterns as part

---

[2] William Goode, *World Revolution and Family Patterns* (London: Free Press of Glencoe, 1964).

of a still more important revolution that is sweeping the world in our time, the aspiration on the part of billions of people to have the right for the first time *to choose* for themselves – an aspiration that has toppled governments both old and new, and created new societies and social movements.

For me, then, the major and sufficing justification for the newly emerging family patterns is that they offer people at least the potentialities of greater fulfillment, even if most do not seek it or achieve it.[3]

At the conclusion of his 1963 book, Goode believed that the simple promise – the mere hint – of more individual fulfilment justified optimism over the radical family transformations accelerating before his very eyes. In nearly every country he studied in the early 1960s, Goode found smaller families, more women working, more equality between husband and wife, more mobility, more education for both sexes – especially for women – and less control by the extended family over the conjugal couple. Goode distinguished between the nuclear family and the conjugal family. The latter was still related to the extended family, but less economically and psychologically controlled by it than in earlier times. He used the phrase 'nuclear family' as an idealised construct to describe a theoretically possible couple more radically disconnected from community and extended family – something that Goode actually thought could not be systematically achieved without the use of political force.[4] Everywhere, however, that the conjugal family spread, Goode believed that couples were freer to choose one another, freer to dissolve the marriage, freer to control their procreation, and freer to control individually their relation to the world outside the home.

Three decades later when Goode wrote *World Changes in Divorce Patterns* (1994), his optimism was tempered. The comfortable fit between the conjugal family and industrialisation described in his earlier work is now perceived as breaking down. Yes, there were still world trends toward the

---

[3] Goode, *World Revolution*, p. 380.
[4] Goode, *World Revolution*, pp. 370–1.

conjugal family and, yes, the conjugal family had the mobility and flexibility to serve the ever more dynamic engines of modernisation. But industrialisation and modernisation were now seen to be playing dirty tricks on the conjugal family. Modernity's speed of change, its capacity to subdue all face-to-face human interactions, whether families or small communities, to the dictates of efficiency and rational production, and its newer ability to shift with breathtaking ease both labour and capital around the world without respect for the elementary requirements of enduring human relations – all of this and more has now made the old friend modernisation at least a testy neighbour if not an outright enemy of the conjugal family. All Western and many non-Western societies are becoming what Goode calls 'high-divorce societies'.[5] Furthermore, he was aware that cohabitation and out-of-wedlock births have dramatically increased in all Western societies. Hand in hand with these movements have been the growing poverty and declining well-being of large numbers of women and children. This 'feminisation of poverty' has had negative effects in wealthy countries but even more devastating consequences in poor ones. In developing societies, family disruption further aggravates poverty and overpopulation.[6]

The formula seems to go like this. The conjugal family helped create industrialisation and modernisation and for a few decades there seemed to be a compatible fit between them. Then, suddenly, modernisation turned and began devouring the conjugal family. From one perspective, Friedrich Engels seems correct in his prediction that modernisation in the form of a market economy would destroy families.[7] Engels did not understand, however, that the bureaucratisation of life by socialist societies would have an equally devastating impact on families.

[5] William Goode, *World Changes in Divorce Patterns* (New Haven, CT: Yale University Press, 1993), p. 336.

[6] Goode, *World Changes*, p. 321; for early insights into the feminisation of poverty and how family disruption contributes to it, see Lenore Weitzman, *The Divorce Revolution: The Unexpected Social and Economic Consequences for Women and Children in America* (New York: Free Press, 1985).

[7] Friedrich Engels, *The Origin of the Family, Private Property, and the State* (New York: International Publications, 1972).

But, as Goode points out, there is no straight line between modernisation and the rise of a high-divorce culture. For instance, as Japan industrialised its divorce rate actually declined. The nineteenth-century Japanese practice of early marriage and patrilocality of the young couple frequently ended in divorce, generally due to conflicts between bride and mother-in-law.[8] This practice had few negative social consequences because the bride returned to the custody of her parents, generally had not yet produced a child, and often got married a second time. But this divorce tradition came to an end as a result of government pressures. The restoration of the Meiji ruling family brought with it the marriage code of 1898 that discouraged divorce and gave government sanction to a patriarchal *samurai* and neo-Confucian marriage pattern.[9] Hence, the power of governmental decree actually stabilised the family for decades during rapid Japanese industrialisation, albeit along highly patriarchal lines.

Goode presents other examples of stable high-divorce societies. Most Arab countries permit men easily to divorce their wives even though the Koran actually discourages the practice. But the father, brothers and uncles customarily rally to protect the divorced woman, saving her from poverty and loneliness. Furthermore, most Arab countries have been high-remarriage societies because of cultural values that define marriage as the only viable role for women.[10]

But there is another model of a stable, high family-disruption society. Goode nominates most Scandinavian countries, especially Sweden, as examples of this model. Sweden's extensive system of social supports for divorced or never-married single mothers holds these women and their children together, at least financially, even if there is no husband or father in the house. It is clear that something like the Swedish model is what Goode envisions, sooner or later, for the entire world, i.e., a stable high-divorce and family-disruption system for all countries, rich or poor, East or West, North or South, with the welfare, extensive bureaucracy, and

---

[8] Goode, *World Changes*, pp. 220–3.
[9] Goode, *World Changes*, pp. 224–5.
[10] Goode, *World Changes*, pp. 251–7.

potential decline of both marriage and civil society that generally accompanies this strategy.

David Popenoe and Alan Wolfe

Goode is not the only sociologist who has examined global trends in family formation and dissolution. Both American sociologists David Popenoe and Alan Wolfe have reviewed the trends. Popenoe in his 1988 *Disturbing the Nest: Family Change and Decline in Modern Societies* primarily compares family disruption in the United States and Sweden, with shorter forays into the traditionally stable societies of New Zealand and Switzerland.[11] Alan Wolfe in *Whose Keeper? Social Science and Moral Obligation* (1989) compares indices of increased family disruption in the United States and Sweden.[12]

Here are samples, and something of an updating, of the kinds of marriage and family statistics that worry Popenoe and Wolfe. Since the 1960s, the divorce rate has more than doubled in the United Kingdom, the United States, France and Australia.[13] Non-marital births range from around one-third of all births in the UK, USA and France to nearly one-half of all births in Sweden.[14] In the USA since 1960 the rate of out-of-wedlock births has increased tenfold in the white community to the present rate of 25% of all births and has increased three times in the black community to a rate of 70%.[15] The marriage rate in all advanced countries has significantly declined, there are fewer second marriages, and more people live longer periods of their lives in the single state. The number of couples cohabiting has increased eight times since 1970 in the USA.[16]

[11] David Popenoe, *Disturbing the Nest: Family Change and Decline in Modern Societies* (New York: Aldine De Gruyter, 1988).

[12] Alan Wolfe, *Whose Keeper? Social Science and Moral Obligation* (Berkeley, CA: University of California Press, 1989).

[13] Kevin and Margaret Andrews, 'Family Composition and Worldwide Trends', *Marriage, Family and Society* (Autumn 1999), p. 10.

[14] Andrews and Andrews, 'Family Composition', p. 11.

[15] Tom Smith, *The Emerging 21st Century American Family* (Chicago, IL: National Opinion Research Center, University of Chicago, 1999), p. 3.

[16] Linda Waite, 'The Negative Effects of Cohabitation', *The Responsive Community*, X (Winter 2000), p. 31.

Studies show that cohabitation is much more unstable than marriage and correlates with higher divorce rates for couples who do go on to marry.[17] Recent research has shown that in the USA, at least, a significant portion of the children born out of wedlock actually occur in cohabiting relationships – relationships that are on average much more fragile than legal marriages.[18] Studies in Sweden of cohabiting couples with one child indicate that the dissolution rate is three times as high for them as it is for legally married couples with a child.[19] In view of such statistics, sociologist Professor Linda Waite and journalist Maggie Gallagher conclude in their *The Case for Marriage* (2000) that a couple's public and legal commitment to the formal institution of marriage seems to contribute to the stability of the union.[20]

These are the kinds of facts that have preoccupied Popenoe and Wolfe. I want, however, to consider the theoretical commitments that lead them to interpret such data as they do. Popenoe accepts for the most part the modernisation theory of William Goode, i.e., that industrialisation has struck back at the conjugal family and dealt it a near-fatal blow. But Popenoe also believes that cultural values such as expressive and utilitarian individualism (to use the categories of Robert Bellah) are the main factors, independent of the social processes of industrialisation, which further fuel family disruption.[21] This leads Popenoe to hope for a cultural conversion – a world-wide renunciation of over-determined individualistic aspirations and the birth of a new familism. The idea of handling the world disruptions of the family by imitating Sweden's relatively stable high-divorce society, as William Goode would urge, is an option

---

[17] David Popenoe and Barbara Dafoe Whitehead, *Should We Live Together? What Young Adults Need to Know about Cohabitation before Marriage* (New Brunswick, NJ: The National Marriage Project, Rutgers University Press, 1999).

[18] Pamela Smock, 'Cohabitation in the United States: An Appraisal of Research Themes, Findings, and Implications', *Annual Review of Sociology*, 26 (Summer 2000).

[19] Popenoe, *Disturbing the Nest*, p. 173.

[20] Linda Waite and Maggie Gallagher, *The Case for Marriage* (New York: Doubleday, 2000), p. 18.

[21] David Popenoe, *Life without Father* (New York: Free Press, 1996), pp. 46–8; Robert Bellah et al., *Habits of the Heart* (New York: Harper & Row, 1986), pp. 32–5.

that Popenoe has carefully considered, finds somewhat attractive, but in the end rejects.

Wolfe rejects the Swedish alternative as well. Wolfe uses the colonisation theory of Jürgen Habermas to show how different expressions of modernisation are almost identical in their negative effects on families. By coining the intriguing word 'colonisation', Habermas (and Wolfe) are employing Max Weber's concept of technical rationality, an idea that was central to Weber's famous theory of modernisation.[22] Technical rationality is the use of means–end, consequentialist, and control-oriented thinking and practice to guide the efficient production of wealth.[23] Habermas' metaphor of colonisation contains within it an interpretation of modern history, i.e., that it has become dominated by the spread of technical rationality into all of life. More specifically, coloni-sation theory holds that the efficiency logic of technical rationality has increasingly come to dominate face-to-face inter-personal life in neighbourhood, local communities, and even families.

Colonisation theory maintains that the spread of technical rationality into the social space of daily interactions – what Habermas calls the 'lifeworld' – comes from two directions. From the market comes the increasing absorption of both men and women into the wage economy and the subsequent decline of time for parenthood and stable marital relations. From state bureaucracy comes the control of the education of our children, the rise of the welfare state, its pre-emption of family functions, and its subtle encouragement of the transfer of dependencies from family to the state.

Wolfe argues that Sweden is the leading example of coloni-sation of the lifeworld from the perspective of bureaucratic expressions of technical reason and that the United States is the leading example of colonisation from the perspective of market rationality. Wolfe calls the family in Sweden an example of the state or 'public family' and the family in the USA an example of

[22] Jürgen Habermas, *The Theory of Communicative Action*, Vol. II (Boston, MA: Beacon Press, 1987), pp. 333–5; Alan Wolfe, *Whose Keeper?* p. 20.
[23] Max Weber, *The Protestant Ethic and the Spirit of Capitalism* (New York: Charles Scribners, 1958), p. 182.

the market or 'private family'.[24] In the end, the results for families of these two forms of colonisation are approximately the same – more divorce, more out-of-wedlock births, and the declining well-being of children. Although Popenoe does not use the language of colonisation, he implicitly agrees with Wolfe's use of it for analysing the world comparative situation of families. Both Wolfe and Popenoe are distrustful of Goode's great hope for a stable high-divorce society in the Swedish style. Popenoe doubts that the Swedish system is actually helpful to the marriages and families it was designed to support. Furthermore, its growing costs question its long-term viability even in this wealthy country.[25] This raises the issue: can the countries of the world afford a system of stable high-divorce and family disruption in the Scandinavian style? Just how generalisable is Sweden's system to poor countries or, for that matter, to rich countries when global competition has led the latter to tighten their economies to meet the challenge?

Popenoe and Wolfe are unique among social scientists in the USA in calling for a cultural renewal that restores marriage and family. Social scientists, in general, tend to see culture reflecting economic and social-systemic changes. They interpret calls for a change in cultural values as fruitless exercises in sermonising and moralism. In the 1970s and early 1980s, American sociologists such as Jessie Bernard celebrated the new culture of divorce and nonmarriage as promising a future of creativity, experimentation and freedom, especially for women.[26] But by the late 1980s, research on the negative economic consequences of divorce for women by feminist scholars such as Lenore Weitzman and Mary Ann Mason cooled this earlier optimism.[27] By the mid-1990s, reports by demographers such as Sara McLanahan and Gary Sandefur showed that children not living with both biological parents, i.e., children of divorce, out-of-wedlock births, and even children living in stepfamilies, were on average two to three times more at risk on

---

[24] Wolfe, *Whose Keeper?*, pp. 52–60, 133–42.

[25] Popenoe, *Disturbing the Nest*, pp. 243–9.

[26] Jessie Bernard, *The Future of Marriage* (New York: World Publishing, 1972).

[27] Weitzman, *The Divorce Revolution*; Mary Ann Mason, *The Equality Trap* (New York: Simon & Schuster, 1988).

indices such as doing well in school, finding employment, and successfully forming families.[28]

Most responsible family sociologists in the USA acknowledge these sobering facts about the effects of family disruption, but they also believe little can be done to lower divorce and out-of-wedlock births other than mitigating the pain associated with their consequences. For instance, respected demographer Larry Bumpass believes that increasingly when the interests of children and parents conflict, they are resolved in favour of the parents.[29] On the other hand, he also believes that the causes of family disruption are rooted in a centuries-old drive toward individualism in Western societies and for that reason are not likely to be changed.[30]

Popenoe and his colleagues are far more hopeful about prospects of cultural change and reconstruction. They advocate a new moral conversation that will lead to a cultural rebirth of marital commitment.

The Neglect of Religion

The social-science debate just described is notable for its neglect of the religious factor. This is not surprising. Many sociologists associate Judaism and Christianity with patriarchy and its harmful consequences for women. Even Alan Wolfe believes that contemporary religious institutions are impotent to be centres of socially reconstructive moral discourse.[31] Popenoe hopes that religion can help stabilise the postmodern family, but makes little effort to develop a theory of how religious institutions can reconstruct cultural values.

If the family issue is first of all a cultural issue, as Popenoe and his colleagues believe, then religion, as it did in the past, must play a decisive role in the reconstruction of marriage and

---

[28] Sara McLanahan and Gary Sandefur, *Growing up with a Single Parent* (Cambridge, MA: Harvard University Press, 1994).

[29] Larry Bumpass, 'What is Happening to the Family? Interaction Between Demographics and Institutional Change', *Demography*, 23 (November 1990), pp. 486, 489.

[30] Bumpass, 'What is Happening to the Family?', p. 493.

[31] Wolfe, *Whose Keeper?*, p. 6.

14   *Celebrating Christian Marriage*

family ideals. Allow me to make a few generalisations developed by the Religion, Culture, and Family Project that I direct at the University of Chicago.[32] They will show why Christianity is a resource for the reconstruction of marriage and family theory for Western societies and, perhaps, for other parts of the world.

Early Christianity, especially pre-Pauline and Pauline Christianity, was a family revolution. It significantly qualified, although it did not completely dismantle, the honour–shame codes that dominated family and marriage in the Greco-Roman world.[33] By honour–shame codes, I mean a family system in which free men gained honour through exhibiting dominance and agency and were shamed if they lost these qualities. Women, on the other hand, gained honour by restricting their lives to the home and submitting to male protection. They were shamed if they went beyond these boundaries. Christianity, we must remember, existed within a cultural context largely formed by Roman Hellenism, and Roman Hellenism was saturated by these honour–shame codes. Early Christianity fractured and qualified these codes by celebrating male servanthood rather than male dominance, by applying the golden rule and neighbour love to relationships between husband and wife, by requiring males to renounce their sexual privileges with female slaves and young boys, and by elevating the status of women. As the American sociologist Rodney Stark has argued in his *The Rise of Christianity* (1997), pagan women flocked to early Christianity because of its stand against infanticide, its restrictions on divorce (which in antiquity worked to

---

[32] Information about the Religion, Culture, and Family Project can be found at www2.uchicago.edu/divinity/family. The project has published a series of ten books with Westminster John Knox and will publish another eight books with William B. Eerdmans.

[33] For review of the application of the insights of cultural anthropology on honour–shame societies to an understanding of the influence of early Christianity on families, see the following:

Bruce Malina, *The New Testament World: Insights from Cultural Anthropology* (Louisville, KY: Westminster John Knox Press, 1993); Carolyn Osiek and David Balch, *Families in the New Testament World* (Louisville, KY: Westminster John Knox, 1997), Don Browning, Bonnie Miller McLemore, Pamel Couture, Bernie Lyon and Robert Franklin, *From Culture Wars to Common Ground: Religion and the American Family Debate* (Louisville, KY: Westminster John Knox, 1997), pp. 129–54.

the disadvantage of women), its rejection of abortion, and its demand that men be responsible fathers and faithful husbands.[34] The famous Cambridge anthropologist Jack Goody argues that it was not only the Protestant Reformation that gave birth to the modern conjugal and companionate family, as Harvard historian Steven Ozment has claimed.[35] He believes that the seeds of what I often call the 'equal-regard' marriage and family go back to the value of the individual and the emphasis on 'inter-personal, rather than inter-group bonds' found in early Christianity.[36]

This emphasis on the value of the individual influenced eleventh- and twelfth-century Roman Catholic canon law to make mutual consent between bride and groom the decisive factor defining marriage.[37] This development limited the power of fathers arbitrarily to give their daughters in marriage for political and economic gain. According to the historian David Herlihy, this emphasis on the integrity and sanctity of the conjugal couple led to the downfall of polygyny and the elevation of monogamy wherever Christianity spread.[38] Although Luther and Calvin rejected the Roman Catholic idea of marriage as a sacrament of grace, they accepted most of the other accomplishments of Roman Catholic canon law on marriage, especially the emphasis on marriage as requiring mutual consent.

But Luther and Calvin added one important element that the societies influenced by the Protestant Reformation may be losing due to the increasing deinstitutionalisation of marriage and family. Marriage, according to the Reformers, was understood by them as both a public and an ecclesial affair. Marriage for the Reformers was first of all a natural good and a contribution to both secular society and the earthly kingdom. Marriage had

---

[34] Rodney Stark, *The Rise of Christianity* (San Francisco, CA: Harper Collins, 1997), pp. 98–118.

[35] Steven Ozment, *Protestants: The Birth of a Revolution* (New York: Doubleday, 1992), pp. 151–69.

[36] Jack Goody, *The Development of the Family and Marriage in Europe* (Cambridge: Cambridge University Press, 1994), p. 23.

[37] John Witte, *From Sacrament to Contract: Marriage, Religion, and Law in the Western Tradition* (Louisville, KY: Westminster John Knox Press, 1997).

[38] David Herlihy, *Medieval Households* (Cambridge, MA: Harvard University Press, 1985), pp. 61–2.

to be registered and sanctioned by the state, and then blessed and sanctified by the church. It is true: marriage for these Reformers arose out of the love and consent of a couple, but it needed completion by both state and church. Making marriage a public institution gradually brought to an end the so-called clandestine or secret marriage phenomenon, with all of its abuses and manipulations, that arose in the Middle Ages when a couple's private consent was the only thing required to establish a valid marriage. For four hundred years – from the Reformation to the mid-twentieth century – church and state have co-operated to perform a great cultural work in bringing order and coherence to marriage by making it a public institution as well as a personal, consensual and ecclesial one.

Not only did the Christian church develop both an ecclesial and a public theology governing marriage, it contributed a rich and complex symbol system that applied to both tasks. The creation story of ancient Judaism is central to Christian marriage theology and the foundation of the entire Western legal and theological edifice of marriage. The creation of Adam as male and female both carrying God's image (Gen. 1:27), their equal responsibility for procreation and 'dominion' (Gen. 1:28), God's declaration that it is not good that Adam 'should be alone' (Gen. 2:18), the statement that 'a man leaves his father and mother and clings to his wife, and they become one flesh' (Gen. 2:24), and the reaffirmation and recontextuali-sation of these classic scriptures within the gospel message of Jesus in Matthew 19:4–6 – these are the scriptures that time and again were interpreted by Catholic and Protestant theologians and even by jurists up into the twentieth century.

It would be wrong to credit these scriptures, and Christian interpretations of them, as the only source of the Western conjugal and companionate marriage and family. Christian theology interacted with Aristotle's naturalistic view of marriage and family as well as Roman and German law. Roman Catholic canon law and St Thomas Aquinas brought all of these sources together and bequeathed them to the Protestant Reformation where they were reworked but largely retained. I believe that this is a proud heritage that needs to be critically appreciated by Western societies today and critically borrowed from by the rest of the world. Notice that I used the adverb 'critically' in both contexts. This heritage has the seeds of excellence.

Empirically and historically, like everything else in this fallen world, it was often far from excellent in its actual implementation. But in order for it to resist the acids of modernisation discussed in the writings of William Goode, David Popenoe and Alan Wolfe, the church must be a leader in a new multifaceted cultural work designed to revive and reformulate its marriage traditions.

Elements in the New Cultural Work

The cultural work needed to revive marriage must have several dimensions to it. No one approach, no one strategy, no one discipline or institution, can accomplish this task alone. There needs to be a new system of voluntary associations, both national and international, that co-ordinate these complex patterns of intervention. Let me suggest an imaginary name. Let us call such an organisation the Coalition of Marriage Reformation and Revival. Take note that I place the word 'reformation' prior to the word 'revival'. The reformation of the ethics of marriage is the more basic task and must precede revival, or at least go hand in hand with it. Let us assume that there would be national chapters throughout the world and something like an international manifestation as well. These organisations would attempt to devise an interrelated philosophical, religious, economic, legal, educational and psychological strategy to influence public life, culture and religious institutions. They would be based on the best research available in these different disciplines, but the overall task would be practical and hermeneutic, i.e., a matter of understanding, as Hans-Georg Gadamer would say, for the purposes of *praxis*.[39]

Here are some of the elements that would go into such a coalition:

1. Research and reflection on Western religious heritages would be central. But this research would be both appreciative and critical. It also would show how the various

---

[39] Hans-Georg Gadamer, *Truth and Method* (New York: Crossroads, 1982), p. 289.

strands of this heritage – Jewish, Catholic, Protestant and Islamic – interacted not only with each other but with other philosophical, legal and social traditions. Gradually, other religions not identified with the Abrahamic traditions would be invited to participate in the coalition and this task of critical retrieval. The divisive issues of homosexuality and abortion would not be eliminated but would not be centre stage. The more tractable issues of fatherlessness, non-marital births, the declining well-being of children and women and the deinstitutionalisation of marriage and family would be more central.

2. The Western marriage traditions would not only be understood but reconstructed and reformed. Certainly, the most central agenda is to reconstitute marriage on non-patriarchal grounds and to address the emerging work and family issues that face all modern marriages. This is the intellectual task of creating what my colleagues and I have called a 'critical familism' or 'critical marriage culture' or what family social scientist William Doherty is presently calling a 'critical pro-marriage' philosophy.[40]

3. Religious institutions should provide theological rationales for why marriage must continue to be seen, as it has been for the last four hundred years, as an interest of the state. The core of such a public theology can be found in Protestant covenantal theologies where the state is also seen as one of the members of the marital covenant. Catholic subsidiarity theologies also had ways of understanding theologically how the state should support families. The best public theology for marriage eventually will bring the two models together. Marital arrangements need the protections, accountability and public supports that the state has provided over the last few centuries. Young people should be helped to understand and appropriate why the state is a friend of marriage, just as it is a friend of the possibility of driving an automobile safely,

---

[40] William Doherty, 'Health and the Ethics of Marital Therapy and Education', in Don Browning, John Wall, William Doherty and Stephen Post (eds.), *Marriage, Health, and the Professions* (Grand Rapids, MI: Eerdmans, forthcoming in 2001).

having clean water to drink, and having good schools to attend. Marriage is a public institution as well as a deeply meaningful personal and spiritual relationship. In keeping with this, the state should find ways to reward marriage, support the childbearing aspects of marriage with tax breaks, give welfare benefits when needed, and provide state-supported marriage education as now occurs in Australia and in the USA in Florida and Arizona.

4. Both state and church must learn to address work and family issues. Market demands and pressures are leading individuals to delay marriage, absorbing more of their time after marriage, and are factors contributing to divorce. Married couples have little time for each other and less time for parenting. New structural accommodations to provide more part-time and flexitime jobs are needed. Furthermore, a family ideal of no more than a combined sixty-hour work week for a couple with children should be encouraged, as my colleagues and I argued in *From Culture Wars to Common Ground: Religion and the American Family Debate* (1997).[41] To accomplish such an ideal, market and government must work with culture-making institutions such as church, synagogue and mosque to create a new philosophy of leisure and new restraints on the consumerism that drives our compulsion constantly to earn more money.

5. Marriage education is a must for the development of a critical marriage culture. Marriage education should begin in secondary schools. This is another reason why the state must be a partner in the reformation and revival of marriage. There are new curricula now available that help young people navigate the increasingly hazardous years of searching for an appropriate mate. These curricula also begin preparing young people for the institution of marriage. No one part of society can make such educational programmes be successful. They must be established on a complex co-operative process supported by church, school, state and market. They must be informed by critically tested marital ideologies and the best

---

[41] Browning et al., *From Culture Wars to Common Ground*, pp. 326–7.

social-science research to determine what actually helps. In addition to careful education about the spiritual meaning of marriage, the church must also do its share of education for marriage communication. Education for marriage communication and the use of scientifically tested premarital inventories such as PREPARE or FOCCUS should be skills possessed by all ministers, priests and rabbis.[42] A powerful marriage theology such as that celebrated by the major religions helps ground marital commitment. But amidst the turmoil of modern life, such commitment needs to be buttressed with well-internalised interpersonal and communication skills. Furthermore, skills and commitment must be reinforced by interacting marriage-supportive institutions.

In conclusion, let me simply repeat my central message. The forces of modernisation are ambiguous. They bring benefits, but they also can be horribly destructive, especially to marriage and family. But human beings in their freedom and culture-making capacities have the ability to harness and control these forces. They have the ability to reform and revive marriage as both public institution and intersubjective reality. To do this requires a multidimensional work of culture.

---

[42] PREPARE and FOCCUS are inventories widely used in the United States and several other countries to assess marital compatibility and readiness for marriage. PREPARE has been developed by Professor David Olson of the University of Minnesota. It claims to be able to predict with 85% certainty those couples who will still be married after five years. FOCCUS is a similar instrument developed by Sister Barbara Markey and used in Roman Catholic and other circles. The address for PREPARE is PO Box 190, Minneapolis, MN 55440–0190 and for FOCCUS, it is Family Life Office, 3214 North 60th Street, Omaha, NE 68104.

2

Marriage, and the Second Demographic Transition in Europe: A Review

Duncan Dormor

In the last forty years we have witnessed unprecedented change in marital and reproductive behaviour across Europe and beyond: marriage rates have plummeted as the age of first marriage has increased substantially and as a lower proportion of each successive generation marries; divorce has become commonplace ending around 40% of marriages in many countries of Europe; the phenomena of non-marital cohabitation and non-marital childbearing have become widespread and finally fertility levels have been below that required for the replacement of population for a considerable period. As a result of these changes the form of families has diversified and large numbers of children are now brought up by one parent or in stepfamilies. Such change can rightly be termed radical, and is increasingly being treated as constituting a major fracture in social ordering.[1]

Such radical change in primary relationships is of course part of a broader shift in society variously attributed in sociological narratives to 'modernisation', 'privatisation', 'detraditionalisation' or 'pluralisation', and associated with the idea of a shift to a new regime whether characterised as post-

---

[1] E.g., F. Fukuyama, *The Great Disruption: Human Nature and the Reconstitution of Social Order* (New York: Free Press, 1999); D. Popenoe, *Life without Father: compelling new evidence that fatherhood and marriage are indispensable for the good of children and society* (New York: Martin Kessler Books, 1996); but see also, A. Giddens, *The Transformation of Intimacy: Sexuality, Love and Eroticism in Modern Societies* (Cambridge: Polity Press, 1992).

industrial or postmodern or even postmaterialist.[2] In this chapter I hope to outline and evaluate the major narrative proposed by demographers for connecting the evolution of the social system with recent changes in marital and reproductive behaviour over the past forty years, namely the 'second demographic transition'.[3]

Whilst the proponents of the second demographic transition vary in their precise formulation, four elements seem central to its conceptualisation.

1. There is a logical sequence of events relating contra-ceptive, sexual, procreative and relationship formation behaviour over the period.

2. A 'path of innovation' exists with innovative behaviour diffusing from the countries of northern Europe, in particular Sweden and Denmark, to the countries of central Europe and subsequently to those of southern and eastern Europe.[4]

3. There is an inevitability about this process and therefore, notwithstanding a period of greater plurality in the transi-tional phase, there will be an increasing convergence in the nuptiality of European countries. All countries making the transition from industrial to post-industrial or infor-mation societies are expected to reach a similar endpoint.

---

[2] See R. Inglehart, *Culture Shift in Advanced Industrial Society* (Princeton: Princeton University Press, 1990).

[3] D. J. van de Kaa, 'Europe's Second Demographic Transition', *Population Bulletin*, 42:1 (1987); G. Santow, 'A sequence of events in fertility and family formation?', *Proceedings of the International Population Conference New Delhi*, Vol. 3 (IUSSP, 1989), pp. 217–29; R. Lesthaeghe, 'The Second Demographic Transition in Western Countries: An Interpretation' (Paper presented at the workshop 'Gender and family change in industrialised countries', 26–30 January 1992, Rome).

[4] I shall draw on demographic material from a range of countries under the following four broad geographical groupings: *Northern*: Sweden, Denmark, Finland, Norway, Iceland, England and Wales, Scotland, Northern Ireland. *Central*: (Western) Germany, Austria, Switzerland, France, Belgium, Netherlands, Luxembourg. *Southern*: Italy, Spain, Portugal, Greece, Malta, Ireland. *Eastern*: Latvia, Lithuania, Estonia, Poland, Romania, Hungary, (Eastern) Germany, Slovenia, Croatia, Slovakia, Bulgaria, Czech Republic. For demographic reasons it makes sense to divide Germany into its 1946 division. The case of Ireland is so exceptional that it is best grouped with the southern countries.

4. While these developments are positively associated with economic changes, secularisation, increasing levels of education and female emancipation, a major explanatory role lies in ideational change, namely the increasing 'individualisation' of Western society.

The Sequence of Change

A clear catalytic role in this change is played by the advent of new contraceptive methods. In combination with the acceptance of sterilisation as a legitimate method to end a procreative career and the widespread legalisation increasing access to abortion across the industrialised world, the intro-duction of the pill and the IUD in the early 1960s had a profound and yet subtle impact. Effective family limitation, it should be remembered, was, in Susan Watkins' memorable phrase, 'a revolution accomplished with primitive technology and without generals',[5] that is with *coitus interruptus* and in the face of opposition from church and state. Indeed fertility can fall even more dramatically in the absence of modern methods than it did at the turn of the nineteenth century. For example, the *Italian Fertility Survey* of 1979 shows that among married women of 18–44 who were using contraception 59% still used withdrawal compared with a total of 27% for the IUD, diaphragm, condom or pill, yet at that point Italy's fertility had already fallen well below replacement level.[6]

What the new contraceptive innovations brought instead through their effectiveness was a high degree of flexibility and thus a much greater range of possible goals; they could be used within marriage to delay a first birth or to plan and space children in addition to preventing pre-nuptial pregnancy or births outside marriage. In short, the impact of these innova-tions was to make having children a conscious decision, the result of interrupting contraceptive practice to conceive rather

---

[5] A. J. Coale and S. C. Watkins (eds.), *The Decline of Fertility in Europe* (Princeton: Princeton University Press, 1986), p. 435.

[6] M. Castiglioni and G. D. Zuanna, 'Innovation and Tradition: Reproductive Marital Behaviour in Italy in the 1970s and 1980s', *European Journal of Population*, 10 (1994), pp. 107–41.

than making the decision to minimise the risk of conception. Indeed some demographers prefer to speak of the 'second contraceptive revolution'[7] rather than a 'second demographic transition', stressing the crucial role that contraceptive innovation played in decoupling marriage, childbearing and sexuality. Yet whilst it is notoriously difficult to measure, there is a reasonable amount of evidence to suggest, for example, that increasing numbers of couples had premarital sexual experience in the post-war period[8] – a development indicative of a widespread receptivity to the contraceptive innovations and the extension of the sphere of personal choice that they ushered in.

The first important impact of the pill and IUD, in a world in which premarital sex was still counter to prevailing mores, was that it permitted people to marry even younger without a commitment to starting a family. The first demographic intimation of change is therefore an increase within marriage cohorts of the gap between marriage and first birth. This is a crucial step weakening the link between marriage and reproduction, for marriage is thus no longer the automatic threshold for fertility. But as modern contraception spreads to the unmarried, premarital pregnancies fall, 'shotgun' marriages disappear and the age of first marriage begins to rise. In many of the countries of northern Europe in which young men and women leave home and live independently in their early twenties, near-universal premarital sexual experience, 'sleeping together', evolved into the practice of 'living together'. This unconventional choice of cohabitation begins as a minority practice in the 1970s but spreads rapidly throughout the 1980s, such that not only do those who marry directly become the minority, but an increasing proportion of people regard it as foolhardy not to cohabit. When the *International Social Survey Programme* of 1994 asked whether it is 'a good idea for a couple who intend to get married to live together first', 58% of British people interviewed agree that it

---

[7] E.g., the French demographers Henri Leridon and Jean-Paul Sardon.

[8] E.g., E. Lodewijckx, 'First intercourse, contraception and first pregnancy in Flanders: changes during the past 30 years', *Journal of Biosocial Science*, 19 (1987), pp. 439–52; United Nations, *Adolescent Reproductive Behaviour – Evidence from Developed Countries*, Vol. 1 (Washington: United Nations, 1988).

is. This compares with 55% of the Dutch, 86% of Swedes and, perhaps most surprising, 49% of those interviewed in the Irish Republic.[9]

With the spread of cohabitation, marriage and the transition to parenthood were thus postponed, though people frequently still marry when the decision to become parents is made.[10] The final stage in the proposed sequence occurs when this connection between marriage and parenthood is loosened and people decide not to marry upon becoming parents.

There is an increasing appreciation that a key role in this process of radical change in the last few decades in both behaviour and attitude has been played by what van de Kaa calls 'mental cohorts'.[11] Each generation of people passing through the various stages, makes decisions which, he argues, 'limits and enriches the options' for the next cohort, such that each peer group considering their attitudes to sex, relationships and becoming a parent is aware of the acceptability of the different choices open to them as members of a specific sub-group, whether they be deviant, unconventional or fairly normal. Indeed, van de Kaa suggests: 'it is precisely through the choice that people make with regard to such life shaping demographic events as marriage, having a child, and method of contraception, that people express their sense of belonging to a certain sub-group'.[12]

Innovative behaviour, it is then predicted, will spread from those sub-groups holding less conventional and more 'progressive' views, generally the young, the educated, urban-dwelling and less religious, to the rest of society. As a result, it would be expected that at various stages in the 'transition' compositional effects will change the character of what is being

[9] J. Scott, M. Braun and D. Alwin, 'Partner, parent, worker: family and gender roles', in R. Jowell, J. Curtice, A. Park and K. Thomson (eds.), *British Social Attitudes* (Aldershot: Ashgate, 1998), pp. 19–35.

[10] Wanting to have/was having/had just had children, was the second most common reason given by couples in explanation of their decision to marry, having cohabited in Great Britain, 1994/5. (J. Haskey, 'Cohabitational and marital histories of adults in Great Britain', *Population Trends*, 96 (Summer 1999), pp. 13–24).

[11] D. J. van de Kaa, 'Options and Sequences: Europe's Demographic Patterns', *Journal of the Australian Population Association*, 14:1 (1997), pp. 1–29.

[12] van de Kaa 'Options and Sequences', p. 3.

described. This is most clearly the case with non-marital cohabitation: whilst innovators may cohabit out of an ideological opposition to marriage, later cohabitees may see the practice as an essential, even normative path into marriage. As a corollary, premarital cohabitation may therefore be associated with a higher relative risk of divorce than marrying directly when it is a minority practice, and a lower level of divorce once it has become a majority practice.[13]

Review of Trends

Marriage

At the turn of the century, Europe had two distinct marriage patterns divided by an imaginary line from Trieste to St Petersburg;[14] to the west and north couples tended to marry in their mid-20s and a relatively high proportion (10–20%) remained unmarried; to the south and east marriage was earlier and near universal. A shift from this pattern is detectable as early as 1860 in France but becomes established in the twentieth century with a gradual decline in the age of marriage and a greater proportion of people marrying, such that the period 1930–1960 could be described as a 'marriage boom'. This development is linked with economic change, in particular the shift in employment into new occupations. So by the early 1960s there is an unprecedented degree of uniformity across Europe in the basic indicators of nuptiality.

This uniformity begins to change in the late 1960s with the age at marriage rising first in Sweden and Denmark in 1968;

---

[13] See, for example, the contrast between J. Haskey, 'Pre-marital cohabitation and the probability of subsequent divorce: analyses using new data from the General Household Survey', *Population Trends*, 68 (Summer 1992), pp. 10–19, in his analysis of 1980s General Household Survey data and his later work based on 1994/5 data in which he concludes: 'the differences in proportions of marriages ending, between marriages with and without pre-marital cohabitation, is no longer statistically significant' (Haskey, 'Cohabitational and marital histories', p. 19.)

[14] See John Hajnal, 'European Marriage Patterns in Perspective', in D. V. Glass and D. E. C. Eversley (eds.), *Population in History* (London: Edward Arnold, 1965).

then in the other countries of Scandinavia and northern Europe in the early 1970s, followed by most of central Europe in the early 1980s and eastern Europe after the fall of Communism in the 1990s. There are exceptions to this broad sequence of change but it remains a fairly robust generalisation. By 1998, all but four of the thirty-five nations in the Council of Europe, for which we have data, have seen a significant upsurge in the age of marriage.[15] In most of these countries the changes are unprecedented and there is little evidence of either a ceiling in the highest (Sweden and Denmark, which are currently around thirty years), or indeed that other countries might stabilise at a particular level below that. Accompanying these changes increasing proportions of successive cohorts are choosing not to marry, though this does not preclude either a sexually active life, or the formation of a lifelong union, or indeed parenthood.

Fertility

Demographic Transition theory assumed that at the end of the industrialisation process, populations would stabilise such that the Total Period Fertility Rate (TPFR)[16] would fluctuate around 2.1 – an assumption based more on hope than any obvious rational foundation. In fact, fertility started to fall quite sharply towards the end of the 1960s and by 1975 all the countries of northern and central Europe had below replacement fertility: by 1985 this was also the case for the Mediterranean countries. In general the later the fertility decline is experienced the more precipitous that decline, at least as measured by the TPFR, so whilst western Germany experienced the lowest period fertility of the northern and central countries, reaching 1.37 in 1985,[17] the sharpest decline in any of the northern or central countries of Europe, fertility rates in the 'Catholic South' of Europe have

---

[15] Council of Europe, *Recent Demographic Development in Europe 1999* (Strasbourg: Council of Europe, 1999).

[16] TPFR – total period fertility rate – this summarises the age-specific fertility rates for a given year as a hypothetical average number of children per woman.

[17] The TPFR in 'western Germany' rose back to 1.46 by 1988, before falling again to a new unprecedented low of 1.24 in 1994.

fallen to lower levels, at least in Italy and Spain.[18] Even this low fertility has been undercut in the former eastern bloc countries since the collapse of the USSR, with particularly low levels in the Baltic states (e.g., 1.09 in Latvia, 1998) and eastern Germany[19] (1.04 in 1997), though the diversity of fertility experience in this region has been greater with some countries experiencing low levels of fertility over several decades (most notably Hungary).[20]

In general these changes have been brought about by a combination of two main factors: a reduction in larger families (four or more children), and a shift towards an older initiation into motherhood such that fertility has increased among those in their early thirties (30–35) and decreased substantially for those in their early twenties (20–25). While in some countries there has also been a noticeable increase in voluntary child-lessness (Germany, UK, Austria, Finland, Netherlands, Switzerland) this is by no means universal.

Cohabitation and Non-marital Fertility

One of the more difficult developments to chart and indeed interpret over the period in question is that of non-marital cohabitation. There are two main reasons for this: the first is simply a matter of data. Unlike the acts of marriage, divorce or giving birth, a cohabitation does not have to be registered officially, therefore most estimates of the extent of cohabitation are produced through surveys or other indirect means, making comparison between countries extremely difficult. This situation is now changing with the use of *Eurobarometer* data and the *European Fertility and Family Surveys*.[21] The second concerns

---

[18] 1.19, Italy, 1998; 1.17, Spain, 1996.

[19] See Nicholas Eberstadt, 'Demographic shocks after Communism: Eastern Germany 1989–1993', *Population and Development Review*, 20:1 (1994), pp. 137–52.

[20] Fertility has been low since the 1960s in Croatia and Latvia, and TPFRs began to decline in eastern Germany and Slovenia well before 1989.

[21] The *Family and Fertility Surveys* project is co-ordinated by the Population Activities Unit of the United Nations Economic Commission for Europe (ECE). *Eurobarometer* data are produced by surveys conducted by the European Commission.

the definition and meaning of cohabitation: as an essentially private commitment it remains opaque to the researcher. Much early work on cohabitation, for example, was keen to discern whether such relationships were seen as a preparation for, or as alternative to marriage. However, the huge increase in non-marital cohabitation during the 1980s and 1990s in much of northern and central Europe has transformed it from being the unconventional choice of a minority to an integral part of established patterns of partnership formation. This development has transformed both the questions asked and the answers sought by researchers.

Across northern and central Europe, couples are much more likely to cohabit as an initiation into their first partnership than to marry directly. So, for example, in the mid-1990s, over 70% of women aged 25–29 who had embarked upon a union cohabited rather than married in Norway, Switzerland, Austria, France, West Germany and the Netherlands – the figures for Finland and Sweden being 88% and 93% respectively.[22] By contrast in the two southern countries for which we have some data – Spain and Italy – the equivalent percentages are 19% and 11%. The eastern European countries for which we have data tend to divide between those with a Protestant history – Estonia (75%), Latvia (49%) and East Germany (49%) – and those with a Catholic history – Poland (5%) and Lithuania (20%).

Whilst 'we can not yet show how the spread of cohabitation led to the partnership status of the population recently observed in the various countries'[23] through the *Family Fertility Survey*, it is commonly assumed that the phenomenon of cohabitation spreads by a diffusion process from 'innovators', unconventional or progressive individuals prepared to risk a 'deviant' status, first to the educated elite and then to the rest of the population. So, for example, a study of women aged 18–37 in the Netherlands found that urban dwelling, high education, being from a one-parent family and lack of church attendance were strongly associated with cohabitation before

---

[22] E. Klijzing and M. Macura, 'Cohabitation and Extra-marital Childbearing: Early FFS Evidence', *Proceedings of the International Population Conference 11–17 October 1997 Beijing*, Vol. 2 (IUSSP, 1997), p. 891.

[23] Klijzing and Macura, 'Cohabitation and Extra-marital Childbearing', p. 891.

marriage.[24] Similarly in her analysis of FFS data, Kiernan found cohabitees to be less religious, more likely to have experienced the divorce of their parents and to have had greater levels of educational participation than those marrying directly.[25]

With the exception of Sweden, cohabiting unions still tend to be of a short duration, either being dissolved[26] or converted into marriage after two to three years (on average) across much of northern and central Europe. Perhaps the most striking and significant fact to emerge in the last few years is that whilst early studies showed that those who had cohabited before marriage were more likely to divorce after marriage than those who married directly, recent studies have demonstrated that in those countries in which cohabitation is well established, divorce rates vary very little for first partnerships between those who marry directly and those who have cohabited first.[27] This suggests that earlier results reflect primarily compositional effects rather than the experience of premarital cohabitation itself.

A key transition for cohabitational behaviour is when it involves parenthood and here there is a surprising degree of variation between countries with comparable levels of cohabitation. If one considers, for example, the unions women are in at the time when their first child is born, Italy, Switzerland and the Netherlands have very comparable figures (see Table 1, p. 31). Yet around half of the women in Switzerland and the Netherlands of this age group are in a cohabiting relationship, whereas only 5% of the Italian women cohabit. Conversely

[24] W. D. Van Hoorn, 'Relaties en sociale achtergrond', *Mndstat bevolk (CBS)*, 91:9 (1991), pp. 12–13.

[25] K. Kiernan, 'Cohabitation in Western Europe', *Population Trends*, 96 (Summer 1999), pp. 25–32.

[26] Though there is considerable variation between countries, dissolution rates for cohabiting relationships remain considerably higher than for marriages even where cohabitation is most well established, i.e., Sweden. Relative risks of dissolution range from 2.27 in the case of France to 7.73 for Sweden to 10.5 for Great Britain.

[27] See Kiernan, 'Cohabitation in Western Europe'. Indeed in Norway, Sweden, Finland and Austria the relative risk of divorce is lower for those who have cohabited premaritally, though this difference is only statistically significant in the case of Norway p<0.01.

Table 1: *The proportions of women who have become mothers or remain childless between 25 and 39 in selected countries. Women with children are grouped according to whether they cohabit, are married or are not living in a partnership*

Country/Year of survey	Age group	Mothers by partnership status			Childless
		No partnership	Married	Cohabiting	
Italy	25–29	2	33	2	63
1995/96	30–34	4	68	3	25
	35–39	4	77	2	17
Switzerland	25–29	2	34	3	61
1994/95	30–34	3	60	5	32
	35–39	5	66	7	22
Netherlands	25–29	2	29	4	65
1993	30–34	2	61	6	31
	35–39	3	75	5	17
Austria	25–29	16	35	17	32
1995/96	30–34	19	51	15	15
	35–39	21	55	14	10
Norway	25–29	9	40	17	34
1988/89	30–34	9	64	11	16
	35–39	13	73	4	10

Data based on national FFS Standard Recode Files and/or Country Reports, table 4, and derived from Klijzing and Macura, 'Cohabitation and Extra-marital Childbearing', p. 889.

Austria or Norway which have comparable levels of cohabitation to Switzerland or the Netherlands have rates of cohabitational childbearing three to five times higher.

Central to these differences, as can be seen from Table 1, are the levels of childlessness (or childfreeness) at each age. These profound differences underline the complexity of interrelationships between union formation and fertility. They also show that whilst broad similarities might exist across Europe there may exist different culturally mediated paths through continuing demographic transition.

Divorce and the dissolution of partnerships

The evolution to a mass-divorcing society in the countries of western Europe and beyond took place predominantly between 1965 and 1980. Preceded by a slow rise throughout the twentieth century, with peaks reflecting the disruptive effects of war and what appears to have been a plateauing in several countries[28] during the 1950s, the acceleration of divorce rates during these fifteen years, accompanied by widespread legislation, has been well documented.[29] However, although one in four marriages in the European Union now ends in divorce[30] there remain substantial and persistent regional differences over time. The incidence of divorce in Italy, Spain and Greece is only just beginning to reach the average level in northern and central Europe of 1960, i.e., before the rapid escalation in divorce. Furthermore, when the analysis is broadened, as it has been for Italy in a study by Castiglioni and Zuanna,[31] to include a consideration of the rate of separations rather than divorces, the incidence of marital dissolution increases in a linear fashion merely by a factor of 2 between 1969 and 1990 with no signs of any acceleration in the probability of dissolution.

---

[28] Including England and Wales, France and Switzerland.

[29] See especially W. J. Goode, *World Changes in Divorce Patterns* (New Haven: Yale University Press, 1993), or more briefly, D. J. Dormor, *The Relationship Revolution: Cohabitation, Marriage and Divorce in Contemporary Europe* (London: One Plus One, 1992).

[30] Eurostat, 'About one marriage in four in the EU ends in divorce', *Statistics in Focus: populations and social conditions*, 14 (Luxembourg: Eurostat, 1997).

[31] Castiglioni and Zuanna, 'Innovation and Tradition'.

Moving east, the situation has been quite different. By the beginning of the 1960s, divorce rates had already risen in Hungary, Romania, eastern Germany, Latvia, Estonia, and indeed the Russian Federation, to levels greater than any country in western Europe. While it is difficult to form a conclusive judgement on the limited data available about the incidence of divorce prior to Communist rule, it is almost certainly the case that the high levels of divorce across the East reflect political and economic stresses; they reflect in Goode's expression the 'polity as agent of marital dissolution'.[32] This is a quite different catalyst of marital dissolution from the increasing individualisation experienced in the West. Nevertheless there have been significant differences between former Communist states in developments since the initial increase in the 1950s. In many countries in the East, divorce rates have been fairly static across a long period of time (e.g., Romania, Poland) and indeed in some countries, having risen initially, divorce rates have fallen significantly, most notably in eastern Germany, Croatia, Slovenia and Latvia. Also the existence of strong and persistent differences within a single state (the former Czechoslovakia, within which the Czech Republic has had an incidence of divorce nearly double that of Slovakia) hints at influences beyond or beneath the effects of 'polity'.

Discussion

The extensive changes that have occurred over the last few decades could be discussed and evaluated within a number of overlapping sociological narratives, and a sufficient description, let alone explanation, would require the successful integration of such narratives. While demographers have tended to be more successful at charting trends than explaining them, even this modest task is stumbling in the face of inadequate data, especially when *de facto* marital status or 'social marital status' is considered, such that there is genuine debate whether trends in Europe are converging or diverging.

---

[32] See Goode, *World Changes*, ch. 5.

Nevertheless, such information is crucial to informing public debate about what we desire in partnerships and for the nurture of children as well as discerning what developments might lie in the future. Three points in conclusion, then:

A Marital-fertility Transition

At the heart of the changes described above there lies a radical break with the past, a 'truly Promethean transformation'[33] involving a profound shift of responsibility to the self. The advent of new, highly effective contraception in the 1960s is the catalyst. The change itself is that marriage ceases to be the threshold for procreation as children become increasingly the product of conscious choice. As a result, a series of developments has occurred in which sex, marriage and procreation become 'unravelled', a process which can correctly be identified as a 'marital-fertility transition'. Facilitated by the collapse in 'plausibility' of the religiously based prohibition on pre-marital sexual intercourse, it has occurred across all the countries of Europe (including those predominantly Catholic), and, I suggest, is likely to spread across the industrialised world. The key demographic components of this change are: a fall in fertility; the postponement of both marriage and childbearing (which reflects the enhanced economic and educational possibilities open to women); and the increased sphere of personal decision-making (reflective and constitutive of the 'postmodern' condition) in which there is a reluctance to choose to make long-term commitments.

Whilst these changes have spread broadly following the proposed path of innovation, there has been more variation in the logical sequence of its progression than envisaged by Santow, van de Kaa and others, a fact highlighted by the 'contraceptive backwardness'[34] of some countries which appear to have undergone such change. This marital-fertility transition is then a development parallel to the fundamental shift in marital fertility central to *the* earlier demographic transition,

[33] P. L. Berger, *The Heretical Imperative: Contemporary Possibilities of Religious Affirmation* (London: Collins, 1980), pp. 12–13.
[34] Castiglioni and Zuanna, 'Innovations and Tradition', p. 127.

which took place between 1890 and 1920 across much of Europe.[35] Whereas in this earlier period the crucial change was the earlier termination of childbearing and therefore a fall in higher order births, in this second shift the change concerns the later initiation of a procreative career.

The stability of the man–woman relationship

Divorce rates have continued to rise slowly over the last ten to fifteen years in most countries of northern and central Europe and there is little sign of a 'plateau' or even a 'ceiling' to this[36] (with the possible exception of the Netherlands[37]). Indeed given the extent of cohabitation, the use of the incidence of divorce as the sole measure of the dissolution of adult relationships is now woefully inadequate, and relationship dissolution is without doubt grossly underestimated. Manting,[38] for example, estimates that more cohabitations break up each year than do marriages in the Netherlands and if correct a similar situation is likely to pertain across much of northern Europe. Kiernan, however (drawing on *Eurobarometer* data), paints a slightly different picture, finding that a surprisingly high proportion of women, 70–80%, aged 35–39, whether married or cohabiting, had only ever had one co-residential partner in most of the countries surveyed. This percentage rises to around 90% in Italy and Spain.[39]

The idea that changes in primary relationships are at root caused by something loosely defined as 'individualisation' has been explored extensively in the last decade, facilitated by the wealth of material that has flowed from the *European Values*

[35] Documented by the Princeton Project under A. J. Coale. See Coale and Watkins, *The Decline of Fertility.*

[36] J. Haskey, 'The proportion of married couples who divorce: past patterns and current prospects', *Population Trends*, 83 (Spring 1996), pp. 25–36.

[37] See A. J. de Jong, 'Trouwen en scheiden: lichte restauratie op komst' ('Marriage and divorce: restorative tendencies expected'), *Maandstatistiek van de bevolking* (Netherlands Centraal Bureau de Statistiek, Juni 1999), pp. 8–16; and Centraal Bureau de Statistiek, 'Echtscheidingen, 1994–1998' ('Divorces, 1994–1998'), *Maandstatistiek van de bevolking* (1999/11), pp. 63–72.

[38] Quoted in van de Kaa, 'Options and Sequences'.

[39] K. Kiernan, 'Cohabitation in Western Europe', p. 28.

Survey and the *International Social Survey Programme.* Detailed analysis of such material has, however, shown that whilst marriage has lost much of its 'institutional weight', increased individualisation is not incompatible with either a high appreciation of marriage and family or indeed what might be called traditional family orientations.[40] Indeed de Moor[41] suggests that over the decade 1981–1990 traditional views on family structure gained support in exactly those countries where secular individualism seemed most dominant. This may reflect a re-evaluation of contemporary family forms, not least in light of growing welfare costs.

Persistent regional variation

There is considerable variation across Europe in the propensity of couples to cohabit, to have children before or outside marriage, or, indeed, to split up. Furthermore, this variation is persistent and deeply rooted. So that whilst, for example, the mean age at which women marry or have their first child is similar in, say, Sweden and Italy,[42] the extent of cohabitation varies by a factor of 10 and that of divorce or extra-marital childbearing by a factor of 5.[43] The escalation in divorce, cohabitation and childbearing outside of marriage must then, I believe, be regarded as auxiliary developments, which have taken place in some countries, may yet take place in others, but are by no means inevitable in all. Rather than being witnesses to the transient plurality of countries at different 'stages' of a journey, it is more likely that we will see the emergence of several distinctive marriage systems across Europe. Increasingly studies of changing attitudes towards relationships suggest an

---

[40] P. van den Akker, L. Halman and R. de Moor, 'Primary Relations in Western Societies', in P. Ester, L. Halman and R. de Moor (eds.), *The Individualising Society: Value Change in Europe and North America* (Tilburg: Tilburg University Press, EVS, 1994), pp. 97–127.

[41] R. de Moor, 'Epilogue', in Ester et al., *The Individualising Society*, p. 229.

[42] Mean age at first marriage, 27.1 in Italy, 28.9 in Sweden; Mean age at first childbirth, 28.4 Italy, 27.4 Sweden (figures for 1996).

[43] Extra-marital births: Sweden 54.1%; Italy 8.3% (1997). Total divorce rate: Sweden 0.48; Italy 0.10 (1997). Cohabitation (% of women who cohabit) aged 25–29: Sweden 31; Italy 3; aged 30–35: Sweden 26; Italy 3.

important role for religious practice or heritage.[44] The patterns of change over the last few decades suggest that older historical and confessional cleavages may still continue to influence the demographic trends and paths that countries take through a 'continuing demographic transition':

1. *Scandinavian or northern Europe* It is in this group of countries that the break with the Western Christian inheritance in respect to the ordering of primary relationships is most established with high rates of relationship dissolution and cohabitation and where a significant minority, between one-quarter and one-third of children, are brought up by lone parents or in stepfamilies. Countries in this group (Norway, Denmark, Finland) are predominantly secular but rooted in an exclusively Protestant heritage and are those which have experienced 'the new primacy of individual aspiration over traditional restraints'[45] most acutely. The extent of the dissolution of relationships is great and although only Sweden has, to date, reached the point at which cohabitational childbearing is well established, it should be anticipated that the other nations will follow fairly rapidly. It is in these countries that Anthony Giddens' ideal type, the 'pure relationship', seems to have taken its clearest shape.[46]

2. *Central Europe* This group of countries (Belgium, western Germany, the Netherlands, Austria) similarly has moderate to high levels of divorce. It differs primarily from its northern neighbours in that cohabitation remains very much a precursor to marriage with cohabitational childbearing relatively uncommon given the prevalence of cohabitation. This situation may change in the next decade and follow the trajectory of the northern pattern, but that is by no means certain.

[44] E.g., R. Inglehart and W. Baker, 'Modernization, Cultural Change and the Persistence of Traditional Values', *American Sociological Review*, 65 (2000), pp. 19–51; and Klijzing and Macura, 'Cohabitation and Extra-marital Childbearing'.

[45] D. A. Coleman, *The State of Europe's Population* (Oxford: Oxford University Press, 1996).

[46] Giddens, *The Transformation of Intimacy*.

3. *Southern Europe* This is made up of predominantly Catholic societies (Italy, Spain, Portugal, Malta) with stronger familial commitments and a pattern of low divorce and low to moderate levels of cohabitation and childbearing outside marriage. This demographic region is likely to prove quite robust unless rapid secularisation results in a profound shift in cultural values.

This rather simple tripartite division obscures the fact that individual countries and smaller groupings have and will persist in having distinctive culturally mediated paths of change in nuptiality. France and the United Kingdom, for example, currently lie between the northern and central patterns. We have already noted the historical peculiarity of Hungary. We might also have considered Ireland where cohabitation is increasing rapidly but divorce remained illegal until very recently. Significantly further divergence in demographic trends in the East is likely to emerge with the formerly Protestant Baltic states becoming more 'Scandinavian' in their demographic profile. The more religiously observant Catholic nations of Poland, Lithuania, Slovakia and perhaps Croatia may incline towards a 'Southern Catholic' profile. Hungary and the Czech Republic may begin to look more like central European countries. Perhaps a fourth distinctive group of south-eastern European countries (Macedonia, Romania, Bulgaria, Albania) will emerge where the marital-fertility transition has yet to take hold.

PART 2

Beginning Marriage

Introduction

Part 2 presents three approaches to the beginning of marriage: one historical and practical, one theological, and one a heart-warming account of a highly successful Christian ministry of marriage preparation. A. R. Harcus describes a remarkable innovation he has introduced into the worship of an English parish church – a betrothal ceremony. Harcus shows how betrothal used to belong to the marriage rites of Catholic and Orthodox traditions, and its historical demise has led to an unfortunate hiatus. So Harcus, acting on his own convictions and well within the confines of canon law, has reintroduced one, and it takes place when a couple's banns are called in church prior to the ceremony. Harcus shows how the new ceremony has reshaped the ministry of marriage preparation and enriched couples' experience of their marriage. The betrothal rite which he uses is included in the text.

Adrian Thatcher draws on the sort of social research utilised by Dormor (Ch. 2) in his analysis of European trends surrounding marriage. He produces a detailed 'guide to living together', pointing out many unpalatable consequences of cohabitation outside marriage. He distinguishes between 'pre-nuptial' and 'non-nuptial' cohabitation, and agrees with Harcus' analysis of the place of betrothal in Christian history. Thatcher is prepared to acknowledge that pre-nuptial cohabitors might be regarded much like the betrothed couples of earlier periods, and this conviction leads him to examine the biblical basis for betrothal and indeed the New Testament theology of it. An 'archaeological' reading of a contemporary marriage rite yields traces of medieval betrothal vows. Thatcher describes how the shift in theological understanding of pre-nuptial cohabitors as having already embarked on the passage from singleness to marriage, transforms attitudes to couples who, until recently, would have attracted censure from Christian ministers and congregations.

Philip Newman's account of marriage ministry in an Australian parish church offers a powerful, practical vision of what local congregations can do, and how effective they can be. Here is a church in tune with its locality, eager and able to offer marriage preparation and to advertise its services. The story of the growth of this particular marriage ministry should inspire all ministers who feel impelled to seize upon marriage preparation as an opportunity for much needed pastoral care. The story runs from a basic marriage preparation course, and free computer disks for couples to design (with guidance) their own liturgies, through to preparation courses for *divorced* people who wish to remarry, to the adult baptisms of inquirers, to baptisms of the children of married couples (he reads the birth column of the local newspaper), and to ten-year follow-ups. There can hardly be a more exhilarating case of practical, parish-based, marriage-focused, pastoral care.

3

The Case for Betrothal

Reg Harcus

Few people digest doctrine through sermons, lectures, or even reading. Generally our understanding of Christian teaching comes about indirectly, through the hymns or songs we sing, or from the shape of public worship. In the case of the wedding service, however, something seems to have gone wrong in the communication. Many people continue to find the church's doctrine in this area confused and confusing. This chapter began its life when a group of students examining the liturgies associated with 'rites of passage' began to question their present form. Is it possible that over the centuries something has been lost? What began as an historical review, in one parish has resulted in a practical policy.

Some of the pastoral problems relating to marriage arise because of a confusion of intention. Often neither the couple nor their families are asking about marriage when they visit a priest to talk about a wedding. What has really happened is that a wedding has been arranged. All the energy of preparation is geared to that. There is the need to arrange for the reception, decide on the wedding dress and what the bridesmaids are to wear, the honeymoon plans, and there are often concerns over costs. There is hardly time to consider things that will happen after the wedding day. Perhaps the nearest they come to that is finding a place to live and what furnishings they want.

The essential element in the wedding ceremony has long been the expression in civil law of consent by the two partners. Almost every society has at one time or another regarded this as essentially a private event, the affair of the families involved alone. Today there is much pressure to return to that situation and to regard marriage as purely a private arrangement. Nevertheless, when two people begin living together often they make some kind of informal statement of intention to a small circle of friends or relations. Despite this, the pervading individualism of society encourages young people to suppose that their relationship has nothing to do with the rest of society. It is not that they do not want a ceremony, religious or otherwise, but that they do not feel the need to make any openly public statement about their relationship.

This is too small a vision of the impact that the 'pair bonding' of two people has. It has echoes far beyond the immediate circle of the individuals themselves. The failure to acknowledge this sometimes becomes the source of later problems and injustices. More than a few social problems have their origins in the split up of cohabiting couples. In 1563 the Council of Trent expressed great concern about 'secret marriages' – marriages drawn up properly but in private. The concern then had to do with legal questions relating to the right of inheritance by children of such a marriage. Today our problems are perhaps somewhat similar. In particular we might think of the issues associated with single-parent families. The fact is that marriage cannot remain a private arrangement. It has implications for the whole of the community at large. Hence the marriage compact must be notified to society. It should be entered into publicly.

The Marriage Contract in Christian History

At first in the Christian church there was little need for a marriage liturgy. Pagan converts for the most part were already married before their conversion to Christianity. When already baptised Christians wished to marry, the idea of celebrating such marriages with a separate church ceremony did not at first come to mind. For Judaism, from which Christianity had originally grown, it was already the case that 'many of the customs were largely a matter of local practice rather than Jewish law'.[1] In the same way, for several centuries Christians did much the same thing as their non-Christian counterparts, whether the society in which they lived was Greek, Roman,

---

[1] Solomon Nogosian, 'Judaism, the Way of Holiness', *Crucible* (1986), p. 182.

Germanic, Frankish, or Celtic. The well-known passage from the *Epistle to Diognetus* asserts that Christians 'pass their lives in whatever township – Greek or foreign – each man's lot has determined and conform to ordinary local usage in their clothing, diet, and other habits. They obey the prescribed laws, but in their private lives they surpass and transcend the laws.'[2] Initially, then, the ceremonies and popular customs associated with marriages in contemporary society also formed the marriage ceremonies for baptised Christians,[3] with some minor modification to avoid aspects of pagan belief. Although the Council of Elvira, about 305–6, took an extreme position with regard to the discipline to be exacted on Christians proved guilty of adultery, the canons still presumed that the marriage of the baptised took place in much the same way as for the marriage of unbaptised pagans.

Nor did the recognition of the church by Constantine bring any great change. Christians continued to seal the marriage contract through the regulations demanded by civil law. Pope Nicholas I ruled, 'Let the simple consent of those whose wedding is in question be sufficient as the civil laws prescribe.'[4] The church continued its practice of holding the marriage of its members in high honour and celebrating the event, but, strictly, the church did not *solemnize* weddings. In the early centuries, marriage was perceived as a straightforward secular act. Marriage 'in the sight of the church' (*in facie ecclesiae*) was then unknown.

---

[2] *Epistle to Diognetus* 5.4 in *Early Christian Writings* (Harmondsworth: Penguin, 1984), p. 176.

[3] The two early references to 'church weddings' are not really exceptions. Ignatius, *Epistle to Polycarp* (5:2), says that men and women should not marry without the consent of the bishop. This is an example of Ignatius trying to increase episcopal authority. There is no evidence that his direction was ever followed by anyone. In *On Modesty* (4:9) Tertullian certainly rules that only marriage 'in the sight of the church' is recognised. But this tract was not produced until after Tertullian had become a Montanist and reflects Montanist tradition rather than mainline Christianity.

[4] Quoted in G. H. Joyce, SJ, *Christian Marriage* (London: Sheed & Ward, 1948), p. 609.

Betrothal and Marriage

Ancient practice in many places divided the marriage into two quite distinct parts. First of all came the espousal or betrothal. From the sixth century BCE in Athens, this was essentially an agreement between the bridegroom's family and the 'master' of the bride. The marriage was 'family-business', and might be arranged while the partners were yet still children. Once marriage customs from the East were introduced, the giving of a pledge in the form of an engagement ring quite often sealed the betrothal. Tertullian is the first Christian to acknowledge this custom when he writes, 'No woman was acquainted with any gold except that on one finger which her spouse had pledged to himself with the engagement ring.'[5] The old Roman betrothal ceremony included many elements we would still recognise today that have been transferred to the wedding itself. A kiss and the joining of hands accompanied the exchange of a ring. The betrothal ceremony was also the occasion for the giving of presents. Within Greco-Roman society, the betrothal was understood as a declaration of intent that carried a commitment not only between the two partners, but also between their families.

In the Old Hebrew scriptures, marriage is frequently associated with a prior betrothal. The case of Jacob and Rachel[6] is perhaps the most well-known example. In the Jewish tradition the betrothal was primarily an action of the bridegroom. It signified that the woman was bound to him in a way that meant she was no longer free to marry anyone else. Amongst Germanic people,[7] marriage took the form of two distinct acts: the betrothal and the *Trauung*,[8] the marriage itself. The Franks,

---

[5] Tertullian, *Apol.* 6.4, *Ante-Nicene Christian Library* [ANCL] 3 (Edinburgh: T&T Clark, 1993), p. 22. That this custom is first cited in Carthage may indicate that the Phoenician heritage continued to exercise an influence.

[6] Gen. 29:15–20. Here it is interesting to note the betrothal period lasts for seven years. The case of Mary and Joseph could be cited from the New Testament for the same custom.

[7] See the sources cited by Edward Schillebeeckx, OP, *Marriage – Secular Reality and Saving Mystery*, Vol. 2 (London and Melbourne: Sheed & Ward, 1965), p. 38.

[8] In Germanic law the most important element of the *Trauung* was the handing over of the bride by her father or guardian. This marked the validity of the marriage.

the Iberian races and the Celts all regarded the betrothal and marriage as distinct legal proceedings. The betrothal was a sort of deed of purchase or conveyance between the bridegroom and the tribe or sponsor of the bride. By giving of presents and other sureties the bridegroom placed himself under an obligation to take the girl as his wife and to give her a share of his possessions. Amongst the Celts, the groom gave a present of money to the sponsor of the bride as a way of entrusting her into his keeping to go unharmed until the day of the wedding.

In all of these cultures, the betrothal was more than the modern engagement party. Indeed, it would be more proper to say that the engagement party is the old betrothal ceremony robbed of all its significant elements. The wedding proper was simply that point in time when the bridegroom brought his wife into his home and the couple took their place together in society. Normally the bride and groom were decked out in marriage costumes, wearing garlands or crowns, and in many places, the bride also wore a veil. They joined in the sacrifices and often shared food and drink. Then a torchlight procession followed them to the bridegroom's house where the bride was lifted over the threshold into the bridal chamber.

This was the practice, with a few minor modifications, followed by Christians for many centuries. The two parts of the marriage were observed in the manner of their fellow citizens. Sometimes there was a lengthy period between the two parts. It is almost certain that only very rarely were the two parts run together as one ceremony. The Jewish community has continued to be aware of the two distinct parts to a marriage and to draw the distinction. Among Christians, however, the betrothal and the wedding became confused. In the process something has been lost.

The betrothal was concerned with a statement of intention and an acceptance by society of the marriage. The wedding celebrates the couple as members of the community and a granting of their privileges within society. It is the betrothal that provides the time to reflect on the meaning and purpose of marriage. In Christian terms, it is at that point in the process that the discussion of faithfulness, the permanence of the marriage relationship and the other elements of marriage education have their place. As the wedding ceremony is presently administered it is no longer possible to make clear the theological and pastoral reasons why marriage consisted of two parts.

The earliest 'church weddings' were a reaction against the regulations of Roman law. Under normal Roman law slaves could not marry free persons, nor indeed were their marriages to each other properly recognised as such. They were joined in concubinage, not *matrimonium*. In a few cases, bishops stepped into situations to conduct 'secret or clandestine marriages', not recognised in Roman law but satisfying the consciences of the Christian community. This was a rare event rather than a rule. Part of Hippolytus' complaint against Callistus[9] was that he had introduced this practice of 'marriages of convenience'. Such a custom was not so widespread as to be in any sense universal. Augustine was careful not to become involved in what he thought was dubious practice.[10] When such a secret marriage went wrong, he feared that the blame would be laid at the bishop's door.

'Church weddings' in a proper sense date from the later part of the fourth century. It is likely that they originated in the visit by a priest, or more particularly a bishop, to congratulate a family on the celebration of a marriage. Not unnaturally, in that situation, couples frequently asked for a blessing on their new state in life. Ambrosiaster mentions that this practice[11] was found both in the synagogue and in the church. Church marriage liturgies developed over the passage of time. Even so, the 'real marriage' was the legal ceremony, not the service, which was merely a blessing of what had already happened. According to Gregory of Nazianzus,[12] the prayers were that God should harmonise the marriage already concluded.

Being Wed in Church

It is important to notice that the marriage was conducted regularly in the setting of the home. The canopy that plays so

---

[9] Hippolytus, *Refutation of all Heresies*, 9.12.24, ANCL 6.

[10] Possidonius, *Vita. S. Augustini*, 27.4–5, *Corpus Scriptorum Ecclesiasticorum Latinorum* [CSEL], 138.140.8–20.

[11] Ambrosiaster, *Quaestiones Vetri et Novi Testimenti*, CSEL 50.400.11–14.

[12] Gregory of Nazianzus, *Epistle 231: to his friend Eusebius*, PG, 37.373.

prominent a role in most Jewish weddings represents the home of the couple. Christians were married within the family and at home for the first thousand years of Christian history. It is not until the early twelfth century that there is evidence of many 'weddings at the church door'.[13] There is much to commend some kind of action that would focus on the sanctification of the home in this way.

The liturgy of the Orthodox churches directs attention towards the home as a place which sanctifies the marriage. The ancient garlands have become more definitely crowns. The change is linked with a change in the symbolism. The ceremony, called 'the crowning', is a sign of their becoming rulers in a new kingdom, the 'king' and 'queen' of their own home. Their home is then interpreted as an eschatological sign of the Kingdom of God. Their marriage then becomes a witness of the Kingdom already in the world.[14]

Legal pressures in the West gradually removed most of the home-elements of the marriage and moved the celebration closer to the church building. Already in the twelfth century marriage 'at the church door' had emerged, and by the fourteenth century the Sarum Missal assumes that the church door or porch is the normal place for the celebration of the wedding. Chaucer's Wife of Bath had had five husbands 'at the church door'.[15] The need to produce legal documents changed the practice even further. In most villages the most obviously responsible person to provide a proper legal record was the parish priest. By 1549[16] the whole ceremony had moved inside the building in England. By that time the kaleidoscoping of betrothal and wedding into one ceremony was complete and the celebration of a wedding had a form that most people would recognise still today.

[13] See J. G. Davies (ed.), *A New Dictionary of Liturgy and Worship* (London: SCM Press, 1986), p. 351.

[14] N. Zernov, *Eastern Christianity* (London: Weidenfeld & Nicolson, 1961), p. 254.

[15] Geoffrey Chaucer, *The Wife of Bath's Prologue: The Canterbury Tales* (Harmondsworth: Penguin, 1958), p. 215.

[16] In Germany, Luther's *Traubüchlein* published in 1529 still had pronounced the marriage at the church door. See 'The Order of Marriage for the Common Pastor', in U. S. Leopold (ed.), *Luther's Works,* Vol. 53 (Philadelphia: Fortress Press, 1965), pp. 110–15.

In this very rapid historical survey no mention of the nuptial mass has yet been made. That is not because it is unimportant. It began to be introduced at a relatively late period and there was no uniform pattern in its use. By it men and women declared their intention to ratify their marriage not only in the sight of the public, but also 'in the sight of God'. Just as the Orthodox symbolism made Christian marriage into an expression of something beyond worldly affairs, so too the Western nuptial mass and the movement of the whole ceremony to the church building declared that marriage *as the world knows it* is not finally sufficient for the Christian. As the anonymous writer had said to Diognetus long before, Christians obeyed the laws, but in their private lives they exceeded them.

Strangely, the move into the church and the beginning of marriage 'in the sight of God' provides one reason for today's undue emphasis on the wedding ceremony itself. For those with a weaker commitment to the Christian faith, the focus of interest has to move elsewhere. Increasingly the wedding ceremony has become an elaborate fashion and flower show. It is difficult to see how any revision of a wedding ceremony retaining the kaleidoscoping of the two quite distinct parts of marriage can speak in such a scene where for almost everyone the trappings have taken precedence.

The Place of a Christian Betrothal Liturgy

Many clergy will look to make up the deficiencies in our present liturgy by careful preparation of couples before the wedding. One of the difficulties, however, is that the minds of the young couple are focused first and foremost on the wedding. Talk about the expectancy of married life has no more than a secondary place. Indeed some couples regard anything other than the wedding arrangements as an intrusion into their private affairs.

The introduction of some ecclesiastical equivalent to the old betrothal is of great value in this setting. The fact that the majority of couples do still have an engagement party and purchase an engagement ring or rings suggests they feel a need to make some kind of 'declaration of intent'. The church could well take advantage of this psychology to introduce a liturgy in which the issues are quite clearly about the meaning of marriage rather than the wedding.

Ideally it would happen at the time of the engagement, and if possible as a part of the engagement party. In the modern situation, though, that ideal is basically impractical. However, in England and some other countries there is still the requirement to call banns before marriage. Most brides and grooms see this as a significant moment. They and their families frequently want to be present to hear the banns and go to great lengths to attend. The psychological need to make a public declaration is probably the reason for this, even though the banns is actually only an opportunity to object to the proposed marriage. The first calling of the banns can therefore be a very appropriate moment to include a betrothal rite.

A betrothal rite should provide the opportunity for those intending marriage to declare their understanding of the step they are planning and to announce formally their intent to marry. Their families and the congregation, as the representatives of the local community, should also make clear that the marriage is going ahead with their blessing and support. Such a rite need not be of any great length, and it would extend the first calling of banns only minimally. Nor is it without liturgical precedent. In the Sarum ritual, the final calling of the banns immediately precedes the actual wedding service.

Betrothal in the Parish of St Mary Magdalene, Bolney, England

This has all been given practical expression in the parish of St Mary Magdalene, Bolney, over the last five years. Bolney is a small village in Sussex. It is within easy commuting distance of London, so that most of its population is away from the village for most of the time during weekdays. The population is quite young, consisting of families where the chief breadwinner is making his or her way up the career ladder. Mostly they are already married, and their children still too young to be seeking marriage. All of this means that the number of weddings in the parish church is quite low, a matter of four or five per year.

Nevertheless, in this matter, it is not unlike many other villages in the area.

Those who come for marriage are offered an optional betrothal ceremony at the time of the first calling of the banns as a part of the preparation for marriage. The betrothal rite takes place in the parish eucharist, at the Peace. After an introduction outlining the reasons for marriage given in the Church of England's wedding service, but including an extended note on the social element in marriage,[17] the couple declare their understanding of marriage as a lifelong commitment and go on to express the intention to remain faithful to each other in their married lives. The families of the couple are then invited to give their blessing to the proposed marriage and the congregation are asked to accept the responsibility to support the couple as they prepare for marriage, chiefly through their prayers.

Everyone is invited to pray silently for the couple before their engagement ring is blessed. It is fitted with the words: 'We wear this ring as a sign of our betrothal and of the commitment we make to each other in preparation for our marriage.' The whole rite is concluded with the prayer provided at the beginning of the wedding service in the Church of England's *Alternative Service Book*. Since the tradition of the church is to share the Peace, the couple then go through the congregation shaking hands with those near at hand. After the service, coffee and biscuits are served.

Couples seeking to be married in the church are introduced to the possibility of this act when they first make contact. It is not normally offered to anyone who is to be married in another church. The rite very much links the couple into the life of the parish, and is clearly less appropriate in cases where the ceremony is to be held elsewhere. It has always been offered as an option that may be refused. Once the rationale behind the idea of betrothal has been explained, however, it has been accepted in all but one exceptional case. Parents also appear ready to make the effort to attend, even when it involves a long

---

[17] See the Appendix below, p. 53. The calling of Banns is included in this introduction.

journey, because they feel that they have been given a role to play that has previously been denied them.

Discussion of the wedding is then postponed until after the betrothal. Instead, preparation for the betrothal concentrates exclusively on the meaning of marriage. The various topics and issues can be better divided between that preparation and the later discussion about the details of the wedding ceremony. Of course, the wedding usually follows after some interval, though this is not inevitable. There have been two occasions in the last five years when discussion before and after betrothal has led to the cancellation or postponement of the wedding.

Some twenty-five couples have so far claimed the right to a betrothal rite. Several of them have reported that it helped to focus their attention on their marriage, and that it certainly involved them more than merely hearing the banns called. One mother from within the regular congregation was very anxious that her son and his fiancée should have a betrothal before their marriage precisely because she perceived that it led couples to think more carefully about the step they are about to take. There is some more practical evidence of this too. As we examine together the reasons for marriage in the betrothal, the couple are often provoked to examine their real motives more clearly. On one occasion, a wedding was put off so that the partners could work through some of the differences that had surfaced. On other occasions, they have afterwards explained that the experience of the betrothal gave a dimension to the actual wedding that they had not realised was possible. It is noticeable that those who have been betrothed come to their wedding in a more composed state. They appear more confident and natural because they no longer feel that the building is just somewhere that their wedding is to take place. They recognise it as in some sense *their* church.

One reason for this has been the involvement of the local congregation. Generally speaking, before betrothals began to happen, the weddings in the church were regarded as simply the business of those being married. Now, though, the congregation gets the opportunity to meet the couple. They have become more involved with the people using their church. In more than one case, a newly married couple has become part of the church congregation and helped to set the ground for new betrothals among their friends.

When the experiment of betrothals was first introduced in the church, some people were very doubtful. They felt that it would take up too much time. It would interfere with the general order of the service. It would be seen as an intrusion into private affairs. Experience shows, though, that these doubts were unfounded. On one occasion more than one couple celebrated their betrothal. The questions were simply asked of the couples simultaneously. Even those who were most dubious have found that the advantages far outweigh the disadvantages.

More recently there has been a significant advance in the use of this rite. At the time of the last Lambeth Conference, the Archbishop of West Africa visited Bolney and witnessed a betrothal. He was sufficiently impressed by its appropriateness to ask for a copy and an explanation of the purpose of the ceremony. In the Diocese of Koforidua-Ho in the Eastern Region of Ghana the betrothal has now been introduced as a standard part of the church's marriage provisions. The clergy in the diocese have already expressed appreciation of this development and see it as an integral part of the preparation they have normally carried out. The rite has now been distributed to the other bishops in Ghana. It seems that a small part of the Anglican Communion agrees that the betrothal both meets a psychological need in young people as they prepare for marriage and that its proper celebration encourages a fuller understanding of the church's teaching.

Appendix

BETROTHAL BEFORE MARRIAGE

The Introduction

Dear friends, we are gathered together in the presence of God to witness the betrothal of N. and N., and to rejoice with them as they commit themselves to their forthcoming marriage.

N. and N., marriage is a gift of God and a means of his grace in which a man and a woman become one flesh. It is God's purpose that, as husband and wife give themselves to each other in love, they shall grow together and be united in that love as Christ is united to his Church.

The union of a man and a woman is intended for their mutual comfort and help, as they live faithfully together in need and in plenty, in sorrow and in joy. It is intended that, with delight and tenderness, they may know each other in love, and through the joy of their bodily union, may strengthen the union of their hearts and lives. It is given that they may have children and be blessed in caring for them and bringing them up in accordance with God's will.

Marriage is a lifelong commitment. Husband and wife give themselves to each other, to care for each other in good times and in bad. They are linked to each other's families, and they begin a new life together in the community. It is a way of life that all should reverence, and none should lightly undertake.

In this act of betrothal, N. and N. are declaring their intention to enter this holy state, but first I am to announce the Banns of marriage between N. of x parish and N. of y parish. If any of you know any reason why these persons may not marry, you are to declare it now.

The Betrothal

The couple stand before the celebrant.
N. and N., the Church of Christ understands marriage to be, in the will of God, the union of a man and a woman, for better, for worse; for richer, for poorer; in sickness and in health; to love and to cherish each other until parted by death. Is this your intention in betrothing yourself to one another today?

Man and Woman: **It is.**

N., have you resolved to be faithful to *N.*, forsaking all others so long as you shall live?
Man: **I have so resolved with the help of God.**
Have you resolved to be faithful to *N.*, forsaking all others so long as you shall live?
Woman: **I have so resolved with the help of God.**

The celebrant may address the following question to the two families:
Do you, members of the families of *N.* and *N.*, give your blessing to their forthcoming marriage?
Answer: **We do.**

The celebrant addresses the congregation.
You are the witness of this betrothal now being made. Will you do all in your power to uphold *N.* and *N.* as they prepare for marriage?
Answer: **We will.**

The Sign of Betrothal

The celebrant receives the engagement ring[s] and addresses the congregation.
Dear friends in Christ, let us ask God's blessing on this ring that it may be a sign of the continuing love and care between *N.* and *N.* as they prepare for their marriage.

The congregation may pray silently, then the celebrant says:
Blessed are you, God of steadfast love, source of our joy and end of our hope. + Bless this ring given and received that it may be a sign of the commitment of betrothal made today by *N.* and *N.*, through Christ our Lord. **Amen.**

Man and Woman say together:
We wear this ring as a sign of our betrothal and of the commitment we make to each other in preparation for our marriage.

The celebrant says:
God our Father, you have taught us through your Son
that love is the fulfilling of the Law.
Grant to these your servants, that loving one another,
they may continue in your love to their lives' end,
through Jesus Christ our Lord. **Amen.**

4

Living Together before Marriage: The Theological and Pastoral Opportunities

Adrian Thatcher

The phrase 'living together before marriage' makes certain basic assumptions. One of these is that marriage begins with a temporal event which gives credence to talk of 'before' and 'after': another is that this event is singular (i.e., the only one offered, which fulfils several functions); another is that the event decides when, in a couple's life, they can start living together and having sex. In this chapter I shall argue that these assumptions turn out to be liberatingly *false*, thereby creating ironic opportunities for the churches to recover their traditions and reshape their marriage ministries to accord more with the gospel and with the real lives of marrying Christians.

What then is the argument? Much of it is based on an analysis of the practice of living together before marriage (Section 1). Unless a serious prior attempt is made to comprehend the social situation to which theology hopes to speak, it had better say nothing. The 're-visioning' of the entry into marriage I propose depends on the recovery of the practice of betrothal both in the Bible and in Eastern and Western churches (Section 2). The combination of the *social* analysis of living together and the *historical* analysis of Christian marital tradition leads to proposals for *liturgical* innovation and for developing *theological and pastoral opportunities* among pre-married people (Section 3).

A *'Guide'* to Living Together

A basic distinction must first be made between people who intend marriage and live together first, and people who live together with no intention of marriage. This is the distinction between 'pre-nuptial' and 'non-nuptial' cohabitation. 70% of marrying couples in the UK lived together before their first marriage in the early 1990s (the figure is rising, and is higher still for people who intended further marriage). Many more lived together but did not marry (more about them below). While wishing to incorporate pre-nuptial living together into a Christian framework of marriage, it is difficult to see how Christian traditions could ever incorporate non-nuptial cohabitation into a marital framework. Being 'non-nuptial' it excludes itself from marriage.

What then do we know about living together as a prolegomenon to theological work? Sociologists and demographers have been studying it for the last twenty years so there is a wealth of material available. Here are ten propositions about living together, and I admit in advance that *only the last of them can be used in support of the argument of this chapter.*[1]

1. *In many countries more people enter marriage from cohabitation than from the single state.* In the early 1990s cohabitation remained illegal in some states in the USA. By the late 1990s about 70% of first-time marrying couples lived together first. Many of these couples maintain separate residences. In the jargon they are 'living apart together'. They are 'LATs'. This is known in France as 'semi-cohabitation'. Neither is the practice of informal cohabitation confined to industrialised or 'first world' countries. In parts of South America there are more informal unions than formal marriages.

2. *Cohabitors are as likely to return to singleness as to enter marriage.* These are the ones we don't hear so much about, yet in the early 1990s about as many cohabitees broke up as went on to marry. Data from the British

[1] There is a longer and much more detailed list in my forthcoming *Living Together and Christian Ethics* (Cambridge: Cambridge University Press, 2002).

Household Panel Survey (which has followed a sample of 10,000 adults annually since 1991) predict that out of every 20 cohabiting couples, 11 will marry, 8 will separate, and 1 will remain intact after 10 years.[2]

3. *Cohabitation has weakened the connection between marriage and parenthood since the 1970s.* A startling discovery was made in the early 1990s which has enormous consequences for family formation well into the third millennium. Jane Lewis and Kathleen Kiernan postulated two major changes in Britain with regard to 'reproductive behaviour' in the previous thirty years.[3] The first was a widespread separation of sex and marriage which happened in the 1960s. The second was a widespread separation of marriage from parenthood, which happened in the 1980s and gathered pace in the 1990s. The first of these was greeted by social commentators and radical theologians with optimism; the second 'has given rise to moral panic about lone motherhood'.[4] The key to both changes is the declining importance of marriage. According to this thesis when an unmarried couple conceived in the 1960s, they generally married. In the early 1970s, when an unmarried couple conceived they generally either married or had an abortion. Living together as a prelude to marriage 'began in the 1970s'. In the late 1970s and early 1980s, an unmarried couple upon conception opted increasingly for an abortion or an illegitimate birth. The 1990s has seen a confirmation of this trend. But in the 1990s 70% of women marrying for the first time had cohabited before marriage compared with only 6% in the late 1960s. Cohabitation is

[2] Jonathan Gershuny and Richard Berthoud, *New Partnerships? Men and Women in the 1990s* (Economic and Social Research Council/University of Essex, 1997), p. 4.

[3] Jane Lewis and Kathleen Kiernan, 'The Boundaries Between Marriage, Nonmarriage, and Parenthood: Changes in Behavior and Policy in Postwar Britain', *Journal of Family History*, 21 (July 1996), pp. 372–88. And see Jane Lewis, *Marriage, Cohabitation and the Law: Individualism and Obligation* (Lord Chancellor's Department Research Secretariat, 1999), p. 10.

[4] Lewis and Kiernan, 'Boundaries', p. 372.

therefore 'inextricably linked' both to the decline of marriage and the increase in childbearing outside it.

4. *Some people choose cohabitation as an alternative to marriage, not as a preparation or 'trial' for it.* They avoid it for different reasons, perhaps from a scrupulous boycott of a failing patriarchal institution, or because of dating behaviour described as 'sex without strings, relationships without rings'.[5]

5. *'Trial-marriages' are unlikely to work.* There are plenty of difficulties with trial-marriages, best exposed by asking what is being tried. Some cohabitors are trying out whether they can bear living with someone else – they are trying out whether living together is better than living alone. Others are trying out their suitability for marriage – the 'weeding hypothesis'. Only 'those cohabiting couples who find themselves to be well suited and more committed to marriage go on to marry'. The rest weed themselves out or are weeded out by the experience.[6] But all the research shows that the likelihood of divorce increases with the incidence of previous cohabitation. The unconditional love which in Christian marriage reflects Christ's love for the church (Eph. 5:25) cannot be nourished in a context where it can be terminated if 'things don't work out'.

6. *Men, in particular, are likely to be less committed to the female partners they live with, and much less committed than women to any children of the partnership.* In 1996 extensive research showed that 'the substitution of cohabitation for marriage is *a story of lower commitment* of women to men and even more so of men to women and to their relationship as an enduring unit'.[7] While men wanted

[5] www.smartmarriages.com, 8 June 2000. The report cited is Barbara Dafoe Whitehead and David Popenoe, *The State of our Unions 2000* (Rutgers, NJ: The National Marriage Project, 2000).

[6] See Lynda Clarke and Ann Berrington, 'Socio-Demographic Predictors of Divorce', in John Simons (ed.), *High Divorce Rates: The State of the Evidence on Reasons and Remedies*, Vol. 1 (Lord Chancellor's Department Research Secretariat, 1999), p. 16. See the sources cited there.

[7] Frances K. Goldscheider and Gayle Kaufman, 'Fertility and Commitment: Bringing Men Back In', *Population and Development Review*, 22 (supp.) (1996), p. 89 (emphasis added).

sex and female companionship, they did not want them within a family-making context, and they also valued the amassing of consumer items which took economic preference over household commitments. Men have 'greatly increased aspirations for expensive consumer goods such as new cars, stereophonic equipment, vacation homes, and recreational vehicles' and they prefer these to the responsibilities of settling into a new family. The authors found that 'although marriage is declining in centrality in both men's and women's lives, the centrality of parenthood is declining far more in men's lives'. There has been 'a retreat from children' and most of it has been on the part of men.[8]

7. *Cohabitors with children are very likely to split up.* Unmarried couples with children are much less likely to proceed to marry than couples without children. Work done on the Canadian Family and Friends Survey in 1990 showed that the 'presence and number of children within cohabitation have a strong negative influence on separation for both sexes' and 'a strong negative effect on the transition to marriage.'[9] Work done in Britain for the Research Centre on Micro-social Change (1997) concluded 'that direct comparison between first children born in a cohabitation and those born in a marriage shows that the former are much more likely to end up with only one parent. Starting from the birth of the first child, half of the cohabiting parents have separated within ten years, compared with only an eighth of parents who were married before the baby was born.'[10]

8. *Children raised by cohabiting couples are likely to be worse off than children raised by married parents.* Children of cohabiting parents are worse off economically; they are more vulnerable physically. Cohabiting couples are more violent to each other than married couples. Robert

---

[8] Goldscheider and Kaufman, 'Fertility', p. 90. They complain that men are generally not considered in fertility studies and that little is known about men's attitudes to fathering generally.

[9] Zheng Wu and T. R. Balakrishnan, 'Dissolution of Premarital Cohabitation in Canada', *Demography*, 32:4 (November 1995), p. 528.

[10] Gershuny and Berthoud, *New Partnerships?*, p. 5.

Whelan's study, based on British data in the 1980s, showed that children of cohabiting parents were 20 times more likely to be subject to child abuse. If children lived with their mother and their mother's boy friend who is not their father, they were 33 times more likely to suffer abuse than if they lived with their parents.[11] 'The most unsafe of all family environments for children is that in which the mother is living with someone other than the child's biological father. This is the environment for the majority of children in cohabiting couple households.'[12]

9. *The extent of cohabitation may reinforce the belief that all intimate relationships are fragile and transient.* New research suggests that attitudes to marriage are negatively influenced by cohabitation. The experience of successive cohabitation impacts on attitudes to marriage, making marriage less likely, or, if it happens, less successful.[13] Popenoe and Whitehead conclude that 'The act of cohabitation generates changes in people's attitudes to marriage that make the stability of marriage less likely. Society wide, therefore, the growth of cohabitation will tend to further weaken marriage as an institution.'[14] There may then be a serious compound effect of cohabitation on the wider societies where it is practised. If so, this becomes a strong reason for arguing that the process of legal recognition of cohabitation should be halted.

10. *People who live together with their partner before they marry value fidelity almost as much as married people do.* Once the

---

[11] Robert Whelan, *Broken Homes and Battered Children: A Study of the Relationship Between Child Abuse and Family Type* (London: Family Educational Trust, 1993).

[12] David Popenoe and Barbara Dafoe Whitehead, *Should We Live Together? What Young Adults Need to Know about Cohabitation before Marriage – A Comprehensive Review of Recent Research* (The National Marriage Project, NJ: Rutgers, The State University of New Jersey, 1999), p. 8. See also, Jon Davies, 'Neither Seen nor Heard nor Wanted: The Child as Problematic. Towards an Actuarial Theology of Generation', in Michael A. Hayes, Wendy Porter and David Tombs (eds.), *Religion and Sexuality* (Sheffield: Sheffield Academic Press, 1998), p. 332.

[13] E.g., Alfred DeMaris and William MacDonald, 'Premarital Cohabitation and Marital Instability: A Test of the Unconventional Hypothesis', *Journal of Marriage and the Family*, 55 (May 1993).

[14] Popenoe and Whitehead, *Should We Live Together?*, p. 5.

distinction is made between pre-nuptial and non-nuptial cohabitors, differences in relationship quality disappear. 'Cohabitors *with marriage plans* are involved in unions that are not qualitatively different from those of their married counterparts.'[15] The finding led the researchers to conclude that for this group of cohabitors 'cohabitation is very much another form of marriage'.[16] Cohabitors intending marriage 'likely view their current living arrangements as a stepping stone to marriage or as a temporary arrangement until marriage is practicable'.[17] European Union research in 1993 showed that 66.5% of married respondents and 62.9% of cohabiting respondents endorsed the statement that 'Getting married means committing yourself to being faithful to your partner'. However, less than half of those who had previously cohabited and were currently cohabiting or single endorsed the statement.[18] This finding contributed to the conclusion that 'it is the issue of commitment which appears to be central to understanding the greater instability of marriages preceded by cohabitation'.

Retrieving an Ancient Tradition

Armed with the important distinction between pre-nuptial and non-nuptial cohabitation it is possible to see how the abandoned practice of betrothal would restore a sense of order and direction to living together before marriage. The rite of betrothal is retained in the churches of the East (where it is combined with marriage in a single lengthy rite). It was

---

[15] Susan L. Brown and Alan Booth, 'Cohabitation Versus Marriage: A Comparison of Relationship Quality', *Journal of Marriage and the Family*, 58 (August 1996), p. 674 (emphasis added).

[16] Brown and Booth, 'Cohabitation', p. 677. The group was actually 76% of the total of over 13,000 individuals surveyed (using data from the 1987–88 National Survey of Family and Households). In the 1990s the numbers of cohabitors with marriage plans progressively diminished.

[17] Brown and Booth, 'Cohabitation', p. 671.

[18] *Eurostat, 1995*, in Jenny Reynolds and Penny Mansfield, 'The Effect of Changing Attitudes to Marriage on its Stability', in John Simons (ed.), *High Divorce Rates*, pp. 16–17.

deprived of legal recognition by the Council of Trent in 1563 and in England and Wales only in 1753 (by the passing of the Hardwicke Marriage Act which had nothing to do with theology and everything to do with property). One needs to borrow the methods of retrieval, pioneered by feminist theology, to recover betrothal, since, as it has been written out of marital scripts for several centuries, even the most astute theologians barely refer to it and thereby unwittingly confirm its demise.

Betrothal in the Bible

An early intimation of oddness might be the thoroughly biblical character of betrothal. Given the importance of the Bible in all forms of Protestantism, a strange phenomenon emerges – Protestant marital practice does not conform to biblical norms (meagre though these are). Marital practice is a severely truncated and impoverished version of medieval rites (lamentably reductionist in the eyes of the Orthodox). There are five cases of couples becoming married in the Bible by being first betrothed. They are Rebecca and Isaac (Gen. 24), Rachel and Jacob (Gen. 29), Zipporah and Moses (Ex. 2), Sarah and Tobias (Tob. 6–7) and Mary and Joseph (Mt. 1).

If betrothal is not the beginning of marriage, then Mary and Joseph were not married at the time of the conception and birth of Jesus. Whether they were married depends upon a prior view of when marriage begins. Aquinas and his contemporaries could not have allowed that the Mother of God had undergone the inevitable impurities of sexual intercourse, even with her husband. However, the adoption of the consent theory of marriage allowed them to be considered married since sexual intercourse was inessential to the marriage. Indeed, the 'marriage' of Mary and Joseph was a major influence on the consent theory. What the consent theory did not do was explain how Jesus was born before the nuptials had taken place. So the question whether the marriage was 'a true marriage' remained. Aquinas held a marriage was true if it conformed to its true purpose of producing and training children.[19] The sexless

---

[19] Aquinas, *Summa Theologiae*, 2a2ae.154.2.

marriage of Mary and Joseph was therefore a true marriage,
Aquinas argued, perhaps without knowledge of where his
argument was taking him. If he is right about this, then the
ideal marriage is a sexless one. It also follows that there are true
marriages which do not need and do not receive liturgical
ceremony. This view would seem to endorse millions of
informal marriages, past, present and future.

Recovering the Place of Betrothal in New Testament Theology

Betrothal is the assumed means of entry into marriage in the
Bible, and in Greek and Roman custom. It is also assumed in
the marital imagery of the New Testament. St Paul compares
the Corinthian church to a bride betrothed but not yet
presented to Christ her 'true and only husband' (2 Cor.
11:2–3). It is likely that the lengthy story of Jesus at the well with
the Samaritan woman (Jn 4:1–42) is to be understood as a
betrothal story because it relies on the literary conventions
found in the betrothals of Rebecca, Rachel and Zipporah. John
the Baptist explains he is the 'forerunner' of Jesus and
compares his relationship to Jesus as one of 'best man' to bridegroom. But who is the bride? The betrothal conventions
include:

1. The hero travels to a foreign land far away.
2. The hero stops at a well.
3. A maiden comes to the well.
4. The hero does something for the maiden, showing super-
human strength or ability.
5. The maiden hurries home and reports what has occurred.
6. The stranger is invited into the household of the maiden.
7. Hero marries maiden-at-the-well. (He will eventually take
her back to his native land.)[20]

Jesus, too, travels to a foreign land, Samaria. He too stops at a
well, Jacob's well. A woman comes to the well. Unlike Rebecca

---

[20] James G. Williams, 'The Beautiful and the Barren: Conventions in Biblical
Type-Scenes', *Journal for the Study of the Old Testament*, 17 (June 1980), p. 109.

and Rachel, whose striking physical and virginal attributes are remarked on (by male authors), the Samaritan woman has had five husbands and a live-in lover. Jesus, like Abraham's servant, asks her for a drink. Abraham's servant gives gifts to Rebecca (Gen. 24:22) and her family (24:53). Jesus has 'living water' to offer the woman (Jn 4:10). Just as Rebecca 'ran to her mother's house' (Gen. 24:28), Rachel 'ran and told her father' (Gen. 29:12), and the seven daughters of Reuel returned to him (Ex. 2:18), so the Samaritan woman 'left her water-jar and went off to the town, where she said to the people, "Come and see a man who has told me everything I ever did. Could this be the Messiah?"' (Jn 4:29).

There are other parallels which cannot detain us. In this narrative it is Jesus, not the woman, who has water to offer, and even Samaritans are welcome to drink it. Even the final convention, that of marriage, is not exactly neglected, just adjusted. Jesus does not marry the woman but union with him is possible, even for a Samaritan woman with a chaotic love-life. The use of 'We know' (*oidamen*: 'we ... know that this is indeed the Christ, the Saviour of the world' – King James Version) at 4:42 can bear the suggestion of a sexual, marital union, along with the more cognitive sense of being 'convinced'. The very gift of salvation is to be understood as the self-gift of marriage. It provides a katabatic theology of betrothal in which God takes the initiative of self-giving to all humanity in a relationship of infinite love that is finitely lived out in the loving commitments that make marriage. Christ is the bridegroom. There are no worries about virginal status here. The woman who appears in the guise of his betrothed at the well is immoral, and aware that Jews regard her racial origin as inferior (4:9). Unlike the brides of Ezekiel and Ephesians, who have to be prepared by the beautician in order to be made ready for the nuptial ceremonies, this woman does not conform to type. Such is the depth of the love of God for humanity that no one is excluded on grounds of religion, sex or race. Christ in offering them living water offers himself. Like all the other encounters that began at a well and led to betrothal and the union of marriage, the encounter with Christ the bridegroom leads to a union of faith and knowledge which has its counterparts in betrothed love. An adequate understanding of the narrative becomes achievable once forgotten betrothal practice is recovered and built into it.

Two ceremonies, two sets of vows

Marriage liturgies presume two occasions, each marked by appropriate rites and social events. The first is the *spousals* which Gratian identified as *matrimonium initiatum* or the beginning of marriage. This constituted the intention to enter, at a future time, an irrevocable and permanent pledge of union. It was a conditional promise rendered unconditional by *nuptials* or solemnization of the marriage. The promise was made in the future tense – *de futuro*. Sexual intercourse, or the marriage liturgy (whichever came first!), rendered the conditional promise unconditional. Vows were made in the present tense – *de praesenti*. This was *matrimonium ratum*. Aquinas is clear that betrothal is dissoluble.[21] One ground of dissolution is mutual consent (so if the couple go off each other, no harm is done!).

An 'archaeological' reading of the Church of England Marriage Service in the *Alternative Service Book 1980* reveals a fragment of the old betrothal vows of the first millennium. The bride and bridegroom are each asked two sequential questions. These are: to the bridegroom, '*N*, will you take *N* to be your wife? Will you love her, comfort her, honour and protect her, and, forsaking all others, be faithful to her as long as you both shall live?'; and, to the bride, '*N*, will you take *N* to be your husband? Will you love him, comfort him, honour and protect him, and, forsaking all others, be faithful to him as long as you both shall live?' The answer is 'I will', and then in words of the present tense each of them performatively 'takes' the other with the words 'I take you to be my wife' or husband. It may be doubted whether many clergy and marrying couples are aware that the future tense of the question 'Will you take . . . ?' and the future tense of the response 'I will' is a tangible relic of the first millennium, when the vows (or *weds*, or *troths*) were exchanged by the be*troth*ed in anticipation of their nuptial ceremony sometime in the future. The future and present tenses still retain a 'trace' of the *verba de futuro* and *verba de praesenti* of another age. The *Alternative Service Book* closely follows the 1662 *Book of Common Prayer* which also requires responses first in the

---

[21] *Summa Theologiae*, 3, 'Supplement', q.43.art.3.

future, and then in the present tense. Where does that come from? It comes from the future-tense question in the early Sarum manual, 'Wilt thou have this woman to thy wife?' (with variations in the question put to the woman), and the answer (of both), 'I will'. It can hardly be doubted, says one historian, 'that we see here a survival from a time when the promise of espousal was held to be sufficiently ratified, even after a considerable time, by the nuptial ceremony following'.[22]

The Liturgical and Pastoral Opportunities

Earlier in this section A. R. Harcus described the very positive benefits which have followed the reintroduction of a betrothal ceremony, in an English parish church, at the first calling of a couple's banns.[23] Kenneth Stevenson translates several such rites from Eastern sources.[24] If the betrothal rite were ever to be restored as a separate rite, the present marriage service would also be restored, *de facto*, to its previous temporal position in the couple's life-history, as a culmination of a process rather than a singular event licensing talk of 'before' and 'after' a marriage. The 'solemnization of marriage', as the *Book of Common Prayer* calls it, restores the supposition that a marriage already exists, and that it has now reached the point of no return, of unconditional promise which requires the blessing of God and continuing divine grace to sustain it

A genuine rite of passage

A huge pastoral advantage of the double rite is that the passage from singleness to marriage is marked in the couple's story. Once betrothed they are no longer single. They are beginning marriage, but the unconditional commitment which marriage assumes has not yet been required of them by the church, by

[22] T. A. Lacey, *Marriage in Church and State* (London: Robert Scott, 1912), pp. 48–9.
[23] Above, p. 51; see also, A. R. Harcus, 'Betrothal and Marriage', *The Expository Times*, 109:3 (December 1997), p. 74.
[24] Kenneth W. Stevenson, *To Join Together – The Rite of Marriage* (New York: Pueblo Publishing Company, 1987).

their families and friends, or by each other. They grow into this as men and women grow into their vocations as monks and nuns, leaving final vows to the consummation of a long process. Arnold Van Gennep, in *Les Rites de Passage*,[25] has established that for a rite to be a genuine rite of passage, three stages need to be involved in it. These are 'separation, liminality, and incorporation'. The older scheme provided this. At betrothal the couple mark themselves off as no longer single, while preparing themselves for the unconditional obligations of marriage. This middle ground is precisely 'liminality', the state of being on the threshold of marriage. People marrying today are offered a rite for only the third stage of the process. Kenneth Stevenson (the present Anglican Bishop of Portsmouth, UK) has drawn attention to the inadequacies of the liturgical provision of the Western churches. He thinks that there is a 'deep structure' to marriage which was once provided for liturgically and now no longer is; that proposed liturgical changes (he wrote this in 1987) amount to playing around with surface meanings instead of addressing the theological and psychological hiatus; that marriage liturgies once catered for the deep needs of the human spirit and no longer do.[26] I agree with this. I think the present efforts of the churches to commend marriage are right, but I reluctantly conclude this is proceeding without any real grasp either of the deep meanings of the theological or liturgical past or of the deep social significance of the demographic trends of the present.

Growing into marriage

I hope that by now the theological and pastoral opportunities provided by the growing practice of living together are suggesting themselves. Non-nuptial cohabitation is unlikely ever to be thought consistent with Christian faith if only because God wills only what is best for us, and there are good reasons for thinking that these arrangements are not the best for us, and particularly not the best for women and children.

---

[25] *Les Rites de Passage* (Paris: Librarie Critique, Émile Mourry, 1990).
[26] Stevenson, *To Join Together*, p. 8.

The distinction between pre-nuptial and non-nuptial cohabitation may be precisely the catalyst that assists pastoral carers in helping pre-ceremonial couples honestly to review their relationships. There are *empirical* reasons for suggesting that if they do not intend marriage they may be harming themselves; there are *theological* reasons for suggesting that if they intend marriage they may already have begun it.

Whether or not betrothal is reinstated, recognition of it, even of the absence of it, draws attention to the processive character of marriage. It is a matter of growth where separately and together individuals grow towards each other. Marriage is a particular form of the Christian experience of new life in Christ, whereby endowment in the Christian virtues is a *shared* undertaking. The Western emphases on consent and consummation provided a slight sense of process, but while they were capable of undergirding a theology of marriage at the start of the second millennium, they can no longer adequately do so at the start of the third. The idea that the essence of marriage lay in consent is largely a by-product of medieval debates about how the 'marriage' of the parents of Jesus Christ could be valid, perfect and sexless. If *consensus facit matrimonium*, then it is possible for a couple to be validly married without ever having touched each other (and that is precisely why the Western churches taught it). This should be faced. The Orthodox churches regard the consent doctrine as reductionist and pointedly don't have a place in the liturgies for it to be expressed. The Germanic churches (however sexist) regarded marriage as having begun as soon as the bride was handed over and began living with the groom. There are alternatives. Consummation provides important senses of completion or fruition, achievement and fulfilment, but it is very doubtful if the first act of sexual intercourse could ever achieve this. Consummation might be more appropriately located at the point in the couple's life-history where the decision to make life-long commitments to each other and to children becomes irrevocable. When the couple reach this stage, then it becomes appropriate for them to go public about what is happening.

In *Marriage after Modernity* [27] I offer some friendly criticisms of

<hr/>

[27] Adrian Thatcher, *Marriage after Modernity: Christian Marriage in Postmodern Times* (Sheffield: Sheffield Academic Press, 1999), p. 242.

the Vatican document *Preparation for the Sacrament of Marriage*,[28] precisely because it refuses to allow that sacramental grace can be experienced before the service of marriage. It is not only sex that we can't have before the ceremony – we can't have God's grace either! The realisation that things were once very different would allow the church to look for signs of God's grace in the growing commitment of couples to each other, and in the painful searchings about whether to make it unconditional. 'The exclusion of sacramentality from engagement seems to have disastrous pastoral consequences. The early flowering and blossoming of mutual love is potentially one of the most graced times in people's lives.'[29]

Finally I suggest the biblical symbols of marriage as a covenant and a union counterbalance each other and provide a biblical foundation for marital spirituality. '"Covenant" clearly maintains the separate identities of the spouses as they undertake a common project, whereas the one-flesh union clearly maintains their oneness, a union of hearts and lives.' Spouses need to see themselves as 'simultaneously separate persons and united partners, and to regard their separateness and togetherness as dialectically related'. Although now is not the time even to outline a theory of marital spirituality, the essence of it is the joint project of 'each trying to love the other as God loves them both in Christ, and recognising Christ in each other'. While marital spirituality cannot be derived from what I have said about betrothal, the connecting thread is the life-history of the couple and its goal according to Christian faith. The pre-ceremonial stage of a marriage is as significant as the instructional stage of a catechumen seeking baptism or a nun preparing to take her vows. Ceremonies are events along the way. Most models of spirituality in Christian faith (with highly notable exceptions) are provided by celibate males enduring the path of renunciation. Perhaps the new century will see an explosion of spiritual testimony whereby couples

---

[28] Pontifical Council for the Family, *Preparation for the Sacrament of Marriage* (Vatican City: Vatican Press, 1996). Section 47 states: 'Although *still not in a sacramental way*, Christ sustains and accompanies the journey of grace and growth of the engaged toward the participation in his mystery of union with the Church' (emphasis added).

[29] Thatcher, *Marriage after Modernity*, p. 242.

report becoming closer to God by becoming closer to one another.

I began by noting the growing phenomenon of living together and the prospects for a recovery of an earlier tradition of marriage. I hope to have shown there are 'ironic opportunities' for the churches to recover their traditions and reshape their marriage ministries to accord more with the gospel and with the real lives of marrying Christians. The churches should have few qualms about pre-nuptial cohabitation, while to non-nuptial cohabitors they are able to suggest a better way.

5

An Holistic, Parish-based Marriage-Ministry

Philip Newman

St John's Anglican Church in Toorak is an 1860 bluestone church set in pleasant gardens and surroundings in an upper-middle-class suburb about five kilometres from the centre of Melbourne. It has always been popular for weddings, averaging between eighty and ninety a year until recent times. It should be noted that neither the Anglican Church nor the Government in Australia provides any geographic limitation as to where a marriage may take place, and the only church requirement is that one party to a marriage should have been baptised in some Christian tradition.

One of the conditions on which I accepted the incumbency of the parish in December 1988 was that we would endeavour to find the money to employ someone, initially intended to be a priest, who would assist with marriage preparation and conduct some of the weddings. The parish was particularly supportive of this because it had come to regard marriages as being an unfortunate distraction which occupied too much of the parish priest's time and took him away from his pastoral duties in the parish. This was both because the priest took all the weddings, and because he gave such marriage preparation as took place. For this ministry he received the wedding fees (which were not inconsiderable).

In preparing to come to this parish, and in the first few months after I arrived, it became more and more apparent that there needed to be a complete rethink of the opportunities presented in the conduct of marriages, starting off with the question of why we wanted to be, or believed it was important for St John's to be, involved in this area, and what specifically the church had to offer.

We came to the view that we had four things that St John's could contribute.

1. *A warm welcome* No priest or parish is required by church or state to take weddings, and many refuse to take them for other than active parishioners. However, we as a parish could welcome people where they were – we are not an exclusive club catering for ourselves, but a church that delights in sharing who we are and what we have with the community.

2. *Help with human relationships* In today's chaotic world more and more people are finding difficulties with their relationships, and in particular in their marriages. This is a need we believed we could meet.

3. *Marriage preparation* Civil celebrants might refer to this, but we could require it. We believed absolutely in its value for all couples, and not as optional value for some, and we knew we could do it well.

4. *Encouraging faith* In a relatively, and often overtly, godless society, issues of faith are often not raised even by two people preparing for marriage. Nevertheless, most people probably have some appreciation of the divine, and we aimed to help couples talk through their faith and its implications. Many were seeking after 'spirituality' and we as a church desired to share in that journey.

We believe that Christian insights have a great deal to contribute to relationships and marriage (as of course do those of other religions), and we are conscious of the fact that probably most of those coming to St John's to be married are not active or even nominal Christians. However, we are convinced that it is important for them to understand the basic insights of the Christian service of marriage that will be used, and it is in this context that we present the Christian message. In our marriage preparation courses, apart from the introduction to the marriage services, we do not necessarily speak about faith issues unless they are raised, although we say at the beginning that this viewpoint underlies all that we do.

The initial objective of employing an additional staff person was fairly limited: it was to do marriage preparation and to help with taking some of the weddings. However, soon other things were added to this priest's responsibilities. Some of the people he prepared for marriage sought additional counselling and others came back later for the same reason. His wife was a trained psychologist and he referred these people to her practice. In preparing the couples for marriage a lecture style was used with notes given out. Each session ended with a question-and-answer time. These courses were much appreciated and we began to have people from neighbouring Anglican parishes, and from other traditions, sending people to us for marriage preparation.

The Current Situation

At present we make ourselves known by advertising in the Saturday morning newspaper, marriage expos, local papers and magazines. We have developed a website explaining our marriage ministry and inviting responses. After four years the marriage minister retired, and we needed to find someone else. The person we employed came from being the co-ordinator of a diocesan marriage ministry in another state. Her title is 'Co-ordinator of Marriage Education and Counselling' but she is often referred to as our 'marriage minister'. She was and still is a member of the National Executive of the Marriage Educators' Association of Australia, a state trainer for *Prepare* and a skilled and experienced marriage counsellor. At St John's she has developed the preparation courses very considerably both in content and process, and a number of options are offered.

The Basic Marriage Course consists of five two-and-a-quarter-hour sessions, the contents of which are:

Session 1	The changes in society
	The influence of family of origin
Session 2	Effective communication skills
	Identity and self-esteem
Session 3	Resolving conflict constructively
	The marriage service
Session 4	Budgeting
	What increases and decreases love
Session 5	Creating intimacy
	Contemporary issues for your marriage.

In addition, we run a parallel series of group courses for couples where one or both have been previously married and there are children. Besides the group preparation we also offer *Prepare*, an educative tool which through a detailed question-naire, filled in separately by couples, gives a profile of the relationship highlighting strengths and work areas. In two or more succeeding sessions a trained *Prepare* educator works with the couple on their relationship. It is sometimes suggested to a couple who have done a group preparation course that they may benefit from doing *Prepare* as it helps them to focus on particular issues that may be causing difficulties.

Courses are held on weekday evenings, Sunday afternoons or over a weekend. In fact we now offer some fourteen basic courses, and three or four remarriage courses a year, preparing some three hundred couples.

In the last twenty years in Australia marriage preparation has become a major concern of the churches, especially the Roman Catholic Church, and to some extent the secular marriage counselling services. Much thought and research has gone into how relationship skills and insights can be learnt. Our marriage minister came to St John's informed about new approaches that emphasised adult learning methodology and the use of trained marriage educators. She immediately began recruiting and training marriage educators and now all our courses are run by at least two trained people. In relation to marriage preparation courses, she sees herself primarily as the trainer of trainers and the supervisor and supporter of these able volunteers.

These volunteers give of their time, in broad terms, for two reasons. First, people come because marriage preparation is an area in which they are interested, and they see it as an oppor-tunity to serve. Most of the educators at St John's give their time for this reason. We have found having a good number of educators is important because of the time demanded of them. Most volunteers can only run three or four courses a year. The second reason people come is because they want to be trained and gain experience as marriage educators so that they can use their training elsewhere. Thus we trained a social worker with the Greek Orthodox Church who now runs courses for that denomination. We also regularly train officers from the Salvation Army and pastors from Seventh-Day Adventist churches on this basis.

Our philosophy of adult learning accepts that every adult has insights into life and human relationships. The educative process involves creating opportunities for adults to reflect on this prior learning in order to facilitate growth and change. Content is given but the emphasis falls on interaction and reflection. In our marriage courses matters such as conflict, or the impact of family of origin, or the management of finances are not dealt with by giving information in a lecture but by getting couples to work together, often with the aid of a handout, on these things. At the end of every course a detailed response sheet is given out and filled in. Those present are asked to assess how well the educators ran their course and of what value it was to them. These response sheets consistently score our educators and our courses very highly, and help us to modify and develop our courses continually.

Once our marriage minister had the group marriage courses established on the new basis, she started developing our marriage-counselling ministry. With her team of trained educators she could give time to this. She now sees a large number of mainly younger couples who have usually gone through our preparation programme but have run into some difficulties. As they come highly motivated and at an early stage, she is able to help many of them find the intimacy and communication in their relationship they are seeking. We have recently had to appoint another woman to counsel one night a week in order to share the heavy workload.

The Wedding Service

During the preparation process we provide couples with a range of materials to help them prepare for their wedding, including:

- an information leaflet
- the two permitted orders of service for them to choose from
- a booklet of suggested hymns
- a booklet of readings (biblical and non-biblical)
- a Bible
- a list of suggested organ pieces for the procession, signing and recession.

In addition couples may borrow or buy a CD or tape of suggested wedding music recorded by our organist. A computer disk containing the two orders of service (each with and without the eucharist) and appropriate hymns is available free of charge to help couples put together their order of service. When they have done this they show it to me and I check it over. Then they have it printed.

We are legally constrained by the state, as well as by the rules of the church, in relation to the wording of the service. The Australian Government has approved the orders of service for use by the clergy of the various traditions, and their licensed marriage celebrants. They are obliged to use the form of words for that tradition and no other. Nevertheless, as much flexibility as possible is offered. We sometimes conduct interdenominational and occasionally interfaith weddings. These place some pressure and limitation on what is permitted by both the state and the church. Some of our weddings are of divorced Roman Catholics, and we have a number of weddings between members of incompatible groups, such as Greek and Macedonian Orthodox, or Chinese and Japanese. We have also devised services that work, to a greater or lesser extent, for Jews, Muslims, Buddhists, and atheists.

Couples are, of course, welcome to have a nuptial eucharist, and in the Australian Anglican tradition all who are able to receive communion in their own church of whatever tradition are welcome to receive it on that occasion. Our organ has recently been reconditioned and is now considered one of Australia's finest. The church bells are rung when the bride arrives and when the bridal party leaves the church, and an avenue of candles down the aisle allows the guests and bride to enter by candlelight. Couples can have weddings at any time, except on Sunday mornings and during Holy Week. Our wedding service has a choice of 'prayers of the people', and some are especially for people who have families from previous marriages. (Three examples of these prayers are included as Appendix 1.)

Wedding parties are warmly invited to use the lawns beside the church (without charge) for photographs, and to serve refreshments during the photographs. The use of confetti, rice, rose petals and pot-pourri is welcome. In inclement weather the parties are welcome to use the large parish hall, unless, of course, it has a prior booking.

Baptisms

One of the consequences of marriage preparation is *adult* baptism. There is no pressure on couples seeking to be married in the church to be baptised (despite diocesan regulations), but baptism is always offered, and each year some 25 to 30 of those intending marriage here are baptised.

We read the birth notices in the papers and send baby congratulation cards to couples who have been married at St John's on the birth of their children. As a consequence of this, together with the warm and welcoming experience of their marriage and marriage preparation, and the marriage anniversary letters, requests for infant baptism are inevitable – and welcomed. For example, of the 136 infants baptised last year, 84 were the children of parents who had been married here. We are not concerned where couples live, although if it is in Australia we will provide the couple with the name and address of their local parish church and parish priest. Some baptisms take place within the Sunday morning service, but about two-thirds take place privately at a time to suit. The most extreme case of this was the baptism of the child of an airline pilot, where two of the godparents were also in the airline industry. There was one thirty-minute period in the middle of a weekday afternoon when people who had flown in from four other countries and interstates were actually going to be in the same place at the same time!

We send birthday cards up until the age of 10 to children who have been baptised here and at the same time send a letter to the parents indicating the appropriate stages of spiritual development and recommending resources. As our random survey indicated, this has very, very warm approval – the only real problem being if one child in a family has been baptised elsewhere and so does not get a card!

Continuing Ministry

A very important part of the follow-up is provided by letters written on a couple's wedding anniversary for each of the first ten years of their marriage. While the letter varies each year, it always contains an invitation for couples to come and talk to a

marriage counsellor if things are not going as well as one or
both of them had hoped. Each week when this letter is sent out
a number of couples avail themselves of this opportunity, for
which there is a charge based upon income. In this letter we
also invite them to do *Enrich* which is a programme for married
couples.

This letter also contains three or four pages of resource
material from the co-ordinator of our marriage ministry with
different material provided each year. The current year's
material contains:

- a personal story from somebody whose marriage was not
  going well, and who participated in marriage counselling
- an examination of barriers to intimacy
- an exercise, 'Your Top Ten Needs'
- some material on the creative expression of anger.

Couples are at the moment also being invited to take part in a
university research study on parenting.

The quality of our courses, and the follow-up letters which
offer *Enrich* or counselling, means we offer a holistic approach
to marriage ministry which has proved to be very effective.
Couples who have been to one of our courses and then receive
a letter offering further help if needed would seem to be much
more willing to seek to come to counselling than is the general
rule. What is more, when they come early it is far more
effective. As far as we are able to tell from a non-scientific study,
the divorce rate of those married five to ten years at St John's is
no more than 10% compared with the Australian average of
approximately 35% for first marriages and 50% for second
marriages. Our follow-up letters also inform couples of other
activities being run at St John's for groups or for couples, and
invites them to consider renewal of marriage vows on
significant occasions, such as their tenth wedding anniversary.

At the heart of this process is the development of personal
relationships, inevitably built around me, although, of course,
there will be others involved. I almost always see the couple
when they come to get the initial information and sign the legal
documentation. I take the part in the marriage preparation
that is connected with the order of service, and I am available
for couples to come and talk with me about their wedding. I
conduct the wedding rehearsal and then the marriage in at

least 90% of the cases. Other Anglican clergy are welcome to take weddings here when they have a particular contact with the couple. Clergy of other traditions are not permitted to take weddings but are welcome to take part.

I visit the couples who are to have their children baptised (if they live in the reasonably close vicinity, say within ten kilometres or less), to talk about all that is involved. I will then conduct the baptism.

This is a significant time commitment of around 440 hours, or four weeks' full-time, for weddings, and about 200 hours, or two weeks' full-time, for baptisms per year. In addition, of course, I have parish duties, I am an Archdeacon with some 43 parishes and have diocesan responsibilities. I am also Director of the Anglican Church of Australia's International Relief and Development Fund, all of which means I live a full and interesting life.

The number of weddings is now running at around 170 a year – probably as many as can comfortably be accommodated in the times and days people want to be married. We always ask why people want to get married here, and increasingly the response is, *because they were recommended, or because they had been to weddings at St John's.* Marriage preparation is a condition for being married at our church, and in a survey conducted of a random sample of those who had been married over the previous ten years (with about a 40% response) the experience of marriage preparation, of the wedding itself and of the follow-up was overwhelmingly positive. Only one of those who responded to the survey found the marriage preparation unhelpful, and only one found the follow-up unhelpful.

We are in it for the long term. We have contact with most couples (unless we cannot locate their address – and we have very sophisticated ways of doing that) for at least ten years, and for those who have children baptised here (which is somewhere between a quarter and a third of those we marry) we will be in contact for perhaps twenty years. We regard these people as being a part of our extended parish community, and so we invite them to significant parish events – last year, for example, it was to the one hundred and fortieth anniversary celebration of the parish's foundation. We also always invite those with children (whether or not baptised at St John's) who live within about ten kilometres of the church to come to special children's services at Christmas and on other occasions. The parish is happy to see all this as a part of its ministry, and while they recognise that it takes me away from them, we have another priest, two licensed pastoral workers and a youth and family worker to work within the parish. A major parish review, which took place two years ago, indicated something like 90% support for this ministry and its continued development, and we are constantly seeking to improve the range and quality of all that we do.

Appendix 1

Some Prayers from Prayers of the People

For the joy of loving:

God our Creator, we thank you for your gift of sexual love
by which husband and wife may delight in each other,
and share with you the joy of creating new life.
By your grace may *N* and *N* remain lovers,
rejoicing in your goodness all their days. Amen.

For an existing family:

God of all grace and goodness,
we thank you for this new family,
and for everything parents and children have to share;
by your Spirit of peace draw them together
and help them to be true friends to one another.
Let your love surround them and your care protect them,
through Jesus Christ our Lord. Amen.

For the healing of memory:

Loving God, you are merciful and forgiving.
Grant that those who are suffering the hurts of the past
may experience your generous love.
Heal their memories, comfort them,
and send them from here renewed and hopeful. Amen.

Appendix 2

Tenth Anniversary Letter

Mr Drewe and Mrs Eliza Bellmaine
11 May Street,
BRIGHTON, VIC. 3186

3 December 2000

Dear Drewe and Eliza,

Congratulations on your tenth wedding anniversary – well done! You are very much in our thoughts and prayers.

A new millennium offers an opportunity for new beginnings in all sorts of ways – and not least in our relationships, and especially marriage. How do we do this? The most important element is to find time. Then do something intentional: for example, take up Lynley's invitation (in the enclosed letter) to do the *Enrich* programme; read and discuss together either of the books she recommends, or perhaps one of the 'Men are from Mars; Women are from Venus' series; and, of course, make use of the resource material accompanying this letter. As you know, we believe that no marriage is as good as it could be, and that any work done on your relationship is valuable.

We are often much better at going to the doctor at the first sign of anything going wrong physically, but not so good at seeking help when the health of a relationship deteriorates! So if things are not going as well as you hoped, do feel free to contact Lynley (or the Anglican Marriage Guidance Council in your area through your local parish if you are out of Melbourne) and arrange to have a talk at a time to suit you; obviously it is better if both come, but that may not always be possible. And while we all have our networks of family and friends who support us, they are hardly objective (thank heaven!), and sometimes it is helpful to have someone who is professional and neutral. Seeking such help is not a sign of failure, but of commitment to one another, and to a mutually fulfilling future.

We warmly commend the idea having a service of Renewal of Marriage Vows, either on a particular anniversary such as this one, or at some other time; this can be a very significant way of renewing your commitment to and celebration of one another.

You can do this on your own, or in the presence of family and friends. Please contact the office for further information, or feel free to give me a call at any time. Do get in touch if we can help.

As you have completed the first decade of your marriage, this will be our last anniversary letter. However, if you would like to hear of our on-going programmes for people married at St John's just let us know – we would be delighted to keep you in touch; we still regard you as a part of our extended family, and remember you in our prayers.

Again, many congratulations, and every blessing on your next year of married life.

Your brother in Christ,
[Archdeacon] Philip Newman

From: Lynley Giles,
        Co-ordinator of Marriage Education and Counselling,
        St John's Toorak

I write just after a very pressured time in my life. I had just too much on my plate. One of the things that puts extra strain and stress on all marriages is excessive busyness. So many of the couples I see in counselling tell me that they are so busy they have little time to do fun things together and relax. This takes its toll on the marriage. When most of our time and attention is taken up with work, or something else, the marriage relationship suffers. Sometimes one party is so dissatisfied with the situation that they tell the other they want to leave. In some cases it is the reason why an affair happens. Someone else offers company, a listening ear and fun times.

Recently I was asked by the Institute of Family Studies to organise a gathering of ten couples to discuss how helpful marriage preparation was for them, and what they would like to see improved in such courses. I enclose a letter from a participant named Ann who has written down her thoughts on this. I think you may find this letter interesting.

In the year 2000 we are offering *Enrich* again as a way for couples to do some work on their relationship. In the first session you fill in a detailed inventory which gives a profile of the strengths and the areas needing work in your marriage. In two follow-up sessions you have the opportunity to work on enriching your relationship. I had some wonderful times with couples who did this last year. It is always a joy to see people finding new depths and rewards in their marriage. We make a nominal charge of $145 for the three sessions.

In 2000 we are also offering a four-night course on marriage and children. The arrival of the first baby and subsequent children changes the marriage relationship and raises many stresses. Couples who would like to reflect on how to negotiate this period of transition may like to enrol. The first course will be Monday evenings, 5th, 12th, 19th and 26th June.

Two good books I would like to recommend are: *Boundaries in Marriage* by H. Cloud and J. Townsend, Strand Pub., and *Family Ties that Bind* by Dr Ronald Richardson, published by International Self-Counsel Press Ltd. Both of these books help us understand ourselves and our partner in the light of our family of origin. The better we understand ourselves and the one we love the better equipped we are to start making small changes in how we relate.

Do give me a ring if I can help in any way.

Yours sincerely,

P.S. Words have the power to make a person into something or to make him or her feel like a nothing.

PART 3

Love and Marriage

Introduction

All major Christian traditions (including, after Vatican II, Roman Catholic) agree that the meaning of marriage cannot adequately be stated without recourse to the complex ideas of divine and human love. All three contributors to this section throw new light on what is involved in speaking of divine and human love within marriage.

Stavros Fotiou provides a comprehensive exposition of the Orthodox view of marriage. Western Christians and churches can hardly fail to derive fresh insights from this ancient Christian understanding. Fotiou's chapter takes the form of an extended meditation on John's account of Jesus turning water into wine at the wedding feast (Jn 2:1–11). This passage is read during the betrothal ceremony of the Orthodox churches (see Chs. 3 and 4). The triune God is a communion of love between Persons; all humankind is summoned to share in this love which God is. The union which is marriage shares in the unity God wills with all people individually and all humankind corporately.

Fotiou explains that desire or *eros* within marriage is simultaneously a desire for God. But human love, unaided by divine grace, can fall victim to the disorders of individualism and selfishness. Married love may degenerate to a satisfaction of biological need and become a type of prostitution (the point of saying this is to maximise the horror of exploitation and violation that may occur in marriages). Divine grace, aided by the practice of spiritual exercises, brings about the death of *eros* only to resurrect it as *agape*. Not only are spiritual exercises fundamental to the sharing which is marriage: marital virginity is the result. Hasty conclusions at this point are likely to be wrong, for talk of the death of *eros* and marital virginity do not at all imply abstinence from sex in pursuit of higher goals. Rather, it is selfish indulgence that is renounced, while marital virginity frees the partners from any degradation or abuse of each by the other. This resurrection of *eros* as *agape* is not confined to the couple, for their love, touched with divinity, transcends the possible exclusivism of two persons (the idolatry of the family) and embraces other people more widely (and perhaps universally).

Thomas Knieps-Port le Roi takes issue with a strand of the marital teaching of the Roman Catholic Church, at least from the Council of Florence to *Familiaris consortio*, that the purpose, or at least *a* purpose, of marriage is to provide children for the church. This strand is at odds with other teaching about the purpose of marriage, not least that of Vatican II. It assumes a relation between marriage as sacrament and the church as sacrament whose continuing influence Knieps-Port le Roi finds distorting both to the picture of marriage and the picture of the church. Karl Rahner's reflections on marriage are used in order to deal with these distortions. For Rahner, the growing unconditional *human* love of partners for each other in marriage already has its basis in the love which is God. Their human love points to God's love, just as a sign points to what it signifies. But, says Knieps-Port le Roi, there is an 'astonishing similarity' between the signifying function of the relation between marital partners, and the signifying function of the relation between Christ and the church, where divine and human love are uniquely mingled. It follows that love is essential, not merely incidental, to the purpose of marriage, and that the marital couple is capable of representing fully the sacramental reality of the church. In this way the pictures of the church, of marriage, and the relation between the two are restored to their original richness and colour.

But while love is indispensable for the Christian doctrines of God, of Christ, of marriage, and much else, love is also a notoriously slippery concept with a range of evanescent and contested meanings. In this respect Philip Mellor's essay is a *tour de force*, for three reasons. It describes the fate of love in much twentieth-century social theory. It offers an argument for the cogency of a particular account of love. And, because Mellor is well attuned to the contemporary debates of theologians, and to the need of theologians for convincing models of love, it offers them encouragement in persevering with talk of love, along with resources drawn from social theory to help them do it.

Mellor considers and rejects three standard treatments of love in the social-science literature. That love is a mask for something else, like personal needs, is comprehensively dismissed: such a view ignores the point that love cannot be accommodated within utilitarian or 'rational' frameworks. That romantic love is a relative, Western phenomenon is similarly dismissed: there is good evidence to suggest that romantic love (though not of course the term) is likely to be a *universal* phenomenon. That love is a product of the biological imperative to get us reproducing ourselves is also dismissed: romantic love occurs even when pregnancy is difficult or impossible. Instead of these sceptical treatments of love, we do well to begin again (conventionally enough) with Durkheim. 'Romantic relationships can be interpreted in Durkheimian terms because they clearly have a strong emotional basis, they naturally give rise to ritual, symbolic and conceptual representations of themselves, and they imbue an experience of social solidarity with a transcendent character.'

Anchored in this tradition Mellor is able to introduce to theologians interested in marriage a range of views which will resonate strongly with their present concerns. They may find it surprising that social theorists consider the merging of two individuals into a single reality; that there is a 'religious bond' between lovers; that the individual self becomes dissolved in the other; that eroticism is a route, not to indulgence, but to transcendence, and so on. This 'underground wing' of sociology leads to Breton's notion of *l'amour fou*, or 'mad love', which is 'transgressive', not in the sense that it is promiscuous or anarchic but in that it resists the 'disrupted utilitarian world-view inherent within the modern project, with its reduction of love and sex to appetites'. Here the languages of social theory and theology converge, for both speak of enduring mono-gamous relationships, of love as a sacrament, of 'revelation', of a 'state of grace', of 'conjugal union' (whether formalised or not), even of infidelity as a profanation of the sacred, and so on. *L'amour fou* is thus vindicated and offered to theologians who might want to 'use aspects of his [Breton's] thought to develop further fruitful, interdisciplinary reflections on religion, marriage and love in the contemporary world'.

6

Water into Wine, and *Eros* into *Agape*: Marriage in the Orthodox Church

Stavros S. Fotiou

The passage that recounts Christ's miracle at the wedding at Cana (Jn 2:1–11) is a synopsis of the Orthodox view of marriage; it is therefore not fortuitous that this passage was selected as the Gospel reading in the betrothal service for the Sacrament of Holy Matrimony. The passage presents the matrimonial relationship in the context of human history: from creation to the fall, and from the fall to the recreation. As such, it sets forth the views of the church regarding sexuality, *eros* (physical love), and *agape* (spiritual love), declaring the church's 'good news' about the significance of marriage in human life.

John the Evangelist begins his account of the miracle at Cana: '*On the third day there was a wedding in Cana of Galilee, and the mother of Jesus was there. Jesus and his disciples had also been invited to the wedding.*'

The God which the church proclaims to humankind is a communion of love between three persons: the Father, the Son and the Holy Spirit; the lover, the beloved and the co-beloved. Before the beginning of time 'I', 'you', and 'the other' all encompassed each other in 'we'. Self-transcendence, self-sacrifice, and continuous giving of oneself: this is the way God exists and lives. Love which is offered freely, and freedom which becomes worthy through love: this is what life means.

Humankind has also been called to share in this communion of love. God created humanity freely and out of love. God's sole aim was that everyone should also freely participate in this communion of love. Consequently, every human being that comes into the world has been summoned to a marriage: unity with God. All human beings are called to experience the joyous impulse to love, to emerge from the self and to offer themselves completely to God.

The love between man and woman is called upon to represent and resemble this marriage between God and humanity, Christ's love for the church.[1] In the matrimonial relationship between man and woman we see depicted 'another yearning, another love: the desire and the love of God for humanity'. Saint Irenaeus explicitly emphasises that when the holy Bible speaks about the creation of Eve from the side of Adam, it does so not to indicate the identity of their natures or the complete equality of honour that exists between man and woman, but to declare the unity and the identity, through grace, that was going to exist between Christ and the church. 'God, through his boundless love and affection for his creation, became a human being and bestowed his grace upon humanity so that it could also participate in divine life, thus enabling God to say, when he looked upon a human being, this at last is bone of my bones and flesh of my flesh (Gen. 2:23), just as a man says when he looks upon his wife.'[2] In their marriage, man and woman are both called upon to experience that unity which does not destroy differences and that dissimilarity which does not divide. In their two-in-one relationship they are called upon to experience, inseparably and indivisibly, the mystery of the three-in-one God.

In this way, all newly-weds, just as the couple at Cana, open themselves up to physical love with the highest expectations and dreams of eternal spiritual love. Two human beings 'unite to face together the difficulties and the tragedy of life. Two worlds pool their wealth and their poverty, their history and their eternity. It is the history of humanity beginning with Adam and Eve that is projected into their frail existence.'[3] My spouse holds the promise of my own completion, the promise that I might become worthy of life. In my spouse's existence I

---

[1] Cf. Clement of Rome, *Epistle 2 on Corinthians*, 14, 2.
[2] D. G. Koutroubis, *The Grace of Theology* (Athens: Domos, 1995), p. 114 (in Greek).
[3] Paul Evdokimov, *The Sacrament of Love* (Crestwood: St Vladimir's Seminary Press, 1985), p. 191.

invest my hope of transcending my own loneliness, of having a taste of androgynous unity, of knowing the maturation and fruition of spiritual love. To a couple in love, everything seems beautiful and ready to turn their dreams into reality. Their relationship will not be like the others, ephemeral and monotonous; none of life's difficulties are going to come between them. Complete participation in *agape*, complete unity of soul and body: this is what each person expects upon entering the communion of marriage.

The Gospel reading continues: '*When the wine gave out, the mother of Jesus said to him, "They have no wine".*'

The wine of human love does not last for very long. Human beings may refuse God's call to love and reject love as the rule of life. When that happens, they fail to achieve the goal of their existence. Love which had been centrifugal becomes centripetal; instead of being directed outward toward another person, it is directed inward toward the self. Instead of aspiring to unity with God and with another human being, such people want to seek self-glorification and to inflate their own self-image.

This egocentric turning in upon oneself undermines every loving bond. Wherever the 'I' is not restrained in order to allow room for the 'you', division and separation appear, along with conflict and strife. All the disorders of *eros* are a tragic consequence of individualism, which introduces alienation into human relationships and estranges people from opening themselves up and encountering another person. Thus, the very thing that brings joy into life and creates happiness disappears, leading tragically to the painful discovery: 'They have no more wine.'

When the wine of *agape* disappears, desire becomes separated from the person, the body from the soul, and sexuality from love. This separation entails objectifying the other person and degrading him or her to the status of a device for satisfying sexual needs. The hungry gaze of the person who has fallen from *agape* objectifies another human being, turning him or her into an apparatus for pleasure. This lustful gaze strips other people naked, in order to categorise them on the scale of sensuality. Faced with this depersonalisation of the human being, a sense of shame is our internal defence. Our external defence is the clothing we use to cover the parts of our bodies that might be objectified. Furthermore, as fallen people we even objectify ourselves, consciously fetishising our own bodies in order to become an object of desire that can satisfy our sexual needs and our unadulterated narcissism. This shamelessness reveals the human downfall; we are stripped of everything that is true.[4] The fallen human being is not a person, he/she is a body.

As a consequence, sexual relationships sink to the level of self-indulgent, biological release and thus, instead of uniting people, do more to estrange them from each other. Egocentrism gives rise to domination, exploitation, appropriation, and possession of another person. The alternation between attraction and repulsion imprisons people in sadomasochism, a vicious circle of pleasure and pain. The search for pleasure for its own sake ends in the pain of despair; eroticism becomes the servant of emptiness and boredom. Quality is replaced by quantity,[5] since the desire of the estranged individual is 'a desire to possess something, to make it serve our own purpose and become part of us. In lust, it is the self which is the centre of attraction, and the object which stimulates it is simply an object and nothing more. That is why lust dies when it is satisfied: it ends with self-gratification, and then disappears until it is rekindled again by its object.'[6]

Naturally, the reason for a relationship's failure is always blamed on the other person. The 'Adam syndrome' is corroborated yet again. Someone who has fallen from *agape* always believes that the other person did not love as much as he or she should have, that the other person was not ready for a serious relationship. There is not a single suspicion that the person laying blame may himself or herself have been responsible, and the one who failed to love. Thus, without any decency or remorse, such a person feels justified in leaving the relationship in order to search for a 'great love' somewhere else, only to see the same sequence of events repeat themselves with someone

[4] Paul Evdokimov, *Woman and the Salvation of the World* (Crestwood: St Vladimir's Seminary Press, 1994), pp. 147–8.

[5] Albert Camus, *The Myth of Sisyphus* (London: Penguin Books, 1975), p. 69.

[6] Philip Sherrard, *Christianity and Eros* (Limni: Denise Harvey, 1995), p. 45.

else. The selfish person, unable to feel love as a deep bond of existence, experiences the despair of loneliness and the reproach of unsociability. People who are alienated in this way are poor when they approach love and even poorer when they leave, cast out into the void.

In the end, this being trapped within the fall and closed up in selfishness results in the death of the spirit.[7] This prison of loneliness, this insistence on individuality and isolated existence – a painful self-punishment which results from the refusal to love – all mean death, being cut off from any sense of unity which might offer wholeness and life. As a consequence, the presence of another person reminds us of our inability to love, while his or her absence reminds us of our inability to become whole. The other person becomes our hell.

The Gospel reading continues: '*Now standing there were six stone water jars for the Jewish rites of purification, each holding twenty or thirty gallons.*'[8]

Faced with this bankruptcy of emotion, this wall of selfishness which separates and divides, people may believe that they will ensure the survival of their marriages by resorting to legal sanction. This solution to the problem focuses on the fair distribution of obligations and rights. The love relationship is thus understood as a business transaction: I give something in order to get something in return. Of course, in comparison with pure egotism the law is a positive step, since it offers mutual power and mutual obligation in place of intractable egotism, which rejects any kind of commitment whatsoever. We pledge that as long as our marriage partners fulfil their obligations, we will fulfil ours. However, as long as our marriage partners fulfil their

---

[7] In *The Possessed*, Fyodor Dostoyevski presents, in the character of Stavrogin, the impasse of autonomous sexuality, which expresses nothing other than the death of God in humanity. See Fyodor Dostoyevski, *Devils* (Oxford: Oxford University Press, 1992), p. 467.

[8] The jars which John the Evangelist deliberately refers to were used by the Israelites for the required daily ablutions dictated by Jewish law. The number six, which is one before the perfect number seven, symbolically indicates the inability of the law to provide life in all its fullness. 'The law didn't settle anything; Mosaic law was insufficient for complete happiness. Nor was it able to fulfill that innate hope for purification and salvation' (Cyril of Alexandria, *Homilies on the Gospel of St John*, 2, 1, PG 73, 229A).

obligations they are also entitled to certain rights. Thus, even sexual union is considered to be a right which can be demanded.

This view of marriage as an equitable legal institution in which rights and obligations can be codified is yet a further manifestation of some people's inability to see their spouses as companions rather than as business associates, for it demonstrates their refusal to support each other under all possible conditions. A love relationship cannot exist when giving of oneself is absent, when selfishness demands a legal safeguard. If a relationship needs the support of the law to thrive, then it is not a love relationship but a business firm in which each partner seeks to realise a profit on their holdings.

The government, of course, considers that the problem has been solved, since the government's only interest is that the external legal structure be maintained. The moral code of the church, however, while not rejecting the usefulness of law and order, goes much further. For the church, the starting point for moral standards is not the action a person takes but his or her free will. For this reason, the church is constantly aware of the danger in allowing the institution of marriage to degenerate into legal and permanent prostitution.[9] For every relationship in which a human being is degraded to the level of an object and used as a palliative for selfishness is prostitution. Consequently, there is no difference whether the object that is being used and abused is the body of a prostitute or the body of a legal spouse. Spiritual violation and physical coercion, as well as the indifference and hatred of the strong for those weaker than themselves, lie hidden behind the social pretence of thousands of such legitimate marriages.

If legal prostitution in the guise of civil marriage represents one extreme of the pendulum, at the other extreme can be found the culmination of personalising human love, the love of a man for a woman and of a woman for a man. Through love the other person ceases to be just anyone, an individual like all the others, and becomes a specific person, unique and unprecedented. Love reveals the complete otherness of the human person; it reverses that equalising logic that claims

---

[9] Cf. Clement of Alexandria, *Stromata*, 2, 23, PG 8, 1093B.

people are all the same, have equal abilities, and are inter-changeable. People in love discover gifts and beauties in their beloved that a third person is unable to see; in this way they transcend the depersonalisation of beings and the objectivi-sation of things. This is a first taste of self-transcendence and self-sacrifice, a first taste of true life.

When people in love experience this well-being they feel an urgent need to exist eternally. Their love is injured by time; their mortal nature implies separation. This death of persons and of love cannot be nullified by any teaching regarding human uniqueness and results once again in the tragic impasse: 'They have no more wine.'

John the Evangelist continues: '*His mother said to the servants, "Do whatever he tells you." Jesus said to them, "Fill the jars with water." And they filled them up to the brim.*'

In order for the miracle to be performed people's co-operation is required. Love is never imposed; it is offered to those who experience it freely. Thus,

> new life enters into the life of man — as a presence, not as an obligation, as a gift and a potential, not as magic — and man remains free to enter the door which is being opened in front of him or to stay where he was in the realm of the 'flesh'.[10]

It is not a new law that is being contrasted here with the old one, but rather a different view of humankind and history, a new way of life. God's love (divine grace) makes up for human inadequacies so that each can achieve harmony and unity with another person.

When that happens, people enter into the life of miracles and the miracle of life. This does not happen magically but is acquired gradually, through daily and persistent spiritual exercise. The husband and wife who apply their efforts through the church toward the coupling of body and soul, sexuality and *agape*, succeed in making all their strength of body and soul serve and express self-transcendence and self-surrender to their spouse. These efforts help the couple to reduce their ego to a minimum and to offer the maximum they can to each other.

---

[10] John Meyendorff, *Marriage: An Orthodox Perspective* (Crestwood: St Vladimir's Seminary Press, 1984), p. 73.

They learn to support each other constantly and steadfastly at difficult moments, to tolerate each other's weaknesses, to be forgiven, and to forgive. Finally, this spiritual exercise restores divine order: as 'an ecclesial hypostasis man proves that what is valid for God can also be valid for man: the nature does not determine the person; the person enables the nature to exist; freedom is identified with the being of man'.[11] A human being, freely and without any physical compulsion, offers himself or herself to the service of others.

Thus, through the church, a biological drive is transformed into the love that is a divine gift, and the natural family is transformed into the ecclesiastical family.[12] The content of the sacrament of marriage is 'the changing, the transfiguring, of human love into a new reality of heavenly origin, which yet through grace takes flesh in this life'.[13] The relationship between man and woman acquires more meaning from the relationship between Christ and the church, the return of love. On the one hand, each spouse gives of himself/herself and even sacrifices himself/herself for the other, following the example of Christ's love for the church. On the other hand, the other spouse returns this love completely, aware of the great gift with which he or she has been honoured. The 'let it be' of the Mother of God finds its response in the 'let there be' of God; love becomes both the giver and the receiver. With the wine of *agape* Christ 'has re-established the wholesome polarity of male and female, he has restored their paradisal splendor, has pacified and illuminated them by the great love which circulates between him and his Church, between him and the earth divinized by the Eucharist'.[14]

[11] John Zizioulas, *Being as Communion* (Crestwood: St Vladimir's Seminary Press, 1985), p. 57.

[12] Zizioulas, *Being as Communion*, p. 61, n. 61. See also Alkiviadis C. Calivas, 'Marriage: The Sacrament of Love and Communion', *Greek Orthodox Theological Review*, 40 (1995), pp. 256–9.

[13] Stephanos Charalambidis, 'Marriage in the Orthodox Church', *One in Christ*, 13 (1979), pp. 206-7. See also Theodore Stylianopoulos, 'Toward a Theology of Marriage in the Orthodox Church', *Greek Orthodox Theological Review*, 22 (1977), p. 249; Stanley Harakas, 'Dynamic Elements of Marriage in the Orthodox Church', in John T. Chirban (ed.), *Personhood: Orthodox Christianity and the Connection Between Body, Mind, and Soul* (London: Bergin & Carvey, 1996), pp. 130–3.

[14] Charalambidis, 'Marriage in the Orthodox Church', p. 209.

Here we encounter marital virginity, which means that one's spouse is never reduced to an object, or in other words is always loved, always recognised as a person. For a married couple, virginity is that integrity of the spirit which prevents any degradation or abuse of the body.[15] The conflict between the sexes comes to an end, and the tyranny of impersonal sexuality is abolished.[16] Sexual union expresses the spiritual communion of husband and wife; it is the physical extension of the osmosis of their souls. Sexuality ministers to the unity of love and to the love of unity; in this way, sexuality, which God has offered to fallen humanity as a means of extricating themselves from their limitations and opening themselves up to others, is made worthy. Sexuality thus becomes

> a dimension of the person, a language of the relation between persons. The vastness of life becomes interiorized in the encounter of two persons and through their mediation receives the divine benediction of the origins, as Jesus recalls it: the amazed face to face of man and woman becoming 'one flesh' (Gen. 2:24; Mt. 19:6). This unity of the flesh denotes not only the union of the bodies but the interwovenness of two lives.[17]

This is why nakedness does not necessarily imply shame,[18] because neither one degrades the other to the level of an object, since 'they do not heed one another with a knavish eye; for wickedness has been abolished'.[19] Here the body becomes a person; that is to say, the whole human being is a person.

---

[15] See William Bazil Zion, *Eros and Transformation* (New York: University Press of America, 1992), p. 350.

[16] Christ performed the miracle at Cana 'so that the weak conviction of the wanton would be transformed into wisdom and prudence' (Epiphanius, *Against Heresies*, 2, 1, 30, PG 41, 941C).

[17] Olivier Clément, 'Life in the Body', *The Ecumenical Review*, 33 (1981), p. 141. And see David C. Ford, *Women and Men in the Early Church: The Full Views of St John Chrysostom* (South Canaan: St Tikhon's Seminary Press, 1996), pp. 46–53.

[18] 'Love does not know shame... Love is naturally unabashed and oblivious to her measure' (Isaac the Syrian, *The Ascetical Homilies*, 51 (Boston: Holy Transfiguration Monastery, 1984), p. 245).

[19] 'They will not look upon each other with an evil eye, for evil will have been taken away' (Pseudo-Macarius, *The Fifty Spiritual Homilies*, 34, 2 (trans. George A. Maloney; New York: Paulist Press, 1992), pp. 103–204).

Within this communion of love, soul and body are able to encompass one another. Two souls are united in one body, and two bodies in one soul. The other person is my other self, 'flesh of my flesh' (Gen. 2:23). The other person is my paradise.

John the Evangelist's account continues: '*He said to them, "Now draw some out, and take it to the chief steward." So they took it. When the steward tasted the water that had become wine, and did not know where it came from (though the servants who had drawn the water knew), the steward called the bridegroom and said to him, "Everyone serves the good wine first, and then the inferior wine after the guests have become drunk. But you have kept the good wine until now".*'

Through the church, this mutual giving by husband and wife matures even further with time, like old wine.[20] This is because *eros* dies on the cross so that it can be resurrected as *agape*: unconditional, all-embracing and eternal love.

There are three aspects of *eros* to die on the cross. The first aspect to die is the prerequisites of *eros*. Eros, at least in its first stages, hides within itself elements of egocentrism. In other words, we love one person and not another because something about our beloved pleases us; because he or she has something that satisfies our own, purely personal requirements. This means that *eros* is offered only to the degree that our beloved fulfils these requirements. As a result, *eros* must be transformed into *agape*, elevated, that is, to that level where we can love with absolutely no preconditions.

This becomes attainable through the church. In the church people can live in the same way God exists, and we can love absolutely freely, beyond any biological or social constraint. Humankind is able to love the way God does, with a love that can reach all the way to the self-sacrifice of death (see Eph. 5:25). This is the highest stage of love, in which a spouse even agrees to descend into hell for the sake of his or her beloved.[21]

---

[20] With this miracle, Christ 'not only made wine, but wine of the best quality. Because such are the miracles of Christ; they are better than any of the things that happen according to nature' (Theophylactus of Bulgaria, *Homilies on the Gospel of St John*, PG 123, 1193B).

[21] 'Loving means humility which puts the lover beneath all creatures (see Romans 9.3), in contradistinction to the superior, "philosophical" love which looks down condolently on others, or even to the "humanitarian," altruistic love which regards others as equals, at most' (John Chryssavgis, *Love, Sexuality and the Sacrament of Marriage* (Brookline, MA: Holy Cross Orthodox Press, 1996), p. 8).

Here the logic of making deals ceases to exist. Here each person is the first to give of themselves.[22] Love allows space and offers time for the other person to reveal his or her inner wealth, to bring God-given gifts into the light of day, and to become blessed by grace. Here

> faithfulness becomes possible. The sacrament, the entry into the light of Christ, helps me to discover the other as God's image. It deepens and stabilizes in me the unique grace to know someone else, soul and body, as a revelation. So that when the other changes, I perceive in him or her that which does not change. I perceive his or her icon, vocation, as if God associated me with the love he has for him or her from all eternity, with the call addressed to him or her from all eternity.[23]

Love forgives the past. At the same time, it lays a wager on the future, on the ability of the other person to change and be transformed, because true love 'is a power that gives birth to love in the other. As is always true, this giving brings to life in the other the capacity to give, but only when it is not looked for to begin with. Thus, the paradoxical truth: the mother is loved when she loves, the teacher is taught when he teaches.'[24]

The second aspect of *eros* to die on the cross is exclusivity, the fatal danger of every form of dualistic love. Exclusivity means that a husband can love his wife and children passionately, a wife can love her husband and children passionately, along with their relatives and friends, and at the time be indifferent to

---

[22] 'Let a wife not wait for her husband to behave with virtue and only then offer her own. For this is nothing great. Nor should a husband expect his wife to be proper and only afterward behave properly. For neither is this a great accomplishment. But each should be the first to offer what is right' (John Chrysostom, *Homilies on the First Epistle of Paul to the Corinthians*, 26, 7, PG 61, 222).

[23] Clément, 'Life in the Body', p. 144. See also Mathias F. Wahba, *Honorable Marriage According to St Athanasius* (Minneapolis: Light and Life, 1996), pp. 180–3; John Breck, *The Sacred Gift of Life* (Crestwood: St Vladimir's Seminary Press, 1998), pp. 69–80.

[24] Joseph Allen, 'Practical Issues of Sexuality', *Saint Vladimir's Theological Quarterly*, 27 (1983), p. 50.

everyone else. This is a love which limits itself to a select circle and number of people, excluding the rest of the world. It amounts to idolatry of the family and is a watered-down form of narcissism: we only love those who love us in return.

Through the church, however, spouses discover that when they love each other truly, wife or husband, then they love everyone. Through the church, love

> becomes a movement of free love with a universal character, that is, of love which, while it can concentrate on one person as the expression of the whole of nature, sees in this person the hypostasis through which all men and all things are loved and in relation to which they are hypostasized.[25]

The person who comes to know cosmic beauty in one person sees this beauty everywhere and at all times. When this happens, physical love for one becomes spiritual love for every other person, for 'the Other'. We become 'magnetized and consumed by the face of the Lord in its tragic and flashing beauty. And in the light of this face the face of the neighbor is revealed as truly non-possessive and personal.'[26]

When exclusivity is transcended, having children acquires a special significance. Having children is an extension of love for one's spouse. With the entrance of a child into the family, biologically and spiritually, the couple emerge from the dyadic relationship of *eros*, which is likely to have been a form of mutual selfishness, in order to open their relationship up to a third member. The couple thus bring a child into the world for one and only one reason: that the child might share in the couple's communion of love. In the image and likeness of the creation of the world by God, having children is the couple's free creation and calls upon the created being to participate in love. Out of love and for the sake of love: this is the one and only incentive for having children.[27]

The third aspect of *eros* to die on the cross is impermanence.

---

[25] Zizioulas, *Being as Communion*, p. 63.
[26] Clément, 'Life in the Body', p. 140.
[27] Zion, *Eros and Transformation*, p. 345.

Through the church a couple's love transcends every division and separation.[28] Nothing can decrease their love and no absence can be permanent.[29] At the culmination of their love, the couple have a foretaste of the transcendence of death. 'I love you, which is why you will not die.' These words of Gabriel Marcel comment on the Song of Songs: 'For love is strong as death, passion fierce as the grave. ... Many waters cannot quench love' (Song 8:6–7).[30] The painful taste of mortality, the subjugation to what is impermanent and passing, is replaced by the experience of resurrection, transcending death and decay, an endless encounter and communion between those who are loved. Human desire has completely achieved its goal: the unity of love with God and with one's co-human being, the eternity of *agape.*

The passage about the wedding at Cana ends as follows: '*Jesus did this, the first of his signs, in Cana of Galilee, and revealed his glory; and his disciples believed in him.*'

With the descent of grace, the married couple experience 'matrimonial Pentecost',[31] the 'sacrament of love'.[32] With the wine of Cana, which is a symbol of the divine eucharist,[33] the married couple experience a divine and clear-headed intoxication 'through which they know the ecstasy that leads from the material to the divine'.[34] Centred within the body of the

[28] 'It is Christ in every marriage who establishes the promise and guarantees the covenant between the spouses so as to change life from a temporal, ordinary level into an immortal and eternal one, through the mystery of God's presence, being thus analogous to the transformation of the water into wine' (Matthew the Poor, 'The Wedding in Cana of Galilee', *Sourozh,* 37 (1989), p. 12).

[29] ' "There is only one marriage", she said, "just as there is only one birth and one death." She did not consider her husband to be dead, as her parents did, but to be living close to God. Furthermore, because of her hope in the resurrection, she thought of him as one who has merely departed. This was why she also considered it wrong not to remain faithful to her one and only departed bridegroom' (Gregory of Nyssa, *Life of Saint Macrina,* PG 46, 964CD).

[30] Evdokimov, *The Sacrament of Love,* p. 106.

[31] Evdokimov, *The Sacrament of Love,* p.128.

[32] See John Chrysostom, *Homilies on the Epistle of Paul to the Colossians,* 12, 6, PG 62, 387.

[33] Cyril of Jerusalem, *Catecheses,* 12, 4, PG 33, 1097B–1100A.

[34] Gregory of Nyssa, *Homilies on the Song of Songs,* 5, PG 44, 873B.

church, their family becomes a 'little church'.[35] For this reason, the married couple are also called upon to abide by the virtues of the church and make the qualities of unity, sanctity, universality, and apostleship a reality in their family life.[36]

The married couple are first called upon to make their life an example of unity, following the example of the Holy Trinity. That is, they are called upon to experience that state of being in which, through their dissimilarity, their equality of honour, and their unity, each fully encompasses the other. In this way they learn through experience that love does not erase differences; on the contrary, it brings them to the fore. Each person remains singular and unique, absolutely incapable of being compared with any other. This respect for difference is expressed through equality of honour. Within this communion of love no one is higher or lower than anyone else; all are simply different. Furthermore, while the persons in this relationship are different and equal in honour, they are simultaneously in a state of total unity. There is no contrast or conflict; there is no muddling or levelling. Each one lives with the other, for the other and by means of the other. The miracle of love 'destroys remoteness, distance, solitude, and gives an inkling of what the mysterious unity of love can be, a heterogeneous identity of two subjects'.[37]

The second dimension of family life is sanctity.[38] The final aim of a family is deification, which means that the family is called upon to become a dwelling-place of God. Sanctity means, on the one hand, a daily struggle to shed egocentrism in order to purify one's inner world. On the other hand, it means being acquainted with God's love, which sanctifies human beings and life as a whole. The family understands that whatever it has – and above all, whatever it is – belongs to God. They don't

---

[35] John Chrysostom, *Homilies on the Epistle of Paul to the Ephesians*, 20, 6, PG 62, 143. 'Let husband and wife make their house a church. For you should not believe that anything will hinder you, thinking that you are only a man and a woman. For it says that wherever two are gathered in my name, there I am also among them' (John Chrysostom, *Homilies on Acts*, 26, 4, PG 60, 203).

[36] A. M. Stavropoulos, 'The Understanding of Marriage in the Orthodox Church', *One in Christ*, 15 (1979), pp. 60–1.

[37] Evdokimov, *The Sacrament of Love*, p. 106.

[38] Clement of Alexandria, *Stromata*, 4, 20, PG 8, 1337A.

consider anything to be their own; everything is a gift from God. This is why they offer everything to God. Their entire life becomes a 'living sacrifice, holy and acceptable to God' (Rom. 12:1). The family lives the church's ethic of sacrifice, knowing that a man or woman is dead unless they die for others.

The family also tries to live according to the love God has for people, which is Christ's love for the church. It thus tries to know love in its universality, as a complete whole, just as each local church experiences the full truth of the church. Here, the part has full knowledge of the whole because it experiences the whole truth. The family knows God's faithfulness towards humanity and receives a taste of his endless philanthropy. Love is not bounded by this world's limits of time and place, but becomes a window that opens on eternity and the final kingdom.

In experiencing this all-embracing love, however, the family also becomes aware of the need for apostleship, so that this love can emerge into the world.[39] Love does not emerge into the world as a result of need, seeking to obtain what it lacks; it emerges from a state of wholeness which desires to give what it is. The family, with all its being, becomes the incarnated evidence of God's love for people, of that love which unites people in a community of harmony and brotherhood.

The family, living as a small church within the larger church, ceases to be a source of conflict, the scene of oppression and rivalry, and is transformed into an icon of trinitarian communion, a way to find unity in diversity. The family thus becomes a place 'where being would have priority over having, where inner fulfilment would be more important than competing for power, and where science and technology would serve life, not death'.[40] Its members thus transform, with the wine of Cana, every aspect of human life: they transform

---

[39] 'If you have love you are an apostle and first among apostles' (John Chrysostom, *Sermo Habitus inscriptionem Actorum Apostolorum*, 2, 3, PG 51, 82).

[40] Elizabeth Behr-Sigel, *The Ministry of Women in the Church* (California: Oakwood Publications, 1991), p. 134. See also Adrian Thatcher, 'Crying Out for Discernment – Premodern Marriage in Postmodern Times', *Theology and Sexuality*, 8 (1998), pp. 92–4.

politics into ministry, economy into philanthropy, work into creation, science into love of beauty.[41]

In this modern world of autoeroticism and consumption, this world of ignorance of others and destruction of relationships, the adventure of marriage as a sacrament of love and freedom, as a starting point for the transformation of the entire world, is the church's call to every potential disciple of Christ.

---

[41] This total transformation of the world through love, with reference to the wedding at Cana, is described by Fyodor Dostoyevski in his masterpiece *The Brothers Karamazov* (London: Penguin, 1993), pp. 413–18.

7

Marriage and the Church: Theological Reflections on an Underrated Relationship

Thomas Knieps-Port le Roi

In what follows I will ask some fundamental questions about the relation between marriage and the church. What relation does the church really have to marriage? What meaning and function has marriage in and for the church?

Children for the Church?

One way of answering these questions would be to examine a range of theological and church historical data, e.g., the development of a liturgical celebration of marriage in the first centuries and of a marriage law in the Middle Ages, with the help of which the church authorities claimed and gradually achieved their exclusive jurisdiction over marriage. There is much to be said, too, about the objection of the theology of Reformation to the ecclesiastical and juridical grip on marriage, which Protestant theologians regarded, in Luther's terms, as a 'worldly affair' having a lot to do with God, but little with the church. Finally there is the phenomenal influence on teaching about marriage of Ephesians 5:22–33, where marriage represents a reflection of the relationship of Christ with his church.[1] My intention is however to approach the subject from a rather different angle.

---

[1] For the evolution of the theology and pastoral practice of marriage see Edward Schillebeeckx, *Marriage: Human Reality and Saving Mystery* (London: Sheed & Ward, 1965); Theodore Mackin, *The Marital Sacrament* (New York: Paulist Press, 1989).

The so-called Armenian Decree of the Council of Florence of 1439 sets out very clearly the church's teaching that the purpose of marriage is the introduction of new members into the church. 'By orders the church is governed and spiritually multiplied, *by matrimony it grows bodily.*'² To the modern eye, this way of defining the relationship of marriage to the church seems very peripheral, even when we take into account the fact that underlying it is Augustine's teaching of the *bonum prolis*, the production and education of children as a primary purpose of marriage. In this conception married couples do undeniably have an indispensable task to fulfil in and for the church, but they do not thereby seem to be able to share in the theological and spiritual mystery of the church. We can assume that this conception remained the official position in Catholic teaching about marriage over many centuries. In the encyclical *Casti connubii* of 1930 Pope Pius XI reiterated it in applying the marital duty to produce offspring, not just to the commission of creation, but to the order of redemption. From this he emphasised the particular obligation of Christian married couples to produce new blood for the church:

> Christian parents should understand ... that their duty is not only to propagate and maintain the human race on earth; it is not even merely to rear worshippers of the true God. They are called to give children to the Church, to beget fellow-citizens of the Saints and members of the household of God (Eph. 2:19), in order that the worshippers of our God and Saviour may increase from day to day.³

Since married couples cannot themselves incorporate the offspring given to them into the new order of salvation – the act of procreation still being particularly subject to the power of sin – they have to present their children to the church to be justified by baptism and to become living members of Christ.

It is true that Christian parents, even though themselves in

---

² N. P. Tanner (ed.), *Decrees of the Ecumenical Councils*, Vol. I (London and Washington: Sheed & Ward and Georgetown University Press, 1990), p. 541 (author's emphasis).

³ *Casti connubii* – *Encyclical Letter of Pope Pius XI* (London: Catholic Truth Society, 1965), n. 14.

the state of grace, cannot transmit their supernatural life to their offspring: indeed the natural generation of life has become the path of death by which original sin is communicated to the children. Nevertheless they do share to some extent in the privilege of the primordial marriage of Paradise, for it is their function to offer their children to the Church so that she, the fruitful Mother of the sons of God, may beget them anew to supernatural righteousness in the waters of baptism, make them living members of Christ . . .[4]

With this argument the impression is strongly conveyed that the only role married couples have in the building up of the church is, metaphorically speaking, to hand over the unfinished raw materials and abandon the further construction work to other responsible architects and builders in the church. Only in the Christian education of the children does marriage retain a genuine ecclesial responsibility, with the spouses being commissioned by the authorities to take care of a part of the whole building.

However, in twentieth-century Catholic theology a concept of marriage has gained acceptance which has largely abandoned traditional teaching about the end of marriage and which is mainly based on the idea of personal commitment. Especially in the Pastoral Constitution *Gaudium et spes* of the Second Vatican Council the spouses' sharing of life and love is given at least equal standing with the procreation and education of children.[5] This new emphasis has been accompanied by a change in terminology. In a clear reference to the way in which the Armenian Decree has systematised the sacraments, the *Catechism of the Catholic Church* of 1993 places ordination and marriage together as 'sacraments of service to others', utilising a clearly modified vocabulary to make the message plain.

---

[4] *Casti connubii*, n. 14.
[5] See *Gaudium et spes: Pastoral Constitution on the Church in the Modern World*, nn. 47–52 in Austin Flannery (ed.), *Vatican Council II: Constitutions, Decrees, Declarations* (Northport, NY and Dublin: Costello Publishing and Dominican Publications, 1996). See also N. Lüdecke, *Eheschließung als Bund: Genese und Exegese der Ehelehre der Konzilskonstitution 'Gaudium et spes' in kanonistischer Auswertung* (Würzburg: Echter, 1989); R. B. Arjonilla, *Conjugal Love and the Ends of Marriage: A Study of Dietrich von Hildebrand and Herbert Doms in the Light of the Pastoral Constitution Gaudium et spes* (Bern: Peter Lang, 1998).

Ordination and marriage 'confer a particular mission in the Church and serve to build up the people of God'.[6]

But has there also been a corresponding change in the underlying concept? What role does marriage play in post-conciliar theology in 'building up the people of God'? Are the commission to the 'mission in the Church' and the service of 'building up the people of God' perhaps to be read as mutually interrelated descriptions of roles characterising marriage and ordination in the same measure? Does marriage also confer a mission in the church as ordination does?

If we look from this standpoint at Pope John Paul II's well-known Apostolic Exhortation *Familiaris consortio*, which in many respects can be viewed as a *summa* of post-conciliar theology of marriage and the family,[7] an ambivalent picture emerges. On the one hand this document describes Christian marriage and the Christian family in clearly programmatic words as a 'specific revelation and realisation of ecclesial community'[8] or as 'a living image and historical representation of the mystery of the Church'.[9] It refers repeatedly to the idea of the *ecclesia domestica*, the 'domestic church', which Vatican II coined in its Constitution on the Church, to emphasise the ecclesiological connection between marriage and church.[10] Thus, the Christian

[6] *Catechism of the Catholic Church* (rev. edn; London: Geoffrey Chapman, 1999), n. 1534.

[7] For the text of *Familiaris consortio* see Austin Flannery (ed.), *Vatican Council II: More Postconciliar Documents*, Vol. II (Northport, NY: Costello Publishing, 1982). An analysis of John Paul II's teaching on marriage and a commentary on *Familiaris consortio* can be found in R. M. Hogan and J. M. Levoir, *Covenant of Love: Pope John Paul II on Sexuality, Marriage and Family in the Modern World* (Garden City, NY: Doubleday, 1986).

[8] *Familiaris consortio*, n. 21.

[9] *Familiaris consortio*, n. 49.

[10] See *Lumen gentium: Dogmatic Constitution on the Church*, n. 11, and also *Apostolicam actuositatem: Decree on the Apostolate of Lay People*, n. 11 in Austin Flannery (ed.), *Vatican Council II: Constitutions, Decrees, Declarations*. M. A. Fahey retraces how the image of the 'domestic church' was introduced at Vatican II; see 'The Christian Family as Domestic Church at Vatican II', *Concilium*, 1995/4, pp. 85–92. See also A. Peelman, 'La famille comme réalité ecclésiale', *Église et Théologie*, 12 (1981), pp. 95–114; M. A. Foley, 'Toward an Ecclesiology of the "Domestic Church"', *Église et Théologie*, 27 (1996), pp. 351–73; F. Caffrey Bourg, 'Christian Families as Domestic Churches: Insights from the Theologies of Sacramentality, Virtue, and the Consistent Ethic of Life' (PhD dissertation, Boston College, 1998).

family is 'grafted into the mystery of the Church to such a degree
as to become a sharer, in its own way, in the saving mission
proper to the Church'.[11] On the other hand there are a series of
expressions in which marriage is treated not as an independent
subject of the saving mission, but much more as the receiver of
the gift of salvation from an official and hierarchically constituted church and as an object of her saving care. For example,
'It is, above all, the Church as Mother that gives birth to, and
builds up the Christian family, by putting into effect in its regard
the saving mission which she has received from her Lord.'[12]

What was described earlier as an active participation in the
mission of the whole church means nothing other than that the
'domestic church' has to insert itself obediently and passively
into that salvation mission which is represented solely by the
church in her official and institutional structure.[13] The consequences of this picture of the church for the understanding of
marriage were already visible in the old theology of marriage:
here as there the marital community always comes into
consideration only as the field of application for a Christian
and ecclesial practice about which decisions are made
elsewhere; it is never valued for itself as a sufficient and
veritable fulfilment of Christian existence and ecclesial
community or even as a sign and instrument of salvation.[14]

---

[11] *Familiaris consortio*, n. 49.

[12] *Familiaris consortio*, n. 49.

[13] M. A. Foley, 'Toward an Ecclesiology', pp. 362–7, comes to a similar
conclusion when she summarises: 'In short, *Familiaris consortio* fails to deliver
on the promise contained in its description of the family as realization and
revelation of church. The primary reason is that it attempts to fit domestic
church into a prior understanding of church which assumes traditional structures of authority. That understanding is still dominated by the Tridentine
insistence on clerical control of Christian life and worship. As a result, church
is too often identified with its leaders, and the laity, including families, can play
a very partial and, at best, imitative role in the church. In the end, the notion
that family can constitute church is not taken seriously' (p. 367).

[14] There is, however, one passage in *Familiaris consortio* which comes close to
a clear vision of Christian marriage and family as a truly active Christian
community: 'For this reason they [Christian married couples and parents] not
only *receive* the love of Christ and become a *saved* community, but they are also
called upon to *communicate* Christ's love to their brethren, thus becoming a
saving community' (*Familiaris consortio*, n. 49). Unfortunately, this idea is not
carried out through the text.

It should now be clearer what is the purpose of our raising the question about the relationship between marriage and the church. It will next be shown that the marital community represents and realises the church in the fullest sense and that such representation must have concrete consequences for our understanding of the church. To what extent can we affirm, of the 'intimate community of life and love' of the spouses, what Vatican II also says of the church, namely that it is a 'sign and instrument of intimate union with God and of the unity of all humankind'?[15]

Secondly our inherited picture of the church will be questioned. Up to now I have shown that the theology of marriage is in considerable measure dependent for its leeway on what was allowed to it by ecclesiology. Where the outward image of the church is concerned, we are chiefly preoccupied today with the question of authority and ministry. But we often overlook the fact that between this area and that of marriage there is a certain structural parallelism. For in both cases we are talking about a particular commitment. And this commitment can be fulfilled in different ways at different periods and by a different type of personnel. Nonetheless commitment remains a timelessly valid task without which the church could not live.[16] Therefore the question about the relationship between marriage and church needs to be restated from the perspective of ecclesiology.[17] The Catholic understanding of the church has a particular need to catch up both in considering the church as the whole people of God, and in seeing marriage and

---

[15] *Lumen gentium,* n. 1. In an ecumenical perspective the following considerations will have to be judged by what Adrian Thatcher has established as the two conditions under which also Protestants could accept the sacramentality of marriage, namely 'with the proviso that divine love is communicated in many other ways and other relationships than marriage, and the institution of marriage whether or not between Christian spouses does not by itself guarantee the experience of God's love at all' (Adrian Thatcher, *Marriage after Modernity: Christian Marriage in Postmodern Times* (Sheffield: Sheffield Academic Press, 1999), p. 236).

[16] See also N. K. Watson, 'Christian Ministry and Christian People: Some Thoughts on Sacramental Theology', *New Blackfriars,* 81 (2000), pp. 89–95.

[17] As a matter of fact, there is practically no, or only marginal, reference to marriage in recent theological works on ecclesiology.

ministerial office as two parallel 'limbs' upon which she rests her visible and institutional reality.[18]

Marriage and the Church – A Mutually Interwoven Relationship?

I base my argument principally on Karl Rahner's article 'Marriage as a Sacrament' (1967).[19] It is well known in Catholic theology that Rahner linked ecclesiology and sacramental theology indissolubly together in that he represented the church as the basic sacrament and the individual sacraments as acts of self-realisation of the church.[20] In 'Marriage as a Sacrament' he applies this concept to marriage. My interest is above all in three lines of argument that build on one another and are of extraordinary significance today for the understanding of the relationship between marriage and church.

First, Rahner defines the nature of marriage as the most intimate and personal unity of love between two individuals. In such a relationship one person commits herself to another in such a way that she surrenders herself totally and unconditionally and in such self-surrender attains to the other in the very deepest and most ultimate levels of his personhood and uniqueness. This is a first, personal, or rather interpersonal, dimension of the love union, which, however, includes a second (in Rahner's terminology) 'transcendental' or simply religious dimension. For that act in which I surrender myself and open myself unconditionally to the 'thou', is at the same time the act in which I experience myself in a radical way and thereby have an experience of my ultimate orientation to the absolute mystery which we call God. Whether I know it explicitly and interpret it rightly or not, a love between two persons which commits itself absolutely to the other has its ultimate basis in the experience of God. Therefore truly human

---

[18] See also my article 'Ehe- und Weihesakrament in der Heilssendung der Kirche', *INTAMS Review*, 4 (1998), pp. 62–71.

[19] Karl Rahner, 'Marriage as a Sacrament', in *Theological Investigations*, X (London: Darton, Longman & Todd, 1973), pp. 199–221.

[20] See in particular Karl Rahner, *The Church and the Sacraments* (New York: Herder & Herder, 1964).

love is always legitimised and supported by divine love, i.e., it is love in which God and human person are in love 'in a mutual interrelationship and according to their respective conditions in such a way that in this relationship the lover achieves his salvation in the event of justification' and in 'this salvation of his he wills salvation for the other also, and in both God is attained to immediately as this salvation in person'.[21]

Beneath the interpersonal and transcendental dimension of the love union of two persons lies a third dimension, a social one. For if I let myself go unconditionally in pure love, I open myself up thereby to all others and preserve this openness even when my self-surrender is responded to by one beloved person. Love for a specific person does not mean self-entrenchment in an 'egoism for two'. It is the love with which one loves all and so it participates also in divine love, in which the whole of humanity is lovingly embraced.

But although Rahner can define married love in this many-layered manner, he does not identify it simply with the intimate personal unity of love. Marriage is not simply this love union, it is basically a *sign*, i.e., a manifestation of this unity of love in the dimension of the physical, of space and time, and of social living. And as with every sign-reality or symbol-reality we find here too a relationship of unity and difference, in that the underlying reality appears and becomes visible only in and through the sign, and yet transcends it. Therefore it can very well happen in some circumstances that marriage does not express what it ought to express, but that it becomes just an empty sign. On the other hand one person may attain to the other in her uniqueness in an intimate personal love union, and thereby come before God and embrace the whole of humanity lovingly, even though he or she does not want or is not able to give expression to this occurrence in marriage.

It would be a misunderstanding, however, if we were to conclude from this analysis of married love that the connection between love and marriage could be conceived on the model of

---

[21] Rahner, 'Marriage as a Sacrament', p. 206. See also Karl Rahner, 'Reflections on the Unity of Love of Neighbour and the Love of God', *Theological Investigations*, VI (Baltimore and London: Helicon Press and Darton, Longman & Todd, 1969), pp. 231–49.

an unchangeable core and its temporally conditioned and changeable shell, so that traditional marriage could give way easily to other and possibly more appropriate manifestations of the personal community of love. To the extent that marriage is thought of here in Rahner's conception as an intimate personal love union, all foundations would be removed from the personal love event if we were to uncouple it completely from married love. What is culturally and socio-historically determined in marriage as an outward form, conditioned by time and so disposable, is far more difficult to judge than the sign theory of Rahner might initially lead us to suspect. One thing is clear after all: what the ultimate essence of personal love is cannot be defined separately from its historical, cultural and social manifestations of which marriage is undoubtedly part. That does not mean, however, that factors which determine the marital relationship in a specific context should not be questioned.

Second, Rahner notes an astonishing similarity between marriage and the church with regard to their respective functions as signs. As in marriage, so in the socio-historically constituted community of the church, there is manifest a love union. The ecclesial community points above all to the love of God by which he communicates himself to all people and which, irrevocably promised and indefectibly received in Jesus Christ, gathers humanity together as the people of God for union and salvation. On this basis the church is 'the sign, at the palpable level of historical and social human life, of the fact that *that* love is being made effective and victorious throughout the whole of humanity which is the love of God for us and of us for God, the love which comprehends and unifies all'.[22] But this signifying function applies unrestrictedly to marriage too, if only the two loving partners do not reduce their bond to being a false sign and instead lovingly include all others in their mutual love. Marriage and the church are thus two different historical manifestations of one and the same loving movement, in which humanity as the people of God attains to the unity of the kingdom of God in love. Herein lies the reason why marriage has a natural sign-character or sacramentality

---

[22] Rahner, 'Marriage as a Sacrament', p. 211.

even *outside the church*. And all of this makes clear what it means when such a marriage is solemnized *in the church*.

If the same love that unites two persons in marriage also forms the church, then it follows that for marriage in the church there is a mutually interwoven relationship. Because it is one of the embodiments of the uniting love of the church, the love of the spouses contributes to the building up and union of the church, as it on the other hand is supported by the uniting love of all the other persons in the church. And yet are married couples in an even more direct way united with the mystery of the church than would be the case if they were just belonging to a co-operative community of persons, who – all loving in their own way – formed the ecclesial community? In that and insofar as their marriage is a sign and occurrence of the love that unites God and humanity, they do exactly that which is characteristic for the church herself, i.e., they not only contribute to build the church in a particular place but truly and entirely fulfil what makes up the essential being and mission of the church. The marriage of two baptised Christians is, in other words, a moment in the self-realisation of the church as such, and the church is truly made present in it. No more and no less is said if we assert that marriage between Christians is a sacrament. Christian marriage points to and embodies that union in love which the church as a whole also points to and realises. Marriage, wherever it emerges in the historical reality of this church, participates in the irrevocable and victorious real promise, on the basis of which the church is the socio-historical, but eschatologically indefectible sign of the unity between God and humankind. Marriage is sacramental because in the sphere of the church the sign-character that naturally inheres in it becomes the representation and actualisation of the ecclesial saving community itself and thereby becomes a constitutive official function of this church. Such marriage is 'really the smallest community, the smallest, but at the same time the true community of the redeemed and the sanctified, the unity among whom can still be built up on the same basis on which the unity of the Church is founded, in other words the smallest, but at the same time the genuine individual Church'.[23]

---

[23] Rahner, 'Marriage as a Sacrament', p. 221.

Third, Rahner reflects on the picture of the church in relation to the model of the Christ–church union which in Ephesians (5:29–32) serves as example for the union of marriage. In this biblical passage the uniting love between two persons 'in one flesh' is said to be founded in creation as the anticipation of the unity between Christ and the church. Consequently, between the marriage-union and humanity brought to unity in Christ, whose historical manifestation is the church, there prevails a relationship like that between the order of creation and the order of redemption. The covenant is the reason for creation and its end insofar as it supports and embraces creation as the setting of the condition of possibility, as the setting of the covenant partner. Creation only is because God willed the covenant, the covenant can, however, only be insofar as the covenant partner is there, with and in creation.[24] In other words: the intimate, personal love union between two persons as creation reality exists only because God in Christ willed to conclude the uniting covenant with humanity. Conversely, Christ can destine humanity to a love covenant with himself only because the human love that grounds the union is already established in creation. Hence there exists not only an outward similarity between both love unions, but a causal, conditional and participatory relationship. The marriage union is founded in the unity of the church, and the uniting of humanity in the church takes place in the love union of two persons to the extent that this human love corresponds to its purpose according to creation.

In the salvific will of God for the unity of humanity, both marriage and the church are thus even originally established as historical signs and instruments of this will, and therefore neither is subordinated to the other. We can at best speak of a temporal priority of marriage over the church, to the extent that it already existed 'in paradise' and is therefore previous to the church to which it points forward. Logically, however, the church is in no way priorly ordered to marriage, even if it must be said that the church is the all-embracing ground from

---

[24] See also Karl Barth, *Church Dogmatics, The Doctrine of Creation*, III/1 (Edinburgh: T&T Clark, 1958), p. 94 ('Creation as the external basis of the covenant') and p. 228 ('The covenant as the internal basis of creation').

which marriage takes its true purpose, since the love union between two persons only really makes sense against the background of the unity of all humanity. To assert this equality of status is meaningful when we think of the way that the church handles marriage in its concrete reality. She cannot possibly think that she can do as she wishes with the marital relationship and then put it to her own use by an act of authority. This is excluded if we truly take seriously the fact that marriage is a sacrament and in itself a constitutive ground and a primary act of self-realisation of the church which she cannot freely dispose of. It is in and by itself that marriage as a divinely-willed creation reality makes manifest the love union, and it does not lose this significance even if it is integrated into the greater unity of love of which the church is the outward manifestation. The personal act in which two lovers pledge themselves and bind themselves to one another is *as such* an ecclesial act which cannot and must not any longer be preceded by any official action of the church.[25] This affirmation summarises the theological essence of the relationship between church and marriage.

A Marital Picture of the Church?

Now it ought to be clearer what relationship the church has to marriage and what meaning marriage has in and for the church. In conclusion let us summon the real insights in both areas – in the understanding of marriage and in the picture of the church – which have resulted from this theological exploration.

First, whatever can be said about marriage from an anthropological, psychological, sociological or juridical perspective, from the Christian theological viewpoint we must when speaking about marriage always deal with the intimate personal

---

[25] For that reason Rahner rightly rejects any attempt to enhance the active assistance of the priest in the liturgical celebration and to raise it to a constitutive function in the concluding of a sacramental marriage (see 'Marriage as a Sacrament', p. 216, n. 33). Since through baptism two Christian spouses are participating in the common priesthood, they are perfectly capable of setting an ecclesial act by pledging themselves to one another.

unity of love which binds two persons together, which touches them in the depths of their personal existence and opens them up to a greater community (of which children are part). Ephesians 5:29–32 provides the time-transcendent programme for this. This, however, does not mean that marriage – always a socio-historically constituted reality that has to be actualised in a specific temporal context – can simply be equated with this ideal love union. On the one hand there are always legitimately other love and life forms alongside marriage which give expression differently and perhaps better to what marriage stands for. On the other hand there are concretely lived forms of marriage which, however Christian they may appear, reduce it to a farce. All this must be prudently acknowledged and stated. But particularly with respect to its ideal meaning, which it is so vital to safeguard, we need to see marriage in the church context raised not to the level of an absolute *norm* but to the level of *a model* (*Leitbild*) remaining permeable and transparent to other forms of partnership. While churches in the Reformed tradition have been using this kind of language for quite some time now, it remains an unfulfilled *desideratum* in the Roman Catholic Church and her theology. The sacramental understanding of marriage ought not to be an obstacle to such a paradigm shift. On the one hand the sacramental form of life on its subjective side is not actually unique and unparalleled, since non-sacramental forms too can give expression to the healing union of love in all its depth and significance. On the other hand in sacramental marriage on its objective side the unconditional pledge of grace from God is bound to a life form which must always be fulfilled by concrete persons in situations of succeeding or failing love. So it too represents 'only' a model – even though the eschatologically indefectible pledge from God is valid for it.

Second, if we in the church really understood and took seriously that the personal self-commitment of two loving persons manifesting itself in marriage and realising itself through a whole life is an original, authentic and official act of the constitution and the self-actualisation of the church, this would fundamentally change our picture of the church. We cannot at this point go into the possible repercussions of a corresponding marriage theology for ecclesiology, which today is a theological building-site around the concept of *communio.*[26] But the kind of change we need is evident at least in respect of the way that the prevailing understanding of the church comes into contact with married couples and families. The point is that the church should no longer regard married persons as objects of a saving care located predominantly in the hierarchy, but should include them as the full subjects of a saving mission whose bearer is the whole people of God. We may then begin to see emerging, a specific competence of married couples, something the church needs pressingly in an ever more secularised environment. I mean the competence to face daily life in love, faith and – if it is true that in marriage (following Rahner) a person opens herself lovingly to the other, persists in radical faithfulness in the face of the often dark mystery of her own existence and that of the other in which God is concealed; and pins her hopes on what will be ultimate and definitive in the existence of them both.[27] The church would then have reason to be more acutely aware of *the married life of Christians* instead of always being preoccupied with the *Christian life of married couples*. For to the extent that the church can be the model for life in marriage, marriage might also be exemplary for our understanding of the church.

[26] See for example J.-M. Tillard, *Église et Églises: L'ecclésiologie de communion* (Paris: Cerf, 1987); M. G. Lawler and T. J. Shanahan, *Church: A Spirited Community* (Collegeville: Liturgical Press, 1995); J. Rigal, *L'ecclésiologie de communion: son évolution historique et ses fondements* (Paris: Cerf, 1997); B. Hilberath (ed.), *Communio – Idealbild oder Zerrbild von Kommunikation* (Freiburg i.Br.: Herder, 1999).

[27] See Karl Rahner, 'Marriage as a Sacrament', pp. 204–5.

8

Sacred Love: Religion, Marriage and *L'amour fou*

Philip A. Mellor

Introduction

Should theologians and church leaders look to the social sciences for insights into the contemporary character and condition of marriage, they will find a great deal of literature concerning power relationships, gender issues, and eroticism, as well as lots of data concerning changing patterns of cohabitation, divorce, and sexual preferences. Nevertheless, given that when people marry they usually do so because of 'love', specifically what might be called 'romantic love', it seems appropriate to consider how 'love' tends to appear in this literature. I suggest its appearance, which is often more elusive than one might expect, characteristically takes three forms.

First, it is discussed as a mythological codification of more basic erotic, personal or economic needs; in short, it is a mask for something else. In the much discussed sociology of Anthony Giddens, for example, 'love' has no independent value, but is simply a 'codifying force' for organising the competing, reflexively determined pursuits of emotional and sexual satisfaction by the two individuals involved.[1] Second, as the anthropologist William Jankowiak[2] has pointed out, 'romantic love' is usually

---

[1] A. Giddens, *Modernity and Self-Identity* (Cambridge: Polity Press, 1991), pp. 95–7.

[2] W. Jankowiak, 'Introduction' to W. Jankowiak (ed.), *Romantic Passion: A Universal Experience?* (New York: Columbia University Press, 1995).

seen as a specifically Western phenomenon, reflecting particular cultural, political (and often 'patriarchal') character-istics of European and American history; it is this view that accounts for what has been, until recently, the virtually total neglect of the study of love in non-Western cultures. Third, apart from their unique association in the modern West, 'romantic love' and marriage are often understood as distinct, sometimes contradictory phenomena, with romantic passion best expressed through adultery or the anti-conjugal demands of Courtly Love.[3]

My chapter aims to challenge all three of these treatments of 'love', and to offer an alternative interpretation, also based mainly in the social sciences, that might provoke further inter-disciplinary reflection on love and marriage. Most contentiously, perhaps, I shall argue that 'romantic love' is a *universal* phenomenon. Even though the theoretical fires of postmodernism may have died down somewhat in recent years, such talk of 'universals' remains deeply unfashionable. Bearing in mind that it is a common human species that inhabits different cultural contexts, however, it is possible to consider an embodied human basis for love that cannot evaporate in the heat of cultural relativism. In this respect, I shall suggest that whilst it is important to be attentive to the significant cultural differences in how love is expressed, we should not confuse these with the common anthropological basis that underpins them. The question of how 'romantic love' relates to 'marriage' can be addressed in terms of this base–superstructure model, but not entirely so. I shall suggest, in fact, that the relationship between love and marriage is not entirely culturally relative.

Lurking in what has been called the 'underground wing' of sociology is the basis for an interpretation of love that does not see it as a codifying force for culturally relative economic or political factors.[4] Émile Durkheim's theory of the sacred[5] allows

[3] S. Lilar, *Aspects of Love in Western Society* (trans. Jonathan Griffin; London: Panther, 1967), pp. 110–11.

[4] R. Collins, 'The Durkheimian Tradition in Conflict Sociology', in J. C. Alexander (ed.), *Durkheimian Sociology: Cultural Studies* (Cambridge: Cambridge University Press, 1988).

[5] Émile Durkheim, *The Elementary Forms of Religious Life* (trans. Karen E. Fields; New York: Free Press, 1995 [1912]).

us to see love, and marriage, not only as expressions of humans' fundamental social impulses but also as phenomena through which reality, meaning and identity are defined in religious terms. He challenged the rationalism and utilitarianism of his time in arguing that human beings have embodied predispositions towards powerful, collectively stimulated emotions that provide the essential foundations not only of religion but also of social life in general.[6] In this chapter, a Durkheimian interpretation of love is developed in conjunction with the surrealist André Breton's notion of *l'amour fou*.[7] This notion, often translated as 'mad love', but best interpreted as 'unreasonable love', is more philosophical than sociological but is consistent with Durkheim's thought in the sense that it rejects rationalist and utilitarian models of love in favour of an argument for its sacred, world-transforming character.

The notion of 'sacred love' developed in this chapter has not, of course, a specifically Christian character, and, barring one or two suggestions, I shall not deal with its relationship to theology here. This task is no doubt best left to theologians anyway, but what I do hope to do is offer an interpretation of love that provides a counterpoint to some of the reductive analyses originating in the social sciences, and thereby offer some fresh spurs to creative thought about love and marriage for theologians and others. I shall begin this by looking at the notion that love is simply a mask for other, more significant, phenomena. This is an important starting point as, left unchallenged, this notion renders further substantive reflection on love problematic, since it implies that we should really be focusing on something else.

Love as a Mask

Whether this notion is framed in sociological, philosophical or biological terms, it tends to assume specific things about the

---

[6] P. A. Mellor, 'Sacred Contagion and Social Vitality: Collective Effervescence in *Les Formes élémentaires de la vie religieuse*', *Durkheimian Studies (Etudes Durkheimiennes)*, 4 (1998), pp. 87–114.

[7] A. Breton, *L'amour fou (Mad Love)* (trans. Mary Ann Caws; Lincoln, NB: University of Nebraska Press, 1987 [1937]).

nature of human beings. Some of the most common conceptualisations of love throughout Western history, for example,
focus upon the satisfaction of *appetites*: from Ovid's concern
with love as a means to secure sexual enjoyment through to
modern sociobiological explanations of love as an attempt
to maximise genetic success, love has been understood as either
a culturally-produced or biologically-driven phenomenon that
exists in order to assist in the satisfaction of sexual, emotional
or reproductive needs.[8] This essentially utilitarian view interprets love as a form of self-delusion or a useful lie that obscures
the real nature of romantic relationships. Into the former
category we can place George Bernard Shaw's comment that
'Love consists of overestimating the differences between one
woman and another';[9] in the latter category there is
Schopenhauer's view of love as a trick played by the Will in
order to compel us to reproduce.[10]

   This utilitarian perspective is also evident in many contemporary sociological studies of love.[11] Giddens' notion of
'confluent love'[12] expresses the idea that modern relationships
are entered into, and sustained, purely as the result of
individuals' reflexive assessment of their needs, desires and
overall life plans, and judgements about whether another
person can assist in the achievement of these. In this
perspective, the transience of many modern relationships
reflects their inherently contractarian, utilitarian character,
combined with the individualistic impulse of late modern life.

[8] See I. Singer, *The Nature of Love*, Vol. I: *Plato to Luther* (1984); Vol. II: *Courtly and Romantic* (1984); Vol. III: *The Modern World* (1987) (Chicago: University of Chicago Press).

[9] H. Fisher, 'The Nature and Evolution of Romantic Love', in Jankowiak (ed.), *Romantic Passion*, p. 25.

[10] A. Schopenhauer, *The World as Will and Representation* (New York: Dover, 1966), p. 536; see C. Lindholm, 'Love as an Experience of Transcendence', in Jankowiak (ed.), *Romantic Passion*, p. 60.

[11] S. Jackson, 'Even Sociologists Fall in Love: An Exploration of the Sociology of Emotions', *Sociology*, 27:2 (1993), pp. 201–20; J. Dunscombe and D. Marsden, 'Love and Intimacy: The Gender Division of Emotion Work', *Sociology*, 27:2 (1993), pp. 221–41; P. O'Connor, 'Understanding variation in marital sexual pleasure: an impossible task?', *Sociological Review*, 43:2 (1995), pp. 342–62.

[12] A. Giddens, *The Transformation of Intimacy* (Cambridge: Polity Press, 1992).

Contracts can be made, and broken, as we seek to pursue our own individual goals and desires. In this view, 'love' has emotional and sexual dimensions but these are contained within a largely cognitive framework centred on the reflexive calculation of different life options. For Giddens, in fact, the reflexive character of modern intimacy is essentially the same as that which characterises global capitalism and modern systems of knowledge. His theory of love is, in short, a theory of modernity.

This view is not unique. A number of studies of marriage and divorce have expressed similar views of the reflexive, utilitarian character of sexual relationships, as have broader theoretical interpretations of romantic love.[13] Of particular note, however, is Van de Vate's argument[14] that expressions of love are actually *policy statements* expressing morally, if not legally, binding commitments with regard to future conduct.[15] Here, 'the couple' has an entirely contractarian basis, and even the most intimate dimensions of our love lives can be analysed as agenda items for a committee of two. The tendency of many sociologists, psychologists and counsellors to emphasise the importance of *talk* in developing and sustaining satisfactory relationships fits in very neatly with this model.[16] Love is not a thing in itself that defines a relationship; it is a codifying myth within which more basic appetites, desires or goals can be organised.

This reductive interpretation of love finds its most extreme form in 'rational choice theory', where all aspects of social experience are explained in terms of a simple utilitarianism:

[13] D. R. Hall, 'Marriage as a Pure Relationship: Exploring the Link between Premarital Cohabitation and Divorce in Canada', *Journal of Comparative Family Studies*, 27:1 (1996), pp. 1–12; C. L. Johnson and F. A. Johnson, 'Parenthood, Marriage and Careers: Situational Constraints and Role Strain', in F. Pepitone-Rockwell (ed.), *Dual-Career Couples* (Beverley Hills: Sage, 1980), p. 146; M. B. Zinn and D. S. Eitsen, *Diversity in American Families* (New York: Harper & Row, 1987); A. Lawson, *Adultery: An Analysis of Love and Betrayal* (New York: Basic Books, 1988); R. Cate and S. Lloyd, *Courtship* (London: Sage, 1992).

[14] D. Van de Vate, *Romantic Love: A Philosophical Inquiry* (Pennsylvania: University of Pennsylvania Press, 1981).

[15] S. S. Hendrick and C. Hendrick, *Romantic Love* (London: Sage, 1992), p. 20.

[16] See Lawson, *Adultery*.

individuals make choices about actions on the basis of a rational calculation of self-interest. Gary Becker,[17] for example, interprets the choice of marriage partner as the rational calculation of benefits and risks in a sexual market, and as therefore essentially the same sort of transaction one might engage in to invest in shares, buy a car, or move house. One of the problems with this view, however, and there are many,[18] is the difficulty in establishing that individuals' choices of marriage partners are 'rational'. To individuals, and often to their families and friends, such choices may look anything but 'rational'. It is true, of course, that many marriages have been entered into for what might be termed 'rational' reasons, such as the need for economic security, but where marriage follows from 'love' rational choice explanations look far from convincing. Aside from the fact that love and *strong emotion*, rather than rational calculation, seem synonymous to many people, love also often appears to have a *gratuitous* aspect. Reflection on these two aspects of love has, within Western history, offered a persistent challenge to the utilitarian view.

Love as Transcendence

As Charles Lindholm[19] has expressed it, this alternative view does not interpret love as a mask for sexual or reproductive appetites, but sees in it the adulation of the beloved *in himself or herself* as a manifestation of something true, good or beautiful. Here, love is bestowed *gratuitously*, rather than as a means to some other end.[20] The relationship between the lover and the beloved is essentially free of any contractarian dimension, and takes on a *transcendent* character. As the young Hegel understood it, individual selves are transcended in an all-embracing unity.[21] This view articulates a sense of the

---

[17] G. Becker, 'The Economic Approach to Human Behaviour', in J. Elster (ed.), *Rational Choice* (Oxford: Blackwell, 1986).

[18] See P. A. Mellor, 'Rational Choice or Sacred Contagion? "Rationality", "Nonrationality" and Religion', *Social Compass*, 47:2 (2000), pp. 265–81.

[19] Lindholm, 'Love as an Experience of Transcendence', p. 66.

[20] Singer, *The Nature of Love*, Vol. I, p. 14.

[21] Lindholm, 'Love as an Experience of Transcendence', p. 67.

transformative character of love, and focuses on its capacity to express some of the most potent and noble of human aspirations, thereby distinguishing it sharply from more mundane human activities.

If utilitarian analyses root their accounts of love in an embodied predisposition towards the pursuit of self-interest, accounts of the transcendent character of love presuppose different human characteristics. Here, humans have a capacity for selflessness that has an incipiently religious quality. Whether this capacity is inherent or learned, however, is a matter for debate. Some sociologists have argued that love is not a universal phenomenon but is a learned one particular to certain cultures, especially that of the West.[22] Furthermore, they have argued that even where love appears to have a self-transcending character the capacity to experience romantic love is actually entwined within broader cultural processes centred on the emergence of a sense of autonomous 'selfhood'. Thus, the development of modern individualism, which has promoted the development of such notions of selfhood to an unprecedented degree, goes hand in hand with the development of romantic love since this encourages the free choosing of sexual partners on the basis that particular individuals can complement one's own unique sense of self.[23]

Lindholm's interpretation of love[24] takes more account of the specifically Christian influence on the West. Although he is also attentive to cross-cultural manifestations of romantic love, he argues that the notion of love as a route to transcendence can be understood as a secularisation of 'Christian notions of God's unconditional, unreserved, and undeserved love for humanity (*agape*), as expressed in the sacrifice of Jesus'. This may contain an element of truth in the sense that certain aspects of Christian theology may indeed have had a significant

---

[22] Hendrick and Hendrick, *Romantic Love*, p. 14.

[23] Hendrick and Hendrick, *Romantic Love*, pp. 16–17; R. C. Solomon, *Love: Emotion, Myth and Metaphor* (New York: Anchor, 1981); Singer, *The Nature of Love*, Vol. III; A. C. Rowntree ' "Johnny Loves Mary Forever": What therapy doesn't know about love', in D. L. Gelpi (ed.), *Beyond Individualism: Toward a retrieval of moral discourse in America* (Notre Dame, IN: University of Notre Dame Press, 1989).

[24] Lindholm, 'Love as an Experience of Transcendence', p. 66.

impact upon the valorisation of certain understandings of love in the West. Nonetheless, as a general account of the phenomenon of romantic love, there are two arguments that can be made against this analysis as well as that centred on the development of peculiarly Western notions of selfhood.

First, it can be argued that romantic love as a non-utilitarian phenomenon is evident not only in Western, Christian, or post-Christian societies, but is perhaps a universal feature of human social life. Second, this cross-cultural evidence suggests a more broadly 'religious' aspect to romantic relationships rather than a specifically Christian one. In Durkheim's terms, these relationships can be understood as religious in the sense that they do not presuppose a highly developed notion of selfhood, but, on the contrary, suggest the transcendence of individual selves through their incorporation into the all-embracing unity of a form of collective life.

Love as a Universal

In relation to the first of these arguments, on the universality of romantic love, an anthropological survey of ethnographic data relating to 166 different cultures has shown that this type of love appears to be a significant phenomenon in 148, or 89%, of them; a result that has led to the suggestion that it is a 'human universal or, at least, a near-universal'.[25] The missing 11%, furthermore, has been attributed to 'ethnographic oversight' arising from anthropological assumptions that romantic love is a characteristically Western phenomenon.[26] Another study, by Hatfield and Rapson,[27] concluded that love occurs in all eras, at all ages, across all ethnic groups, and equally frequently for men and women.

This is not to underestimate the significance of different cultural influences upon the shaping of romantic love in terms

[25] Jankowiak, *Romantic Passion*, p. 5; W. Jankowiak and E. Fischer, 'A Cross-Cultural Perspective on Romantic Love', *Ethnology*, 31:3 (1992), pp. 149–55.

[26] Jankowiak and Fischer, 'A Cross-Cultural Perspective', p. 154.

[27] E. Hatfield and R. L. Rapson, 'Passionate Love: New Directions in Research', in W. H. Jones and D. Perlman (eds.), *Advances in Personal Relationships*, Vol. I (Greenwich, CT: JAI, 1987).

of the choices of lovers and the timing and process of courtship,[28] or in terms of the relationship between this type of love and marriage patterns.[29] In relation to this latter point, however, cultural variations might not be as significant as we tend to assume and can, in fact, support the argument that certain patterns in human relationships have universal characteristics.

One aspect of this cross-cultural data on love, for example, which might be surprising to many people, is the evidence for the massive dominance of monogamy as the preferred form of sexual relationship. According to Van den Berghe's study of patterns of human cohabitation across cultures,[30] monogamy is the norm for both men and women. In 99.5% of cultures women marry only one man at a time. For men, monogamy is the prescribed social form for relationships in only 16% of cultures; in 84% polygamy is permitted, and in 44% it is the preferred marriage form. Nevertheless, in most of these cultures only about 10% of men actually practise polygamy, leading to the conclusion, also endorsed by Murdock,[31] that monogamy dominates in nearly every known human society.[32]

While monogamy appears to be a cross-cultural norm, similarities in the broad patterns of romantic stimulation and attachment in different societies also suggest a limit to the influence of cultural variations. An initial stage of intense, passionate attraction, followed by a further stage of a calmer but secure sense of attachment to a particular individual, has been noted among the !Kung people of the Kalahari desert as

[28] Fisher, 'Nature and Evolution of Romantic Love', p. 26; A. Hinton, 'Prolegomenon to a Processual Approach to the Emotions', *Ethnos*, 21:4 (1993), p. 18; J. Money, *Lovemaps: Clinical Concepts of Sexual/Erotic Health and Pathology, Paraphilia and Gender Transposition in Childhood, Adolescence and Maturity* (New York: Irvington, 1986).

[29] Lindholm, 'Love as an Experience of Transcendence', p. 63; P. Grimal, *Love in Ancient Rome* (Norman: University of Oklahoma Press, 1986); see M. Mead, *New Lives for Old: Cultural Transformation – Manus, 1920–1953* (New York: Morrow, 1956).

[30] P. L. Van den Berghe, *Human Family Systems: An Evolutionary View* (Westport, CT: Greenwood, 1979).

[31] G. P. Murdock, *Social Structure* (New York: Free Press, 1949), pp. 27–8.

[32] See Fisher, 'Nature and Evolution of Romantic Love', pp. 30–1.

well as among modern Americans.[33] The explanations offered
for these similarities fall into two basic camps, however, the
biological and what might broadly be called the *anthropological.*

The biological view is another variant on the idea that what
we call 'love' is really something other than it appears to be. For
Liebowitz,[34] for example, these two stages of love are
explainable in terms of the human brain's capacity to release
endorphins that promote a sense of well-being. In this view, we
become attached to particular individuals, and feel terrible
when we lose them, because of the habitual triggering of neuro-
hormones stimulated by contact with the beloved; a view that is
rooted in broader evolutionary biological arguments
concerning the development of physiological processes that
encourage us to form and maintain sexual unions that are
conducive to the successful production and rearing of children.
In short, love is the result of a particular balance of endorphins
arising from genetic imperatives.

The problem with such biological explanations, however, is
that while their account of physiological processes may seem
plausible, in some respects, the simple link between the
evolution of these processes and the need to reproduce cannot
account satisfactorily for the fact that romantic love occurs even
where pregnancy is undesired or impossible. Lindholm's
analysis,[35] in contrast, draws upon anthropological studies to
question both the biological association of love with sex, and,
despite his secularisation argument, the sociological view that
love is a uniquely Western phenomenon. Drawing on examples
as diverse as medieval notions of Courtly Love and a number of
contemporary cultures in the Middle East, he does not dismiss
the idea that sexual desire may have a biologically driven utilitarian character, but he asserts that numerous cultures not only
exhibit strong evidence for the near universality of romantic
love, but also attest to the fact that love cannot simply be
equated to sex.

Following the Weberian tradition of German sociology, he

[33] M. Shostak, *Nisa: The Life and Words of !Kung Woman* (New York: Random House, 1981), p. 268; M. Liebowitz, *The Chemistry of Love* (New York: Little & Brown, 1983); Fisher, 'Nature and Evolution of Romantic Love', p. 28.

[34] Liebowitz, *The Chemistry of Love.*

[35] Lindholm, 'Love as an Experience of Transcendence', p. 64.

interprets romantic love as a response to existential conditions facing human beings.[36] Here, love is a quest for transcendence, an attempt to escape from the contingency and solipsism of individual existence, which cannot be reduced into biological instrumentality. In seeking to expand upon how this quest for self-transcendence is worked out, however, he draws upon the work of writers such as Bataille and Alberoni whose interpretations of love owe much to a different sociological tradition, namely that of Durkheim.[37] It is Durkheim's work that enables us to see an inherently religious dimension to romantic love.

Love as Sacred

Central to Durkheim's *The Elementary Forms of Religious Life*[38] is an analysis of the intimate relationship between social life and various collective experiences and representations of the sacred. For him, the very possibility of society is contingent upon collective, emotionally charged experiences that become channelled into ritual, symbolic and conceptual cultural patterns. The experience of what he calls 'collective effervescence', the sense of solidarity associated with it, and the collective representations of these processes through symbols and concepts, are the very essence of the sacred and of society itself. The experience of the sacred arises from the collective stimulation of powerful emotions which individuals experience as a form of self-transcendence, and which allow them to be integrated into either a larger social whole or smaller collective bodies.[39]

Romantic relationships can be interpreted in Durkheimian terms because they clearly have a strong emotional basis, they naturally give rise to ritual, symbolic and conceptual representations of themselves, and they imbue an experience of social solidarity with a transcendent character in the sense that they

---

[36] Lindholm, 'Love as an Experience of Transcendence', pp. 68–9.

[37] G. Bataille, *Eroticism* (New York: Marion Boyars, 1987 [1962]); F. Alberoni, *Falling in Love* (New York: Random House, 1983).

[38] See note 5 above.

[39] Durkheim, *Elementary Forms of Religious Life*, pp. 422ff.

'connect us with something that surpasses us'.[40] A romantic relationship creates and nurtures not a 'committee of two' constituted by shared policy aims, but a *society of two*, with its own models of sacred and profane, and rules of moral obligation.

Randall Collins[41] follows this Durkheimian model in his suggestion that in modern societies there is a 'cult of the dyad', which encourages patterns of courtship where couples are structurally isolated, becoming intensely focused on each other, so that whatever emotions they feel are intensified through the ritual mechanism of the cult and attached to symbols of the relationship itself.[42] In developing this model, Collins challenges contemporary theoretical and pastoral approaches to relationships, and relationship breakdowns, that focus on the importance of *talk*. He believes these to be inattentive to the emotional and ritual foundations of relationships that operate below the level of cognitive reflection.[43] In Durkheim's terms, the couple is a 'moral community' with an inherently sacred character.

Sasha Weitman's study of *eros* and solidarity[44] develops on a similar basis. According to Weitman, the logic that governs lovemaking is the same logic that governs sociability in general; a logic he finds reflected in Durkheim's theory of religion. Associating lovemaking with the connection to a 'sacred' reality sharply distinguished from the profane routines of day-to-day life, Weitman sees it as being essentially the same sort of social phenomenon as the religious rituals that imbue religious

---

[40] É. Durkheim, 'The Dualism of Human Nature and its Social Conditions', in R. N. Bellah (ed.), *Emile Durkheim on Morality and Society* (Chicago: University of Chicago Press, 1973 [1914]), p. 161.

[41] R. Collins, 'Love and Property', in *Sociological Insight: An Introduction to Non-Obvious Sociology* (New York: Oxford University Press, 1981); Collins, 'The Durkheimian Tradition'.

[42] Collins, 'The Durkheimian Tradition', p. 120.

[43] Collins, 'The Durkheimian Tradition', p. 121; R. E. Dobash and R. Dobash, *Violence against Wives* (New York: Free Press, 1979); see P. A. Mellor and C. Shilling, 'Confluent Love and the Cult of the Dyad: The Precontractual Foundations of Modern Contractarian Relationships', in J. Davies and G. Loughlin (eds.), *Sex These Days* (Sheffield: Sheffield Academic Press, 1998).

[44] S. Weitman, 'On the Elementary Forms of the Socioerotic Life', *Theory, Culture and Society*, 15:3–4 (1998), pp. 71–110.

worshippers with the sense that they are members of something vaster, more real, and more enduring than they themselves are simply as individuals.[45] Both Collins and Weitman, then, use Durkheim to understand how the emotional and physiological factors inherent within sexual relationships come to form a 'religious' bond between the lovers. What they are interested in is the merging of two individuals into an overarching, transcendent totality.

When Weitman uses the term 'lovemaking' rather than 'sex',[46] he does so in order to emphasise that he is not talking simply about copulation, but about an all-embracing engagement between two people that Alberoni has called *le grand érotisme.*[47] Alberoni calls falling in love 'the simplest form of collective movement',[48] and talks of the dissolution of the distinction between duty and pleasure, signalling that the sexual aspects of a relationship can become integrally entwined within a broader transformation of identities and experiences. This transformation is centred on the dissolution of the individual self and its reconstitution on the basis of a new form of collective life. The exploration of these processes is central to the work of Georges Bataille, whose account of 'eroticism' is also about far more than sex.

Love as Dissolution

Also using Durkheim's theory of the sacred, Bataille draws our attention to the capacities of the erotic to bring about a 'fusion of beings with a world beyond everyday reality'.[49] In contrast to Giddens' emphasis upon the individualistic character of modern sexual relationships, Bataille sees in eroticism a route towards transcendence and away from 'our random and ephemeral individuality'.[50] In Bataille's work, eroticism refers to an intense experience that transgresses the self, wiping away

[45] Weitman, 'On the Elementary Forms of the Socioerotic Life', pp. 71, 75.

[46] Weitman, 'On the Elementary Forms of the Socioerotic Life', p. 72.

[47] F. Alberoni, *L'Érotisme* (Paris: Ramsey, 1987).

[48] F. Alberoni, *Falling in Love*, pp. 7, 23.

[49] Bataille, *Eroticism*, p. 18.

[50] Bataille, *Eroticism*, p. 15.

the discontinuities that separate individuals. As Bataille notes,[51] eroticism has the ability to substitute for the individual's isolated discontinuity a feeling of profound continuity: 'the unity of the domain of eroticism opens to us through a conscious refusal to limit ourselves within our individual personalities'.[52] For Bataille, an erotic, effervescent exuberance can rupture us from the profane 'world of things' and put us back in contact with an experience of self-dissolution that allows us to regain touch with the sacred. As Lindholm expresses it, 'instead of resembling a biological drive, falling in love is more akin to religious revelation'.[53] The self-dissolving potentialities of eroticism in Bataille's work are essentially the same as the effervescent, self-transcending encounter with the sacred that Durkheim sees as the basis of social life.[54]

If Collins and Weitman use Durkheim's theory of religion to see the couple as a microcosm of social order, however, Bataille's development of it sees the couple as a microcosm of the universal human condition; a sacramental, but also somewhat tragic, experience of continuity in a world of discontinuity. The experience of a sacred continuity of two beings transgresses conventional social orders, but is inherently transient and the profane 'world of things' soon reasserts itself. In his own words, 'if love exists at all it is, like death, a swift movement of loss within us, quickly slipping into tragedy and stopping only with death'.[55] In this respect, at least, Bataille's understanding of love diverges from Durkheim's analysis of the sacred. What this understanding lacks, from a Durkheimian point of view, is a sense of how an effervescent eroticism can be channelled into enduring forms of social life that persistently challenge the profane, utilitarian world of day-to-day life. Breton, however, the founder of surrealism, offers an account of love that shares some continuities with that of Bataille, but also challenges very strongly the idea that love is inherently transient.

---

[51] Bataille, *Eroticism*, p. 15.
[52] Bataille, *Eroticism*, p. 24.
[53] Lindholm, 'Love as an Experience of Transcendence', p. 67.
[54] Durkheim, *Elementary Forms of Religious Life*.
[55] G. Bataille, 'Writings on Laughter, Sacrifice, Nietzsche, Un-Knowing', *October*, 36 (Spring 1986), p. 239.

Love as Transgression

Surrealism, led by Breton, was an artistic, poetic and, in some respects, political movement that sought to challenge modern rationalism and, especially, that aspect of modernity identified by Breton as the *hatred of the marvellous*.[56] In all its various spheres of activity, surrealism saw as its moral purpose the revitalisation of a sense of wonder and awe; the revitalisation of the sacred, in fact, to challenge the profane utilitarianism of modern societies. Breton's espousal of *l'amour fou* as the most potent source of such a confrontation with modernity[57] mirrors Bataille's concern with the transgressive nature of love, but is shorn of its tragic overtones. For the surrealists, love was the essential path towards *exaltation*.[58]

Lindholm's account of love as a route to transcendence[59] not only emphasises the *experience* of this exaltation, but the *imagining* of it: love is an act of the imagination, as individual minds attempt to reach out beyond the limits of the self. For Breton, love transforms the lives of individuals, but it also has a collective and even a universal dimension. Herbert Marcuse has defined the 'imaginary' as a collective defence of human aspirations towards wholeness in the face of the inhibitions of reason.[60] This definition expresses very clearly the surrealist sense that union through love points towards a broader union with nature and, even, the survival of humanity itself.[61] As Anna Balakian has pointed out, if surrealism can be understood as a 'spiritual union' its origins can be traced to a 'spiritual crisis' in European civilisation.[62] Born between the two World Wars, and having to confront European complacency towards the rise of fascism in Germany, surrealism rejected what it saw as the bankruptcy of the modern project. Contrary to modern

---

[56] A. Breton, *Manifestoes of Surrealism* (Michigan: Ann Arbor/University of Michigan Press, 1972), p. 14.

[57] Breton, *L'amour fou*.

[58] A. Balakian, *Surrealism: The Road to the Absolute* (3rd edn; Chicago: University of Chicago Press, 1986), p. 235.

[59] Lindholm, 'Love as an Experience of Transcendence', p. 67.

[60] H. Marcuse, *Eros and Civilisation* (Boston: Beacon Press, 1955), pp. 142–3.

[61] Balakian, *Surrealism*, pp. 2–3.

[62] Balakian, *Surrealism*, p. 213.

rationalism, surrealism sought to expand the experience of reality, and revitalise the European 'imaginary'.

Like Bataille, Breton is interested in the transgressive character of passionate relationships, but this has nothing to do with sexual experimentation or promiscuity, which he saw as dehumanising phenomena. As André Thirion points out,[63] although their private lives did not always match their proclamations, the surrealists condemned the licentiousness of artistic circles in Paris, and promoted the idea of a faithful, passionate love between two individuals. As a central part of their determination to re-evaluate modern social and personal values, they challenged the utilitarianism and cynicism surrounding love and sex, and 'sought to recompose an experience of the sacred – of the marvellous possibilities of life – within the framework of the sexual encounter itself'.[64] For Breton, in particular, this experience of the marvellous meant that, for couples, love and sex should not be separated, because without the affective element relationships would be reduced to the satisfaction of biological needs. For him, passionate relationships were encounters with the *other*, the transformation of life through the union with another unique human being. They were therefore 'transgressive' in the sense that they disrupted utilitarian world-view inherent within the modern project, with its reduction of love and sex to appetites.[65]

In contrast to Bataille's emphasis on the transience of sacred love, in fact, Breton emphasises the sacred character of an *enduring*, monogamous, relationship, asserting that the commitment to the idea that love is *forever* is 'the master key' to the surrealist transformation of reality.[66] For him, the meaning of life is to be found in the love for one unique being, and, again in contrast to Bataille, this meaning is not only to be found in bed.[67] The sacred is to be found everywhere, but love

[63] A. Thirion, *Revolutionaries Without Revolution* (London: Cassell, 1976), p. 92.

[64] M. Richardson, 'Seductions of the Impossible: Love, the Erotic and Sacrifice in Surrealist Discourse', *Theory, Culture and Society*, 15: 3–4 (1998), p. 379; R. Benayoun, *Erotique du surréalisme* (Paris: Jean-Jacques Pauvert, 1965), p. 11.

[65] Richardson, 'Seductions of the Impossible', pp. 378–9.

[66] Breton, *L'amour fou*, p. 114.

[67] Breton, *L'amour fou*, p. 42.

is a kind of sacrament, a privileged means through which truth, beauty and goodness enter our lives. Speaking of the 'revelation' of the unequalled emotion that individuals encounter in love, he challenges the disenchanting impulse of the modern project,[68] and calls love a 'state of grace'.[69]

This notion of love as a 'state of grace' challenges two aspects of the modern assumption that love is an inherently transient phenomenon. First, in associating love with revelation rather than illusion it rejects the idea that 'the phantasmagoria of love is uniquely produced by our knowing the beloved being so little'.[70] Second, it rejects the idea that love is driven simply by sexual desire, so that, with the accomplishment of the sexual act, love inevitably weakens. Many psychologists,[71] sexologists[72] and evolutionary biologists[73] tend to support the notion that familiarity eventually results in indifference, but, for Breton, the idea that love lays itself open to ruin to the very extent that it pursues its own realisation is one of the most deadly of modern myths.[74]

Drawing upon both Engels and Freud, Breton associates monogamous, passionate love with a moral imperative that transcends cultural differences,[75] and the promotion of a collaborative way of living that challenges modern egoism.[76] The 'recolouration' of the world through love does not merely affect the two lovers themselves then, but, in unleashing the sacred into the world as a whole, reminds everyone of the availability of beauty and truth to all if we open ourselves to their presence.[77] In short, Breton's *l'amour fou* is not merely a vehicle of transcendence for two individuals, but a medium through which social life in general can be reshaped.

---

[68] Breton, *L'amour fou*, p. 40.

[69] Breton, *L'amour fou*, pp. 83–4.

[70] Breton, *L'amour fou*, pp. 52–3.

[71] D. Tennov, *Love and Limerence: The Experience of Being in Love* (New York: Stein & Day, 1979).

[72] J. Money, *Love and Love Sickness: The Science of Sex, Gender Difference and Pairbonding* (Baltimore: Johns Hopkins University Press, 1980).

[73] Liebowitz, *The Chemistry of Love*.

[74] Breton, *L'amour fou*, pp. 52–3.

[75] Breton, *L'amour fou*, p. 77.

[76] Breton, *L'amour fou*, pp. 34–5.

[77] Breton, *L'amour fou*, p. 79.

Love as Marriage

It is because love has these revolutionary implications that it has an ambivalent relationship with modern social orders. On the one hand, as Collins suggests,[78] romantic love as a relational form is apparently encouraged in modernity, and those studies that have suggested it is a uniquely Western phenomenon have tended to focus on the social and cultural patterns that appear to manifest this encouragement. On the other hand, however, for Breton, the *full* characteristics and implications of love are often systematically denied. The widespread opinion 'that love wears out, like a diamond in its own dust' is therefore symbolic of the broader modern tendency to assume the inherent transience of all things.[79] In this view, Giddens' notion of 'confluent love'[80] might capture something significant about the modern view of love, but it does not tell us much about what love really is.

If Breton's account of love expresses its ambivalent relationship to modern social orders, however, it also raises the question of its relationship to social orders more generally. Even if it can be established that romantic love is a universal phenomenon, and that, despite cultural differences, monogamy tends to be the preferred relational form, it is also undeniable that the relationship between love and marriage is historically and culturally variable. Marriage has often been arranged, and in some cultures still is, in the interests of political alliances or advantage, economic security or advancement, and a range of other decidedly non-romantic interests. In these circumstances, romantic love tends to have a clandestine character, and is often perceived to be a threat to established social orders.[81] Applying Durkheim's analysis of the sacred to love, however, combined with Breton's account of its enduring, world-shaping character, suggests that the relationship between love and marriage has a more organic character than examples of cultural differences might suggest.

---

[78] Collins 'The Durkheimian Tradition'.
[79] Breton, *L'amour fou*, p. 100.
[80] Giddens, *Modernity and Self-Identity*.
[81] Lindholm, 'Love as an Experience of Transcendence', pp. 64–5.

Pursuing this line of thought, Suzanne Lilar has argued that *l'amour fou* is the real basis of the couple, even though cultures have a persistently ambivalent attitude to it,[82] and she calls the couple bound together through this 'unreasonable love' a 'conjugal union', whether it has been formalised or not. Following Durkheim, Collins' analysis of the ritual channelling of emotion in the 'cult of the dyad'[83] expresses the same sense that the sacred character of love implies the spontaneous emergence of what might be called a 'conjugal' structure, regardless of whether this is institutionalised as 'marriage'. In other words, love and marriage are not, in a sense, the distinct phenomena imagined in the traditions of Courtly Love, certain forms of Romanticism, and modern presuppositions concerning the dichotomous relationships between interior feelings and external institutions. While love may or may not lead to marriage in terms of the legal requirements of church or state, its essential character tends towards a personal, social and religious bond that is captured better by the word 'marriage' than by terms that imply a looser form of association.

It is surely the recognition of this inherent character that has led so many different religious forms to attempt to incorporate love into a broader, more formalised religious structure. The Catholic conception of marriage as a sacrament is merely one of the most obvious examples of this incorporation. Although it may initially seem somewhat bizarre to compare Breton, the so-called 'pope of surrealism', with Pope John Paul II on the subject of love, the latter's understanding of the nature of marriage is not essentially in contradiction to Breton's conception of *l'amour fou*. In *Familiaris consortio* the Pope emphasises that marriage should not be understood as the imposition of an external form on the interior realities of individuals, but as the public affirmation of what are already the inherent characteristics of a relationship he terms 'conjugal'.[84] Where he differs from Breton is not in his concern for the importance of this public affirmation, but in terms of his emphasis on the

---

[82] Lilar, *Aspects of Love*, p. 12.
[83] Collins, 'The Durkheimian Tradition'.
[84] R. Lawler, *Catholic Sexual Ethics* (Indiana: OSV, 1985).

broader theological significance of the relationship, and therefore his subsequent specifically Christian arguments as to why the marriage form should be supported, maintained and valued. In this respect, one can also note that Hans Urs von Balthasar's theology of marriage expresses a similar sense of the 'interior mystery' of marriage,[85] and proposes an account of love as a transcendence of the egoism and utilitarianism of modern life that echoes some of Breton's thoughts quite closely.[86]

Love as a Problem

Nevertheless, even if it is possible to draw on the magisterium of the church, one of the founding figures of sociology, and the *avant-garde* of French philosophy to argue that love and marriage have a more organic relationship than is often assumed, the evidence of contemporary societies would seem to suggest that such an argument is unsustainable. This evidence points towards increasing divorce, a developing preference for patterns of cohabitation rather than marriage, life-cycles marked by serial monogamy rather than unbreakable bonds, a fairly robust separation of love and sex, and the assumption that relationships are interpersonal opportunities for self-realis- ation rather than transpersonal forms that reshape self-identities in the interests of a collective form of life.[87] As the conservative cultural critic Allan Bloom has expressed it, sex and meaningful relationships have replaced love.[88]

Nevertheless, and without minimising the significance of these trends in terms of how we experience, observe and reflect on modern relationships, it is possible to question the assumption that love is a *totally* relative phenomenon that can

[85] H. U. von Balthasar, *The Glory of the Lord. A Theological Aesthetics*, Vol. I. *Seeing the Form* (trans. Erasmo Leiva-Merikakis; Edinburgh: T&T Clark, 1982).

[86] See P. A. Mellor, 'Objective Form and Subjective Content: Marriage and the Transcendence of Self in Roman Catholic Theology', *Irish Theological Quarterly*, 56:2 (1990), pp. 136–49.

[87] Johnson and Johnson, 'Parenthood, Marriage and Careers'; Hall, 'Marriage as a Pure Relationship'.

[88] A. Bloom, *The Closing of the American Mind* (New York: Touchstone, 1988), p. 230.

arise, disappear or radically alter its form in the light of cultural changes. Lilar,[89] for one, follows Breton in arguing that talk of the 'death of love' is empty: what has died 'is not so much love as the honour in which love is held'. Given that it is a single human species that populates different cultural contexts, and bearing in mind the evidence for a universal, embodied disposition towards romantic love, it may be more appropriate to talk of culturally relative attitudes, dispositions and practices in relation to love, rather than of the relativity of love itself. From this point of view, many of the problems surrounding love and marriage in the contemporary Western world can be understood as indications of a failure to understand love, and therefore to understand those things, within our grasp, that will help us lead happy and fulfilled lives, rather than as indications of more fundamental human transformations. That, I think, is what the tradition represented by Breton is telling us.

A consequence of adopting this view is not only the encouragement of scepticism concerning modern treatments of love, but also scepticism about modern assumptions of secularity. If love is sacred, although our culture might consistently promote its profanation, then this might cause us to reflect again on other religious aspects of our lives. It is notable, in fact, that sociologists such as Giddens, who tend to promote the idea that modern changes in relationship patterns are immense and radical, also tend to overestimate consistently the uniqueness of modern societies in relation to other historical and contemporary forms. An inescapable component of this uniqueness, for Giddens, is the desacralisation of all areas of social and cultural life.

In this respect it is notable that Lilar, in charting the demise of the value we attach to love, argues that the present 'crisis of the couple' is merely one aspect of the broader crisis of the sacred. In other words, the penchant for demythologisation that has undermined much of the beliefs and values of more conventionally 'religious' forms has spread even into the most intimate areas of our lives. Giddens, in his vision of modernity's promotion of an ever more pervasive, chronic reflexivity, would concur with Lilar on this point. Where she differs from him,

---

[89] Lilar, *Aspects of Love*, p. 13.

however, is in not accepting that our contemporary cultural predispositions regarding love are necessarily accurate, let alone desirable, ways of understanding a phenomenon that most of us will have some experience of at some point in our lives, regardless of cultural and historical differences.

In drawing on Breton to propose unreasonable love as the foundation of the couple, Lilar argues that contemporary rationalisations and demythologisations of relationships tend to exacerbate many of the problems they attempt to explain or mitigate.[90] Interpreting infidelity as a profaning of the sacred, for example, she argues that the notion of an 'open relationship' is a contradiction in terms: the rationalisation of promiscuity endorses the repeated profanation of the sacred foundation of the relationship. Consequently, the development of what she calls a 'legitimate jealousy' is as assured as the demise of the couple's relationship.[91] Collins' account of the sacred basis of relationships expresses a similar view.[92] For him, this basis is ordinarily manifest in positive bonds, such as tenderness and self-sacrifice, but can be expressed as violence, jealousy and hatred when the ritually constituted moral bond is violated through sexual or affectional infidelity. What is clear here is that this way of interpreting relationships does not simply offer a model for how relationships should be, or how they might work in some ideal typical situation. What it offers is a way of analysing how they come into being and are sustained, but also how they can break down and, by implication, how they can be repaired.

Conclusion

In conclusion, the general sense of a 'crisis' in contemporary relationships should not lead us to dismiss Breton's account of love as an unrealistic vision of an ideal beyond the reach of most of us, or as something that cannot tell us anything worthwhile about marriage in the modern world. Viewed within the context of Durkheimian sociology, it is arguable that the

---

[90] Lilar, *Aspects of Love*, p. 12.
[91] Lilar, *Aspects of Love*, p. 191.
[92] Collins, 'The Durkheimian Tradition', p. 121.

notion of *l'amour fou* not only has sound anthropological foundations, but also throws fresh light on modern relationships and attitudes to other areas of religious concern. This tradition of thought tells us that love, like the sacred in general, is inherently 'unreasonable', and will therefore have an uneasy place in the heavily rationalised environment of modernity, where things are often measured in terms of their utility. In so doing, it challenges utilitarian accounts of love, in their biological and sociological forms, and thereby offers a warning to those reflecting on love, marriage and religion in modernity not to confuse cultural presuppositions with more foundational questions about human capacities and propensities. In particular, it can be argued that this tradition might encourage theologians to remain dubious in the face of some of the more reductive analyses of love developed in the social sciences and elsewhere. Breton himself, it must be said, tended to see theologians as part of the problem surrounding the modern view of love, rather than its solution. Nevertheless, theologians might remain sceptical here too, and use aspects of his thought to develop further fruitful, interdisciplinary reflections on religion, marriage and love in the contemporary world.

PART 4

The Marriage Relationship

Introduction

Part 4 moves from the meanings attached to love in marriage, to the quality of the married relationship. The emphasis on relationship should not be taken to mean that any of the authors is advocating that marriage should not also be treated as an *institution*: rather they have simply chosen to write about different aspects of the marriage relationship which demand sympathetic treatment.

All five authors write from overt theological positions. John Wall writes as a mainstream, Christian, North American theologian. Wall enters into a positive, mutually critical, conversation with the marriage education movement. The marriage relationship cannot be sustained by skills alone. While careful not to undermine the achievements of the movement, he draws attention to shortcomings within the movement and argues that there are traditions of Christian marriage which might complement the movement at just these particular points of weakness. First, a feature of the movement is that stronger marriages can be actively promoted by the teaching of interpersonal communication skills. While this is desirable, it fails to identify marriage as more than a personal relationship, i.e., as a social institution in which everyone has a stake. Wall utilises Roman Catholic subsidiarity theory at this point to show that marriage cannot be extrapolated from the wider social goods with which it is bound up.

A second feature of the marriage education movement is that its understanding of marital commitment generally amounts to partners becoming committed to making their marriages more fulfilling for themselves. Wall utilises Reformed covenant theory at this point to show that if marriage is understood as a covenant which mirrors God's own covenants with humanity, the commitments of marriage partners are not just utilitarian but also obligational, responsible and long-term (even if not indissoluble). Less obviously, but more profoundly, these commitments are social, because marriage is viewed as an order of creation which supports, and receives support from, the wider community. A third feature of the movement is its general lack of recognition of social and political oppressions which damage marriages by enforcing unequal gender roles and marginalising the needs of children. Wall utilises liberation theology at this point to introduce a larger vision for marriage which locates it in the redemption of society 'at the level of its very deepest political and economic structures'. Without gainsaying the achievements of the movement Wall gently interposes Christian theological traditions at particular points in order to provide a missing depth, breadth and vision to the secular project.

Lisa Isherwood writes as a feminist theologian who tackles directly the horror of domestic violence against women and children, which she renames 'domestic torture'. Isherwood amplifies the contribution of liberation theology to a re-thinking of marriage, hinted at in Wall's chapter. Her paper was the only one at the conference dealing with violence, a reflection perhaps of the shame and embarrassment that the topic creates, thereby reinforcing the culture of silence. (It is easier to treat marriage as a sacrament.) Christian faith is deeply implicated in the 'moods and motivations' which lead to witch-hunts, legally sanctioned wife-beating and marital rape. The dogma of complementarity discourages any independent growth on the part of wives: the demand that women are submissive to men leads to enforcement and, when there is disobedience, to punishment. The agenda of many right-wing Christians represents a return to female submissiveness, and since women now expect greater equality, this agenda makes violence against women yet more likely.

The obvious crisis in masculinity is deepened and not addressed by popular images of masculinity and by pornography. Like Eve, women are to blame for this crisis. 'Texts of terror' are still used against women and patriarchy has subverted the very heart of Christian faith. The cross itself is able to be seen as an act of divine child abuse, the glorification of pain and the inevitability of victimhood: the demand for forgiveness of the perpetrators becomes a further psychological abuse, and the demand of selfless love is easily rendered by the 'possession mindset' of patriarchal men as disesteem, loss of self-worth and misery. The 'underside' of marriage has a corresponding 'underside' in theology, and this is exposed. Isherwood is nonetheless not against marriage! Her uses of 'justice', 'incarnation' and 'mutuality' indicate that better theologies of relationships (including marriage) are available.

Jack Dominian writes as a psychiatrist and Roman Catholic layperson. In his chapter he makes available the experience of over forty years of professional counselling and shapes it into an overall model. Dominian analyses three types of factors which contribute to marital breakdown – global, sociological and clinical. He believes these factors are irreversible and warns against conservative attempts to dismantle them. In the second half of the chapter Dominian describes three phases of marriage, and briefly examines each according to the five dimensions they exhibit. These are social, emotional, sexual, intellectual and spiritual. The dynamics of married life are thereby opened up in a way that enables trouble to be predicted, understood and countered. Dominian warns against over-sophistication in an area that is still 'full of obscurities'. Nonetheless his model is certain to provide a cognitive and professionally tested framework for counsellors and marriage ministry.

George Lotter writes from a Protestant, Reformed perspective, concerned with the male midlife crisis. This, and some of the forms it takes, is described from medical, psychological and social points of view. The theological and pastoral treatment can then begin. Lotter first describes how the Christian virtues of faith, hope and love are able to reach men in crisis, and then offers characteristically Protestant insights into the possibility of transformation. Men in midlife crisis are distracted by their declining powers, failed ambitions, etc. They are preoccupied with themselves (or with their unrealistic self-images). This is a state which is disturbing both to them and to the people around them. God's grace, however, accepts people as they are in all their unattractiveness, and operates to bring about a renewal of personal life based on increasing faith in God. Freed from self-preoccupation, the journey of faith is able to be restarted, and Lotter provides guidelines for pastors working with men exhibiting these problems.

Aldegonde Brenninkmeijer-Werhahn writes as a Roman Catholic layperson on marriage and becoming old. Her starting point is the increasing age of populations and the implications it poses for social and economic policy. Growing old in marriage together is itself an 'art' which recognises there may be a new beauty in ageing and a new depth of love in the midst of a more quiescent sex life. Retirement becomes an opportunity for negotiating new boundaries between partners, while the demands of caregiving to older parents and relatives cry out to be more justly shared between partners. Journeying together can be a form of growing into eternity, but this journeying itself needs social support, and able defences against what Brenninkmeijer-Werhahn calls 'the Moses feeling', i.e., the sense of not being admitted to a better future. Marital spirituality involves not simply prayer but critique, active resistance to cultural currents that disvalue and patronise elderly people.

9

The Marriage Education Movement: A Theological Analysis

John Wall

This chapter will use theological resources to assess and critique the 'marriage education movement', a social phenomenon that has risen to prominence in the past decade in North America and Europe, and which seeks to strengthen contemporary marriages by educating couples in marriage communication skills. Marriage education of one form or another has almost certainly existed for as long as there have been marriages. Couples about to get married, or seeking to improve their marriages, have always been able to find counsel, interest and support from such parties as parents, extended family members, experienced members of the community, and paid professionals like clergy, doctors and lawyers. The new marriage education movement is unique, however, in that it grows out of the profession of marriage therapy, a profession typically associated with helping marriages only when they are in trouble. This new approach involves imparting therapeutic communication skills designed to prevent marriages from becoming severely disrupted in the first place.

The thesis I will develop here is that while the marriage education movement provides valuable tools for couples to strengthen their marriages, it cannot be sustained effectively on its present, largely *therapeutic* basis. To help marriages in a meaningful and lasting way, marriage education needs to expand its horizons to include more socially – and spiritually – oriented marriage education traditions like those found in Christian theology. These marriage traditions have today been largely forgotten, by therapeutic and religious communities alike. Nevertheless, they are responsible for the profound intuition, at least in Western societies, that strong marriages are not just *interpersonal relations* but also in some important sense *social institutions.* While the institutional nature of marriage is still today widely assumed, it is precisely this social and public dimension of marriage which a therapeutic perspective at once relies upon but cannot, on its own grounds, provide adequate training in. Today's marriage education movement will fall short in its goal of strengthening contemporary marriages if it cannot develop a richer and more careful understanding of marriage as, first, not just a private but also a public institutional commitment; second, aimed at not just personal but also social and institutional goods; and, third, not just an interpersonal bond, but also one that is embedded in the larger institutional frameworks of law, economics, extended families and potential parenthood.

Rather than making a *confessional* critique of marriage education therapy, in which a Christian witness is brought against therapeutic ideology, I will instead enter into what the great twentieth-century Protestant theologian Paul Tillich called a mutually critical *correlation* or *conversation.* My goal is not to discredit the marriage education movement, but rather to place it in its larger context and to show ways in which major Christian marriage traditions could help *reform* it so as to better meet its own fundamentally laudable goal of strengthening contemporary marriages. To this end, I will first briefly examine the present marriage education movement itself and the therapeutic ideals and values by which it is driven. Then I will develop three Christian analyses of these ideals, from the perspectives of, respectively, Catholic subsidiarity theory, the Reformed Protestant covenant model, and the more recent possibilities emerging out of liberation theology. These analyses are not meant to be exhaustive of all possible theological perspectives, but rather to illustrate both the kind of dialogue Christians might enter into around marriage education, and the thesis that this dialogue would seek to reform the present marriage education movement to include training in marriage as a public and social institution.

The Marriage Education Movement and Its Ethic of Health

The marriage education movement itself has now grown into a diverse cultural phenomenon involving not only therapists but also clergy, rabbis, school and college teachers, business executives, and leaders of government. These various groups are united by their desire to strengthen marriages in whatever ways they can, preferably before and during their formation. They want to stem the tide of what social scientists now widely believe are the enormous personal and social costs which result, on average, from weak and broken marriages. These diverse groups form a *movement* in the best sense of the term. They are a grassroots up-swelling in multiple sectors and levels of society which have joined together around a common and pressing goal, and a broadly agreed-upon set of instruments for reaching it.

Despite its diversity, however, the origins of this movement and its driving ideals lie squarely in the profession of marriage therapy. In the early 1990s, a group of marriage therapists began to grow increasingly frustrated at having to treat couples whose marriages were already too far gone for help. Out of this frustration grew the now international Coalition for Marriage, Family, and Couples Education (CMFCE) directed by Diane Sollee,[1] as well as a rash of new books and research on the skills couples should use to prevent their marriages from getting to the point of no return. These therapists and therapy researchers adopted the language of 'education' in order to emphasise their goal of teaching couples the skills and tools needed to build and maintain healthy and long-term marriages for themselves.

By the end of the 1990s, the marriage education movement had been joined by a wide range of other professionals with similar frustrations. There were clergy and rabbis who increasingly saw the couples they joined in holy matrimony separated a short time later. There were teachers in schools and colleges who sought educational means to counter increasing confusion among youth about what a good marriage looks like. And there

---

[1] See the CMFCE web site at www.smartmarriages.com for a view of this organisation's stunning breadth and power to effect social change.

were public policy makers and government leaders, including most notably Tony Blair and Bill Clinton, who saw in marriage education a means for attacking trenchant social problems like youth crime, educational decline, and workplace inefficiency.

What attracts all these groups to the marriage education movement is the idea that strong marriages can be promoted by teaching couples better *interpersonal communication skills.* Communication skills are therapeutically grounded techniques for handling marriage's inevitable problems and conflicts. The classic communication skill taught is the so-called 'speaker-listener technique', famously described in the classic co-authored book, *Fighting for Your Marriage: Positive Steps for Preventing Divorce and Preserving a Lasting Love.*[2] The speaker-listener technique helps couples to hear and understand each other's point of view during contentious marital disagreements. Couples can be trained in this skill by being handed a single piece of square tile representing 'the floor'. They then practise discussing a sensitive issue in their relationship allowing only one partner to 'hold the floor' at any given point in time, during which the partner without the floor can only summarise and repeat back what the first partner says. Partners then switch holding the floor back and forth until both are satisfied that they have been adequately heard and understood. While marriage educators do not expect couples subsequently to carry a piece of tile around with them at all times, they do expect them to internalise the basic skill of taking turns listening to one another with care and attentiveness and repeating back significant points.

The marriage education movement is not monolithic in the communication skills it teaches. An alternative and sometimes complementary technique is for couples to learn how to separate out 'problem discussion' from 'problem solution', so that the full dimensions of a conflict can be probed calmly without either partner prematurely closing the discussion off.[3] By contrast, the respected marriage researcher John Gottman

---

[2] Howard Markman, Scott Stanley and Susan Blumberg, *Fighting for Your Marriage: Positive Steps for Preventing Divorce and Preserving a Lasting Love* (San Francisco: Jossey-Bass Publishers, 1994), pp. 63–72.

[3] Markman et al., *Fighting for Your Marriage*, pp. 82–8.

argues that couples should be taught, among other things, how to begin discussion of difficult issues with a 'softened start-up', which involves learning communication 'rules' like not placing blame, being concise in one's expression of problems, and starting all statements about problems with 'I' rather than 'You'.[4] Still other marriage educators promote techniques in such things as a 'fair fight for change'[5] or, as in the title of one popular book, 'getting the love you want'.[6]

These and other communication skills are meant to be applicable to almost any kind of situation that may come up in a marriage, and they can be taught not just by therapists but also by anyone else concerned about marriages. Many clergy, for example, now teach these skills in three to eight short sessions for couples who want to get married in their churches.[7] Some lawyers are now trained to introduce these skills when couples enquire about marital dissolution, and the American Bar Association produced a widely used video for youth about what steps they can take to prevent their marriages from ending in divorce (even lawyers, apparently, are growing tired of divorce).[8] Some business corporations are now starting to introduce marriage communication skills into employee training in order to head off conflicted marriages' possible drags on worker productivity. Public officials are also in on the act. Government leaders in Grand Rapids, Michigan, in the United States, for example, in 1997 started the first broad-scale 'community marriage policy'. Here the whole range of marriage professionals is organised into a co-ordinated and

[4] John Gottman, *The Marriage Clinic: A Scientifically-Based Marital Therapy* (New York: W. W. Norton & Company, 1999), pp. 224–6.

[5] Lori Gordon, *Passage to Intimacy* (New York: Simon & Schuster, 1993). This book is the basis for the widely popular PAIRS programme, information about which can be found on its web site at www.pairs.com.

[6] Harville Hendrix, *Getting the Love You Want: A Guide for Couples* (New York: Pocket Books, 1993).

[7] One prominent example in the United States is the 'Great Start' programme developed by Robert Cueni at Country Club Christian Church in Kansas City, Missouri.

[8] The video, titled *Partners for Students*, was created by Lynne Gold-Bikin, then Director of the Family Law Division of the American Bar Association, and is now used widely in high schools and colleges in the USA. See the video's web site at www.abanet.org/family/partners/home.html.

well-advertised city-wide effort to make sure that communication skills are imparted in one way or another to all marrying couples.

If one asks, finally, what such communication skills are meant to bring about – that is, what a 'good marriage' on this view would look like – the dominant consensus among marriage educators is that it means both partners enjoying greater personal fulfilment, satisfaction, and health. The language of 'health' is a therapeutic, and originally medical, metaphor which the marriage education movement has embraced as standing for a range of personal and private goods. As sociologist Linda Waite puts it, marriage 'matters' because on average it provides both partners – male and female alike – with better sex, more emotional fulfilment, and greater physical health and longevity than they would otherwise enjoy.[9] On the whole marital fulfilment and health are viewed as highly related to the personal wishes and needs of the individual partners involved. The book *Fighting for Your Marriage* concludes with the following summary:

> We've tried to provide tools that you can use to build a relationship that brings long-term fulfillment, and to protect your relationship from naturally occurring storms. But, like anything, once you have the tools, it's up to you what you do with them. As the ad says, 'Just do it.'[10]

A marriage is therefore 'good', on this view, insofar as it leads to greater long-term satisfaction and fulfilment *for you as an individual.*

Catholic Sacramental Subsidiarity Theory

Given the enormous success of this movement and its obvious potential benefits for individuals and society alike, what could a Christian perspective add that would be of any value? Let us look first at Catholic subsidiarity theory, one of the most

---

[9] Linda Waite, 'Does Marriage Matter?', *Demography*, 32:4 (November 1995), pp. 483–507. See also Linda Waite and Maggie Gallagher, *The Case for Marriage* (New York: Doubleday, 2000).

[10] Markman et al., *Fighting for Your Marriage*, p. 315.

powerful but least well-known models of marriage in the Christian tradition. The term 'subsidiarity' was first introduced into official Catholic teaching by Pope Pius XI in 1931 in the context of the international labour movement.[11] Its roots lie in Thomas Aquinas and the deep classical tradition of natural law theology. Subsidiarity is a Latin term which literally means 'furnishing help', and it refers broadly to the theory that larger and more powerful institutions in society should furnish help to less powerful social institutions without, however, taking over the natural functions which more specialised social institutions are uniquely suited to perform.[12] It is an expression of Aquinas' powerful and influential natural law theology within the context of the greater appreciation for plurality in modern society, where a diversity of interdependent and specialised social institutions is needed in order to fulfil the diversity of the natural human goods created by God.

Applied to marriage, subsidiarity theory affirms at once the uniqueness of the goods of marriage and the dependence of these goods for their fulfilment on social institutions outside of marriage. Marriage on this view exists for the purpose of such human goods as the direction of sexual desire toward mutuality and love, the procreation and raising of children, and the uniting of families around common emotional, social and economic ends.[13] Marriage on this view is also one of the seven Catholic sacraments, in that, like baptism, it participates in the *spiritual* good of the union of Christ and the church.[14] The great insight of a subsidiarity theory of marriage is that the fulfilment of the private goods of marriage is deeply inter-twined with the fulfilment of larger kinds of social and sacred goods as well.

---

[11] Pope Pius XI, *Quadragesimo anno (Forty Years After [Rerum novarum])* (1931). *Rerum novarum* (1891) is Pope Leo III's influential encyclical on the condition of labour workers.

[12] For a good broad definition of 'subsidiarity' see National Conference of Catholic Bishops, *Economic Justice for All* (Washington, DC: US Catholic Conference, 1986).

[13] Thomas Aquinas, *Summa Theologiae* 2:2 (London: R. & T. Washbourne, 1917), q.26; *Summa Theologiae* 3, 'Supplement' (New York: Benziger Brothers, 1948), q.41; *Summa Contra Gentiles* (London: Burns, Oates & Washbourne, 1928), 3, ii.

[14] Thomas Aquinas, *Summa Theologiae* 3, 'Supplement', q.42.

There is a certain sense in which subsidiarity theory blends nicely with the marriage education movement's emphasis on the good of personal marital fulfilment. It is no accident that Catholics have been amongst the movement's most vigorous and active supporters. One might even suggest that subsidiarity theory could learn from marriage education therapy not to assume a grand natural ordering to marriage and instead accept a greater relativity of possible marital goods. However, the strength of subsidiarity theory with respect to marriage education is that it insists on viewing marital goods as not merely the pursuit of whatever private and individual aims each partner may happen to desire. Rather, marriage education should help couples pursue the specific goods which are peculiar to marriage itself, goods which by virtue of marriage being an institution are not only private but also public and social.

What this means concretely is first that marriage education should not ignore the greater social goods with which marriage is implicitly caught up. Marriage draws individuals beyond themselves into participation in wider and publicly shared social ends. For example, it includes building a new kind of life together between the couple, the potential social good of raising children, each partner's participation in fulfilling certain goods of their spouse's extended family, the couple forming a single unit of economic consumption and productivity, and even the marriage becoming a basis for socially active goods like adoption. Marriage education therapists might well protest that whatever larger social goods are furthered through marriage should be the personal choice of each individual partner. However, the fact is that these social goods lie at the core of what defines marriage as an institution. In an important sense marriage *should* be formed with the *possibility* of children in mind (even if couples individually do not choose or are not able to have children), with an understanding of what it means to become an economically and legally bound unit, and mindful of the fact that each partner is joining not just another person but also their larger familial and social community. Therapists unnecessarily and unhelpfully limit the scope of what it means to have a *fulfilling* marriage by assuming that fulfilment can only refer to private and personal goods like sex, fun and intimacy. *Marital* fulfilment is by definition also social, intergenerational and communal.

But also, second, subsidiarity theory suggests that since marital goods are at once private *and* public, they cannot adequately become fulfilled without help furnished by larger sectors of society. The marriage education movement implicitly acknowledges this by exhorting couples to seek profession-alised therapeutic marriage skills training. In addition, experiments in cities like Grand Rapids, Michigan, seek to ensure such training through the support of governments and communities. Interestingly, the most widespread and successful effort to involve communities in marriage education is, in fact, the Christian-based Community Marriage Policy organised by Michael McManus.[15]

However, these community supports for marriages are still largely limited only to helping couples to help themselves. They are primarily oriented around teaching couples how to apply therapeutic skills to their own relationship. While such help is all to the good, no marriage could in fact survive on the basis of communication skills alone. Especially in an age like ours where marriages are increasingly isolated from their public contexts, marriage educators are in a position to help couples explore the support and help that may be furnished not only by marriage educators themselves but also by extended families, places of worship, workplaces, schools, neighbourhoods, and other such communities. There is no reason why marriage education should not develop a more expanded vision in which couples are trained to seek help from these broader parts of society as valuable sources of support for their marriage as a partly public institution.

The Protestant Covenant Model

A different Christian perspective on the institutional nature of marriage comes out of the Protestant Reformation tradition

---

[15] For a description of this programme see Michael McManus, *Marriage Savers: Helping Your Friends and Family Avoid Divorce* (Grand Rapids, MI: Zondervan, 1993), ch. 13; or visit the Marriage Savers website at www.marriage-savers.org.

originating in John Calvin. This Reformed approach under-stands marriage as essentially a social *covenant*. It shares with subsidiarity theory the view that marriage is not only a private relationship but also a public institution inextricably related to larger elements in society. But this public dimension in covenant theory has less to do with marriage participating in larger social goods, and more with marriage's responsibilities and commitments as part of society's basic moral foundations. Marriage on this view is not just one specialised institution, but one of God's three ordained 'orders of creation' – alongside the state and the church – which together constitute society's basic institutional structure.[16]

Protestant Reformers like Calvin applied the Hebrew Bible's *vertical* covenant between humanity and God to a *horizontal* covenant between two human beings in marriage.[17] Covenant marriage is not viewed as a sacrament because it does not establish a sacred union with God. It remains inextricably bound up with the fallen human order still in need of God's redemption. Rather, covenant marriage is a human and social relationship in which God participates *indirectly* through his chosen agents on earth.[18] In marriage, the couple covenants under God to commit themselves not only to one another, but also to their ordained role in the social order. At the time of the Reformation, marriage in the West became for the first time a fully *public* and *legal* institution, requiring the explicit witnesses of the state, the family, the church, and the community. The marriage covenant not only suggests but requires the couple to share their joint properties under the laws of the state; to seek out the spiritual counsel offered by the church; publicly to honour the concerns and interests of their extended families; and to raise their children to be worthy and productive members of the community.[19] While the marriage covenant for the Reformers shares some features with the kinds of 'covenant

---

[16] John Calvin, *Calvin's Commentaries*, 47 vols. (Edinburgh: Oliver & Boyd, 1843–59), Comm. Eph. 5:22, and Comm. Mal. 2:14.

[17] John Witte, Jr, *From Sacrament to Contract: Marriage, Religion and Law in the Western Tradition* (Louisville, KY: Westminster John Knox Press, 1997), p. 95.

[18] See for example Calvin, *Calvin's Commentaries*, Lev. 19:29; Eph. 6:1–3; 1 Thess. 4:3.

[19] Witte, *From Sacrament to Contract*, pp. 94–8.

marriages' now emerging in the laws in parts of the United States, they were intended, more profoundly, to secure the duties of marriage as essential to the very peace and preservation of society.

It is perhaps no accident that therapeutic approaches to marriage grew up in largely Protestant countries, for a covenant view when taken too far can surely subject couples to enormous social burdens that are detrimental to individual health. What is more, the assertion of marriage as an 'order of creation' opens it up to patriarchal interpretations. Nevertheless, the covenant model remains useful in articulating an essential institutional dimension of marriage which marriage educators do not adequately address, namely the couple's implicit and very real *commitments* and *responsibilities* toward one another, their potential children, and society.

Marriage educators do in fact speak of the value of marital 'commitment', but upon closer inspection what they typically mean is that each partner should dedicate themselves to the task of making their marriage more personally fulfilling for themselves. Commonly, the marital commitment is compared to the stock market, where each partner makes an 'investment' in the marriage so that they may receive a high 'return' in personal satisfaction.[20] The marriage educators Markman et al. famously distinguish 'dedication' commitment from 'constraint' commitment. Dedication commitment is to be affirmed, because it helps couples think of their relationship as long-term and important in their lives. Constraint commitment, however, is on the whole to be discouraged, because it keeps couples together on the basis of negative factors like economic interdependency, social pressure, and, most telling of all, 'concern for children's welfare'.[21]

The covenantal perspective on marriage helps us understand the commitments couples make toward each other and society as more than a long-term, utilitarian, market-like calculation. It views the marital commitment as one toward a vital and socially

---

[20] Markman et al., *Fighting for Your Marriage*, pp. 191-7.

[21] Markman et al., *Fighting for Your Marriage*, pp. 170–8. The authors interestingly also include under 'constraint commitment' what they call viewing the marriage as a 'covenant', which perhaps exposes what their therapeutic model really believes itself to be against.

embedded institution. Partners commit themselves to supporting each other in health *and* in sickness. They join not just an economic arrangement which might make them financially better off, but also a unified institution of economic consumption and production. They enter into not just a partnership in sexual exchange, but also a family structure linked to the partners' procreative parents as well as their yet-to-be procreated possible children. And, most importantly of all, they commit themselves not just to a reciprocal exchange of love, but also to a social institution that can support love's trusting growth and maturation, can provide a context – within limits – for genuine forgiveness, and, if necessary, can sustain the capacity to love and raise children.

Marriage educators do a disservice to couples if they suggest that the only commitment they are making to one another is to dedicate themselves to a personally enriching relationship. While marriages obviously should on one level exist for the personal benefit of both partners, this benefit is inextricably linked to a range of vital social responsibilities. A marriage education which obscures these larger institutional commitments fails to help couples learn how to take on the social responsibilities which marriages implicitly entail. By suggesting that marriage has value chiefly as a utilitarian exchange, marriage education as it presently stands in fact contributes to the dissolution of marriages once couples run up against their real and important institutional commitments and responsibilities.

A Liberationist Perspective

Finally, a third kind of conversation could be undertaken between Christianity and the present marriage education movement by introducing the possibilities contained in liberation theology. This third conversation will have to be even more exploratory than the first two, as liberation theology was developed only at the beginning of the twentieth century, and it has not to my knowledge produced a systematic conceptualisation of marriage *per se*. Liberation theology does suggest, however, that marriage may be viewed as a social institution on still a third different level. Marriage is not just tied up with larger public goods, or linked to significant social responsibilities, but also embedded in a greater *political* context of unequal freedoms and oppressions.

Liberation theology originated in a Catholic movement in Latin America which sought freedom for the poor from oppressive social structures of inequality. Liberation theologians like Gustavo Gutiérrez and Juan Luis Segundo hold that all persons have a sacred and equal dignity as children of God. Furthermore, economic and political inequalities are so ingrained in ordinary human life that they can be fought effectively only on the *religious* grounds of working to realise a just Kingdom of God.[22] Liberation theology differs from Catholic natural law and Protestant covenantal theologies by emphasising the *prophetic* call to redeem society at the level of its very deepest political and economic structures. It is now practised widely by non-Catholic Christians as well and around the world, and has been applied not only to poverty but also to other forms of social oppression like racism,[23] sexism,[24] and the plight of children.[25]

A liberation theology of marriage education, as I interpret it, would be concerned with helping partners free themselves from marital practices which support or play into larger economic, cultural and political oppressions. Such oppressions might include women being expected to take on primary responsibility for child care and housework; children receiving too little parental attention in a market-driven economy; and men having unequal legal rights to care for their children after divorce. In each of these cases, marriage is viewed as not just an interpersonal or even social institution, but also an inherently *political* one. Liberation theology suggests that one of the key tasks of marriage is to structure family relationships in a way

---

[22] Gustavo Gutiérrez, *A Theology of Liberation* (Maryknoll, NY: Orbis Books/London: SCM Press, 1973); Juan Luis Segundo, *The Liberation of Theology* (Maryknoll, NY: Orbis Books, 1976). For an accessible introduction to liberation theology see Leonardo Boff and Clodovis Boff, *Introducing Liberation Theology* (Maryknoll, NY: Orbis Books, 1987).

[23] E.g., James Cone, *A Black Theology of Liberation* (twentieth anniversary edn; Maryknoll, NY: Orbis Books, 1990).

[24] E.g., Rosemary Radford Ruether, *Sexism and God-Talk: Toward a Feminist Theology* (Boston: Beacon Press, 1983).

[25] E.g., Adrian Thatcher, *Marriage after Modernity: Christian Marriage in Postmodern Times* (New York: New York University Press, 1999), ch. 5.

befitting the dignity and equality of all persons as children in God's Kingdom.

There is no doubt that in a certain sense a liberationist view would embrace the tasks and practices of improving marriage communication skills. The marriage education movement is in part built upon the premise of liberating couples from the unhealthy marriage practices of our culture of divorce. However, a liberation theology perspective would insist that marital oppression is not *just* an issue of interpersonal communication. It is also an institutional issue tied up with society's larger economic and political structures. For example, good communication skills could help a husband understand that his spouse is angry because she does the bulk of the housework. However, it would take more than just the husband and wife communicating well to change the more profound social expectations and structures that support this problem. No matter how much the partners learn to understand each other's concerns, women in our culture will still be blamed (by others and often by themselves) for messy homes, and both men and women, in our economy, will still have little time for work around the house in the first place.

The liberationist perspective suggests that marriage education should help couples learn how both to *identify* and *actively to resist* the deeper social oppressions into which their marriages play. This more political approach to marriage education could not rest content with the assumption that marital problems are caused by the marriage relationship alone. It would also help partners learn how to examine their marriage in light of its larger cultural and political contexts. What is more, it would teach couples how to develop and maintain substantive ideals for their marriages, whether those ideals involve images of God's intended Kingdom or similar ideals like shared devotion to Krishna or simply some kind of spiritual oneness of humanity. A greater capacity to relate one's marriage to one's spiritual values empowers couples to resist the political and economic oppressions which confront them.

Without this political dimension, the marriage education movement in fact itself risks playing into marital oppression. The current focus on skills aimed at marital fulfilment as the 'be all' and 'end all' of good marriages is itself based on the unexpressed and somewhat dubious cultural ideology of what

Robert Bellah et al. have called expressive individualism.[26] Such a marital ideal is arguably oppressive toward children, who need parents who are committed to more in a marriage than the parents' own personal fulfilment. It could also unwittingly play into oppressions toward women, who in our culture on average have less economic and cultural power in a marriage and hence more to lose from an uncontextualised communicative exchange.[27] The most striking case of the failure of communication skills to make marriages strong is physical and sexual abuse, where communication can only be one part of what the couple should hope to achieve. But this is not an exception to what marriage education should be all about; it is the most obvious sign of the need for marriage educators to address oppressions in all their subtle and not-so-subtle forms.

Conclusion: Toward Education for the Marriage Institution

I will not conclude with any grand synthesis of these three possible Christian perspectives on marriage education, nor with a discussion of how they might be related and ordered. This is a task for further work, even perhaps a new agenda for marriage theology. What is more, there are a great many other Christian and non-Christian religious perspectives that could and should be introduced into the conversation as well. It is sufficient now merely to suggest, as I have done, that these three major Christian perspectives illustrate different levels or layers of the kind of theological analysis which the marriage education movement cries out for.

Instead, by way of conclusion I propose that one of the most

[26] Robert Bellah, Richard Madsen, William Sullivan, Ann Swidler and Stephen Tipton, *Habits of the Heart: Individualism and Commitment in American Life* (Berkeley: University of California Press, 1985).

[27] Some would argue that women in particular need the political protections of marriage as an institution in order to keep the fathers of their children committed and involved. See, e.g., Don S. Browning et al., *From Culture Wars to Common Ground: Religion and the American Family Debate* (Louisville, KY: Westminster John Knox Press, 1997), ch. 6.

pressing tasks before the marriage education movement itself, as it stands today, is to expand its vision of what strengthening marriages really involves. Good communication skills are clearly part of the picture, and these should be embraced and further developed. Communication skills may themselves have important spiritual dimensions, such as forgiveness and the sacred nature of interpersonal love, which theologians should not ignore. However, communication skills as such can be effective only within the context of helping couples form strong marital institutions. Good marriages are more than *just* private exchanges for the purpose of partners' personal health, satisfaction and well-being. They are distinguishable from other kinds of loving relations by also having more highly structured social, public and political dimensions. This means that marriage education should prepare couples not only to communicate well, but also to bear the burden of important social and procreative goods; to support complex familial and intergenerational commitments; to find institutional support from couples' greater public and social contexts; and to develop institutional resistance to larger political, cultural and economic oppressions.

Clergy and religious leaders have a vital and important role to play in leading the way toward this kind of more realistic, helpful, and expansive conception and practice of marriage education. In this they have profound untapped resources in the Christian traditions, and these traditions can be interpreted self-critically into the contemporary marriage situation. Christian approaches to marriage education do not have to remain limited merely to absorbing the latest therapeutic techniques, as they often do,[28] nor to taking a confessional approach which rejects therapeutic perspectives altogether.[29] A truly constructive Christian voice will enter into the kind of dialogue illustrated here, in which theological perspectives are applied to reforming the marriage education movement itself.

[28] This approach is taken for example by the leading marriage educators Scott Stanley, Daniel Trathen, Savanna McCain and Milt Bryan in their influential book *A Lasting Promise: A Christian Guide to Fighting for Your Marriage* (San Francisco: Jossey-Bass Publishers, 1998).

[29] This latter approach is evident, for example, in the negative reactions of some Christian churches and denominations to the 'covenant marriage' laws that were recently passed in Louisiana and Arizona in the United States.

10

Factors which Contribute to Marital Difficulties

Jack Dominian

Everyone is aware that there has been a meteoric rise in marital breakdown in the last thirty years. In 1961 there were 25,000 divorces in England and Wales. In 1998 there were 145,000. This is a huge increase.[1] When spouses and children are added together, nearly half a million people come out of the divorce courts every year. All this amounts to an enormous cost, both financial and human, which has been described in numerous publications. Clearly we are all concerned to find out what we can do to prevent this social wound.

This chapter is concerned with putting together some of the social and clinical data which research has gathered, showing an association between them and marital breakdown. It should be remembered that this is only a statistical association, but it is a powerful one which can help us with prevention. There are three groups of factors. Group one consists of global factors that apply to all Western societies, approximately 40% of the world. A second group is sociological and a third is clinical. This I have put together as a result of my clinical experience.[2]

Global Factors

Social factors influence the life and relationships of men and women. In the case of marriage, the evolution of women's

---

[1] Office of National Statistics, *Population Trends* (London: HMSO, Spring 2000).
[2] Jack Dominian, *Marital Pathology* (London: Darton, Longman & Todd, 1980).

status from dependence on men and patriarchy to greater independence means that women no longer put up with tribulations that they would have tolerated a generation or two ago. Thus they do not accept violence, excessive gambling, alcoholism and infidelity. This change in attitude is shown by the fact that women file nearly 75% of petitions for divorce. This factor, reflecting women's emancipation, is unlikely to change unless something exceptional occurs. It has implications for preventive strategies. There are those who urge society to go back to the past, by which is often meant to the acceptance by women of harsh patriarchal behaviour. Since this will not happen, we should be aiming to encourage men to change their attitudes. This is particularly relevant for Christianity since it has for so long supported patriarchy.

The second global factor is rising expectations. Both men and women have attained minimum material standards, beyond which they want emotional and sexual satisfaction. This is a critical factor. That is to say, what level of emotional and sexual dissatisfaction will they tolerate? Here the prevailing philosophy of society is very influential in the outcome. A philosophy of individualism or, as it is commonly called, the 'Me, Me, Me' attitude to life, prevails and people do not put up with suffering for very long. There is room here for society to re-examine its attitude to what couples will put up with before they seek dissolution. The third global factor is the shift of marriage from an institution to a relationship of love. This change means that traditional roles have given way to an emotional relationship in which feelings are paramount. This vital change is also likely to remain permanent. These three global factors have permeated the whole of Western society and need to be recognised in the home, the school and society. They are fundamental, and no amount of tinkering with the details, which leaves them unacknowledged and unresolved, will be effective.

Sociological Factors

All three of the above factors apply to all marriages in Western society. The following factors apply to individual marriages.

1. Age at marriage

It has been shown quite consistently that marriages are more vulnerable to divorce when the bride is under the age of 20 at the time of marriage.[3] The much higher risk of divorce is increased still further if the groom is also under 20.[4] The references quoted are from the 1970s but recent research confirms this finding.[5] One of the obvious reasons is that as men and women mature their original reasons for marrying no longer apply.

2. Premarital pregnancy

There is also persistent evidence that premarital pregnancy and pregnancy early in the marriage are related to a higher incidence of marital breakdown.[6]

3. Youthful marriage and premarital pregnancy

There is further evidence that a combination of youthful marriage and premarital pregnancy is particularly likely to lead to divorce.[7]

4. Social class, income and education

By and large it has been shown that there is an inverse relationship between social class, income, education and marital breakdown. However, the connections are complex. They have been carefully analysed by a One Plus One study.[8]

---

[3] P. C. Glick and A. J. Norton, 'Divorce and Age at Marriage', *Journal of Marriage and Family*, 33 (1971), p. 307.

[4] R. Leete, *Population Trends* (London: HMSO, 1976).

[5] J. Simons (ed.), *High Divorce Rates: The State of the Evidence on Reasons and Remedies* (London: One Plus One, Marriage and Partnership Research, Vol. 1, 1999), p. 14.

[6] Simons, *High Divorce Rates*, p. 19.

[7] G. Rowntree, 'Some aspects of marriage breakdown in Britain during the last 30 years', *Population Studies*, 18 (1964), p. 147; B. Thornes and J. Collard, *Who Divorces?* (London: Routledge & Kegan Paul, 1979).

[8] Simons, *High Divorce Rates*, p. 21.

5. *Premarital acquaintance*

Hasty marriages are risky propositions. This is understandable because such marriages lack sufficient acquaintance to ensure enough common ground for maintaining the relationship. A unique study of 738 elopements found a happy outcome in only half the couples.[9]

6. *Engagement*

A harmonious engagement could be expected to augur well for marriage. A prospective study confirmed this.[10] Brief courtships of less than nine months, or a stormy and tempestuous courtship are often warnings of an unhappy marriage. The storms in the engagement period are often a reflection of a disturbed personality, which persists in the marriage.

7. *Premarital cohabitation*

It seems common sense that one way of testing the future togetherness is for couples to cohabit before marriage. The incidence of cohabitation before marriage has increased enormously. The so-called 'weeding hypothesis' argues that only those cohabiting couples who find themselves well suited and more committed to marriage will go on to marry. However, in the last two decades evidence has accumulated that cohabiting couples who proceed to marriage are more vulnerable to divorce.[11]

The global factors are really impervious to easy manipulation but the socio-economic factors are subject to demographic control. Effective educational intervention might therefore be productive.

---

[9] P. Popenoe, *American Sociological Review*, 3 (1938), p. 47.
[10] E. W. Burgess and P. Wallen, *Engagement and Marriage* (Chicago: Lippincott, 1953).
[11] Simons, *High Divorce Rates*, p.16.

Clinical Factors

The third set of factors is the longest and is based on the author's clinical experience. Work over forty years in counselling has established some patterns of difficulties that I have assembled in some order and called 'the clinical model'. Those who want a detailed study of this model can refer to my book *Make or Break*.[12]

The clinical model is divided into three phases of marriage, the first phase consisting of the first five years. The selection of the first five years is not random for these years show a great deal of separation that will end in divorce. Given the gap between separation and actual divorce, it is not surprising that nearly half of all divorces occur in the first nine years of marriage.[13] These five years also include many of the pregnancies and births of the marriage. In my first book on marital breakdown over thirty years ago,[14] I showed an association between the first birth and marital breakdown. Subsequent research has confirmed this. Nowadays this phase may be anticipated in cohabitation.

The second phase is between 30 and 50, that is the middle years. These years capture some important events such as the growth, adolescence and departure of the children, the peak of work achievement with its stresses, the menopause and health problems of the middle years. The third phase covers the years between 50 and the death of one of the spouses. Although divorce is primarily an event of the first and second phases, it continues in the third phase. This phase is life without children at home, retirement, sexual decline and is punctuated with ill-health.

The Phases and Dimensions of the Clinical Model

These three phases are part one of the model. Part two is an analysis of the relationship using five dimensions, the social, emotional, sexual, intellectual and spiritual.

---

[12] Jack Dominian, *Make or Break* (London: SPCK, 1984).
[13] Dominian, *Marital Pathology*, p. 8.
[14] Jack Dominian, *Marital Breakdown* (London: Pelican, 1968).

When we speak of marital problems it is right to use the plural for breakdown is never the result of a single factor. It is the interaction of the personalities of the spouses and one or more of the five parameters I have mentioned. Common personality factors which are to be found in those who divorce are a high degree of sensitivity to criticism, a paranoid make-up, jealousy, quick temper, aggressivity, impulsiveness and extroversion. There are of course other elements, but these are the most common. Marital problems arise when a husband or wife is hurt to the point of considerable frustration and anger and, despite repeated requests or efforts, the behaviour of one or both partners does not change.

First phase

Social dimension

(a) Parents

One of the principal characteristics of marriage is that the partners leave the family home and unite to form a new household. In this household they will consult each other and reach their own mutual decisions. One of the problems is when one of the partners does not really leave their family. Such men and women bypass their spouse and discuss crucial matrimonial questions, not with each other but with their parents. They ring home several times a day and spend weekend after weekend with their original families. In other words, although married, they have not left the dependence on the support of their family. They still remain children dependent on their parents. This is an intolerable situation for the other spouse and very often the tension escalates until it ends in divorce. An over-dependence on parents of the family of origin is a common problem. If a child is born in this situation the problem may be aggravated because the child is not managed in the marital home but in the household of one set of grandparents, and tension may arise between the two sets of in-laws.

(b) Housing and home management

One of the principal needs of a new couple is to have their own home, which, however small, gives shape to their unity and

independence. When the couple have their own home, how
they run it can be a source of difficulty. Men may promise the
moon when they are courting but may not live up to their
promises in reality. Research suggests that, despite the
increasing involvement of men in household chores, women
are still left with the major responsibility of household work.
When this is coupled with outside work and children, the
accumulation leads to tiredness and fatigue, a decreased libido,
tension, frustration and marital difficulties.

(c) Money

It is not often that you listen to a marital distress story without
money raising its head among the mutual grievances. Very often
these are: for the wife that she is not given enough; and for the
husband that his wife is financially inept. The reason money is so
important is because it has several meanings. First is the obvious
economic one. Secondly, and rarely appreciated, it has
emotional overtones in the sense of feeling, 'If you loved me, you
would not keep me short.' Thirdly, money is a source of power.

(d) Work

There is ample evidence that both unemployment and
excessive hours at work are associated with marital difficulties.[15]
Unemployment is associated with depression and low self-
esteem, both damaging to the relationship, and long hours
at work often by the husband leave the wife lonely and
disengaged.

(e) Leisure

It is well established that time spent together by the couple
cements their relationship.[16] In the early years of marriage,
some men in particular want the advantages of home and also

---

[15] Simons, *High Divorce Rates.*
[16] Jack Dominian, *Marriage* (London: Heinemann, 1995), p. 76.

to continue to pursue their own leisure pastimes. Wives are often left at home on Saturdays while the husband goes to the football match or in the evenings when he goes to the pub with his mates. These patterns can cause great distress.

These are the five social factors that cause difficulties.

Emotional dimension

Still within the first phase we move to emotional factors. Courtship or cohabitation should assume emotional compatibility, but in a paradoxical way men and women show themselves in the best possible light under these testing conditions, only to find a little later on that their spouse may be a totally different person. Early exit from marriage may be due to the fact that either spouse when married feels stifled, caged-in or oppressed. They cannot stand intimacy. Or spouses find that their partner falls short of their expectations. In practice they are not what they promised to be. They are far more dominant, aggressive, mean, intolerant, oversensitive or moody, lose their temper easily. In brief, spouses may not survive the transfiguration from the initial idealisation to reality.

Sexual dimension

Sexual problems in all phases fall into two categories, physical and emotional. The commonest physical sexual problem is non-consummation. Modern sexual therapy can help with this. Pain on intercourse and lack of orgasm are two rare female difficulties, both of which can be helped. Emotional problems have been extensively examined by sexual therapists and include a history of sexual abuse in childhood, difficulties in relating to parents, excessive anxiety or latent homosexuality.

In the first five years there is often the birth of the first child. After childbirth it has been shown that women experience reduced libido for some months, and many have no desire for sex for some time.[17] In some very rare instances there is an early extramarital relationship.[18]

---

[17] Dominian, *Marriage*, p. 170.
[18] Dominian, *Marriage*, p. 164.

Intellectual dimension

The mutuality of intellectual needs is met by similarity of social and educational backgrounds. Occasionally class and educational similarity is breached when a man marries primarily a body and a woman marries money. In these circumstances they soon find in practice that they have little in common and the marriage does not last.

Spiritual dimension

In a society where overt religion is not highly prized, the religious affiliation of the spouses matters little in marriage. A generation ago it mattered a lot and mixed marriages were problematic. Nowadays it is the values the couple hold that matter. The greatest conflict is between spouses when one holds a materialistic outlook and the other an altruistic one. Money or quality of life can divide couples, but other values can also separate them. It depends whether the quality of the relationship is stronger than the differences of their values.

Second phase

We move to the second phase, the years of marriage which cover the ages between 30 and 50. Crucial events during these years are the growth of the children, their adolescence, promotion at work or unemployment, mid-life crises, the menopause and the departure of children from the home. One factor, however, stands out and that is change. As we traverse these years we change in our personality, work, needs, values and so on. Once again I take the five dimensions, social, emotional, sexual, intellectual and spiritual, with change in mind.

Social dimension

Social status may change during these years either by an upwardly mobile move or a downward one. Upward mobility may be due to promotion, or increase in financial status, power or authority. The danger here is that the other spouse may be left behind and outgrown. Downward social mobility may be the result of unemployment, ill-health, gambling, alcoholism or crime. The common factor here is poverty, combined with social disgrace, and a drop in self-esteem. The couple turn their frustration into mutual hostility or disenchantment.

Emotional dimension

These two decades are critical for emotional development. We grow from emotional dependence on our spouse to independence. We now want to take control of our lives, socially, economically, emotionally, intellectually and the key to marital stability is whether our partner allows us to be the person we have become or whether they insist on treating us as a dependent child. We also move from insecurity to security, and we are less dependent on our partner for survival. The outcome once again depends on whether our spouse can accept our new-found confidence. This change is in growth and the key is the mutual adaptation of the spouses.

Sexual dimension

As I mentioned before, sexual difficulties are either physical or emotional. Physically, during this phase, we see the beginnings of impotence or premature ejaculation in the male and the persistence of vaginal pain, lack of orgasm or persistent loss of sexual desire after childbirth in the female.

The couple may become disenchanted with each other sexually because they are emotionally no longer attracted to each other. These are the years of adultery which may affect 40% of men and 20% of women. Adultery may result in the end of the marriage but many marriages survive a first extramarital affair.

Intellectual dimension

At the intellectual level couples also change. Their social, political and economic views may alter. They may agree to disagree but in association with other factors this is the disagreement that may break the camel's back.

Spiritual dimension

Just as with intellectual values so with spiritual ones, unilateral changes may take place. Spouses may give up their religious faiths or they may embrace new ones. They may come to see the meaning of life in diametrically opposed views. Whether they go their separate ways depends on their underlying emotional and sexual relationship.

Third phase

Finally we reach the third phase from the age of 50 to the death of one of the spouses. Although divorce continues in this stage of marriage, most of it has taken place at an earlier stage.

Social dimension

The main social events are the departure of the children from the family home and the retirement from work of the spouses. If the husband has occupied himself primarily with his work and the wife with the children, then, when these two activities cease, the couple look at each other and see a stranger. In these circumstances there is no unifying force in the marriage.

Emotional dimension

The growth process from dependence to independence continues in this phase and the couple may experience further alienation. But the majority of couples adapt to one another and become interdependent. Some couples hold on to each other in the absence of emotional cement in an empty structure. Mutual physical care and ill-health may hold them together.

Sexual dimension

For the woman the main sexual event is the menopause. Some women find this a relief. For some it is a loss and a reminder of the end of their childbearing years. But sexual intercourse continues. For the man the main concern is increasing impotence which can play havoc with his sexual life. Occasionally in this phase a man leaves his wife for a younger woman.

Intellectual and spiritual dimensions

Again in this phase the couple may develop different views and values but these do not often lead to marital difficulties.

Conclusion

The clinical model, with its phases and dimensions, is not intended to be a dictionary of marital breakdown. The factors included, although extensive, are only an outline, but they are meant to shed light on a subject that strikes families suddenly and is still full of obscurities.

For those who do marriage counselling, it may provide a useful framework and for pastors some help in their pastoral work. Those who are responsible for education may be helped in their work and everyone else helped to deepen their understanding of what is still an obscure but vital concern.

11

The So-called 'Male Mid-life Crisis' and Marriage

George Lotter

Introduction

Female menopause is a well-known phenomenon.[1] There is a high degree of concurrence amongst the clinical disciplines as to its causes and consequences. Until relatively recently, the common assumption was that such a midlife transition was characteristic of women, but not of men.[2] Research has shown that there is a growing body of evidence which suggests that increasing numbers of men experience something *similar* to, if not identical with, menopause.[3] The syndrome manifests physically, psychosocially and spiritually.[4]

[1] R. D. Chessick, 'Mental Health and the Care of the Soul in Mid-life', *Journal of Pastoral Care*, 37:1 (1983), p. 5; J. Thompson, 'First Aid in Pastoral Care: VI Midlife', *Expository Times*, 95:2 (1984), p. 356; 'Male Mid-life Crisis', see http://www.health.iafrica.com/psychonline/qa/selfimage/malemidlife crisis.htm; D. V. Bejian and P. R. Salomone, 'Understanding Midlife Career Renewal: Implications for Counseling', *Career Development Quarterly*, 44 (September 1995), p. 57.

[2] N. Coetzee, 'The So-called Male Mid-life Crisis. Theory and Praxis for the Pastoral Ministry' (unpublished MA dissertation, Potchefstroom, South Africa: Potchefstroom University for CHE, 1997).

[3] C. W. Stewart, 'Mid-life Crisis from a Faith Perspective', *Quarterly Review*, 2:3 (1982), p. 65; J. Conway, *Men in Mid-life Crisis* (Elgin, IL: David C. Cook Publishing Co., 1990), p. 27; cf. D. C. Gould, R. Petty and H. S. Jacobs, 'For and Against: The Male Menopause – Does it Exist?', *British Medical Journal*, 320, Issue no. 7238 (25 March 2000), p. 858.

[4] A. Kruger, 'The Midlife Transition: Crisis or Chimera?', *Psychological Reports*, 75 (1994), pp. 1299, 1301; T. G. Plante, S. Yancey, A. Sherman and M. Guertin, 'The Association between Strengths of Religious Faith and Psychological Functioning', *Pastoral Psychology*, 48:5 (2000), p. 405.

Hermans and Oles have a good definition of the midlife crisis.[5] It is 'a process of intensive transition of the self including the reinterpretation of time perspective, reevaluation of life values and goals, confrontation with death as a personal event in the future, and planning of the second half of life'. In addition to the intrapsychic pain experienced by a man in the grip of such a crisis, marriage, family and other social relations also appear to be adversely affected by this phase in men's lives.[6] From the side of practical theology as subject [7] and from Christian counselling itself there is a great challenge to address the issue, in close co-operation with the other relevant disciplines (physiology, psychology, sociology etc.) but with a distinct focus: faith and religious values, issues which are essential and pivotal in the counselling of men in this phase of their lives.

By not being sensitive to the possibility of the male midlife issue, many a good counsellor might be 'barking up the wrong tree' in their counselling. In the counselling of couples in their midlives it is imperative that *not only* the husband should be counselled once it is ascertained that this might be the problem, but also the wife in order to educate her on how her husband should be dealt with in this often difficult stage of his life. In this chapter perspectives from a medical as well as a psychosocial view will be discussed and evaluated briefly. Pastoral counselling of these persons will also be addressed and finally guidelines for pastoral care and ministry will be proposed in dealing with the male midlife crisis.

A Medical View

From a medical perspective different words can be used to describe the male midlife: *male climacteric, viripause,*

---

[5] J. M. Hermans and P. K. Oles, 'Midlife Crisis in Men: Affective Organization of Personal Meanings', *Human Relations*, 52:11 (1999), p. 1403.

[6] A. Song, 'Understanding Mid-lifers and Their Frustration: A Practical Theology Response', *Praktiese Teologie in Suid-Afrika* (Journal of the Society for Practical Theology in South Africa), 12:1 (1997), p. 42.

[7] Cf. J. W. Fowler, *Faith Development and Pastoral Care* (Philadelphia: Fortress Press, 1987), p. 15; L. M. Heyns and H. J. C. Pieterse, *A Primer in Practical Theology* (Pretoria: Gnosis, 1990), p. 10.

andropause.[8] Terms like *mid-life crisis*[9] or *midlife transition*[10] are also used. It all adds up to the issue of the definite changes that take place between a certain age: roughly between 40 and 50,[11] although there are many other theories about the age bracket.[12] Hence, there is no real agreement on the exact age of the onset and continuation of male midlife crisis. A safe choice would be between 35 and 50.

A range of different changes takes place in midlife. *Physical changes* include balding, loss of hair and the distending of the 'stomach where the "middle age spread" resides',[13] overall fat deposition and reduced muscle mass and strength.[14] *Endocrinal changes* include a lower concentration of testosterone (hypotestoteronaemia) which can be connected to erectile dysfunction.[15] *Sexual changes* result in men performing less well than they did in the past. This can be triggered by an array of causes: fatigue, insomnia, depression, an addictive lifestyle like excessive drinking and smoking, too little leisure, and burnout.[16] Coetzee[17] indicated in his research that 23 out of 28 midlife men questioned had a loss of libido. Many extramarital relationships start with midlife men who think they have to prove themselves sexually to younger women.[18] Kruger[19] refers to 'a good analogue of Valliant's "renegade minister who leaves behind four children and the congregation that loved him in

[8] Coetzee, 'So-called Male Mid-life Crisis', p. 7.

[9] Conway, *Men in Mid-life Crisis*, p. 17.

[10] M. B. Radebe, 'A Phenomenological Study of the Midlife Transition as Experienced by Some Professional Black Men and Women', (unpublished PhD thesis, University of South Africa (UNISA), 1993), p. 64.

[11] Kruger, 'The Midlife Transition', p. 1300.

[12] Bejian and Salomone ('Understanding Midlife Career Renewal') put it at 35–45; Song ('Understanding Mid-lifers', p. 40) chooses 35–65; Stewart ('Mid-life Crisis', p. 64) 40–65; Thompson ('First Aid in Pastoral Care', p. 356) at 45 onward and M. Schachter (*The Male Andropause* (http://www.healthy.net/library/articles/schachter/andropas.d.htm)) at 40–55.

[13] Song, 'Understanding Mid-lifers', p. 40.

[14] Gould, Petty and Jacobs, 'For and Against', p. 859.

[15] Gould, Petty and Jacobs, 'For and Against', p. 860.

[16] Cf. Stewart, 'Mid-Life Crisis', p. 65; Thompson, 'First Aid in Pastoral Care', p. 358.

[17] Coetzee, 'So-called Male Mid-life Crisis', p. 78.

[18] Cf. Stewart, 'Mid-life Crisis', p. 66.

[19] Kruger, 'The Midlife Transition', p. 1303.

order to drive off in a magenta Porsche with a twenty-year-old striptease artiste"'.

A Psychosocial View

The term 'psychosocial' includes everything connected to the psychological effects and/or social circumstances that midlife men face. These areas will be discussed separately.

Psychological

According to Oliver[20] men *generally* have seven factors bringing them to counselling. These are: incomplete identities, unfaced fears, unmanaged anger, undiagnosed depression, struggles with loneliness, misunderstood sexuality, and faulty conflict resolution skills.

If one looks at midlife as such, some of the signs are: restlessness, unhappiness, shortness of temper, dissatisfaction with oneself or one's circumstances.[21] Hermans and Oles[22] even mention that the high crisis group in their investigation expressed a 'highly reduced self-enhancement motive'. External factors in this age bracket also adversely influence the psychological well-being of men, like job-losses, early retirement, affirmative action (especially a hot issue in South Africa at this point because it is directed especially at middle-aged men), work-separation trauma,[23] and cause them to doubt their own abilities or usefulness. Song[24] mentions the word *cyberphobia* which means 'having to cope with younger people who are more familiar with modern forms of tests'. Cyberphobia 'puts the older man at a distinct disadvantage: he is simply less "test wise" than the modern youth'. The flip side is, of course, also true. Many a man may experience a *midlife career renewal.*[25]

[20] G. J. Oliver, 'Are You Man Enough? Exposing the Masculine Myth', *Christian Counseling Today*, 3:1 (Winter 1995), pp. 17–18.
[21] *Male Midlife Crisis* (web site), p. 1.
[22] Hermans and Oles, 'Midlife Crisis in Men', p. 1418.
[23] Bejian and Salomone, 'Understanding Midlife Career Renewal', p. 58.
[24] Song, 'Understanding Mid-lifers', p. 43.
[25] Bejian and Salomone, 'Understanding Midlife Career Renewal', p. 53.

In his analysis of 28 questionnaires, Coetzee[26] shows that psychological issues were pervasive: 26 suffered from depression, 24 from anxiety bouts, 20 from avoidance of responsibility, 20 from fits of rage/temper, 20 from introspection, 17 from loss of confidence, and 17 from sulking. These results have to be seen within a certain context and should not be generalised. However, the literature is clear overall that there are psychological issues *sui generis* attaching to the midlife and these indications should be recognised in any counselling of midlife men.

Social

The social side of male midlife reflects mostly in family life and career. Issues include: a strained relationship (with the wife going through her own menopause); teenage and other grown-up, demanding, children in the house; the care of parents who became dependent either emotionally, physically or financially; the greater demand to 'produce' at their jobs for both the husband and wife since they (perhaps both) may move into managerial positions and the ultimate crisis: the affair.[27]

A case of a distant relative which the author counselled in 1996 had all the ingredients for disaster. Only by looking back does one realise that this man was in the throes of a male midlife crisis: he started to exercise excessively in the gymnasium; he wanted to hang out with girls half his age; he suddenly started wearing 'mod' clothes and enjoying late-night parties with younger men and keeping up with their drinking, etc. His whole pattern of life reflected what one later realised was the case-book example of male midlife transition which of course had disastrous results on his marriage and on relationships with his children who were already college students when this started. He was divorced and lost his business. As Hermans and Oles put it: 'conflicts between different values, the disorganization of the valuing process, re-evaluations, and lowered sense of realization appear to contribute to midlife crisis'.[28]

[26] Coetzee, 'So-called Male Mid-life Crisis', p. 78.
[27] Conway, *Men in Mid-life Crisis*, p. 98.
[28] Hermans and Oles, 'Midlife Crisis in Men', p. 1065.

The literature on male midlife or transition abundantly indicates that marriage is one of the areas in which the male midlife has a profound effect.[29] Song describes this aptly:

> Wives complain of being neglected and husbands complain of being overworked and unappreciated at home. This period becomes very tenuous for marriages which may not have been adequately anchored in earlier years. Thus when the empty nest syndrome occurs with the young people out of home, couples may feel free to extricate themselves from what they consider as 'an unhappy relationship'.[30]

It is therefore imperative that special attention should be given to the husband in male midlife in connection with his marriage (see below).

Since the midlife is often described as the time to change one's perspective from *time since birth* to *time left to die*,[31] it is understandable that it will be a time 'for reviewing the hopes and dreams of youth and perhaps accepting that some of them will never be achieved'.[32] This should necessarily lead to a reinterpretation of the 'future self, with special emphasis on the planning for the second half of life'.[33] The midlife is a time to reflect on one's position in society, especially on what has been achieved personally, but also on what failures there were.

In conclusion, the man in midlife has many social changes to adapt to. Some of these are of his own making; others are external over which he has no control.

Pastoral Counselling

Pastoral counselling is viewed as *per se* Christian counselling from the context we work in, and is distinctly different from

---

[29] Bejian and Salomone, 'Understanding Midlife Career Renewal', p. 57; Coetzee, 'So-called Male Mid-life Crisis', p. 73; Hermans and Oles, 'Midlife Crisis in Men', p. 1418.
[30] Song, 'Understanding Mid-lifers', p. 42.
[31] G. D. Cohen, 'Human Potential Phases in the Second Half of Life', *American Journal of Geriatric Psychiatry*, 7 (February 2000), p. 3.
[32] *Male Midlife Crisis* (web site), p. 1.
[33] Hermans and Oles, 'Midlife Crisis in Men', p. 1405.

other kinds of therapies[34] since it operates from specific biblical principles. Habermas[35] summarises it by saying: 'The God of the universe invites believers to view the myriad details of life from his eternal vantage point. It is applied to topics like worry, suffering, dealing with others, wealth, our journey through life, and even death.' The Christian is in many ways different from the person not believing in the Triune God of the Bible. For one thing, there is the dimension of hope. Hope is one of the most important aspects of the Christian life[36] and it reaches beyond the self. Richardson[37] suggests four processes for working with hope in therapy: hope as an experiential process, as a spiritual or trancendent process, as a rational thought process, and as a relational process.

One of the basic premises of the Christian faith is the 'very fact of salvation: God's faithful love';[38] another premise is the righteousness the Christian has in Christ.[39] While these presuppositions do not lessen the difficulties of life, they provide another perspective and the knowledge that one need not go this way alone.

The uniqueness of Christian counselling is set forth in Meier, Minirth and Wichern.[40] As they say, the Bible is accepted as final authority; there is dependence on the indwelling power of the Holy Spirit; Christian counselling deals effectively with the counsellee's past by working with forgiveness and guilt; it is based on God's love; it deals with the whole person and takes cognisance of the physical and psychological as spiritual aspects of human

---

[34] J. F. Macarthur and W. A. Mack, *Introduction to Biblical Counselling. A Basic Guide to the Principles and Practice of Counselling* (London: Word Publishing, 1994), p. 368.

[35] G. R. Habermas, 'Top Down Thinking. Heaven and the Problems on Earth', *Christian Counseling Today*, 6:2 (1998), p. 27.

[36] J. Calvin, *Golden Booklet of the True Christian Life* (Grand Rapids, MI: Baker Book House, 1982), p. 67.

[37] R. L. Richardson, 'Where There is Hope, There is Life: Toward a Biology of Hope', *Journal of Pastoral Care*, 54:1 (2000), p. 75.

[38] D. J. Louw, *Illness as Crisis and Challenge. Guidelines for Pastoral Care* (Halfway House: Orion Publishers, 1994), p. 158.

[39] R. S. McGee, *The Search for Significance* (Houston, TX: Rapha Publishing, 1997), p. 171.

[40] P. D. Meier, F. B. Minirth and F. Wichern, *Introduction to Psychology and Counseling. Christian Perspectives and Applications* (Grand Rapids, MI: Baker Book House, 1982), p. 292.

beings. The recognition of the power of prayer,[41] and the *koinonia* and support of other believers should also be included.[42]

Pastoral Guidelines

General guidelines

For a start, the man in his midlife crisis will have to realise that his 'point of control' is wrong. His well-being should neither be determined by his career, his standing in society, his wife, children or any other thing in this world. What is needed is summarised by Welch: 'Fear God and know your duty'.[43] This is also a biblical formula: 'Now all has been heard; here is the conclusion of the matter: fear God and keep his commandments, for this is the whole duty of man' (Eccles. 12:13).

It seems that the biggest problem men have in their midlife is the fact that they anchor themselves to all kinds of *human* expectations, such as what *other* people think of their body (or what they themselves *perceive* other people to think about their body!); whether they achieved in their careers what *normally* would have been expected of someone in a career; whether their wives think they are good husbands; whether their children perform well in school and life; whether they can perform sexually any more, and so on. All these and many more concerns about the male midlife crisis should be addressed in a biblical way and according to biblical standards and guidelines.

Specific guidelines

These are divided into two parts: intra-personal and inter-personal. The first is the relationship with one's self, and the second the relationship with one's spouse.

[41] Ps. 18:6 – cf. also G. A. Lotter, 'Counseling Divorcees on Forgiveness' (unpublished DMin project, Philadelphia: Westminster Theological Seminary, 1987), p. 118.

[42] Heb. 12:1 – cf. also D. J. Louw, *A Pastoral Hermeneutics of Care and Encounter. A Theological Design for a Basic Theory, Anthropology, Method and Therapy* (Cape Town: Lux Verbi, 1998), p. 70.

[43] E. T. Welch, *When People are Big and God is Small. Overcoming Peer Pressure, Co-dependency, and the Fear of Man* (Phillipsburg, NJ: P&R Press, 1997), p. 219.

Intra-personal counselling

It is important in dealing with the male midlife crisis to start with the most important relationship one has: with God. Calvin[44] describes it the following way: 'It must be our desire, therefore, if we want to be disciples of Christ, to fill our minds with such a great reverence for God and with such an unrestrained obedience that we may triumph over all contrary inclinations, and submit to his plan.' The picture is clear: if the midlife male starts with the most important relationship there could be, other areas of concern can also change. One is reminded of Matthew 6:33: 'But seek first his kingdom and his righteousness, and all these things will be given to you as well', and what is written about Solomon (1 Kgs 3) when he requested wisdom and all the other things had been given to him anyway, because he started at the right point: going to God and requesting the 'basic' thing.

In starting with the relationship with God, one should ascertain that the midlife male does not have to perform (like in so many other areas), but that by *grace* he is accepted fully and can live from that vantage point. MacDonald[45] calls it the 'granting of restorative grace' which is of course the same thing *and* different than 'original grace'. The man in counselling should be reminded 'that he is deeply loved by God, completely forgiven, fully pleasing, totally accepted, and complete in Christ, resulting in a life of love and depth and meaning'.[46] There is ample proof that religious faith is important to overcoming difficulties and gives meaning to life. Plante, Yancey, Sherman and Guertin point out that 'those with stronger degrees of religious faith tend to be significantly less interpersonally sensitive, exhibit a greater belief in personal control, and maintain higher self-esteem than those lower in faith'.[47]

The first step then is to guide the man in question to 'grow in faith' and help him with the necessary spiritual

[44] Calvin, *Golden Booklet*, p. 63.

[45] G. MacDonald, *Rebuilding Your Broken World* (Nashville, TN: Highland Books, 1982), p. 206.

[46] McGee, *The Search for Significance*, p. 144.

[47] Plante et al., 'The Association between Strengths of Religious Faith', p. 406.

discipline. By doing that the man will get to know himself better, because he now does not mirror himself in others or the world, but in God – a mirror which is truthful and comprehensive.

From a counselling point of view, the aspects like background, history, physical, emotional, relational and other relevant matters which the counsellor deems important should also be looked into and not neglected, but for real change, the starting point should be the person's relationship with the Triune God. This has been observed by the author in fifteen years of counselling.

Inter-personal counselling

Since the focus of this chapter is on marriage, the main emphasis will be on the man's relationship with his wife in marriage from which other relationships will flow: children, grandchildren etc. Without going into detail, there are wonderful guidelines and 'counselling' homework to give couples for marriage enhancement.[48] Priorities should also be structured in the marriage, and Covey[49] could be helpful. Wheat[50] points out three dimensions of a successful marriage which can be discussed with the couple in this part of the counselling: an emotional climate of love and nurturing, with a growing intimacy; the creation of a smooth-working, satisfying partnership; a shared faith which provides meaning, direction, and unified purpose for their marriage, and spiritual resources.

These things – being a good starting point – should be spelled out in practice for the couple and specific homework should be given, as well as directed assignments about *how* to do it. The spouses will have to be 'checked' carefully since they

---

[48] W. A. Mack, *A Homework Manual for Biblical Counseling,* Vol. 2: *Family and Marital Problems* (Phillipsburg, NJ: P&R Publishing, 1980), pp. 42, 60; *Your Family God's Way. Developing and Sustaining Relationships in the Home* (Phillipsburg, NJ: P&R Publishing, 1991), pp. 3–17.

[49] S. R. Covey, *First Things First* (New York: Simon & Schuster, 1994); *The Seven Habits of Highly Effective Families* (London: Simon & Schuster, 1997).

[50] E. Wheat, *The Power of Your Secret Choices. How to Settle Little Issues Before They Become Big Problems* (Grand Rapids, MI: Zondervan, 1989), p. 19.

might have unlearned to do these things. They may need hands-on guidance, for as the adage goes: 'people don't do what we expect, but what we inspect'.

Conclusion

In this chapter it has been shown that there is something like a male midlife crisis although it cannot be likened to the female menopause in the strict sense of the word. Literature is clear on the issue: something like this phenomenon does exist and cannot be ignored. It should be looked at from different angles: medical, psychological and sociological. The pastoral counselling of men in the throes of a so-called male midlife crisis has also been discussed and the need for counselling from a biblical point of departure has been stressed. Finally, guidelines for the counselling of these men were proposed.

12

Lifetime as a Virtue: Changes in Marriage over Time

Aldegonde Brenninkmeijer-Werhahn

The elderly have always been with us. What is new today is that the number of those who reach an advanced age is greater. Sociological research speaks of an 'age of the elderly'. What can we or must we do to ensure that dying can consistently occur without loss of freedom and dignity? This great challenge cannot be met solely by recourse to technological and social-structural innovations. We shall need a determined mobilisation of moral powers if society is not eventually to grow ominously weary of her elderly folk. In 1982 in Vienna the United Nations drew up its first plan of action on ageing. A few years later they published eighteen principles for older persons and decided that every 1 October should be celebrated as the Annual World Day for the Elderly. 1999 was the International Year of the Older Person, with its theme 'Towards a Society for all Ages'.[1] The time is approaching fast when one person in five will be a pensioner and one in ten aged over 75, when there will be only three people of working age to support each pensioner and when old-age pensions may account for one-fifth of national income. An investigation by the United Nations in March 2000 shows that Europe has a need of 3.4 million immigrants per year in order to balance

---

[1] Kofi Annan, the UN Secretary General, declared in his message for the 1998 World Day of the Older Person that 'a society for all ages is a society which, far from caricaturing older people as retired and infirm, considers them on the contrary as agents and beneficiaries of development' (Pontifical Council for the Laity, Rome, *The Dignity of Older People and Their Mission in the Church and the World, Briefing* (10 March 1999), London, p. 11).

the relation between the working population and the pensioners.

In elderly care work and in the different Christian churches people have been struggling hard to resolve this problem and there are many studies on it.[2] But today each individual is faced with the challenge of reflecting on the issue of growing old. In present-day society time is not usually devoted to planning the future on the basis of an acceptance that we must age, or to taking into account that life will change as we grow older. We are born and grow to young adulthood, when we enter into a period of active independent life that gives way to an age of dependence and frailty. Finally we surrender life and allow death to happen.

I do not wish to give the impression that I have a superior expertise in this area, for the truth is that I am only just seriously getting to grips with it. This chapter is intended to act as a reminder to individuals of their own ageing process and then to remind hierarchies in society, politics and economics of the pressing question of the ageing society. Growing old *together* is a process that begins right from the first year of marriage. Living a satisfying life is a question of practice from the early years.[3] And so I have narrowed my chapter down to six small sections.

The Time Dimension

The current situation[4]

To understand our current situation it is vital to be attentive to the times we are living in. A report to the Fourth European

---

[2] The Church of England General Synod, *Ageing* (London: Church House Publishing, 1990); Pontifical Council for the Laity, *The Dignity of Older People and Their Mission in the Church and the World*; John Paul II, *Letter to the Elderly*, *Briefing* (10 November 1999), London.

[3] Different aspects are: 1. Enjoying everyday activities. 2. Discovering meaning in everyday events. 3. The awareness of having attained one's most important goals. 4. Having positive self-esteem/self-knowledge. 5. Having a generally optimistic attitude. Social interaction helps us to lead a satisfactory life (Alfons Auer, *Geglücktes Altern, Eine theologisch-ethische Ermunterung* (Freiburg, Basle, Vienna: Herder, 1995)).

[4] The World Health Organisation tells us that today there are 580

Congress for Gerontology in 1999, *Growing old in Europe – European aging*, stated that the 'oldest continent' is Europe.[5] Here every fifth person today is over 60, in twenty years it will be every fourth person. And of these 'older persons' every fifth one will be seriously old – over 80.[6] Alan Walker has listed a number of tasks that will need to form part of national policies: maintaining economic security, preventing poverty among the elderly, preserving the solidarity of the generations and fighting ageism, particularly in the workplace.[7] Furthermore the care and support of the needy elderly must be kept up. Their rights should be extended and they should be integrated better into society – not only as receivers of assistance and pensions, but with all their skills and experiences as givers too. Thus Alan Walker sees Europe as a giving continent in spite of its ageing.

Social justice and human dignity

In the near future older people's problems will become problems for us all. Just think of the injuries to the dignity of the person – the marginalisation, the reduction of income, the lack of human contacts, the abandonment, the loneliness and isolation. This too is a kind of impoverishment. On the other hand, why do we not allow the elderly to participate in decision-making processes and enable them to influence the policies that concern them both as persons and as citizens? Could they not themselves be involved in the relief of the ageing situation

---

million people over 60. In the year 2020 the number will have risen above a billion. The surprising thing is that more than 700 million of them will be living in the developing nations. For the average life expectancy is climbing very steeply there too; at the beginning of the 1950s it stood at 41, in 1990 at 62 and in 2020 it should hit 70. The whole world is growing older, and that has all sorts of problematic consequences, even though it is also a sign of growing prosperity (*Frankfurter Allgemeine Zeitung*, 157 (10 July 1999), p. 10).

[5] *Frankfurter Allgemeine Zeitung*, 157, p. 10.

[6] Today the expression 'third age' is used to refer to those who have retired from active employment while still being able to contribute to the common good. These are the 'young old' (65–75). The 'fourth age' are those who are 75 and older, and the term 'old age' is applied to them.

[7] *Frankfurter Allgemeine Zeitung*, 157, p. 10.

in society? And what about educational programmes for older people? Not enough help is provided to give them ongoing training and re-skilling so that they can keep pace with the rapid progress of technological development and derive material benefits from it – for example, learning to use the Internet. There is also a need for fresh thinking in the whole voluntary sector – is there no way that the wider community could gain more benefit from a healthy elderly population?

Growing with Change

Divorces and second marriages

Couples live longer now and therefore divorces and second marriages are increasing among the elderly after the departure of children. These events bring to the fore other issues such as the reactions of adult children, the question of inheritance, and adjustment to additional family members where previous emotional difficulties may still be unresolved.[8] Later-life divorce has specific consequences, with psychological, economic and social/relational aspects. Divorce at any age leads to a deep sense of loss; however, such feelings may have a greater personal impact as a decline of self-esteem in later life. Many older women who divorce suddenly find themselves without economic support and have to find employment.[9]

Widowhood

As spouses grow older they are inevitably faced with the possibility of death – their own or that of their spouse. Being widowed is among the most difficult of all losses experienced in life, and younger family members have to understand and

---

[8] 'The phenomenon today will be that the extended family is unfortunately not anymore a collection of aunts, uncles and cousins, but also of step-parents and half-brothers and sisters, or of stepbrothers and sisters with no blood connection at all' (Charles Handy, *The Age of Unreason* (London: Century Business, 1992), p. 206).

[9] Terry D. Hargrave and Suzanne Midori Hanna, *The Aging Family: New Visions in Theory, Practice and Reality* (New York: Brunner/Mazel, 1997), p. 186.

accept the parent's need to grieve. Loss of a spouse after many years of communal living can be extremely painful, and it represents a very demanding task for widowhood; for many bereaved persons, this may be the most difficult task of all. For them, it feels as though life stopped when the spouse died, and this pain has to be acknowledged and worked through. It is crucial that widow(er)s can express the normal feelings of sadness, anger and loss. But friends and family members should also always remember to 'honour widows who are real widows' (1 Tim. 3:5).

Moreover, profound social changes occur after the loss of a spouse, such as loss of self-esteem, companionship, income, home and often independence in relation to the children. The death of a parent has many implications for the family: a widowed parent may experience new dependency needs, both physical and emotional, and the adult children may not have the time or inclination to meet all those needs. For believing families their Christian faith can surely be a huge comfort. When we experience suffering and darkness, God is with us. God's presence does not eliminate the suffering but it does help us to cultivate the right attitude towards the things we cannot change in life.

The Art of Growing Old in Marriage

The body

There is an old Taoist parable about a carpenter and his apprentice who saw a huge oak tree.

> The carpenter said to his apprentice: 'Do you know why this tree is so big and so old?' The apprentice said: 'No ... Why?' Then the carpenter answered: 'Because it is useless. If it were useful it would have been cut down, sawed up and used for beds and tables and chairs. But, because it is useless, it has been allowed to grow. That is why it is now so huge that you and I can rest in its shadow.'[10]

---

[10] Henri J. M. Nouwen and Walter J. Gaffeny, *Aging* (Garden City, NY: Doubleday, 1974), p. 71.

Let us now move to a deeper level and take a closer look at how we can learn positively from changes brought about by ageing. Take your hand and look at your fingers. Each finger has a different length. The Greek Church Father Ephraem the Syrian compared our life to the fingers of the hand. Each different finger has its particular character, and each finger represents steps by which a person advances.

The beauty and attractiveness of the body decline with age. The way in which men and women experience ageing – e.g., the loss of a firm and muscular body for men, of beauty and attractiveness for women – is not generally welcome and may be a source of distress. The physical charms of someone over 70 are clearly less attractive and exciting than those of younger persons, except that the face of the elderly person may be more interesting than the young face. On the face of the elderly person life has written many stories. The multitude of wrinkles are not always repellent, but show what the person really is. If we look at the last self-portrait of Rembrandt we discover a depth that was not there before. We marvel also at the last works of Michelangelo and realise they are actually the best; or the old Albert Schweitzer, the piercing eyes of the elderly Einstein, or the gentle face of Pope John XXIIII.

With increasing age another beauty appears. Sensitivity often grows, the capacity to sense the state of mind of others better. Young people generally have such a strong ego that they have difficulty picking up subtler movements in the souls of their fellows, which they tend not even to notice.

Sexuality

Undoubtedly sexual intimacy and the way the spouses share and live their love is deeply affected by the ageing process. Sexuality does not of course disappear with age, but for older married couples it inevitably has a different quality. Love shows itself in a very different way. In old age it may be possible to reactivate youthful love relationships, but in general that kind of thing diminishes. In old age love experiences something else, something deeper and perhaps more important. In married love between the elderly man and woman the capacity fully to experience pure and total love often grows. Biology, aesthetics, and social prestige no longer have the power to add spice to love at this age. Such pure deep love can, for example, be expressed by a husband who cares faithfully for his wife who is confined to bed with MS. This love has another, perhaps even a higher status than the love between Romeo and Juliet. We Christians would say that in love we see the *eternal soul*. We see through into the deeper dimension of what the person whom we love really *is*. Love in older married life has the capacity to see, to experience and to love a person as he or she is. It is often impossible to describe what is seen in this eternal soul by the loving spouse and not by other people. Love in old age makes us no longer blind but seeing.[11]

Retirement

Retirement is a time of trial, especially for men. In addition to potential distress arising from reduction of income, it is often experienced as the loss of a meaningful social role and of social relationships. It can contribute to stress in relationships and it can cause low self-esteem. It also affects women. A wife's daily routine is inevitably disrupted by the need to find a new way of being together with her spouse for so much more time than before. This demands that the couple negotiate new boundaries and meanings in their relationship as well as with their adult children. It is important that the spouses negotiate and share common interests, that they redirect their interests into new spheres so as to find new ways of living together. This whole sector should be looked at with new eyes and a new resolve.

Voluntary work

Our desire to acquire a job, to forge a good career, to own a house, stocks and shares, to have good relationships, to acquire a huge amount of all kinds of knowledge, has become central to our motivation for living. We have to be careful not to slide into a social mentality in which a civilisation of 'being' is in fact

---

[11] Adolf Guggenbühl-Craig, 'Liebe im Alter und das Hoheleid', *Familiendynamik*, 4:24 (Jahrgang 1999), pp. 411, 416.

considered less important than 'doing' and 'having'. Consider the problems related to voluntary work. Many people start experiencing themselves as old when certain institutional arrangements such as mandatory retirement place them outside the circle of those who identify themselves primarily with what they do, have, or can acquire. Those who can no longer participate in this state of rivalry and competition are doomed to experience themselves as less human. They become the sad 'fall-out' of our society. This is particularly true of economic life. On the other hand, if through hard work elderly persons have acquired enough money to enjoy a secure old age, they still tend to feel less valued when they can no longer earn their own living. So many elderly persons feel that they are only acceptable members of society if they are getting paid for what they do. It is indeed a strange paradox that in a culture which creates more and more free time, 'voluntarism' carries little prestige. However, we should at all costs avoid the idea that moving towards the end of the life cycle is a fundamentally morbid reality. If we persist in thinking this, then all our concerns for the elderly become like almsgiving with a guilty conscience, like friendly gestures to people imprisoned by age.

The intergenerational situation

In this twenty-first century we shall increasingly face the phenomenon of the intergenerational situation. The need to care for ageing parents calls on all our reserves of flexibility and adaptability. Often the care-givers are middle-aged and pressures may emerge both from the ageing parents and from their offspring. When couples in midlife have to fulfil their responsibilities to their ageing parents at the same time as coping with the demands of their employment and their household responsibilities, the workload becomes formidable.[12] Because women tend to be the main care-givers all through, they may burn out in later life with the increasing demands made on them by the physical, emotional and

---

[12] Jeffrey S. Turner, *Encyclopaedia of Relationships across the Lifespan* (Westport, CT, London: Greenwood Press, 1996), p. 42.

spiritual needs of a frail elderly relative. Because women feel a
sense of obligation to care for loved ones, family members may
take it for granted that they will act as care-givers. Men on the
other hand have not been expected to assume the nurturing
role in their relationships – whether as father, husband or son.
But there are a number of reasons why care-giving may be
entirely appropriate for men in the post-retirement stage of the
life cycle.

Suffering

Suffering is another facet of growing older – not just physical
but also psychological suffering. The approach of the end of
life is one of the best opportunities for the family to settle old
issues, heal wounds, and develop love and trust. Responsibility
for such issues should be shared among all the family members.
It gives the entire family an opportunity to share the burdens as
well as the blessings.[13]

In modern culture physical suffering is very much devalued.
Our society prefers to live without suffering and tends to seek
for the sedation of all pain – of all suffering present and future.
Researchers speak of our generation as the 'valium generation'.
To deny suffering is to deny an inherent element of life and
the meaningfulness of human experience. Yet reflecting on the
meaning of life in general and suffering in particular is not an
easy thing to do. Older people tend to feel suffering more
deeply, not simply because of the restraints imposed by
sickness, but also because they are more isolated from their
communities, friends, and relatives and lack the physical
strength to cope with that isolation. This is often aggravated by
the experience of pain, illness or dying. Human beings need
therefore to be surrounded by caring and loving people.

Could euthanasia be a solution for such difficult situations?
Or does the debate over euthanasia not undermine confidence in family members and doctors or nurses who see their
patients suffering? There is 'aggressive medical treatment'
which some may choose to reject, there are forms of treatment

[13] Hargrave and Hanna, *The Aging Family*, p. 26.

to alleviate pain which fall within normal medical care in the case of terminal illness, and then there is euthanasia – understood as directly causing death – which is a different matter entirely.

There are as many ways of dying as there are of living. Nothing is so personal as dying, even though dying is a common human experience. Despite the death-phobic culture in which we live, it is fundamental to accept the reality of loss in death as well as the experience of pain and grief. Death makes a person into that 'particular individual' who will begin a personal life in and with God: in concrete terms, bringing God into dialogue with ourselves and practising prayer.

Journeying Together

The responsibilities of the wider society

There is an old Balinese story:

> It is said that once upon a time the people of a remote mountain village used to sacrifice and eat their old men. A day came when there was not a single old man left, and the traditions were lost. They wanted to build a great house for the meetings of the assembly, but when they came to look at the tree-trunks that had been cut for that purpose no one could tell the top from the bottom: if the timber were placed the wrong way up, it would set off a series of disasters. A young man said that if they promised never to eat old men any more, he would be able to find a solution. They promised. He brought his father, whom he had hidden; and the old man taught the community to tell top from bottom.[14]

There cannot be any doubt that for many people growing old is a way to destruction and darkness. But there are also many others – maybe less visible – for whom growing and maturing in years is growing into eternity. The wider society of which elderly

[14] Simone de Beauvoir, *The Coming of Age* (New York: Doubleday, 1966), p. 77.

persons are a part could be helped to value the art of 'telling top from bottom' in their families, or elsewhere in the midst of our fragmented society. In our over-busy world they offer their sustaining without any thought of a return. But this is increasingly difficult, for we have all grown to adulthood in a society in which everything has to be earned: career, recognition, affection and even love. Even as small children we discover that everything has to be earned and that has marked our lives. But faith is different. It tells us that the love of God is poured out *gratis*.

Do we not sometimes forget what the elderly do for others and for their families as well as for the wider society? One such task is handing on the faith.[15] They help to pass on the traditions which are an important element for culture.[16] If we allow our sense of history to be diminished, we are more likely to repeat its errors. Years ago I read in a publication of the German Demographic Allensbach Institute that role models play a key role in families in which faith and culture are passed on. As the Balinese story reminded us, the elderly can have an important influence in the process of making our society and culture more human and more precious.[17]

The Moses feeling

Just as Moses never entered the Promised Land, so many people at the beginning of the new century may feel, or be told, that they will never enter the promised land of new opportunities which the century affords. This feeling deserves the name 'the Moses feeling'. The difficulty lies in learning to say goodbye to yesterday, moving forward to new,

---

[15] Families in whom faith is alive usually do a lot together and communicate rather better than families in which the handing on of the faith has not taken place (Unpublished paper of Institut für Demoskopie Allensbach, 'Thesen zur Weitergabe des Glaubens in der Familie' (undated)).

[16] We inherit strong customs and family festivals as well as recognisable signs like prayer. Here a foundation stone can be laid for the child for interest in others through interest in his own childhood and the way of life of his own parents and grandparents. The child also becomes better able to bear responsibility in society.

[17] Pope John Paul II, *Letter to the Elderly*, p. 13.

unknown experiences, understanding that the years, weeks, days and hours do not belong to us for ever. It is a gentle reminder that we are called to give not only love and work but life itself to those who follow us and who will take our place. This is a kind of poverty, a quality of the heart which makes us relate to life as a gift to be shared. With the Psalmist we can say: 'You have taught me, O God, from my youth, and till the present I proclaim your wondrous deeds. And now, till I am old and grey, O God, forsake me not, till I proclaim your strength to every generation that is to come' (Ps. 71:17–18).[18] Old age can be seen as a truly 'favourable time' for bringing life and God's plan for each person to its fulfilment, time when everything comes together and enables us to grasp the meaning of life better and attain to a true 'wisdom of the heart'. [19]

Marital Spirituality: Fulfilling Time Together

Culture and spirituality

It is difficult to speak about a specifically marital spirituality when we can't seem to define the culture of the modern times in which couples live. I mean that spirituality develops not just within the lines of Christian tradition but also within the culture of our society, the culture of living, of professional life, married life, family life – and with all this it engages in constant interaction. This is what I understand by 'lay spirituality'. Therefore to formulate the principles of a marital spirituality for today both a good knowledge of the history of spirituality and a clear understanding of modern culture are required. On the other hand spirituality is not simply a child of its culture, it is also a critical attitude towards certain assumptions of modern

[18] Abraham was a privileged old man, and God made a great nation out of him (Gen. 12:2–3). Moses was old when God entrusted to him the mission of leading the people out of Egypt (Ex. 23). Elizabeth and Zechariah the parents of John the Baptist (Lk. 1:5–25, 39–79) were old; Simeon, an old man, blesses God and proclaims the Nunc Dimittis, a passage in evening prayer(Lk. 2:29). And Anna, a widow of 84, a frequent visitor in the temple had the joy of seeing God (Lk. 2:38).

[19] Pope John Paul II, *Letter to the Elderly*, p. 8, no. 8.

culture, in that spouses are seeking to express genuine faith in a supernatural being.[20]

The search for spirituality

Although we have only one life cycle to live, although it is only a small part of human history which we will cover, to do so gracefully and caringly as a couple is a supreme vocation. Hence for every human being, young or old, it is a privilege to be able to ask the question of meaning. The task of discovering our baptismal meaning belongs in a particular way to all Christians and certainly to ageing couples. Seeking and finding meaning has also to do with particular events of daily life in which God, nature, fellow human beings and ourselves are involved. If believing baptised elderly couples can look back on a satisfactory life together, on their difficulties and on how they have managed them, their marital history can be very inspirational and a valuable guide to others.

Reconciliation with the past

As we grow old the foundation on which our life is built usually becomes visible. The awkward question then raises itself as to whether that foundation can bear the whole building of life. Is it strong enough to face up to the shadows too? We first become mature when we know this.[21] It can become the perfect opportunity for reconciliation with the past. Often this process is accompanied by feelings of guilt associated with lost opportunities and past failings.

Such a situation can become a time of fulfilment, a special time that the Bible writers call *kairos*, a time when a person can take care of unfinished business with him/herself, with others and with God. Ageing couples and families need to do the work of communicating about, reconciling with and coming to terms

---

[20] Martin Gray, *A Book of Life* (New York: Seabury Press, 1975), pp. 43–4; Leo Missinne, *Reflection on Aging: A Spiritual Guide* (Liguori, MO: Liguori Publications, 1990), p. 78.

[21] Piet Van Bremen, 'Eine Spiritualität des Altern', *Geist und Leben*, Heft 1(1997), Echter Würzburg, p. 362.

with the past. In this way the groundwork for trustworthy relations is constructed for the couple itself as well as for their children and friends. Thus, older couples have the opportunity to be an example to the younger generation and an inspiration to their peers.

Precious Gifts of Old Age

For all its diminishment and decline, ageing has many gifts to bring that are positive and even holy. *Humour* is a gift of knowledge with a soft smile. Old people often fill the house with good humour, they make the serious businessman all caught up in his great projects sit down and laugh. Humour is also helpful because it helps us to keep things in proportion and enables us to laugh at ourselves. Humour helps to integrate what life has brought me, what I have received and what I have worked out. Humour influences and alters our conception of humanity and our relationship with God. *Thankfulness* conveys the gift nature of life, something to be valued and celebrated. Thankfulness means that what is granted to me is to return to the source; I am not to receive it as self-evident or as pure chance but to acknowledge the one source of all good.[22]

A marriage built on wishes is in constant danger, but a marriage built on *hope* is open-ended and full of possibility, since it is the partners themselves who count and not what they can do or have. The conversion from wishes to hope entails the slow process of detaching ourselves from the many little things of the moment and opening our arms to the future. C. G. Jung expresses it like this:

> The noon of life is the moment of greatest deployment, when a man is devoted entirely to his work, with all his ability and all his will. But it is also the moment when the twilight is born; the second half of life is beginning ... At midday the descent begins, determining a reversal of all the values and all the ideals of the morning.[23]

[22] Van Bremen, 'Eine Spiritualität des Altern', p. 361.
[23] C. G. Jung, *Modern Man in Search of a Soul,* quoted in Nouwen and Gaffeny, *Aging,* p. 68.

Every time life asks us to give up a desire, to change our direction, or redefine our goals; every time we lose a friend, break a relationship, or start a new plan, we are invited to broaden our perspectives and to deepen our hope. Humour, thankfulness and hope can give rise to a new vision. The vision which grows in ageing can lead us beyond the limitations of our human self. It is a vision that makes us detach ourselves not only from preoccupation with the past but also from the importance of the present. It is a vision that invites us to a total, fearless surrender in which the distinction between life and death slowly loses its pain.

Conclusion

It is not only at the level of relationships that the problem of ageing emerges. We should all be urging on church and state a social, structural and economic approach. That is the approach toward marriage taken by several authors in this book.

Without the presence of old people we might forget that we are ageing. The elderly are our prophets: they remind us that what we see so clearly in them is a process in which we all share. So we should not be content with mere written words about ageing, but start to challenge the division of the world into strong and weak, helpers and helped, givers and receivers, independent and dependent. Only then will real caring be possible and a blurring of the dividing lines that cause so much suffering. Through the dangerous and hopeful events of the cultures in which we live today, not only must we safeguard our personal lives, but also the whole society in which we live, so important is it for our relationship with God.

13

Marriage: Haven or Hell?
Twin Souls and Broken Bones

Lisa Isherwood

. . . With my body I thee worship . . .
>Every three minutes a woman or child is raped.
>In many countries rape in marriage is not a crime.[1]
>There is a rise in reporting rates and a dramatic fall in conviction rates.
>1 in 4 women will be raped in their lifetime; 1 in 5 by her husband/partner.
>Less then 5% of the perpetrators will be convicted.

. . . in sickness and in health . . .
>Suicide is 12 times higher amongst battered wives/partners.
>Battered women are hugely over-represented amongst female alcoholics, drug addicts and sufferers of mental illness.

. . . till death us do part . . .
>In Scotland 50 women a day, with their children, leave abusive partners.
>In 1997, 15,000 Russian women were killed by their husbands.
>In Britain 2 women a week are killed by husbands/partners.

---

[1] Rape in marriage became a crime in 1991 in Britain and already there are those calling for a repeal of the law. They suggest it is not in the interests of women since it is hard to prove and has a detrimental effect on the prosecution of other forms of rape.

In the USA that figure is 12.

... for mutual society, help and comfort ...

In Britain 6 out of 10 men regard violence against partners as an acceptable option.

20% of British men aged 15–25 believe it is acceptable to force sex on women, especially girlfriends/wives.

Many men consider rape an acceptable way of putting women back in their place.[2]

This litany of terror clearly shows that when we are sold the romantic myth of marriage, and, in addition as Christians, told that God ordained marriage for the mutual benefit of individuals and the continuation of the species, we are being told half the story. A global picture is emerging that suggests women are at risk at home and in the embrace of the family. This chapter does not argue for the abolition of marriage but rather for an honest engagement with the reality of marriage for many women. In addition I hope to show that the churches cannot claim immunity from blame in the creation of a culture that allows the abuse of women and children. I will also make some suggestions as to how that situation can be challenged by Christian theology.

Trouble and Strife

It is all too easy to reduce the impact of the figures given by relegating them to the private sphere where they become to some degree tamed by the application of the term 'domestic violence'. We are able to imagine an unfortunate woman married to a drunk, a madman or just a bad sort. We can pity her but with our British reserve and our notion that an Englishman's home is his castle the likelihood is that we will do nothing about what we see or hear. Underpinning this may be a slight wondering about what she did to deserve it. In other

---

[2] The figures in the 'litany' are from material provided by the Conference of European Churches and have their origin in data collated by the United Nations Division for the Advancement of Women. Additional data is from Shere Hite, *Women as Revolutionary Agents of Change: The Hite Reports: Sexuality, Love and Emotion* (London: Hodder & Stoughton, 1994).

words we can contain it within the home, preferably of others, and place it lower down the list of pressing concerns than, say, fox hunting.

This privatisation and marginalisation of domestic abuse has long concerned feminists who understand the ideology of privacy to be a major cause in the continuation of the abuse and a central component in the devaluation of research in the area and of the allocation of funds to address the problem. Since 1878[3] feminists have argued that domestic violence is rightly named 'domestic torture' and that so naming it would change the face of the debate and the time given to it. This is no mere wordplay but rather an attempt to highlight the political nature of male violence against women. In other words, feminists do not accept that some women are just unfortunate and marry the wrong man. They think that we live in a culture which breeds that violence and makes women the 'natural' targets. By the use of the term domestic torture it is hoped that the brutal reality will be exposed as well as the failure of national and international communities to protect their citizens from torture. Despite the widespread nature of this torture many governments and most religious institutions have failed to address it in any systematic or sustained way. The churches have for generations spoken up for victims of torture under political regimes around the world. The reality is that the violence that many women suffer is as brutal and psychologically more devastating (since a loved one carries it out), but the churches have, until very recently, remained silent.

It is not only the way we view domestic violence that changes once we call it torture. It also takes on a different legal status. There are a number of international conventions on human rights, for example, the Convention for the Elimination of all Discrimination Against Women,[4] which lay out the responsibility

---

[3] Frances Cobbe Powers' article 'Wife Torture in England' (1878) had a great impact on public opinion and the Matrimonial Causes Act of 1878 was passed which enabled women to separate from abusive husbands and have restraining orders placed on them. The article has been reprinted in Jill Radford and Diana E. H. Russell (eds.), *Femicide: The Politics of Woman Killing* (Milton Keynes: Open University Press, 1992).

[4] This is a United Nations Convention that was signed by this country twenty years ago. Therefore the UK is in contravention of this declaration by failing to protect women.

of nation states for the protection of women. Therefore governments that are inactive in the passing of tougher legislation to
protect women adequately are in fact guilty of compliance in the
torture of their citizens. This is a violation of human rights and
a crime. It seems absurd that conventions, which can be used for
the protection of women in the public sphere, are not used in
the private sphere when the actions carried out are so similar.
Once we understand that what happens to many women in
these intimate situations is no less torture than if carried out by
strangers, then we are also able to bring into play many more
statutes and conventions since torture is outlawed on the international stage. If women's safety were simply a case of laws there
would be enough that could be enacted for us to feel safe. The
fact that this does not happen leads us to suspect that something
else is going on.

I am not suggesting a conscious conspiracy against women
but rather a set of 'moods and motivations', which make it very
easy to marginalise and overlook violence towards them. These
lie deeply buried in our culture and are easily accessed as stereotypes, which justify abusive behaviour. 'Woman' as culturally
created carries a great deal of negative baggage, which makes us
distinct from the norm, man, and therefore suspect, defective
and devious. In an androcentric world our place is always
prescribed for us and we will often get it wrong. How cultures
are formed and enacted is a topic way beyond the scope of this
chapter, but it is not too contentious a claim to suggest that
Christianity has been a dominant force in the creation of
Western culture. Despite the decline in church attendance we
would be unwise to assume that many of the moods and motivations of Christianity have been totally eradicated from our
culture. Secularism still operates from many of the assumptions
inherent in Christianity but the danger is that in particular cases
the origin of an assumption has been forgotten and so lives on
as a given, and not a disputable suggestion. I hope to show that
while most abusers of women are not Christian they still operate
from a set of moods and motivations that have their roots deep
in Christian culture. In addition if we are as Christian
communities going to declare domestic torture to be wrong we
have to examine and eradicate the causes of that violence within
our own belief systems. Churches Together in England are
calling for gender inequality to be addressed since this is one of

the underlying causes of violence to women.[5] We have to admit that Christian theology and religion has been and is still guilty of many systems and beliefs that encourage division between the sexes, rather than mutuality and respect.

Eve and Mary – Patron Saints of Wife Beaters

So why have the Christian churches remained silent for so long about the abuse of women? Well, of course, one answer is that they have themselves been instrumental in the perpetuation of the abuse through witch-hunts aimed at independent women who did not conform quite enough,[6] or in the domestic sphere where husbands have been encouraged to beat their wives. One manual even described the dimensions of the stick to be used (it was to be bigger for the wife of a minister).[7] Also there are Christian marriage manuals of the 1960s which read more like rapist manuals than lessons in loving mutuality.[8] They encourage the muscular Christian to take his wife by force the first time so as to set the tone of the marriage and put in place the power relations. He is told she will object and may feel pain but she will be glad of it in the end, as she can feel safe in the knowledge that he is in charge. It is not difficult to see then that the churches may have been unable to see clearly enough through their own preconceived diatribes in order to delineate a problem and condemn it. There is neither time nor space to examine minutely the litanies of contempt that have been spewed out at women from the churches over the centuries, or to delve into the libraries of books about how to deal with a wife. However, it is necessary to look at some of the more general ways in which a set of moods and motivations damaging to the health and well-being of women is inherent in Christian theology.

[5] Unpublished paper available from Churches Together in England, 27 Tavistock Square, London WC1H 9HH.

[6] See, e.g., Robin Briggs, *Witches and Neighbors: the Social and Cultural Context of European Witchcraft* (London: Viking, 1996).

[7] A ruling of the Council of Toledo (587).

[8] See for examples of these references E. Wilson, *Only Halfway to Paradise* (London: Methuen, 1980); J. M. K. Bussert, *Battered Women: from a theology of suffering to an ethic of empowerment* (New York: Lutheran Church of America, 1986).

Of course we get off to a bad start being represented as the secondary creation, issuing from the rib of Adam and placed here to be his helpmate. We are named by him along with everything else that he is to have dominion over and our role is a complementary one. In addition the secondary creation proves her defective status by transgressing, and the scene is set for centuries of mistrust and blame. St Paul has the solution, however, which is that in Christ there is neither male nor female. Contemporary readings[9] suggest that this means an extinction of women as the wayward rib slips back into the original and glorious creation of man. Until such time as this occurs we are to be obedient to our husbands who have a duty to rule over us as Christ rules over his church. The role of Mary further confirms that we are to be docile and submissive. 'Be it done to me according to your word' could be the mantra of many Christian women.

Those who work with abusers have found that the complementarity model as well as the authority model are foundational in acts of violence against women. Adam Jukes who works with both Christian and non-Christian men has found that men who are told that they need women to be whole, they need their other half, can become extremely frightened if their wives or partners show signs of independence. This threatens their own sense of self and many become violent in order to control the situation.[10] Despite papal rhetoric about the virtues of the complementarity model of the sexes, it allows for a world of difference but without recognising or commending equality. Such rhetoric divides us within ourselves and between ourselves in a very unhealthy manner and leads us into all kinds of insecurities and feelings of inadequacy if we do not have that all-important other half, who is of course of the opposite sex. It has never been a model that thrives on equality nor could it be since we live in an androcentric world.

Christian theology needs seriously to challenge this unhealthy model and encourage a grounding in the incarnation that

---

[9] See Kari Borresen, *The Image of God: Models in Judeo-Christian Traditions* (Minneapolis: Fortress Press, 1995).

[10] Adam Jukes, cited in Anne Borrowdale, *Distorted Images: Christian Attitudes to Women, Men and Sex* (London: SPCK, 1991), p. 108.

allows for a joyful embrace of our own completeness and incompleteness. It is the chaotic partialness of being alive that signals creative incarnation, not an ideal form of wholeness that has to be mirrored in human relations. Christian theology needs to ditch Plato and grasp reality. We all need to learn to glory in our own incarnation and not look to others for wholeness. This would lead to a much healthier environment in which to form relationships. Of course this raises a very serious Christological challenge and one that the churches may not wish to embrace. There are questions here of autonomy and the situating of the divine in the messy incompleteness of life. We need a Christology that encourages self-empowerment rather than the giving away of one's power to others, even if that other is a creator God. That kind of patriarch sets a very dangerous patterning in place. We are in need of a divine image that is not threatened by us taking power for ourselves in an adult way. The violence that springs from a model of complementarity poses a very significant challenge to theology and I hope we will be able to embrace it and develop a more realistic model of humanness, which reduces risks of violence.

Of course the authority model is as destructive and dangerous for women as the complementarity model. Jim Wilson who works with batterers puts it plainly: 'domestic violence comes from two things; the authority you believe you have over your wife and the services you expect to get from her'.[11] It is therefore not surprising that 'Bible-believing' Christians are highly represented amongst batterers since they believe their wives should be submissive (1 Pet. 3:5–6). Scripture therefore gives them high expectations and a great deal of control. Susan Brocks Thistlewaite worked with fundamentalist Christian women and found that levels of battering and rape were as high as in non-Christian families.[12] Yet the denial runs deep. In addition Christian women will often

---

[11] Jim Wilson, cited in Borrowdale, *Distorted Images*, p. 107.

[12] Susan Brocks Thistlewaite, 'Every Two Minutes', in Judith Plaskow and Carol Christ (eds.), *Weaving the Visions: New Patterns in Feminist Spirituality* (New York: Harper Collins, 1989), pp. 302–11. Her statistics are taken from the United Methodist Church's Programme of Ministries with Women in Crisis (1980–81) and read as follows: 1 in 27 wives admitted they had been raped, 1 in 13 had been abused and 1 in 4 received verbal and emotional abuse.

accept the blame for the violence far more readily than non-Christian women. One participant in Thistlewaite's programmes summed up the feelings of many of the women by declaring that God gives women more pain, an allusion to Genesis 3:16. Further, the notion of conjugal rights is alive and well in many Christian homes despite legislation to the contrary. This does not in all cases lead to forced rape (although Thistlewaite's figures do show a significant amount) but rather to coercion through emotional pressure and a model of expectation that is just as abusive.

Rather than breaking down this authority/expectation model many churches are bolstering it. This is graphically illustrated by the Religious Right in the USA which is constantly attempting to reduce the rights of women in the areas of contraceptive and abortion choice, as well as wishing to stop sex education for them. Indeed, educational opportunities for girls are thought unhealthy and marriage education is considered to be the only education they need.[13] It will be interesting to see what form the British government places on the marriage education it feels to be necessary. Divorce costs Britain £17 billion a year, so we should not be surprised that marriage for life is encouraged. Another movement that appears to have a hidden agenda is The Promise Keepers, an American group of mostly Afro-American men who have declared they will take control of their families. Womanists have not embraced this movement with unreserved joy since in many cases it has meant the reintroduction of violence into the home along with the no longer wayward Christian husband. It seems that many forms of Christianity have not yet been able to address the question of post-feminist masculinity and still rely on the old models of authority and expectation. In a world where women now expect more equality of treatment, this will inevitably lead to greater potential for violence. Indeed, one minister reasoned that violence is on the increase because men are no longer masters in their own homes; his solution was that wives should learn submission.[14]

---

[13] These measures were put forward in the Family Protection Act in USA in 1981. They were not passed but the Religious Right is still trying.

[14] Susan Faludi, *Backlash: The Undeclared War Against Women* (London: Vintage Books, 1992), p. 264.

There is a desperate need for many more male theologians to examine models of masculinity that thrive through mutuality and move away from the muscular Christianity of their fathers and grandfathers. This model is not only outdated but also damaging to women and men.

I think a starting point is to image mutuality as sexy. It has not been portrayed as such, as we see from all kinds of pornography, from the mildest to the worst. There the domination/submission model is alive and well. Instead of condemning it because it is sex it would be more constructive if the churches engaged in a debate about images that enhance relationship and allow the performance of masculinity in non-aggressive/thrusting and dominating ways. The churches need to issue a challenge to the phallocentric world in which we live for this is a world that places great pressure on men to perform their sexuality/gender correctly. It is this performance model of ownership and conquest that feeds the culture of violence in which women suffer.

It is not only pornography that is full of crazy images of masculinity. Popular culture of all kinds is brimming over with the indestructible male facing and overcoming the odds. Man the saviour is played out from Robocop to Nintendo and the acts of non-emotional heroism are nauseating. What is a man to do when a mere woman stands up to him or refuses to play the damsel in distress? How is he to cope if she is in a well-paid job and he is not? His real world, that of sexually charged celluloid heroes, is under threat and the cause is the woman who does not know the rules. Many men who inflict violence on women name their feelings of resentment and inadequacy as the reason for the violence. It is a frightening fact of life that 'woman as threat' may become 'woman as target'. It is even more frightening that woman is created as threat by the media, which are incapable of imaging masculinity beyond narrow boundaries. What are the churches doing to balance this? The answer is nothing. There are some gay theologians[15] who are attempting to examine what it means to be male but their attempts are not being met with joy by the churches. In the

[15] Robert Goss, *Jesus Acted Up: A Gay and Lesbian Manifesto* (New York: HarperCollins, 1993).

shadow of the AIDS crisis predatory/performative and conquest models of sexuality had to be seriously reworked. In their place many gay men developed playful, full-bodied and imaginative relationships, which took them beyond patriarchal expectations and rituals. They have found that less emphasis on performance has meant there is greater opportunity for mutuality and empowerment. This new pleasure-seeking has brought many gay men to a deeper understanding of selfhood through a more honest engagement with others.[16] This is not a model that Christianity has actively encouraged: indeed at times in its history it has advocated the exact opposite, with men showing their dominance in the marital bed. There is a crisis in masculinity in our time, the old models of power over/dominance/submission will no longer do, and one of the results is an increase in violence to women. There is a desperate need for the churches to become more realistic about sexuality and gender relations and they could do worse than listen to voices from the margins where accepted norms have already been challenged.

Underlying much violence to women is the notion that all women are sluts, temptresses, deserving and desiring what befalls them. Many a familial act of battering or rape has sprung from this idea – an idea that Christianity has been instrumental in embedding in our culture. From the moment Adam passed the blame to Eve there was a precedent set which has still to be successfully challenged. Male sexual desire is the fault of women. They are the ones who through dress, speech, presence and looks turn men into sexual beings unable to control themselves. This rhetoric, while it is to be expected in the defence statement of any rapist, was in fact the way the church fathers spoke of women. Of course, there is confusion here between an act of domination, rape, and sexual desire which is not the cause of rape. For example, the youngest reported rape victim in the UK was 4 months old. She died. The oldest was 97. She died. Both were in the privacy of their own home and it is difficult to imagine how dress, speech and looks applied in these

---

[16] See Martin Stringer, 'Expanding the Boundaries of Sex: An Exploration of Sexual Ethics After the Second Sexual Revolution', *Theology and Sexuality*, 7 (1997), pp. 27–43.

cases. The old lady was asleep and the child having her nappy changed by her father who was the perpetrator.[17] Once we accept that rape is a crime about power we can perhaps begin to understand the statistics that tell us that 77% of sexual abuse against children is carried out by fathers.[18] The turn-on is not the body of their daughter who may be months old, but rather the power they believe they have. In many traditional Christian families the power of the patriarch is supreme and this makes him dangerous. He has the power but she is the temptress.

A crucial part of any theology of masculinity has to be, not only the uncoupling of the erotic from violence, but also the halting of sexual scapegoating. Woman is not the devil's gateway and she is free to walk in the street or sit in her home as she pleases. The responsibility lies with the man to respect her space and to acknowledge his own feelings and why he has them. Along with the scapegoating goes an unconscious 'possession mindset', which encourages men to think that all women are theirs for the taking – we belong to them. The standard male defence, that she did not mean 'No', graphically illustrates this.

Christian sexual ethics have over the years alienated people from their desires, and this has led to a world in which we find it difficult to be present with our needs and desires, to own them as ours and to enjoy them. Desire can never be removed but it can become misplaced and misshapen. While both women and men have suffered this Christian intrusion into their sexual psyches, men have had women to blame for desire and the guilt that can accompany it. This has, in my opinion, led to greater alienation and a fear of intimacy. This is clearly seen in the writings of many of the church fathers and some more contemporary notables, but is also worryingly shown in psychological research. Carol Gilligan shows that young men will often invent violent situations in order to avoid intimacy.[19]

---

[17] These figures came from my work with a Rape Crisis Centre in 1990.

[18] These statistics are from the US Health and Human Services Department and presented in Joanne Carlson Brown, 'Because of the Angels: Sexual Violence and Abuse', in Elisabeth Schüssler Fiorenza and Mary Shawn Copeland (eds.), *Violence Against Women, Concilium*, 1994/1, pp. 3–10.

[19] Carol Gilligan, *In A Different Voice: Psychological Theory and Women's Development* (Cambridge, MA: Harvard University Press, 1982).

The situations can be bizarre, such as aliens landing, but never-theless a significant number prefer such fantasy to the prospect of intimacy (not to be confused with sex). How have men become so alienated from their feelings and their bodies? While sex continues to be understood as 'something out there that takes possession of me' and it is her fault, the stage will continue to be set for violence of all kinds. Christianity urgently needs to embrace a more body-friendly sexual ethic, one that moves away from dualistic fantasies and encourages real engagement with real bodies in a mutual and empowering way.

Unholy Writ and Unjust Doctrines

A further problem for those addressing the question of violence to women is that the churches still use what Phyllis Trible calls 'texts of terror',[20] that is texts in which women are the victims of terrible violence, as teaching texts. The Bible is full of stories about sexual violence to women. Sadly they are not used to illustrate the evil of violence to women but rather some greater plan of God in which the abuse of the women is just one component. The stories of Lot's daughters and the Levite's concubine are examples of how it is not questioned that men have the power to hand over women to the abuse of others. Lot's daughters escape the violence but the concubine is raped and tortured all night and dies as a result of her ordeal. At no point does the story suggest sympathy for her and the focus is that of the Levite's honour. I do not wish to get into a debate about biblical ethics here since my point is that these stories are still used in churches. Through this use a dangerous connection is made between the abuse of women and the working out of God's purpose.

Susan Brocks Thistlewaite is scathing in her criticism not only of the way the Bible is used but of the stories themselves. She says, 'For women whose religious beliefs include extremely literal interpretations of the Bible as the norm, no authority except that of the Bible itself can challenge the image

---

[20] See Phyllis Trible, *Texts of Terror: Literary-Feminist Readings of Biblical Narratives* (Philadelphia: Fortress Press, 1984).

contained in these texts of women as silent, subordinate, bearing the children in pain and subject to the absolute authority of their husbands.'[21] For these women, feminist biblical exegesis is an urgent ethical task. They need to see that the Bible can also encourage them to respect themselves and to acquire a little holy rage at the situation in which they find themselves. I would go further than Thistlewaite and argue that stories of abuse and submission be removed from the canon of holy scripture, because they are not holy stories. They do not simply tell of times gone by because Christians have a strange relationship with their past as laid out in the pages of the Bible and they tend to bring it into the present and use them as ethical standards. While there is of course huge variation in how this is done it still seems to me to be problematic to have stories of abuse as part of the life of the church. Further, traditional interpretations of scripture have led us to believe that there is an absence of women in authority. This has led to the notion that only men have power. Contemporary readings that challenge this idea are very welcome and are flowing abundantly through feminist scholarship. The Bible is not a neutral book, nor is it without influence. The way it is used is therefore of the utmost importance.

Of course, one deeply problematic area is the way that scripture and tradition have imaged the suffering and death of Jesus. Traditional interpretations have proved to be a gift for abusers of all kinds. Traditional 'theologies of the cross' have not only presented us with a model of divine child abuse but also with a strong obedience and dependency model. In an androcentric world this is bad news for women. The 'supreme' example of the suffering of Christ has held many women in abusive situations and has been the pastoral response of too many clerics. Christine Gudorf[22] has demonstrated how the sacrifice of surrogate victims does not interrupt violence but rather by rechannelling it the perpetrators are protected from the protest of those they abuse. By ritualising the suffering and

---

[21] Susan Brocks Thistlewaite, in Plaskow and Christ, *Weaving the Visions*, p. 305.
[22] Christine Gudorf, cited in Fiorenza and Copeland, *Violence Against Women*, p. xv.

death of Jesus, Christian theology has disempowered the oppressed and therefore encouraged the continuation of the cycle of violence.

The only way that the suffering and death of Jesus can be 'good news' to the victims of abuse is by it being proclaimed an outrageous act of socio-political torture. That is, it was an act that was neither willed by God nor necessary for the work of God. It should inspire rage and praxis against oppression, and not be seen as an action to emulate. Despite the fact that many contemporary Christologies have moved from the more gruesome understandings of this doctrine there still remains a residue of the 'goods of suffering'.[23] There are none.

Of course, intimately connected with 'theologies of the cross' are notions of forgiveness. These have kept many women in abusive relationships and have been instrumental in damaging the self-esteem of women. What is needed is a theology of resistance, one that encourages women to be angry and to value themselves sufficiently to take the necessary steps to stop the abuse. Being encouraged to love enemies and not to resist evil creates a mindset in which victims remain victimised. Worse still, the damage to self-esteem leads to a self-blaming and self-loathing that can result in alcohol abuse, drug abuse or suicide. Certainly it creates family patterns that are more likely to make children open to victimisation. A theology of resistance is one rooted in incarnation and the goodness of creation; it celebrates the awesome glory of the human/divine nature and demands spaces of liberation and mutual relationships that enable flourishing. Theologies of the cross as we have them will never do this.

Selfless love, which has been underpinned by the theology of Jesus' suffering and death, is a problem for women. At its worst it leads to their death, emotionally and physically. However, before it reaches that point it sets the scene for non-reciprocal relationships and an acceptance of such patterns. These relationships overlook the lived experience of women and perpetuate the myth that love poured out by one can overcome

---

[23] This is not to say that sacrifice is an outmoded concept. It is clear in the world that if the West would sacrifice its rampant capitalism then all would benefit but this is not the same as imposed suffering.

the lack of love by the other. This not only means that there is an unequal relationship but it also encourages the abuser to keep abusing. It is psychologically true that 'more of the same leads to more of the same', in other words if the pattern of lack of respect, commitment and mutuality is allowed to continue the behaviours will continue to be abusive. The pattern is reinforced by lack of action. This is not to blame abused women for their situation, since in reality once the situation has escalated, they are vulnerable and have limited choices.

In order to avoid that situation arising theology would do well to see love as justice seeking rather than self-sacrifice. Theologians and ethicists such as Margaret Farley, Carter Heyward, Beverley Harrison, Delores Williams and others[24] have all problematised self-sacrificing love and called for an understanding of love as justice. While churches seem to have no difficulty in accepting this and including it in their rhetoric in the public realm there seems to be reluctance to apply it to the so-called private sphere, that of intimate relationships and family lives. This simply illustrates how important it is to do away with the private/public distinction.

For Farley, 'just love' is an expression of the equal worth of those loved.[25] It is an affirmation of their needs and a refusal to reduce their space through sex-defined stereotypes and prejudices. Along with other theologians Farley is calling for a remoulding of Christian ethics to include justice in an ethic of love. Intimacy in relationship can no longer be an excuse for overlooking the demands of justice. This, of course, will require a new look at the unit we call family and a re-evaluation of its place in the public arena. In addition the question of power within the family will need urgent attention and may call for models that are both challenging and frightening. The

[24] See Carter Heyward, *The Redemption of God: A Theology of Mutual Relation* (Lanham, MD: University Press of America, 1982); Beverley Wildung Harrison, 'The Power of Anger in the Work of Love', in Ann Loades (ed.), *Feminist Theology: A Reader* (London: SPCK, 1990), pp. 194–214; Delores Williams, *Sisters in the Wilderness: The Challenge of Womanist God-Talk* (Maryknoll, NY: Orbis Books, 1993).
[25] Margaret Farley, 'New Patterns of Relationship: Beginnings of a Moral Revolution', in Walter Burkhardt (ed.), *Woman* (New York: Paulist Press, 1977), p. 67.

Christian church has tended to adopt whatever model of family relationship was prevalent at the time. This is clearly seen with the adoption of the Roman model under Constantine. The time seems right, in the face of failing marriages and disinterest in the religious aspects of the institution, to break loose from convention and engage in radical alternatives. What exactly would a justice-seeking space for women, men and children look like in a world drowning under the worst excesses of patriarchy: abuse, sexism, capitalism, and so on? Families pledged to equality, respect and counter-cultural living would be a welcome change to the unimaginative units we call home! Surely, if a notion such as the Christian family is to continue it cannot simply underpin the *status quo*. What is Christian about that? When the Religious Right speaks about family values, what we actually have placed before us is an agenda for return to a world that existed before Civil Rights movements, a world of white male privilege and bigotry. Justice, if not traditional Christian love, demands that we resist such a model and the life it propels us into.

Once the private space is politicised there is no excuse for lack of engagement with the world. The nuclear family is the backbone of advanced capitalism and as such it is in many interests to keep it intact. There is much violence done to the environment and to the lives of third world women, men and children in the service of this many-headed beast called multinational capitalism. The Christian family as a space of justice would need to be aided by a radical theology of work and economics if it were to make a difference. This would not only make the family a unit of justice within the global economy but would also deal with one of the causes of wife battering throughout the world. Economics within the family is one of the factors in abuse yet the churches have not always made the link between the public and the private in a creative and helpful way. There is a great deal of work to be done on this issue but theology, as always, is slow to respond.

'I came that you may have life ... abundantly'

I have attempted to show that domestic abuse/torture is not simply a private and therefore pastoral problem; it is rather a public/systemic reality and as such is a theological and ethical problem. The words and the actions of Christianity have been incongruent. 'Love one another as I have loved you', when placed against the background of willed crucifixion, is not necessarily a call to liberated mutuality, while the call to be one flesh can be a call to emotional or physical extinction for women in a patriarchal world. The lives of those who are abused can never be the same again; the simple Christian formula of forgiveness does not restore the lost potential of the unbattered.

Statistics seem to vary according to who publishes them but the thing that is indisputable is that women and children do suffer domestic violence at the hands of the men they love. These men are often husbands and often Christians. It would be quite wrong to get sidetracked by a debate about numbers. One is too many. Encouraging women to marry by telling us that we are safer married than single is not that big a deal when 72% of female homicide is in the home and battering is the single greatest cause of deadly injury.[26] There has been a conspiracy of silence and the time has come for the abused and the not-yet-abused to speak out in both anger and hope: anger that a religion of incarnation and liberation has remained silent for so long, and hope that it may repent and change the systems that underpin the devaluing of women; a devaluation that has led to the torture and death of millions of our sisters over the centuries.

[26] Fiorenza and Copeland, *Violence Against Women*, p. ix.

PART 5

Children and Marriage

Introduction

Are children necessary to an understanding of the purposes of marriage in Christian faith? While the birth of children remains one of the reasons for marriage according to most marriage liturgies, is the birth of children so fundamental to marriage that married couples who *choose* childlessness intentionally frustrate God's purpose for the institution they have entered? The two contributors to this section give highly divergent answers to this question. The positions they take, the analyses they provide, and the conclusions they reach, are controversial, topical, and a base for further theological research.

Helen Stanton begins with a recent reassertion, by an Anglican bishop, of the traditional view that children are fundamental, and not merely optional, to the purposes of marriage. She next contrasts two studies, one of them her own, into the reasons why some couples *choose* childlessness. The first study gave, among the reasons for choosing to be free of children, postponement of the decision to have them, an absence of maternal instincts, negative attitudes to parenthood, the disruptive effects of children on the home, and an aversion to risk and change. The second study, although small scale, examined reasons committed Christians gave for choosing childlessness. These were very different, and included the lack of a vocation to parenthood, and 'commitment to Christian, political and pastoral causes'. The results of this study prompt Stanton to re-examine traditional Christian teaching about procreation and to advance some theological reasons which support a possible *vocation* to childless marriage.

Stanton describes a transition in Christian liturgy and theology towards voluntary childlessness in marriage. Pope

John Paul II's attack on chosen childlessness is seen to be undermined by the responses given in her study. These Christian women exemplified neither the death-dealing 'contraceptive mentality', nor the individualism or consumerism lamented by the Pope. Without children, they believed themselves better able to work for the reign of God. Stanton offers further reflections on these women's testimony. Perhaps, now reliable contraception is here to stay, marriage but not children is a vocation: children and parenthood may be a sub-vocation. Children remain a gift in any adequate theology of children, but not all gifts need to be, or can be, actualised. There are other ways by which one might be fertile in 'giving life for God'; and the re-establishment of the priority of discipleship over the raising of biological families may be a prophetic act.

While Stanton's starting point is the reassertion of traditional teaching, Jon Davies begins with the lack of consideration for children which is pervasive in Western societies and which has exercised a baleful influence on liberal theology, Christian ethics and liturgy. The consequences, *for children*, of their parents having them without wanting or being committed to them, are shown to be horrendous and often unrecognised. This *is* individualism, and Davies mounts a savage polemic against it in the name of those children whose interests are unacknowledged by their (biological) parents. Davies mocks the condition of a society which on the one hand allows rampant individualism in the area of sexual choice (among others), while insisting that social support be provided for the sustaining of incomplete families who have not exercised the responsibilities that accompany the freedoms they take for granted.

Whereas Stanton is able to welcome documented theological and liturgical changes which lead to children becoming a voluntary purpose of marriage, Davies firmly rejects them. In placing children first among the purposes of marriage the *Book of Common Prayer* was theologically right and pastorally astute. The rite proclaimed 'the communal interest in what is going on: this is a public institutional act because the production of babies is not only a private concern'. Davies here echoes the concerns of Don Browning (Ch. 1) and John Wall (Ch. 9) for the public, communal interest in marriage. No one gains from the alternatives to lifelong, monogamous marriage, least of all single mothers and their children.

What, then, do these contrasting chapters hold in common? The differentiation of the aims of each is a necessary first step towards answering the question. Stanton raises a genuine pastoral question: is it legitimate that some Christian marriages be childless? Her reflections lead her to re-examine parenthood as a vocation and children as a *renunciation* in favour of Christian commitments of a different kind. These considerations would seem to escape the strictures of both Pope John Paul II and Davies, since they embody neither 'the culture of death' nor the selfish individualism of the worst excesses of the secular world. Is the vocation to marriage, but not to parenthood, sustained by contraception, and, if so, is the distinction sound? Davies, however, grounding his concerns in the plight of children who are neglected by their biological parents, starts with a broader social analysis. While Stanton and Davies will find much to disagree about (not least the reasons for, and the impact of, changes in Christian theology and liturgy with regard to the place of children), they can agree there is a vast difference between renunciation and neglect, between devotion to God's reign and abandonment to hedonism. While devotion to God's reign may unite Christians, differences about what that means and entails will continue to divide them.

14

Obligation or Option?
Marriage, Voluntary Childlessness
and the Church[1]

Helen Stanton

In March 2000, the Anglican Bishop of Rochester, the Rt Revd Michael Nazir-Ali, published in the Rochester diocesan newspaper an article, 'Marriage, the Family and the Church', in which he expressed concern about the state of family life in England. The article identifies 'increasing individualism' as a key factor in family breakdown, and Nazir-Ali also asserts that 'the development of effective contraception has led to the view that women and men have been liberated from the traditional structures of the family'.[2] Nazir-Ali develops this theme later:

> In an age of excessive self-regard and encouragement on every side to the new religion of the 'me', it is very important for the church to continue saying that having children and their nurture is a basic good of marriage and not an optional extra. Just as marriage is not complete without mutual support, companionship and love, so there is a real lack if the intention is never to have children, regardless of circumstances.[3]

---

[1] I recognise the pain, frustration and unhappiness experienced by people who wish to have children but are unable to do so, or who have decided not to do so for medical reasons. I hope that nothing which is written here will be seen as diminishing respect for their situation and feelings.

[2] Michael Nazir-Ali, 'Marriage, the Family and the Church', *Rochester Link* (March 2000), para. 2.

[3] Nazir-Ali, 'Marriage, the Family and the Church'. Even the *Church Times* leader felt that Michael Nazir-Ali's comments not only lacked realism but were unjust (*Church Times*, 10 March 2000, p. 10).

Nazir-Ali was restating the traditional teaching of the church about marriage and procreation, a teaching which has a long history and which is still explicit within the Roman Catholic Church and implicit in the Church of England. Some of the Free Churches, as I shall make clear later, seem to have more open views about this. Behind much of the reiteration of traditional arguments about marriage and procreation lies a concern about increasing cohabitation, the high divorce rate, family breakdown – which is often perceived as a breakdown of society – and perhaps a sense that if voluntarily childless marriages are fully acceptable, gay and lesbian marriages will be unpreventable in the long run.

This chapter addresses the issue of voluntary childlessness as a growing phenomenon, drawing upon the key 1998 study, *Choosing Childlessness*,[4] and upon conversations which I have had with a small group of voluntarily childless couples within the churches. I will then summarise some of the teaching of the historic English churches in this area, and finally reflect on some of the issues raised.

The Social Phenomenon of Voluntary Childlessness

Fiona McAllister and Lynda Clarke's 1998 study *Choosing Childlessness* analyses the projection made by the Central Statistical Office in 1993, that 'one in five women of child-bearing age may remain childless'.[5] Their research highlights the complex experience which may lie behind the idea of voluntary childlessness, not least that very few of the people they interviewed had made an early decision about child-lessness from which they never wavered. They also emphasise the profound significance of delaying conception:

[4] Fiona McAllister with Lynda Clarke, *Choosing Childlessness* (London: Family Policy Studies Centre, 1998).

[5] McAllister with Clarke, *Choosing Childlessness*, p. 7. McAllister and Clarke's study was based upon in-depth discussions with thirty-four women aged between 33 and 49 who identified themselves as voluntarily childless, from initial British Social Attitudes Surveys of 1994 and 1995. Eleven male partners of these women also took part in interviews. McAllister and Clarke's principal aim was to gain 'access to people in a wide range of marital and socio-economic circumstances' (p. 21).

The recent increase in the proportion of women experiencing childlessness in Britain is not without historical precedent and is not unique to this country. What is different to previous cohorts of women is the role played by choice, deliberately or unwittingly. The lack of marriageable partners may no longer be an obstacle to childbearing but the pursuit of other immediate goals may preclude this choice until a later stage. What may matter more than a desire to avoid childbearing in determining the level of childlessness are motivations that delay the decision to start a family or give it a low priority. The decision may not be faced until it is too late – women find they have 'forgotten' to have children because of other immediate priorities – or that when they do take this decision, they find they are infecund.[6]

McAllister and Clarke note that 'choosing childlessness has often been portrayed as an integral part of a shift away from "traditional family values" ',[7] and their research reveals a range of values and attitudes which lie behind the decision not to have children for their respondents. Among them are 'lack of interest in traditionally female pursuits or an absence of "maternal instincts"', negative attitudes towards parenthood, 'the sacrifice of spontaneity and freedom and a dislike of what was perceived as a "parenting lifestyle" ',[8] commitment to the creation of a beautiful home which would, or might, be compromised by children;[9] and 'an aversion to risk and change in their lives', linked to a sense of having achieved a desired lifestyle and reluctance to see it undermined.[10]

Commitment to work or a career, however, was not especially significant: 'there is no straightforward relationship between rates of female participation in the workforce and fertility trends in particular countries'.[11] Specifically within the scope of

[6] *Choosing Childlessness*, p. 19.
[7] *Choosing Childlessness*, p. 21.
[8] *Choosing Childlessness*, p. 27.
[9] *Choosing Childlessness*, p. 38.
[10] *Choosing Childlessness*, p. 36.
[11] European Commission, 1994, quoted in McAllister with Clarke, *Choosing Childlessness*, p. 40.

McAllister's and Clarke's study, 'Two-fifths of respondents were clear that it [work] has *never* come first for them.'[12]

> Only five of McAllister and Clarke's respondents agreed that work had always been quite or very important or a major priority for them (four women and one man) while six women and two men felt that it had never been a priority for them. Five women felt that their work had become more important over time, in contrast with almost half the group who thought work grew less important over time. This confirms the overall impression that work is not the main priority for most of the people interviewed.[13]

This finding is in stark contrast to the group of married Christians whose experience I will refer to later. Even for McAllister's and Clarke's respondents, however, career or work factors were an influence in the *delay* of childbearing, which often developed into a decision not to have children. 'By moving beyond the surface categories of how important work was and attending to the detail of respondents' accounts, it was possible to discern some trends as to the timing of when work was important and the reciprocal effects on remaining childless.'[14] Marriage in this study was found to be a highly significant indicator of the desire to have children, however:

> Being married increases the likelihood of childbearing, in spite of increases in both cohabitation and births to unmarried women. Childlessness in general is associated with being unmarried and marriage remains an important predictor of becoming parents. In this context, couples who have made an active decision not to have children are particularly unusual.[15]

McAllister and Clarke found emphasis upon the quality of a relationship to be of prime importance for their respondents. They found evidence of this in other studies too. Morrell, for

[12] *Choosing Childlessness*, p. 41.
[13] *Choosing Childlessness*, p. 41.
[14] *Choosing Childlessness*, p.41.
[15] *Choosing Childlessness*, p. 32.

example, notes that 'the voluntarily childless wives in her study stressed "supportive and deep friendship" with their spouses, and that the oldest women in her study equated having children with leaving paid employment and staying at home, a sexual division of labour, economic dependence and erosion of power within marriage'.[16]

Marriage as an institution was not insignificant, however: 'The value of legal marriage and permanence to childless people reflected their concern for a predictable future.'[17] This theme of predictability is in marked contrast to those with whom I had conversations, and to whom I now turn.

Christian and Voluntary Childlessness

Throughout this chapter it is important to remember that no method of contraception is wholly reliable, and therefore 'choice' is not a wholly accurate description in relation to voluntary childlessness. It is also important to recognise that voluntary childlessness is an option for a highly privileged minority, and is something which is virtually unknown, for example, in the two-thirds world. This is perhaps especially true of the group of twelve people with whom I had the conversations from which this chapter arose. The twelve consisted of five couples, plus two women whose partners were unable or unwilling to participate. All were in professional employment, although five identified themselves as having been brought up in working-class families. All were educated to degree level, and five were academics with doctorates. Ages ranged from 33 to 55. Eight were Anglicans, two Methodists and two Baptists. Four were ordained, including one clergy couple. The sample is therefore small and unrepresentative.

Some of the reasons given for choosing to remain childless echo those of McAllister's and Clarke's respondents, not least a universal rejection by the women of traditional roles.[18] One of

---

[16] Carolyn M. Morrell, *Unwomanly Conduct: the challenges of international childlessness* (London: Routledge, 1994), cited in McAllister with Clarke, *Choosing Childlessness*, p. 37.

[17] *Choosing Childlessness*, p. 37.

[18] Another unusual aspect of this group was that only two of the women shared a surname with their spouse, and all the women, and four of the men, identified as feminist or pro-feminist.

the women also related to fears about a relatively equal partnership becoming very unequal should children be born. There was a universal rejection of the creation of a beautiful home as a reason for not having children,[19] and there was some anger expressed by two people at a view (expressed in a recent *Woman's Hour* radio programme) suggesting that 'leisure lifestyle' lay at the heart of some people's decision not to have children. The avoidance of risk and change was also rejected as a reason for choosing to be childless, for there was a sense that risks were already being taken, with the stress of hard paid employment, political and church commitments. The potential, and, in some cases, actual, detrimental effects of this upon marriage were recognised.

The group did relate to a sense of the huge sacrifices required by parenthood, but this was not so much accompanied by negativity about parenthood, as a sense that it was not possible to 'have it all', and of the absence of a vocation to parenthood: 'It's not really me', 'I feel called to other things.' In four cases this was accompanied by an expression of lack of empathy with children, though others were enthusiastic about other people's children. Although four of the group had considered having children at some point in their lives, all now felt disinclined. One woman said: 'It never occurred to me that I would ever have children.' All twelve were certain, however, that they would not have a termination should there have been, or be (in some cases), an 'accidental' conception.

Overwhelmingly, and in contrast with McAllister's and Clarke's findings, issues of work, of vocation, and of commitment to Christian, political and pastoral causes were given as the primary reason why members of the group had chosen not to have children. These other callings were felt very strongly, and seen as incompatible with the perceived high calling of commitment to be parents. There were also echoes of traditional arguments for a celibate priesthood in some of what was said, e.g., 'being available to other people', 'having an open home', 'being able to prioritise the things of the Kingdom'.

---

[19] In some cases amid much mirth as we sat in a study piled high with papers and books.

One couple described their marriage as 'a stable centre from which to go out'.[20]

So, given the traditional teaching of the churches, and the expectations of society about children as a 'natural', 'God-given' part of marriage, why had these people married? Universally the twelve said that this was to do with making a life-long commitment to a partner whom they felt in some sense had been given to them by God. One priest said: 'Would the bishop have given me a licence if I'd cohabited with my partner because we didn't want to have children?' In all cases it had been important to make this commitment in church, despite, especially for the older couples, having to cope with the *Book of Common Prayer*'s views on the purposes of marriage.

Expectations about children both from the church and society were seen by the whole group as optional, rather old-fashioned, and something which they felt free to resist. Some recorded, however, being angered by some of the things which people said to them, and excluded by events like Mothering Sunday which reinforced traditional expectations.

Christian Teaching

All the historic churches in England have made some move in recent years away from seeing marriage primarily in terms of procreation and the avoidance of sin, to emphasising positive aspects of the quality of married relationships and the positive role of sexual expression within marriage. This almost certainly reflects an increasing understanding of those who are unable to have children, or who chose not to do so for medical reasons, and for whom, therefore, a stark proclamation of marriage being for children might be alienating. I suspect, too, that the realities of contraception are also taken into account,

---

[20] In response to Michael Nazir-Ali, Sue Walrond-Skinner says much the same thing: ' "We for one, as a couple, do not have children, and we see our vocation as a married couple nevertheless as extending out to others, to be including others into our family and to be creating a family in a different kind of way." Christian couples in today's over-populated world could well see that as their vocation, she said.' Cited in Pat Ashworth, 'Children not "optional extra" for couples', *Church Times*, 10 March 2000, p. 3.

but it is not clear how far the concerns of couples *planning* not to have children at all are being accommodated. Despite this movement, however, the place of children remains central to the purposes of marriage in the teaching of the churches.

The Roman Catholic Church

With its ban on artificial contraception, the obligation of children is most strongly developed by the Roman Catholic Church where children are generally accepted as one of the 'givens' of marriage. This is despite significant changes in favour of the value of the married relationship and of sex as a valid part of the married relationship, and a very positive stance in relation to those who cannot have children.[21] Choice about children for Catholics is to be God's not a couple's: 'By its very nature the institution of marriage and married love is ordered to the procreation and education of offspring and it is in them that it finds its crowning glory.'[22]

The Church of England

Authorised teaching is not a great feature of the life of the Church of England, and its marriage liturgies, therefore, are of especial importance in gleaning how doctrines have changed. In the 318 years between the *Book of Common Prayer* and the *Alternative Service Book* there is a huge change of emphasis. The *Book of Common Prayer* offered procreation, the avoidance of fornication, and only then 'the mutual society, help and comfort' as 'the cause for which matrimony was ordained'.[23] The *Alternative Service Book* significantly rearranged the order of

---

[21] 'Spouses to whom God has not granted children can nevertheless have a conjugal life full of meaning, in both human and Christian terms. Their marriage can radiate a fruitfulness of charity, of hospitality and of sacrifice' (*Catechism of the Catholic Church* (London: Geoffrey Chapman, 1994), p. 370, para. 1654).

[22] *Gaudium et spes*, 48, in Austin Flannery (ed.), *Vatican Council II* (Northport, NY: Costello Publishing, 1982).

[23] *Book of Common Prayer*, p. 171. Part of early Anglicanism's distinct identity was to reject the sacramental nature of marriage.

1662, so that comfort and help comes first, the avoidance of fornication is dropped and replaced by a celebration of married sex, not least as an important part of bonding, and finally marriage 'is given that they may have children and be blessed in caring for them and bringing them up in accordance with God's will, to his praise and glory'.[24] Marriage here is not 'for' children as it was in 1662, but there is, at least, an expectation. The 2000 *Common Worship* continues this stance.[25]

Three other Church of England documents may be significant to this discussion. First, *Marriage – A Teaching Document from the House of Bishops of the Church of England* (1999), reinstates the order of the purposes of marriage of the *Book of Common Prayer* and something of its tone.[26] Like much other contemporary theology the teaching document also recognises the importance of the quality of married relationships and that the unselfish love which is central to marriage may extend to a wider group than the immediate family. Second, the 1995 report, *Something to Celebrate*, which is primarily about family life, makes some interesting observations. It challenges the idea that children are a problem,[27] and criticises stances which suggest children are an economic burden, or limit the freedom of adults, or even add to social security costs. It calls upon married people to recognise that sexual intercourse is not for themselves alone, but that through it new life is made possible. Children are 'one of the most important ways couples can achieve happiness and fulfilment'. However, the report significantly states that '... having children is thought of in the

---

[24] *Alternative Service Book* (Cambridge: Cambridge University Press, 1980), p. 288.

[25] 'It is given as the foundation of family life in which children are (born and) nurtured ...' (*Common Worship: The Marriage Service* (London: Church House Publishing, 2000), p. 3).

[26] Although it also uses the rider 'are traditionally described as', the purposes of marriage are 'the procreation and nurture of children, the hallowing and right direction of natural instincts and affections, and the mutual society, help and comfort which each affords the other in prosperity and adversity' (House of Bishops, *Marriage* (London: Church House Publishing, 1999), p. 8).

[27] Something strongly echoed in Adrian Thatcher, *Marriage after Modernity: Christian Marriage in Postmodern Times* (Sheffield: Sheffield Academic Press, 1999), p. 65 and *passim*.

Christian tradition as a special calling which people ought not to enter upon unadvisedly'.[28] This special calling of parenthood is not presented as an intrinsic part of the special calling of marriage for everyone.

Third, the 1991 House of Bishops statement, *Issues in Human Sexuality*, acknowledges marriage as having a patriarchal history, not least in the perceived necessity of sons, while it yet remains 'the best home for our children'.[29] Marriage is not, however, wholly for children; it is a spiritual as well as a physical and social partnership. There is less of an insistence upon procreation here than elsewhere in Church of England documents, and married people 'can form a partnership which is both a blessing to the whole community and also the stable and loving environment in which children need to be brought up'.[30]

The Methodist Church

The United Kingdom Methodist Church reveals a greater degree of movement in recent years. Whether from pastoral concern, or from a greater sense of the voluntary nature of procreation, the 1975 *Methodist Service Book* asserts that 'such marriage is the foundation of true family life; and when blessed with children ...'.[31] Here children may be a blessing, but they are neither an inevitability, nor an obligation. This tone is continued in the 1999 *Methodist Worship Book* which states: 'It is the will of God that marriage should be honoured as a way of life, in which we may know the security of love and care, and grow towards maturity. Through such marriage, children may be nurtured, family life strengthened, and human society enriched.'[32] Again there is a sense of voluntariness with regard

[28] Board for Social Responsibility, *Something to Celebrate* (London: Church House Publishing, 1995), p. 86.

[29] House of Bishops, *Issues in Human Sexuality* (London: Church House Publishing, 1992), p. 21.

[30] *Issues in Human Sexuality*, p. 19.

[31] *The Methodist Service Book* (Letchworth: Methodist Publishing House, 1975), p. E4.

[32] *The Methodist Worship Book* (Peterborough: Methodist Publishing House, 1999), p. 369.

to children, and other expressions of the wider 'public' implications of marriage are also offered.

The 1979 Methodist Conference statement, *A Christian
Understanding of Human Sexuality*, also teaches that the fruits of
marriage 'are mutual growth in maturity, creativity and inter-
dependence, and often in the gift of children'.[33] The 1992
Methodist Church Division of Social Responsibility statement *A
Christian Understanding of Family Life, the Single Person and
Marriage*, while emphasising the importance of parenthood,
does not make it an obligation on married people. Future work
is planned on the area of childlessness, however.[34]

The United Reformed and Baptist Churches

In these two denominations where authority is highly devolved
it is difficult to pinpoint what may be called 'official teaching'.
However, the Wedding Service in the United Reformed Church
Service Book may give some clues. In a series of four paragraphs
describing the purposes of marriage the third paragraph reads:
'God has given us marriage for the birth and nurture of
children, so that they may grow up in the security of love, and
come to experience the freedom of faith.'[35] This is the only
example of a liturgy proclaiming that marriage is 'for' children,
though alongside the other three paragraphs it seems less
prescriptive than may at first appear. In the light of this it is
notable that during the prayers the only section in parentheses
consists of these words: ' (Bless them in the gift of children: may
they be loving, wise and caring parents.) '[36]

[33] Quoted in Jack Dominian, *Marriage, Faith and Love* (London: Darton,
Longman & Todd, 1981), p. 23.

[34] The Methodist Church Division of Social Responsibility, *A Christian
Understanding of Family Life, the Single Person and Marriage* (Methodist
Conference, 1992), p. 1.

[35] *The Service Book, The United Reformed Church in the United Kingdom* (Oxford:
Oxford University Press, 1989), p. 52.

[36] *The Service Book*, p. 58. The United Reformed Church and Society
Department also referred me to *An Ecumenical Guide for Marriage Preparation*
(London: Churches Together for Families, Churches Together in England,
1998), which nowhere implies children as an obligation of marriage, though it
encourages couples to 'explore the part they hope/expect children to have in
their future life together' (p. 25).

The Baptist Church also provides few clues. However, the 'Declaration of Purpose' from the *Order of Service for Christian Marriage* uses the threefold form of comfort and help, bodily union and finally (in a very weak form) children: 'It is given so that the stability it imparts to their relationship may be a source of strength to others and the foundation of a secure family life for any children they may have.'[37]

Giving Life for God

Both *Something to Celebrate* and Adrian Thatcher's *Marriage after Modernity* challenge thinking which regards children as a problem or an irrelevance.[38] Both these sources assert that children are a cause for celebration and an appropriate good of marriage: 'Children are seen as a miracle, a gift, an achievement ...'[39] This is also made explicit in most of the material which was consulted in preparing this chapter where children are primarily seen as a gift, as a source of delight and enrichment, and, not least, of growth for parents.[40] These positive assessments are emphasised even when the hard work of child-rearing, its disruptiveness and its potential threat to the marriage relationship are taken seriously. Much is written which echoes the judgement of the *Catechism of the Catholic Church* that 'it is in children that marriage finds its crowning glory'.[41]

Echoes of the charge that children are a problem can be heard, however, among both groups of voluntary childless people discussed in this chapter. For those represented in McAllister's and Clarke's study, economics and the limitations of freedom did seem to play a part, although economics did not feature explicitly among the groups of voluntarily childless Christians I spoke to – perhaps because they were relatively affluent. There was nonetheless an echo of a desire not to limit

---

[37] Cited in John Weaver, *Water into Wine* (Baptist Union of Great Britain, undated), p. 16.

[38] Thatcher, *Marriage after Modernity*, p. 65 and *passim*.

[39] *Something to Celebrate*, p. 101.

[40] E.g., *Catechism of the Catholic Church*, p. 366, para. 1641.

[41] *Catechism of the Catholic Church*, p. 370, para. 1652.

freedom through having children. This emphasis on freedom is at the heart of Pope John Paul II's condemnation of what he calls 'contraceptive mentality'; 'a corruption of the idea and the experience of freedom, conceived not as a capacity for realising the truth of God's plan for marriage and the family, but as an autonomous power of self-affirmation; often against others, for one's own selfish well-being'.[42] Contraception, which he inextricably links with abortion, is for John Paul II fundamentally an option for what is death-dealing rather than life-giving and as such it is linked with other death-dealing values like consumerism. For John Paul II the link in McAllister's and Clarke's work between the preservation of freedom and the desire for a beautiful house would be an obvious one.

The Christians to whom I spoke, however, did not link their choices with consumerism. Indeed they would all have described the undermining of consumerism as fundamental to their Christian calling and a requirement of God's reign.[43] Rather, using the language of vocation, they identified other demanding commitments which might also have been described as limiting freedom, though perhaps not to the extent that raising a family would. There was not a hint of selfishness 'against others', though there was some sense of autonomy in the confidence of making a choice, of following a personal sense of vocation.

It is notable that in the teaching of the churches it is the language of gift not vocation which primarily applies to children. This may well reflect an overwhelmingly positive stance towards children on the part of the churches, at least in theory,[44] rather than a rejection of the vocation model. Also, it should be remembered that for most of the history of humanity, reliable contraception did not exist, and so children were almost inescapable in marriage, not only a good of it. The concept of vocation with regard to having children is inevitably a new one. In the past, however, the vocation to marriage was a common concept, which fundamentally subsumed the vocation

---

[42] John Paul II, *Familiaris consortio*, 6.
[43] For a critique of 'contraceptive mentality' see Thatcher, *Marriage after Modernity*, pp. 199–200.
[44] In practice churches do not always accommodate or encourage children.

to children within it. Now, because of contraception, it does not necessarily do so and contemporary theology has begun to develop a language of vocation in relation to children in marriage.

Outside of the Roman Catholic Church, in the popular theological resource of Christian marriage preparation, there is an emphasis upon a couple agreeing whether to have children. Reaching accord on this issue is seen as vitally important, while having children is regarded as an option. There is a hint of a vocation to parenthood in the Church of England teaching document *Marriage*, which assumes children, but asks some apparently vocational questions of those considering marriage: 'a couple needs to consider what will be demanded by the tasks of parenthood and mutual support, and what the implications may be for the career of each. Nobody can enter through this door without closing others ...'[45] Is it legitimate within a marriage, in so far as it is possible, to close the door upon children in order to open other doors? *Something to Celebrate* thinks it is: 'Sometimes remaining childless is a self-sacrificial choice undertaken to allow the couple greater freedom to commit themselves to the needs of the Kingdom of God.'[46]

In discussing the models of gift and vocation it may be significant to note that in the case of many other gifts choices have to be made, for not every gift can be exercised or developed. Many clergy, for example, have neglected or abandoned their giftedness for music or painting, or medicine or teaching, in order to follow their vocation to ordination. Perhaps the gift of fertility, where it exists, may also be abandoned in pursuit of other vocations. If vocation is a religious way of speaking about the deepest longings of human beings, this suggestion may indeed be legitimate, though the charge of an over-individual and personal approach to vocation may also be relevant here. However, eschewing the potential gift of children may be, I believe, for some married people, part of the way of holiness.

In much of the history of Christianity, the pursuit of holiness has been portrayed as something more readily attainable by

[45] *Marriage*, p. 11.
[46] *Something to Celebrate*, p. 194.

those who are celibate, and especially celibate priests and religious, than by married people. This reflected, amongst other things, a negative attitude to sexual expression deriving from dualistic philosophies, together with a sense that professional Christians had more time to practise holiness than lay people. Fundamentally, however, holiness has been judged by the quality of Christian prayer and the fruits of this. Holiness is, at least in part, about outcomes. If giving life for God through children is a fruit of marriage to be celebrated, it is not the only fruit, as this chapter makes clear. May not then other forms of giving of life also be the approved fruits of marriage even if children are absent?

Marianne Katoppo's reinterpretation of virginity may be relevant here, where a mature woman who abstains from sexual expression, and is therefore childless, becomes 'fertile, she gives life for God'.[47] Abstinence from sexual expression within marriage is not well attested,[48] but it may be that mature married people who choose not to have children may also be said to be fertile, to give life for God. Somewhat in this vein Carter Heyward, too, challenges, from a lesbian perspective, the idea 'that only procreation is truly creative'.[49]

A pursuit of holiness which is fruitful in areas other than child-bearing and rearing may in fact contribute an important antidote to a church where it may not be contraception which is 'death dealing', but the hegemony of family life. Elizabeth Stuart uncovers how the church has 'allowed itself to become identified with the bourgeois family and thereby implicated in the economic, social and cultural structures that created and have sustained it through shifting patterns for generations'. In Stuart's view, these elements have had a dire effect upon the church, and she laments: 'How far the churches have lost sight of ecclesial personhood is evident in the virtual collapse of

---

[47] Marianne Katoppo, *Compassionate and Free* (Geneva: World Council of Churches, 1979), pp. 21–2.

[48] Though Thatcher commends a less phallocentric/penetrative approach to heterosexual love-making prior to marriage (*Marriage after Modernity*, pp. 173–6). Of significance here also may be the concept of spiritual marriage in the medieval church.

[49] Carter Heyward, *Our Passion for Justice* (Cleveland: Pilgrim Press, 1984), p. 91.

Christian discipleship into marriage and family life that is evident in recent church pronouncements on sexuality, and in the steady theoretical marginalisation of the religious life, even in the Roman tradition.'[50] Her critique of this phenomenon finds its force in the New Testament assertion that discipleship takes priority over family life. More than that, 'St Paul ... was convinced that the freedom wrought by Christ ... decentres the family. In particular the resurrection obviates the need to produce heirs, for in the resurrection all will be re-membered and remembered. Karl Barth, as a great Pauline scholar, could assert that "the idea of the family is of no interest at all for Christian theology".'[51]

Despite sympathy with Barth's argument, I suggest that Paul's teaching about marriage belongs in an apocalyptic framework which is no longer a valid starting point.[52] Nonetheless, apocalyptic writings and apocalyptic frameworks can provide important prophetic messages for the church. Perhaps, as Stuart suggests, a prophetic and counter-cultural stance should be taken by some couples, in order to undermine the universality of the bourgeois family and its dominance in the church.[53]

Conclusion

This chapter is but a small contribution to the discussion of the growing phenomenon of voluntary childlessness. It is an important discussion which needs to be continued, not least, in order to reassert a Christian discipleship which is not wholly identified with family life. The call to follow the way of Jesus within committed partnerships without children is significant for a range of people, for those who choose not to have children, gay, lesbian or straight, and for the one in ten couples

---

[50] Elizabeth Stuart, 'Sexuality: The View from the Font', *Theology and Sexuality*, 11 (Sept. 1999), p. 16.

[51] Stuart, 'Sexuality', p. 16.

[52] For a more thorough answer to these arguments see Thatcher, *Marriage after Modernity*, pp. 166–7.

[53] I am grateful to David Hewlett for pointing out, however, that the New Testament also decentres marriage.

who are infertile, and who need to find a way of life not forever overshadowed by the absence of their own children. Marriage, and other covenanted relationships, which do not include procreation, can, I believe, legitimately be affirmed as another way of following Christ. They may perhaps, but not always, enable a wider availability to people, to political causes, and to the building of the Kingdom of God. It is important, however, that – unlike theologies of celibacy in the past – there is no hierarchy of merit established, but that diversity of callings is respected, and everyone is recognised as playing a part in giving life for God.

Perhaps Stuart's vision of an ecclesial theology of sexuality can be applied to all Christian discipleship and vocation: 'It must begin with a desire to complete the story of ascent to union with Christ which is prefigured and begun in baptism among the tragedy of human existence. This is both an individual and a corporate desire. It can be worked out in a number of ways ...'[54]

[54] Stuart, *Sexuality*, p. 17.

15

Welcome the Pied Piper

Jon Davies

New Wheels for Old

Once upon a time a society decided that it had had enough of
boring old round wheels and decided to go in for wheels of more
exotic shapes: square ones, triangular ones, oblong ones, all
attached by axles made of chewing gum to woollen carts lacking
all motive power, as the new-Wheelites decided to rely for
propulsion on Wish rather than on physical effort or engines:
Because we Want them to move they Will move, they said, sitting,
Wishing, on their triangular-wheeled chewing-gum-axled
knitted carts. Not a lot of locomotion took place. Seeking to
know why this was so the new-Wheelites saw that a small number
of people had in fact stuck by the old wheels and were moving
around quite nicely. 'It's *because of them* that we aren't moving',
they said; and they stopped the deviant-traditionalists from using
their round wheels. Then Zero Locomotion took place ...

Once upon a time another society was bothered by a plague
of rats. A Pied Piper said that he would, for a fee, get rid of
them – and, having been promised his fee, did so. The Piper
lured the rats into the river where they all drowned. Then the
society refused to pay the fee. So the Pied Piper played his pipe
again and all the children followed him to a mountain which
swallowed them all up (except for a lame child and a deaf child
who could not keep up or hear the pipe). Suddenly, a child-free
society! What bliss!

It is a sure bet that 80% of the words thrown into the air by
this book will assume the existence of an adult-only world and
the primacy of adult interests and appetites. In this, this book
will be on all fours with the bulk of theologico-psychologico-

240

sociologico writing on 'the family' and on sexual matters. In such an adult-only world, composed of autonomous self-directing adults, there is no reason whatsoever why such adults should be prevented from making whatever sexual or ideational relationships they choose. In the felicific calculus of self-regarding adults, relationships conducive to Happiness (authenticity, self-fulfilment, personisation, independence, whatever) can be held to be both internally and externally self-justifying: individuals will be Happier in themselves, in whatever variant, or variants of Happiness they choose; and an Invisible Hand will integrate all these Happinesses in an amiable happy Community. Even when, occasionally, someone comes a cropper then that's OK as adults are expected to be responsible for their failures as well as for their successes. Needless to say, radical adultness of *that* sort rapidly fades into demands for 'communal' support for such failures; and by 'communal' is meant compulsory.

Children destroy the comfort and symmetry of this utilitarian theology. They are not participants to the social contract, being absent when it is signed, and as a-responsible agents they cannot sign such contracts anyway. They are dependent, not independent; vulnerable, not autonomous; inchoate, not finalised; ignorant, not wise; wrong, not right.

There are various ways of dealing with the Children Problem. A recent survey conducted by the British polling organisation MORI, for the National Family and Parenting Institute, reported that whereas 70% of the children interviewed said that their parents' relationships affected them and that they would be unhappy if their parents did not get on well, only 33% of parents thought that their relationships had an impact on their children's happiness.[1] How convenient. Adults are assiduous in finding ways of minimalising the Children Problem. In earlier essays[2] I have dealt with three of these, i.e., Stop Having Them,

---

[1] *The Guardian*, 12 June 2000, p. 5.
[2] J. G. Davies, 'From Household to Family to Individualism', in J. G. Davies (ed.), *The Family: Is it just another lifestyle choice?* (London: Institute of Economic Affairs, 1993), pp. 63–107; 'A Preferential Option for the Family', in S. Barton (ed.), *The Family in Theological Perspective* (Edinburgh: T&T Clark, 1996), pp. 219–36; 'Sex These Days', in J. G. Davies and G. Loughlin (eds.), *Sex These Days* (Sheffield: Sheffield Academic Press, 1997), pp. 18–34.

Nationalise Them, Treat them as Pretend Adults. All of these tactics are both in use and easily justified by contemporary theology and the vested interest which that theology represents — the Adult Orgasm Association (ADORASS). I may though be allowed to comment that in those essays I contend (hugely platitudinously to my mind) (a) that society (*any* society, human, vegetable or animal) needs children (more, for example, than it needs same-sex 'marriages' or authenticated transsexuals); (b) that caring for children collectively is tantamount to caring for them less; and (c) that to pretend that children can be treated as adults is nonsense and, in pandering to the predatory self-interest of adults, is likely to lead to the infantilisation of adults as well as to the degradation of children. This last theme was well expressed in that tragic film *The Full Monty* (tragic in part because it was received and reviewed *as a comedy*!), a film well and truly of and for our time. The only 'adult' in the film was a male child, appropriately (given what he could see going on around him) named Nathan.

An Insurance Policy for a Foetus

Succinctly, it must be the case that a foetus pondering its about-to-be arrival in the world, and looking for an insurance policy which would give it the best, or least worst (not, note, *the perfect*) start in life would be advised, by any reputable seller of life assurance, to enter into a domestic unit composed of its biological parents monogamously and permanently married to each other. *Any* other domestic unit would give it a worse start in life; and some of the domestic units (which we seem to be encouraging) would be positively dangerous. Insurance policies, it should be noted, are based on the *probabilities* of actuarial tables: that is, they offer no guarantees but policies of 'more or less' – *this* policy is more likely, and *that* one is less likely to do what you want, there are no guarantees, things go wrong. Indeed that is precisely why you need insurance. This means, for example, that while children in a household consisting of a never-married mother living with a 'partner' who is not the biological father of her children are more likely to suffer abuse, including being killed, than children living with both their biological parents monogamously married, it does not mean either that *all* children in the former household will suffer abuse or that children in the latter type of household *never* experience abuse. It is simply a matter of higher and lower probabilities; and this is the best we can expect of human institutions. As far as children are concerned, the vast bulk of the evidence we have is that, in all probability, they are better launched into the world through and in the stable marriage of their biological parents. If you want to diminish the life-chances of children then simply increase the statistical incidence of 'alternative' household types – and this is precisely what we are doing. No sensible foetus would take *our* advice on a life assurance policy.

What has the church to do with all of this? The conference which gave rise to this book took place in an Anglican establishment, and I will restrict my remarks to that bit of the Christian tradition. Caught between its prophetic and pastoral responsibilities, and with a *Guardian*-newspaper-welfarist view of what 'pastoral' means, the Church of England will in its *theological* pronouncements slipperily erode any genuine support for the moral (never mind practical) superiority of procreational, marital, sex: as Elizabeth I told her Puritan interlocutors and would-be instructors, theology of this type is 'ropes of sand and sea-slime to the moon'.

Liturgies and Children

A more adamant or 'harder' form of commentary on sex, marriage and their purposes lies in the liturgy of the church(es). Of all forms of religious utterance, liturgy is the most meticulous, representing hundreds of man-(person-) hours of pernickety head-scratching, phrase-making and syllable-shuffling – all to get as close as possible to an exact expression of what the proper form is. Generally, liturgies are aimed outside ordained clergy, aimed that is at the laity. The *Book of Common Prayer* (BCP) is a vade-mecum for practical day-to-day this-worldly living.

Funnily enough, until the *Alternative Service Book* (ASB) of 1980, the Anglican Church has never had a '*marriage* service'. The Reformation Settlement gave us the BCP. It deals with sex and procreation in the 'Order for the Solemnization of Matrimony', itself a service derived from the medieval 'Sarum'

Orders. The medieval Orders of matrimony were unusual in the Roman liturgy in that they were written in the vernacular: they were meant to be understood and not simply 'witnessed'. The 'Order for the Solemnization of Matrimony' of the BCP remained under that title (the proposed revision of 1928 retained the title) and became 'The Marriage Service' only with the ASB of 1980. So for hundreds of years before the BCP, and for three hundred years or so after it, our society entered into 'matrimony', not 'marriage'. A quibble? Perhaps: but then liturgies are a quibble – about serious meanings. 'Solemnization of Matrimony' meant that the sexual relations which the Order legitimated were being entered into within an institutional framework designed to facilitate and buttress motherhood – the having of babies within a setting in which both their safety and welfare and the safety and welfare of the woman-about-to-become-mother would be made less, rather than more, difficult and dangerous. Everyone knows that in the secular worlds of all these centuries the position of women, at every level of society, was 'less eligible' than that of men. Everyone knows that men are by nature not naturally very good at being domesticated (though they are major beneficiaries of that state). This is precisely why the Order stresses the necessity to wrap liturgical urgencies and imperatives around the business of having babies. In the context of the sexes and of procreation, doctrines of perfection are most seriously practical.

While the BCP inherits from the Sarum Rite the title 'Order of Matrimony', it adds to the service an introductory Homily which lays down the 'causes for which matrimony was ordained. First, it was ordained for the procreation of children.' In giving two other reasons (to enable people unable to do without sex to have it without sin or fornication; and for the 'mutual society, help and comfort' of the two participants) the BCP would appear to be laying out a set of priorities rather than just a list of matters of more or less equal status. There is some dispute about this, but the writers of the ASB clearly felt that they were dealing with a set of priorities when, in addition to introducing *for the first time* the word 'Marriage' into the title of the rite, they reversed the set of priorities in the list, putting children third. For the first time, the concerns of adults take centre stage. In this, of course, the writers of the ASB were on all fours with the trends, promotional activities and ambitions of secular society. 'Marriage' derives from the Latin *maritus*, meaning man or husband, only rarely *marita*, woman or wife. 'Matrimony', obviously, derives from the Latin for 'mother' or 'motherhood'. In this, the rite of matrimony introduces and emphasises the persistent ritual comprehension of the relationship as one in which procreation rehearses and replicates the act of Creation.

It should also be noted that the BCP 'solemnizes' matrimony, i.e., it confers religious approval on an arrangement already entered into. Generally, such arrangements would be made between families and friends of the woman and man concerned – they would supervise or facilitate the betrothal. The sound sense in this, of course, is that a kinship or social group ignored by two people insistent on getting married 'no matter what' would for that reason be less able to call on family and friends at some later stage when, as is the predictable trail of human affairs, things failed to go according to the couple's starry-eyed plans. However, the rite itself assumes the voluntary assent of the two, i.e., we are not here looking at coercion; and in inviting 'any man' (i.e., not just family) to provide reason why the union should not go ahead the rite proclaims the communal interest in what is going on: this is a public institutional act because the production of babies is not only a private concern. Everything in the rite is aimed at according primacy to the having and nurturing of babies in such a way that their nurture is best looked after by the structured support of motherhood; and the rite *knows* that this aim is best accomplished by providing firm institutional support for (including restraint of) the biological parents. The boy and girl concerned will be more likely to achieve social maturity by becoming parents, one of life's most difficult tasks; and will best do this, in no matter what circumstances they find themselves, by putting their own concerns second. Children, not adults, are centre stage.

Perfect? Obviously not! Golden age-ism? On what possible grounds, when the liturgy shares with the theology from which it derives a sense of the precariousness and patchiness of human accomplishment? Better things have always to be worked for and can be laconically invented neither in the past nor in the future. Tough on women? Certainly – but not as tough as having babies outside of wedlock, and certainly not as tough on the babies themselves: why make things tougher?!

Hypocritical irresponsible men? Certainly – but not as licensed in their irresponsibility as they are now. Socially repressive? Certainly – but for quite good reason, unless the cost of any and all repression can always and everywhere be shown to outweigh the benefits. Out of date, as we don't need babies any more, or the state will look after them, and the world is overpopulated? Well, don't we need babies more than we 'need' transsexuals or than we 'need' to provide same-sex couples with the babies they can't have on their own? And what benefit will the world derive from the collapse into demographic solipsism of the more successful economies of the world, which already indirectly import the labour of, for example, children in the third world and whose spokesmen are now talking of selectively and directly importing those 'more useful' members of poorer countries? However, it is the child-free vocabulary of ADORASS that now dominates and children as our direct responsibility will steadily disappear as both subject and object of social discourse.

For Whose Good?

Who benefits from the child-free world created by the Pied Piper? Unlike rain, the costs and benefits of social change do not fall equally on the just and on the unjust alike. Generally, those who are weaker or poorer will experience an undue share of the disbenefits, although there are some exceptions to this rule. Men, as a species-group, have been historically privileged, deriving from their involvement with matrimony both considerable material and demographic benefits as well as a degree of licence to absolve themselves from its responsibilities. Men are now in a rather ambivalent position. On the one hand, the endless availability of sex without marriage, and even paternity without marriage or commitment, confers upon all men the carnal delights hitherto enjoyed only by sexual athletes and philanderers. Yet men unattached to a house (*hus*bands, that is) also suffer from various enhanced forms of pathology (alcoholism, accidental injury, lowered life expectancy, suicide etc.) as well as representing, as criminals and street louts, a profound threat to 'society' as a whole. Marriage rates for higher social-status males are slowly increasing, as these men at any rate realise where their interests lie.

Women? Women have been the main drivers of sexual-social change, as is indicated by the fact that they initiate divorce proceedings very much more often than men. Again, better-off women in the professional classes, for example, are probably well placed to operate as single mothers or as divorcees, as their comparative affluence enables them to buy in the labour-and-skill equivalent of a husband, without the discomfort of a permanent presence in bed and at board. Poorer, less-educated girls or women, living in less amiable surroundings and badgered by importunate 'liberated' loutish males, and getting pregnant by them, are a large reason why poverty is being feminised. A recent report in the medical journal *The Lancet*[3] stated that lone parents (most of whom are women) are 70% more likely to die prematurely than those living with a partner, and that even when financial resources are standardised, they are still 20% more likely to die prematurely than women who are married or cohabiting. After all adjustments, the authors conclude that for lone mothers 'there was a significant increase in all-cause mortality, suicide, inflicted violence and alcohol-related mortality'. Interestingly, the authors do not distinguish between married and cohabiting couples although they appear to have had the relevant data.

In the United Kingdom three million 'dependent' children live in lone-parent households, where income is on average less than one-half the income of two-parent households. For both the women in lone-parent households and the children, this represents a major social handicap. As for children, the vast bulk of the data we have shows that in every respect children who live in anything other than a two-biological-married-parental house-hold are, in all probability, more likely to experience difficulties in life than the children who do live in such a conventional household. Pamela Wells[4] refers to American data[5] showing that

[3] G. R. Weitoft et al., 'Mortality among Lone Mothers in Sweden: A Population Study', *The Lancet*, 355 (8 April 2000), pp. 1215–19.

[4] Pamela Wells, 'Sarah B. Hardy's Mother Nature', *Times Literary Supplement* (7 March 2000).

[5] M. Daly and M. Wilson, 'Evolutionary Psychology and Family Homicide', *Science*, 242 (1988), pp. 519–24; 'Some differential attributes of lethal assaults on small children by stepfathers as opposed to genetic fathers', *Ethnology and Sociobiology*, 15 (1994), pp. 1–11.

a child under two living in a household in which there is no genetic father present but where there is stepfather or other unrelated man present has a 70 times greater chance of homicide than a child living in a household where the biological father is present. Robert Whelan also shows that the physical risk to children (including murder) grows exponentially the further the domestic environment of the child diverges from that of a married relationship of his or her two biological parents.[6] This is now about as factual a statement as it is possible to make. Anyone who thinks that 'The State' can do much to ameliorate the mess resulting from ignoring such a fact is an idiot.

On top of all of this we pour greater and greater tolerance of various forms of 'leisure' pursuits which involve excessive use of alcohol and drugs ('sex, drugs, and rock and roll'), an increased insistence on self and appetitive satisfaction, a massive increase in crime both petty and large – all of this in a world manageable, perhaps, by adults but crushing, by temptation, children. What 'society' now offers anxious parents is more worry, not support. It is not surprising that visitors to our society ('the West') from Islamic or African countries find us to be depraved – and stupidly rather than intelligently so.

'There is No Such Thing as Society'

Lady Thatcher was vilified for saying that there is no such thing as society. Yet her critics are busy making her comment (usually misquoted) come true. It was around children that we, once upon a time, and very slowly and precariously, created the institutions of civil society – the family, chapels and churches, schools and other communal facilities attendant upon children and family life, the locations of primary socialisation in which we learnt the pleasures and problems of self-indulgence and self-control, of proper and improper behaviour, of the boundaries between self and other. An adult-only world, the world of ADORASS, has no need of the institutions of civil society. It operates with Individuals on the one hand and the State

---

[6] R. Whelan, *Broken Homes and Battered Children: A study of the relationship between child abuse and family type* (Oxford: Family Education Trust, 1994).

(usually these days called 'the Community') on the other. Illogically, perhaps, but very humanly, the most adamantly self-regarding individual will immediately call upon the aid of others (the Community) when his or her folly gets him or her into trouble. Since voluntary acts (in a society composed of legitimately self-regarding individuals) of altruism are rather hard to come by, the call becomes one for compulsory altruism: the fiscal powers of the State (called Community) are to be used to compel me to pay for your orgasm and its oops-consequences. I might, of course, not like having my own self-maximising trajectory derailed in this way . . .

That this is an illogical and perhaps unsustainable system is perhaps camouflageable by the sheer amount of wealth that the system appears to be able to create. More probably, though, it will be the task of liberal theology over the next decades to devise a liturgy under which we can all have everything that we want without seeming to be doing that and without having to pay for it. Then, the Pied Piper's task will be complete and the rats can come back again as pets.

PART 6

Single-Sex Marriage

Introduction

There are few questions as deeply divisive in the churches as lesbian and gay unions and/or marriages. Indeed there remains controversy even over the framing of the questions about them. Each writer in this section contributes originally both to the clarification of the questions and to fresh answers that a new generation of Christians may be able to give.

Elizabeth Stuart provides a comprehensive and authoritative overview of the subject from the all-important perspectives of lesbian and gay theologians themselves, and offers her own analysis of the contemporary debate and its possible future direction. She finds that gay theology is not very interested in marriage. The issue of monogamy (versus non-monogamy) has been more pressing: while monogamy for several writers has been an ideal state, marriage has been seen as a heterosexual institution. Several writers have taken up the notion of covenant or 'covenanted union', but Stuart shows that, while these unions are regarded as, or equivalent to, marriages, there is considerable reluctance to admit this. Alternatively, committed gay relationships are said to sacramentalise God's reign or to be particular manifestations of friendship.

The verdict of lesbian theology on marriage is very clear: where patriarchy is the theory, marriage is the practice. The feminist virtues such as mutuality and equality cannot thrive inside it. Issues of monogamy and of friendship (including the extent of its sexual nature) re-emerge in lesbian theology, but Stuart finds serious flaws in both lesbian and gay theology that force her to move beyond both. The main flaw is the uncritical acceptance of 'homosexuality' and 'heterosexuality' as foundational categories for these theologies. Social constructionism

251

shows this assumption to be mistaken. On the other hand
'queer theology' accepts 'the free-floating relation between sex,
gender and desire' whereas lesbian and gay theologies remain
trapped in essential assumptions. However, the agenda for a
queer approach to marriage draws on surprisingly traditional
theological assumptions. Personal identity is established by
baptism: for Christians the 'primary community' is the church,
and sexual relations can, and should, bear its four marks.
Indeed marriage itself in queer perspective is thought to be
better able to mirror the love between Christ and the church
than a fixed heterosexual understanding of marriage. If
Christians conform to Christ, then received notions of gender
are certain to be subverted.

John Boswell's pioneering work on *Same-Sex Unions in
Premodern Europe* (1994), together with the reactions it caused,
is the starting point for Alan Bray's careful and meticulous
study. Boswell's conclusion was that a rite traditional among
Greek Christians (the *adelphopoiesis* — literally a rite for the
'making of brothers' or 'sisters') had functioned in the past as
a homosexual marriage ceremony. Bray's chapter opens by
exploring the problem that the unreserved rejection of John
Boswell's thesis can itself be open to the same charges of
anachronism as the thesis itself. These considerations merely
set the scene for Bray's chapter, which looks at the eucharistic
rite that corresponded to this Greek rite in the West. The
question he explores is how these rites can be understood in
historical rather than contemporary terms; and from that
vantage point outside contemporary culture, he then turns to
how that understanding might or might not illuminate the
possible liturgical recognition of friendship today.

Why did individuals participate in this rite? Bray reviews some
of the answers to this question that have been proposed. His
criticism is that they have characteristically and anachronisti-
cally selected only part of the evidence (and rejected the rest),
whether in the suggestion that the rite was used only for the
resolution of disputes, for the purposes of armed aggression,
for profit or as in Boswell's proposal. The historical context for
the rite, Bray argues, was the diverse – but potentially
overlapping – forms in which kinship could be formed in the
world that these rites inhabited. This frame did not obliterate
the boundaries of the family in the sense of a group of parents

and their children; it rather befriended it; and the sworn brotherhood or sisterhood of this rite was a part of that frame.

Is this history relevant to the church today? Its relevance, Bray argues, lies in its ability to question the adequacy of sexual ethics as a framework in which to consider the possible liturgical recognition of friendship today. The question it raises from its distinctive perspective is rather how homosexual friendship might appropriately be drawn in and contribute to the existing families of the two friends today.

Would the church be compromised by such a liturgical recognition – where the engine power that drives the contemporary debate is currently precisely in such sexual terms? Here Bray's paper avoids some of the pitfalls both sides of this debate fall into when discussing the question of liturgy. The eucharistic rite he describes was not an unreserved endorsement of the friendships it addressed and sought to shape: it was rather a response to them and one addressed to the potential good in them. If the first implication of Bray's highly original paper is to question the terms in which this debate is being conducted, the second is to point to the potential role of the liturgist in this debate: the arguably irreplaceable role of liturgy in negotiating those dangers of mutual appropriation that are always present when church and world come together.

16

Is Lesbian or Gay Marriage an Oxymoron? A Critical Review of the Contemporary Debate

Elizabeth Stuart

Whenever friends of mine get hitched I always write the same words of wisdom on the card that accompanies the gift: 'Never go to bed on an argument ... stay up and fight'. If Christians are good at nothing else they are accomplished fighters. We endlessly fight with each other and the very word 'homosexuality' seems to spark a ruck. David Sollis in an article on the representation of the 'homosexuality debate' at the 1998 Lambeth Conference of Anglican bishops in the British print media has noted that the debate was stereotyped and inaccurately reduced to two issues: the ordination of gay and lesbian clergy and same-sex marriage.[1] The media and, indeed, the opponents of greater inclusion of lesbian and gay people and their experiences into the churches give the impression that the theological and legal recognition of their relationships as 'marriage' is an important and urgent issue for lesbian and gay Christians. This chapter seeks both to test that assumption and to analyse what has been written about marriage in the body of theology known as lesbian and gay theology. Is this a burning issue for lesbian and gay theologians themselves and what does the issue, as a theological construction, constitute?

---

[1] David Sollis, 'Bearing False Witness: The Media and the Gay Debate', *Theology and Sexuality*, 12 (March 2000), pp. 109–19.

The Development of Lesbian and Gay Theology

Gay theology, theology done by self-affirming gay people, began to emerge in the USA and in Britain in the mid-1970s when gay Christians began to reflect theologically upon the gay liberation movement. The gay liberation movement, whose creation myth is the Stonewall Riots of June 1969, marked a shift in consciousness because men and women classified by the medico-legal establishment as 'homosexual' rejected both the label and the pathologising of their lives and claimed their own voice, subjectivity, moral agency and right to self-definition and deter-mination. They also began to question heterosexual normativity. Gay theology, when it first emerged, was dominated by men (with one or two notable exceptions like Sally Gearheart) who felt able to do theology about and on behalf of lesbians as well. In its very earliest manifestations gay theology tended to be apologetic in tone and intent and liberal in its methodology but as it developed in the 1980s under the influence of Latin American liberation theology and feminist theology, the apolo-getic dimension gave way to something far more confident. From liberation theology gay theologians absorbed the notions that God is always on the side of the oppressed, who have a privileged theological epistemology, and that theology consists of critical reflection upon active involvement in the struggle for political and social justice. Lesbian theology emerged out of gay theology under the influence of feminist theology and has tended to be more radically deconstructive of the tradition than gay theology. However, both lesbian and feminist theology exercised a strong influence over most gay (male) theology produced in the 1990s.[2] Lesbian and gay theology is currently in the process of a radical transformation and I will return to this in due course.

Gay Theology

I begin my discussion of the issue of marriage in lesbian and gay theology with an analysis of the theology written by gay men

---

[2] For a critical overview of the development of lesbian and gay theology see Elizabeth Stuart, 'Christianity is a Queer Thing: The Development of Queer Theology', *The Way*, 39:4 (October 1999), pp. 371–81.

between the mid-1970s and mid-1990s. The first point to note is that it is not in any sense a dominating issue in gay theology during this period. Major texts such as Gary Comstock's *Gay Theology Without Apology*[3] and Richard Cleaver's *Know My Name*[4] do not deal with the topic in any form, nor did Comstock and Susan Henking in their anthology *Que(e)ring Religion*[5] feel that it had been a sufficiently dominating issue in lesbian and gay theology to figure as an issue in the selected papers. This is surprising considering the fact that in the USA, from which most gay theology has hailed, the issue of gay marriage became a hot political issue in the early 1980s when the 'family values' rhetoric of the Christian right produced a reverse political discourse in which gay and lesbian people claimed their relationships as marriages and families and sought societal recognition for them. In Britain the Thatcherite homophobic rhetoric of 'the pretend family' created a similar climate.

Jim Cotter

What we find in gay theology is a tendency to reflect on the theo-ethics of gay relationships in terms of monogamy versus non-monogamy with little reference to marriage. Where it is referred to this is in terms that suggest it is essentially a hetero-sexual estate, to which gay relationships may be equal but different.

Jim Cotter, in *Towards a Theology of Gay Liberation* (the first work of gay theology to be published in Britain), exemplifies this approach.[6] Cotter draws attention to a reality which may well have had a profound effect on many gay approaches to marriage, namely that in the past many gay people have been forced into heterosexual marriage as a means of hiding or

---

[3] Gary Comstock, *Gay Theology Without Apology* (Cleveland: The Pilgrim Press, 1993).

[4] Richard Cleaver, *Know My Name* (Louisville: Westminster John Knox Press, 1995).

[5] Gary Comstock and Susan Henking, *Que(e)ring Religion* (New York: Continuum, 1999).

[6] Jim Cotter, 'The Gay Challenge to Traditional Notions of Human Sexuality', in Malcolm Macourt (ed.), *Towards a Theology of Gay Liberation* (London: SCM Press, 1977), pp. 63–79.

denying their same-sex desire. Marriage has therefore been constructed by society and by gay people themselves as a space in which same-sex desire is absent or unable to breathe. Cotter writes appreciatively of marriage, arguing that it reminds us that relationships need time to develop and that a formal commitment guarantees such a time, a guarantee that is necessary for people to evolve, to project and to face their own demons. But

> a gay person may here challenge the traditional notion of such a commitment necessarily being exclusive and for life. Many will claim that their primary commitment is enhanced by other relationships that include *eros* genitally expressed. Here the challenge is to work through those feelings of jealousy and possessiveness which are characteristic of most relationships and even close up a marriage completely. Also the challenge is to emphasise the quality of a relationship rather than its quantitative length: there may come a point beyond which two people can no longer grow together.[7]

Faithfulness, Cotter argues, is not necessarily identical to monogamy. Faithfulness involves trust, vulnerability and, of course, faith, the necessary conditions for love to expand and flourish.

> It may be that if I love B deeply, then I am also freed to love C (and both may be sexual loves). For love is not a cake with larger and smaller pieces: only time is the cake which has to be apportioned with care and sensitivity. Love may grow exponentially! ... Most of us probably feel safer when *eros* is limited in its genital expression to one person, but that may be because we have not really learned how to love. For the Christian, too, all human relationships are secondary ... The Christian's primary relationship is, in the end (which may be very much in the future as we stumble on the way of loving, reluctantly letting go of many an idol *en route*) with God. And under God's rule, we read, 'there is not even marriage or giving in marriage' (Mark 12:25).[8]

---

[7] Cotter, 'The Gay Challenge', p. 69.
[8] Cotter, 'The Gay Challenge', p. 71.

The notion that same-sex relationships which do not follow a monogamous marriage model might in some way incarnate an eschatological space beyond marriage is a theme that we will see is taken up in other writings in this genre.

Michael Keeling and Michael J. Clark

Michael Keeling offers a slightly different approach.[9] Whilst not wanting to posit monogamy as the sole moral norm for gay relationships, and drawing upon John MacMurray's definition of chastity as emotional sincerity,[10] Keeling argues that Christianity in marriage presents a monogamous relationship as the ideal which gay people concerned with building up meaningful relationships might aspire to, for such relationships catch us up within the practice of death and resurrection: 'Every commitment is in a sense a "death" to other possibilities. It is only through such deaths that the resurrection to new love can take place.'[11] Other forms of non-monogamous sexual activity need not be viewed as wicked as such but because they have no relationships to express they are meaningless in themselves.

These two early essays flag up what were to become some common features in much gay theological reflection upon same-sex relationships: an assumption that marriage is a heterosexual estate, one not superior to monogamous gay relationships but which nevertheless in some way embodies the Christian standard for all sexual relationships, a refusal to dismiss non-monogamous relationships as necessarily sinful and rather shallow theological analysis. There is a profound lack of interest in what marriage is and more generally what theological underpinnings human sexual relationships might have.

The work of Michael J. Clark makes an interesting case study. Clark was one of the first gay male theologians to adopt a

---

[9] Michael Keeling, 'A Christian Basis for Gay Relationships', in Macourt (ed.), *Towards a Theology of Gay Liberation*, pp. 100–7.

[10] John MacMurray, *Reason and Emotion* (London: Faber & Faber, 1935), pp. 128–32.

[11] Keeling, 'A Christian Basis for Gay Relationships', p. 106.

liberationist methodology, which he combined with process and feminist theological approaches. His early work written in the shadow of the AIDS pandemic is fiercely resistant to unthinking assumptions about the superiority of monogamy and the need to imitate heterosexual relationships. Clark here argues that honesty and faithfulness to particular relational commitments, whatever they may be, is rather what is required. He is critical of the romanticisation of monogamy and marriage which obscures the key ethical questions to be asked of any relationship, namely is it just and mutually empowering? Clark follows Foucault in arguing for a friendship model of relating among gay men because it is not dependent upon heterosexual models of relating. It is particularly appropriate for Clark because it resonates with the body of work on male friendship to be found in the Christian tradition and most particularly with the work of Aelred of Rievaulx whose theology of spiritual friendship Clark states was 'clearly coloured and informed by his gay perspective'.[12] In his later work Clark is converted to the merits of monogamy over non-monogamy, arguing that AIDS has forced gay men to question their reduction to sex, a reduction he attributes to post-Second World War heteropatriarchal culture.

> Only gradually did we surface from an underworld delimited by heterosexist parameters to realise that what we really need is not more sex but more love, love in committed relationships and in friendships based on justice in right relation, regardless of whether anything genitally sexual is involved.[13]

The pragmatic response to this need is monogamous sexual relationships based upon friendship which do not imitate heterosexual relationships but which better embody the virtues of right relation – equality, mutuality and reciprocity.

Clark's work, despite the fact that it involves shifts towards a monogamous model of relating, is an example of theo-ethics in which theology is almost totally eclipsed by ethics. The foundational principles of these ethics are pragmatism and a desire to

---

[12] J. Michael Clark, *A Defiant Celebration: Theological Ethics and Gay Sexuality* (Garland: Tangelwüld Press, 1990), p. 70.

[13] J. Michael Clark, *Defying the Darkness* (Cleveland: Pilgrim Press, 1997), p. 68.

avoid the imitation of heterosexual relationships, whilst seeking the most responsible model of sexual relating in which friendship can flourish. Here marriage is again simply assumed to be in essence a heterosexual relationship and one, indeed, that gay people should not want to imitate because its patriarchal structures work to discourage real friendship between the couple.

John J. McNeill

The Roman Catholic gay theologian John J. McNeill offers a more nuanced approach to the whole subject. In his earliest work, which was apologetic in character, McNeill followed the line of argument in many early works of gay Christian apology in arguing that the church should support and bless monogamous gay relationships as a means of discouraging promiscuity and providing a space for God's grace to transform love into ever less selfish forms.[14] In a later work, *Taking a Chance on God,* which is much more liberationist in its approach, McNeill, whilst recognising that many gay people choose other models of relating, argues that to be human is to need what Genesis 2:18 calls a 'helpmate'. In other words, committed monogamous relationships provide the ideal context in which human beings can grow into emotional maturity. This, he asserts, is not about imitating heterosexual relationships. AIDS brought gay love 'out of the closet', making gay and lesbian couples much more visible and undermining the homophobic myths of promiscuity and selfishness. For McNeill in this book, the relationship portrayed in the Song of Songs provides the biblical model for sexual relationships, playful but committed, and in both aspects mediating a mystical experience of the divine. Since there is nothing here that cannot be present in lesbian and gay relationships, 'there is no reason why their sexual unions should not be as accepted, respected, and valued by the church and by society'.[15]

---

[14] John J. McNeill, *The Church and the Homosexual* (3rd edn; Boston: Beacon Press, 1988), pp. 183–4. See also Norman Pittenger, *A Time for Consent: A Christian's Approach to Homosexuality* (London: SCM Press, 1976), p. 78.

[15] John J. McNeill, *Taking a Chance on God: Liberating Theology for Gays, Lesbians, and Their Lovers, Families, and Friends* (Boston: Beacon Press, 1988), pp. 135–6.

In his latest work of theology McNeill devotes a chapter to
'covenanted unions'. He dislikes the term 'marriage' because it
is 'derived from a French root referring to husband' and he
dislikes the term 'union' on its own because it can suggest the
kind of fusion in which people lose their own identity. The
term 'covenanted union', on the other hand, 'encourages us to
see a give-and-receive relationship that seeks, with the help of
God, the fulfilment of two individuals'.[16] McNeill's implicit
argument is that marriage is simply a label that has been given
to heterosexual unions but in fact the underlying relationship
is the same as a gay covenanted union. Gay as well as straight
relationships, he argues, fulfil the divine purpose of companionship set out in Genesis 2:18. Since the papal encyclical *Casti
connubii* (1930) recognised mutual love as the primary purpose
of marriage, the status of homosexual relationships in the eyes
of the church should have changed (in theory if not in
practice). McNeill draws on the work of the gay historian John
Boswell to argue that, in requesting a rite to recognise a
covenantal union, gay Christians are 'only reclaiming what is an
ancient tradition in the Church'.[17] So McNeill does what
Boswell is actually careful not to do and assumes that the liturgical ceremonies for spiritual brotherhood that Boswell
uncovered in the tradition are 'holy unions or marriages for gay
persons'.[18] The need for a contemporary public rite, McNeill
argues, is a need for affirmation of God's grace and celebration
by the whole community of which a couple are part. McNeill
appears to be suggesting that covenanted gay unions are
marriages, in that what have been called marriages are in fact
covenanted unions, although he never makes this claim
explicit. His understanding of what marriage consists of is
essentially companionship in which the couple grow together
and towards God.

[16] John J. McNeill, *Freedom, Glorious Freedom: The Spiritual Journey to the Fullness
of Life for Gays, Lesbians, and Everyone Else* (Boston: Beacon Press, 1995), p. 84.
   [17] McNeill, *Freedom*, p. 86.
   [18] McNeill, *Freedom*, p. 86. See also John Boswell, *The Marriage of Likeness:
Same-Sex Unions in Premodern Europe* (London: HarperCollins, 1995).

Jeffrey John

The notion of gay relationship as covenanted union is found
elsewhere in gay theology. The British Anglican theologian
Jeffrey John, in a largely apologetic work devoted entirely to the
issue of the theological status of lesbian and gay relationships,
has a different argument to McNeill's. He seeks to persuade his
readers that, while heterosexual marriage may be the ideal,
there is an equivalence of status between such a marriage and
permanent, faithful and stable gay relationships. This is
because these relationships constitute the ideal form of
relationship for those for whom heterosexual marriage is not
an option. John suggests that, morally speaking, same-sex
partnerships are on a par with infertile heterosexual marriages.

John takes his definition of marriage from the *Alternative
Service Book* of the Church of England, arguing that gay and
lesbian couples can fulfil all the purposes of marriage outlined
there with the exception of childbirth. This cannot be why in
the first edition of his book he resists applying the term
'marriage' to gay relationships, because he applies it to infertile
heterosexual couples. He states that 'at the physical level at
least, it [a gay relationship] is clearly not the same thing [as a
marriage]'.[19] But he never explains what he means by this.
Lesbian and gay relationships fulfil all but one of the purposes
of marriage but for some unclear reason they are not
marriages, even though they have the moral equivalence of a
gay marriage. What same-sex relationships are, according to
John, are *covenants*, a reflection of a faithful covenanting God,
and that is why 'our sexuality is meant to express faithful,
covenanted commitment to one partner'.[20]

Monogamy is the key for John and therein lies the equiva-
lency to marriage. He vigorously rejects the friendship model of
lesbian and gay relationships because 'friendship and a
relationship of sexual commitment are qualitatively different.
One may have many friends; one may not, within any moral
framework which remotely links with Christian teaching, have

[19] Jeffrey John, *'Permanent, Faithful, Stable': Christian Same-Sex Partnerships*
(London: Affirming Catholicism, 1993), p. 18.
[20] John, *'Permanent, Faithful, Stable'* (1993), p. 18.

many sexual partners.'[21] In the second edition of his work (2000) John retitles 'Friendship or Covenant?', the section in which he discusses the friendship model, as 'Friendship or Monogamy?' and the covenant model is mentioned only intermittently. This section now becomes an extended critique of the friendship model advocated by Michael Vasey and Elizabeth Stuart.[22] John believes that heterosexual marriage embodies the distinctively Christian understanding of sex and therefore must provide the moral structure for same-sex relationships. Friendship is an inadequate model. John advocates the liturgical blessing of such relationships as long as the vows taken are promises of permanence and faithfulness. He argues that such a recognition 'does not overturn the institution of marriage and the family, it affirms and extends it'.[23] Indeed, John now no longer draws a sharp distinction between same-sex relationships and marriage. In fact he seems to be arguing for the inclusion of lesbian and gay people in marriage, on the grounds that

> the Church understands marriage as a covenant within which two people are called to find their truest selves by giving themselves always in love to one another. It is a 'mystery' or sacrament of God because it potentially reflects the mystery of self-giving love, which is at the heart of the Trinity, the dynamic, creative interchange of love which binds persons in one, yet such that they become more fully themselves. At the same time, the couple are a cell in the Body of Christ, the Church ... both marriage and the Church are God-given training-grounds for learning Trinitarian love. Both can 'work' equally for homosexual people – if they are allowed in – because homosexual people are no less made in God's image than heterosexuals and no less capable of loving in his image.[24]

John seems to have ultimately concluded that it is because monogamous same-sex partnerships are covenanted unions

---

[21] John, *'Permanent, Faithful, Stable'* (1993), p. 18.
[22] Jeffrey John, *'Permanent, Faithful, Stable': Christian Same-Sex Partnerships* (2nd edn; London: Darton, Longman & Todd, 2000), pp. 31–8.
[23] John, *'Permanent, Faithful, Stable'* (2000), p. 51.
[24] John, *'Permanent, Faithful, Stable'* (2000), pp. 52–3.

that they are not just equivalent to, but are in fact marriages. He never states this explicitly, but he seems to have ended up in much the same position as McNeill.

Chris Glaser

Chris Glaser employs the covenant model to different effect. He too argues that it is on the covenant between God and his people that sexual relationships must be modelled and since relationships are in fact covenants (i.e., mutually agreed sets of promises) which must of necessity allow for a certain degree of creativity, it is the content of the covenant rather than the form that should be of moral concern. The contemporary heterosexual practice of writing one's own wedding vows is testimony to the plastic nature of a covenant.[25] God's covenant with us reveals four key elements to the content of a covenant – steadfast love, faithful love, sacrificial forgiveness and unconditional love. Steadfast love is love which persists through change and which is always available though not demanding or smothering. This love leads to faithful love, faithfulness to *the covenant*. Defining faithfulness as covenant faithfulness allows, Glaser argues, for the possibility of faithful non-monogamous relationships. Covenants must be sustained by a willingness to be sacrificially forgiving and unconditionally loving. Glaser suggests that heterosexual marriages and same-sex partnerships are the same thing – covenanted unions – and that it is gay people who have perhaps understood the nature of a covenant as a negotiated relationship, where content influences form. In other words, the couple must work out which kind of relationships will enable steadfast love, faithfulness, forgiveness and unconditional love to grow between them. Just as the covenant between God and Israel was reinterpreted in Jesus Christ so covenants can be renegotiated.[26]

---

[25] Chris Glaser, *Come Home! Reclaiming Spirituality and Community as Gay Men and Lesbians* (San Francisco: Harper & Row, 1990), pp. 100–3.

[26] A similar approach is adopted by Larry Uhrig who argues that what is needed is a new understanding of marriage which resists traditional gender roles. He does not use the term 'marriage' for covenanted lesbian and gay relationships, however, employing the term 'Holy Union' instead. See Larry J.

McNeill, John and Glaser all seem ultimately to agree that same-sex relationships are marriages, in that they are covenanted unions, although all three are remarkably reluctant to state this explicitly. For McNeill and John the covenant lies in monogamy, for Glaser it lies in the certain qualities of love. Although this approach is more theological, in that there is an explicit attempt to ground models of relating in scripture and tradition, the focus continues to be largely ethical. And the fact that there is an evasiveness around identifying gay relationships with marriage suggests an uncomfortableness with 'going that far', a residual belief that marriage is in some sense a hetero-sexual relationship. There may also, of course, be a pragmatic political dimension to this evasiveness in reaction to the hostility that the term 'gay marriage' evokes in many Christian and non-Christian circles.

Robert Goss

Robert Goss has written perhaps the most explicitly libera-tionist work on lesbian and gay theology.[27] His theological reflection is deeply rooted in reflection upon the transgressive politics of lesbian and gay communities in the United States of the early 1990s. It is firmly anti-assimilationist and resistant to compulsory heterosexuality. It is inclusive (at least in theory) of all those marginalised on grounds of sexuality, not just gay and lesbian persons – Goss uses the word 'queer' to represent this wider group. Goss attempts to rescue from the Christian tradition the dangerous memory of Jesus as the practitioner of God's reign in a specific historical context which, at the resur-rection, is universalised and eternalised:

> Jesus' *basileia* message and praxis signified the political trans-formation of his society into a radically egalitarian, new age, where sexual, social, religious, and political distinctions would be irrelevant. Jesus struggled for *basileia* liberation in

---

Uhrig, *The Two of Us: Affirming, Celebrating and Symbolising Gay and Lesbian Relationships* (Boston: Alyson Publications, 1984) and *Sex Positive: A Gay Contribution to Sexual and Spiritual Union* (Boston: Alyson Publications, 1986).

[27] Robert Goss, *Jesus Acted Up: A Gay and Lesbian Manifesto* (San Francisco: Harper, 1993).

his siding with the humiliated, the oppressed, and the throw away people of first-century Jewish society.[28]

At Easter this Jesus entered into solidarity with the oppressed and marginalised in every age and context, practising his transgressive *basileia* action among them. So in contexts of homophobia and heterosexism Christ becomes the 'queer Christ' and Christians are called to incarnate such solidarity. Queer Christians in our age, faced with a refusal by most Christian communities to disentangle themselves from homophobia and heterosexism, are called to embody *basileia* in queer base communities – local communities of resistance. This involves, among other things, sacramentalising, that is, performing symbolic representations of the *basileia* that incarnate it. It is important that queer Christians sacramentalise because 'ecclesial sacraments have been used to demand obedience, sanction a hierarchical deployment of misogynistic/homophobic power, and punish infractions'.[29] Queer sacramentalising of experience resists such exclusion and turns queer experience into a performance of God's reign. The blessing of same-sex unions is such a practice within an ecclesial and societal context which steadfastly refuses to separate procreation from sexuality. Same-sex unions testify to a fecundity that is not narrowly procreative and a gratuitous celebration of love that symbolises God's grace in a particularly powerful manner. They often incarnate the *basileia* values of equality and mutuality more effectively than heterosexual unions and as such form a 'prophetic model of relating for the Christian community'.[30] The blessing of such unions recognises them as *basileia* practice. Whether Goss regards these relationships as marriages is completely unclear. At the outset of the discussion he speaks of 'gay/lesbian marriage, domestic partnerships, or unions',[31] describes marriage as being 'so narrowly construed as to exclude gay/lesbian relationships'[32] and takes time to demonstrate the life-giving nature of gay and

[28] Goss, *Jesus Acted Up*, p. 73.
[29] Goss, *Jesus Acted Up*, p. 127.
[30] Goss, *Jesus Acted Up*, p. 138.
[31] Goss, *Jesus Acted Up*, p. 136.
[32] Goss, *Jesus Acted Up*, p. 136.

lesbian relationships. But Goss does not examine the theological nature of same-sex unions at all, with the result that exactly how they constitute *basileia* practice remains ultimately unclear. Is it because they extend and remodel marriage or because they offer an alternative way of relating altogether?

In a later volume Goss describes how, when he himself formed a same-sex partnership, he and his lover rejected the model of heterosexual marriage on the grounds that it was 'too patriarchal an institution, based on archaic, economic, and oppressive notions of sex property. We felt that marriage was too dysfunctional a model, patterned after rigid heterosexual stereotypes and unequal power relations.'[33] Searching round for an alternative model, and since they had both come from the Society of Jesus, they adapted the Jesuit model 'of friendship, service, and community to comprehend our sexual relationship. We described our sacramental partnership and friendship as a "community of two".'[34]

Michael Vasey

The British evangelical gay theologian Michael Vasey argued that, whilst it is understandable in the absence of other social scripts that gay people should look to marriage as a pattern for their relationships, 'it also marks the extent to which modern culture has abandoned the ancient idea of society as a network of friendships, held together by bonds of affection'.[35] Vasey's whole approach to the issue of sexuality is a historical, social constructionist one. He argues that the tendency of contemporary church and state to structure themselves around marriage shows their compromise with modernity rather than being a biblical witness. While modern society structures itself around competition between nuclear families, pre-modern

---

[33] Robert E. Goss, 'Queering Procreative Privilege: Coming Out as Families', in Robert E. Goss and Amy Adams Squire Strongheart (eds.), *Our Families, Our Values: Snapshots of Queer Kinship* (Binghamton: The Harrington Park Press, 1997), p. 5.

[34] Goss, 'Queering Procreative Privilege', p. 6.

[35] Michael Vasey, *Strangers and Friends: A New Exploration of Homosexuality and the Bible* (London: Hodder & Stoughton, 1995), p. 233.

Christian society understood friendship to be the basis of human society. Which is why both Augustine and Aquinas value marriage as a particular form of friendship. The scriptures do not limit the concept of covenant to marriage but also apply it to the political order and to same-sex friendship. The love of friends is shown again and again to create bonds of kinship, as it did between David and Jonathan, Ruth and Naomi, and Mary and the Beloved Disciple. This was worked out most obviously in Christian history in monastic communities and is probably the context in which to understand the rites uncovered by Boswell.[36] For Vasey, then, marriage is a particular manifestation of friendship which has the particular task of bearing children; lesbian and gay relationships are not marriages but they share a covenantal nature. They are different manifestations of the friendship that is essential to the Christian vision of society and which has been obscured by modernity. For Vasey gay relationships are, in Goss's terms, *basileia* practices, because they constitute a reminder that society should be based upon friendship, not competition, and that there are other ways of scripting gender than the ones required for industrial Western society.

Of course this approach is open to criticism. The difference that sex makes to a friendship is not explored in these theologies of friendship (and all the models held up by Goss and Vasey are non-sexual relationships). It is clear that in terms of marriage the difference is procreation but the difference for lesbian and gay relationship is never addressed. John's claim that a friendship model of relating inevitably leads to promiscuity[37] is, I think, unjustified, but he is right to question the nature of sexual friendships and how they fit (if at all) into the symbolics of Christian doctrine. This is something that neither Vasey nor Goss addresses.

---

[36] Boswell, *The Marriage of Likeness.*

[37] So that he even dares to connect Vasey's death in 1998 with his theology (John, *'Permanent, Faithful, Stable'* (2000), p. 38). In fact Vasey did not die of AIDS. He had a heart attack but was found to be HIV positive after his death.

Robert Williams

There is one gay male theologian who has argued explicitly for the nuptial nature of lesbian and gay relationships and that is the late Robert Williams. Williams, writing from an Episcopalian perspective, challenged the argument used on all sides that marriage is by definition a transaction between a man and a woman. This argument, to Williams, 'sounds suspiciously like one of the objections we heard to the ordination of women: that a woman cannot be ordained because ordination is, by definition, something that is conferred on a man'.[38] Nor is he in favour of an equal-but-different kind of approach, arguing that the 'something else' that lesbian and gay relationships would be designated as would always be regarded as something less than marriage. Taking the definition of marriage from the canons of the Episcopal Church in their 1988 version, Williams argues that same-sex relationships fulfil all elements – companionship, mutuality and the desire for a lifelong union. Some also seek to be or already are parents, but, just as the Episcopal Church will marry heterosexual couples who never intend to have children (and alter the liturgy accordingly), the non-procreative nature of lesbian and gay relationships cannot be held up as an obstacle to the recognition of their relationships as marriages.

Williams goes on to construct a theology of marriage rooted in the concepts of companionship and mutuality. He argues that what the issue of lesbian and gay relationships has exposed is the lack of a theology of marriage in the Anglican Church; the church has been content to bless a fundamentally legal contract. He argues that marriage must be regarded as a sacrament with three dimensions. First, marriage is a sacrament of redemption in which our alienated and estranged condition is embraced by a loving relationship which causes love to grow and overflow – it thus mirrors and incarnates the process of redemption. Second, marriage is a sacrament of justice in

---

[38] Robert Williams, 'Toward a Theology of Lesbian and Gay Marriage', in Adrian Thatcher and Elizabeth Stuart (eds.), *Christian Perspectives on Sexuality and Gender* (Leominster and Grand Rapids: Gracewing and Wm B. Eerdmans, 1996), p. 281.

which mutuality between two people grows and flourishes. The biblical witnesses to covenanted relationships of mutuality are same-sex relationships, David and Jonathan, Ruth and Naomi. Williams understands marriage to be a covenant which, unlike a contract, is not dependent upon one party fulfilling their obligations. People place themselves under obligations from which they are not released if the partner does not fulfil theirs. Third, marriage is a sacrament of incarnation. It is a bodily union which bespeaks our 'intense and inevitably frustrated desire to transcend the boundaries of our skin and be truly at one with another person'.[39] This is itself a manifestation of our desire for union with God. Sexual passion and orgasm enable us to 'occasionally catch glimpses of the eschatological promise of such union'.[40] There is precedent, Williams argues, for the church to bless marriages that the state will not recognise. The early church recognised relationships between free citizens and slaves, and, more recently, American Anglican clergy often officiated at the marriage of slaves.

Williams has presented a clear and theologically (rather than ethically) grounded argument for same-sex marriage. Why then, we may ask, has it by and large failed to convince other lesbian and gay theologians? Since it is church officials who control access to the sacraments, Williams' argument may not engage lesbian and gay theologies because they are not the ones with the power to change things. The answer may also lie in reality, in the divorce statistics, in the fact that marriage is not living up to its own publicity. And, returning to Cotter's point, it is hard to persuade people that an institution which has been used to exclude and marginalise them is in fact theirs for the taking and the royal road to the divine. This is particularly evident in lesbian theology.

Lesbian Theology

Lesbian theology has tended to be constructed by women strongly influenced by North American and British feminism.

---

[39] Williams, 'Toward a Theology of Lesbian and Gay Marriage', p. 297.
[40] Williams, 'Toward a Theology of Lesbian and Gay Marriage', p. 297.

Feminism has long maintained that, if patriarchy is the theory, marriage is the practice, which is to say that the theo-social construction of marriage has often served as the principal means by which unequal power relations between men and women have been enforced and preserved. It would be fair to say then that there has not been much enthusiasm for constructing lesbian relationships as marriages among lesbian theologians.

Carter Heyward

Carter Heyward has been the most influential lesbian feminist theologian, to the point that her identification of the divine with the erotic – a deep body knowledge and power that propels people towards a sense of self-worth and mutuality in relation with others – and her understanding of Christian living as a living out of this radically immanent relational power have achieved the status of an unquestioned orthodoxy in lesbian (and, indeed, in much gay) theology.

Heyward does not address the issue of marriage as such; her concern is with monogamy. She argues that, because we value the erotic as sacred power, we may choose to reserve expression of it to one person but, because we value it as sacred power, we may wish not to withhold it from the friends with whom we are 'most mutually involved'.[41] Such sexual friendships are moral if they are examples of right relation, that is, if they incarnate the power of the erotic by being mutual, reciprocal and are conducted in a context of fidelity. Fidelity is 'a matter of making a commitment to love, rather than simply drifting into "love" or being run over by it'.[42]

> Fidelity to our primary relational commitments does not require monogamy. But learning to value sexual pleasure as a moral good requires that we be faithful to our commitments. This is always an obligation that involves a willingness

---

[41] Carter Heyward, *Touching our Strength; The Erotic as Power and the Love of God* (San Francisco: Harper & Row, 1989), p. 121.

[42] Carter Heyward, *Our Passion for Justice: Images of Power, Sexuality, and Liberation* (New York: Pilgrim Press, 1984), p. 184.

to work with our sexual partner, or partners, in creating mutual senses of assurance that our relationships are being cared for. Thus we are obligated to be honest – real – with each other and to honour rather than abuse each other's feelings.[43]

Whilst monogamy can be 'a resource of remarkable relational empowerment' if it is an unexamined commitment, it can 'become a canopy for unspoken hurt, lies, and, in time, the dissolution of friendship'.[44] For Heyward friendship is a synonym for right, mutual relationship:

> This is because, for many women, friendship is the most exact experience we have of mutual relationship. For many of us, heterosexual as well as lesbian, our friendships with women, whether lovers or not, are more genuinely erotic than our marriages or relationships with male lovers.[45]

This is a view echoed by Mary Hunt who is deeply suspicious of the arguments for gay marriage, regarding it as a way of simply 'detouring' the trend towards individualism rather than 'rerouting' society towards community.[46]

Elizabeth Stuart

Elizabeth Stuart is also deeply suspicious of what she terms the idolatry of marriage in the Christian community. The uncritical worship of marriage serves to obscure its changing history, its patriarchal construction, the problem of domestic violence, its part in bolstering capitalism, and other possible models of relating.[47] Like Vasey, Stuart believes that the pre-modern Christian tradition presents friendship as the relational ideal, but also that that relational ideal is always embodied in scripture in same-sex covenants. To say that these friendships

---

[43] Heyward, *Touching our Strength*, p. 137.

[44] Heyward, *Touching our Strength*, p. 136.

[45] Heyward, *Touching our Strength*, p. 188.

[46] Mary E. Hunt, 'Variety is the Spice of Life: Doing it Our Ways', in Goss and Strongheart (eds.), *Our Families, Our Values*, p. 100.

[47] Elizabeth Stuart, *Just Good Friends: Towards a Theology of Lesbian and Gay Relationships* (London: Mowbray, 1995).

are not sexual and therefore cannot be used as a model of sexual relating (as John does) is, she argues, to buy into far too narrow an understanding of what counts as sexual. Stuart prefers the term 'passion' to 'the erotic', on the grounds that it more easily avoids an easy reduction to genital activity, contains within it notions of tragedy and pain, and has a history of being attached to types of friendship. She argues that passion is the motor of all right relationships and so clear boundaries cannot be drawn between sexual and non-sexual relationships.

Stuart also considers the issue of non-monogamy but she is more circumspect than Heyward.[48] She argues that, on the one hand, being able to love without boundaries could be regarded as an experience of realised eschatology, a place beyond marriage and family in which love is released from all limitation.[49] On the other hand, however, Stuart is sceptical whether it is possible to attain the passionate radical vulner-ability of friendship with more than one person at a time, in a context of finitude and structures that encourage us to objectify and abuse each other.[50] It is of course possible to have sex without passionate radical vulnerability, but it is for such a relationship that people long. Because we need time to unlearn all our inherited patterns of relating, it is important to mark out the space of such a relationship through a covenant commitment.

Stuart fiercely resists the labelling of these relationships as anything other than friendship. She rejects taking them out of the nexus of friendship and making them essentially different from other forms of relating. They are an intensive form of friendship, an ideal form of friendship, and the kind of loving we long for with everyone but which will not be possible this side of the rainbow. The same standards of faithfulness, justice and care are required in all our relationships. Marriage, she suggests, should be redefined as 'a relationship in which two

---

[48] And certainly more circumspect than Jeffrey John suggests. See John, *'Permanent, Faithful, Stable'* (2000), pp. 31–8.

[49] Stuart, *Just Good Friends*, pp. 190–1. See also Elizabeth Stuart, 'Sex in Heaven: The Queering of Theological Discourse on Sexuality', in Jon Davies and Gerard Loughlin (eds.), *Sex These Days: Essays on Theology, Sexuality and Society* (Sheffield: Sheffield Academic Press, 1997), pp. 184–204.

[50] Stuart, *Just Good Friends*, pp. 220–1.

friends of the opposite sex enter into a covenant of passionate radical vulnerability'.[51] Stuart accepts that Williams and non-gay theologians such as Adrian Thatcher have proved their case that gay and lesbian marriage is not an oxymoron; what she rejects is that marriage is the Christian ideal to which lesbian and gay people should aspire. Rather, it is friendship which as a model encompasses sexual and non-sexual relationships, whether gay, straight or celibate, in the same project of the building up of a new type of kindom.

There are obvious problems with a theology of friendship. The category is too vast and often stretched so far as to become meaningless. None of the advocates of a theology of friendship draws clear enough distinctions between sexual friendships and other types of friendships, and when (like Stuart) they do, they tend to suggest that some relationships are actually more than friendships. Advocates of theologies of friendship (with the exception of Stuart) tend to posit marriage as an essentially heterosexual relationship and one which, as it is constructed, is deeply antithetical to the Christian feminist virtues of mutuality, equality, justice and community building.

Virginia Ramey Mollenkott

A contrasting approach is taken by the evangelical lesbian theologian Virginia Ramey Mollenkott. She never explicitly identifies lesbian and gay relationships as marriages but working from scripture argues that the biblical model of sexual relationships is a covenantal one which manifests the qualities of one-fleshedness, namely, justice and caring. She too quotes MacMurray's definition of chastity in this context. She goes on to argue that, since 'marriage was not formalised by either church or state in the biblical culture; so the current Christian insistence on marriage is an unbiblical insistence'.[52] However, the biblical ideal is for a lifelong monogamous relationship in which one-fleshedness of the partners is achieved through mutuality and reciprocity (and procreation is decentred).

[51] Stuart, *Just Good Friends*, p. 234.
[52] Virginia Ramey Mollenkott, *Sensuous Spirituality: Out from Fundamentalism* (Crossroad: New York, 1993), p. 115.

Lesbian and gay people are more than capable of embodying this ideal. Indeed those who seek to force celibacy upon them stand under the judgement of heresy, according to 1 Timothy 4:1–4, and deny them God's creation gift to humanity – the gift of companionship.

The only lesbian theologian prepared to argue explicitly for same-sex marriage that I have come across is Amy Adams Squire Strongheart. Taking as her starting point Jesus' intellectual tussle with the Sadducees about marriage, she concludes that marriage is a temporal social construct of not ultimate significance and is therefore transformable.[53] She defines marriage as 'a covenant of love between two consenting adults who must be committed to the covenant as they are to each other, and they must live out their covenant on a daily basis'.[54] And that is the depth and scope of her argument.

Lesbian and Gay Theology: Conclusions

This survey of lesbian and gay theology demonstrates two things: that marriage is not generally a dominating issue for lesbian and gay theologians, but where it is discussed in one way or another there is always something rather unsatisfactory in the approach. I want to suggest that this inadequacy stems from the theological methodology behind lesbian and gay theology. Lesbian and gay theology is fundamentally liberal and/or liberationist in its character and in its assumptions. Whilst liberal theology is effective in demythologising and deconstructing dominant theologies, it tends to do so on the basis of an uncritical adoption of modernist assumptions, including a shallow and one-dimensional modernist reading of scripture and tradition. Lesbian and gay theology has been extremely effective in highlighting the problematic dimensions of dominant 'theologies' of marriage. It has in fact forced some hard thinking on the topic from non-gay theologians. It has been far less successful at proposing a convincing alternative.

---

[53] Amy Adams Squire Strongheart, 'The Power to Choose: We're Here, We're Queer, and We Want to Get Hitched', in Goss and Strongheart (eds.), *Our Families, Our Values*, pp. 82–3.
[54] Strongheart, 'The Power to Choose', p. 83.

The reduction of theology to a system of ethics detached from any cosmology or dogmatic foundation is a characteristic of much liberal theology and renders the Christian voice indistinctive and purely reactive. The liberationist emphasis on experience is problematic in many ways, especially for lesbian and gay theology. Liberal and liberationist lesbian and gay theologians, and pro-gay heterosexual theologians, share the assumption that homosexuality and heterosexuality really exist, that they are truth, that they are matters of ultimate concern and are therefore strong enough concepts to bear the weight of theological reflection. This modern assumption is becoming increasingly difficult to maintain and its passing takes away the foundation of lesbian and gay theology and the basis of a great deal of other theological reflection upon marriage.

The Challenge of Queer Theory

Queer theory is chiefly associated with Michel Foucault and the development of his ideas by Judith Butler.[55] Foucault questioned some of the central notions upon which post-Enlightenment theory and theology of sexuality have been based. The most important is the notion of a fixed, essential identity, sexual or otherwise. Foucault argues for the social construction of sexual identity through discourse and constant redefinition. The second notion is the idea that power is something held by dominant groups and used against others with less power, for example, women, gay people, the poor, etc. Foucault argued that power was fluid and present in all parts of society and could be deployed by any group. Where power was exercised there was always resistance to it, which itself was a kind of power.

These ideas are developed by Judith Butler. She argues that feminism has made a fundamental error in continuing to assume that there is an identity of 'woman' somehow bound up with the female body which is stable enough to make some (though perhaps not many) generalisations about. This is a

---

[55] Michel Foucault, *The History of Sexuality*, Vol. 1: *An Introduction* (New York: Random House, 1978); Judith Butler, *Gender Trouble: Feminism and the Subversion of Identity* (London and New York: Routledge, 1990).

paradoxical position for most feminists to take, considering their antipathy to the 'biology is destiny' approach to gender. Butler seeks to question the 'natural' connection between sex, gender and desire, arguing that gender and desire are unstable. Indeed, she famously asserts that gender is not expressive of some inner nature but is instead performative. We learn to become a woman or a man by following the gender scripts that our culture hands out to us and each performance reinscribes that gender upon our bodies. It is only when some people throw away the scripts or perform them badly or subversively that the non-natural nature of gender is revealed.

Butler argued that the parodic performance of gender by drag queens or butch and femme lesbians most clearly demonstrated and disrupted the connection between sex, gender and performance. She called for a resistance to the gender scripts that are handed out to us and for a proliferation of subversive performances of gender. But she also noted the difficulty of resisting such scripts because no one stands completely outside of them. This is then the 'essence' of queer theory, that there is no essential sexuality or gender. 'Queer' then is not actually another identity alongside 'lesbian' and 'gay' (although it is sometimes confusingly used to convey a radical coalition of lesbian, gay, bisexual and transgendered persons[56]). It is a radical destabilising of identities and resistance to the naturalising of any identity.

Queer theology then is properly identified as that theology which has a Foucauldian and Butlerian understanding of the free-floating relation between sex, gender and desire, and which seeks to reflect theologically from that perspective. It need not be done by lesbian or gay people nor be purely concerned with issues of sexuality and gender. Queer theology is in its infancy but already it has produced work which demonstrates a radically different approach to the whole issue of marriage.

---

[56] This is certainly how Goss uses it in his work and how it is used in Elizabeth Stuart with Andy Braunston, Malcolm Edwards, John McMahon, Tim Morrison, *Religion is a Queer Thing: A Guide to the Christian Faith for Lesbian, Gay, Bisexual and Transgendered People* (London and Herndon, VA: Cassell, 1997).

Kathy Rudy

Kathy Rudy draws upon queer theory to argue that for Christians the only stable identity is that of a member of the people of God, the church, conveyed by baptism and constituted by God's self.[57] No identity should take precedence over Christian identity. Within the church then, gender cannot be a determining factor in assessing what kind of sex constitutes moral sex. Baptism and not biology is the means by which one becomes Christian. In Christ there is 'no male or female': gender is radically decentralised.

In order to establish what a degendered notion of moral sex might look like Rudy turns to the Christian tradition and the persistent understanding that sex must be unitive and procreative. In insisting that sexual activity must be unitive the church requires that it involve the blurring and transcending of the boundaries of the self, which is what all Christians are called to accomplish in the body of Christ. Indeed, sexual love is part of the process of building up the communion of the church. The procreative principle sought to ensure the unitive dimension by making every act of sexual love open to the generation of a new member of the church. In recent years, however, there has been a move even among Roman Catholic moral theologians to argue that procreation need not necessarily be completely identified with reproduction. This is evident in the shift towards the theory of complementarity among both Protestant and Roman Catholic theologians. The theory of complementarity, however, is thoroughly gendered and lacks an ecclesial dimension. It also marginalises the celibate and single along with those involved in lesbian and gay relationships. Rudy is equally critical of her fellow lesbian theologians who advocate mutuality as the criterion for moral sex. Rudy finds such an approach unrealistic: power is an element in all relationships and sometimes a positive one, and none of us is free from inculturation. There is no 'pure' form of sex completely free from any kind of influence.

Rudy seeks to reconfigure the procreative principle around

---

[57] Kathy Rudy, *Sex and the Church: Gender, Homosexuality, and the Transformation of Christian Ethics* (Boston: Beacon Press, 1997).

the biblical notion of hospitality. Sexual activity must be hospitable, both in terms of opening ourselves to another and in terms of that relationship helping us to open our lives to the stranger among us. All Christians are called to be hospitable in every aspect of their lives because the body of Christ is a hospitable body. Moral sex is then unitive and hospitable, building up the body of Christ by breaking the boundaries of the self and propelling us towards the stranger. It has nothing to do with gender. Rudy is insistent that for Christians the church is their primary community. Indeed the church makes marriage unnecessary for no one is single in the church: all belong to each other. This is why the early church was able to make the radical claim that the celibate state was at least as honourable as the married one. Through baptism Christians are incorporated into a new family which fulfils the companionate dimension of human nature. Sexual relationships then are moral when they build up the Christian community by creating community through unitivity and hospitality.

Elizabeth Stuart

In her most recent work Elizabeth Stuart has moved from a lesbian to a queer theological perspective.[58] Like Rudy she argues that baptism relativises all other identities. Drawing upon Butler's notion of parody, defining it as repetition with critical difference, Stuart argues that the parodic performance of gender is an essential element of Christian discipleship precisely because gender is destabilised by baptism and decentralised in Christian morality. The performance of maleness and femaleness by the baptised must be strange (and has often been in the Christian tradition) because it must constitute a cultural critique of gender. Also like Rudy, Stuart seeks to ground a Christian sexual morality in ecclesiology, arguing that chaste relationships in the body of Christ should bear the four marks of the church. They should be *one* in the sense of being unitive; they should be *holy* in that they should manifest the

---

[58] Elizabeth Stuart, 'Sexuality: The View from the Font (the Body and the Ecclesial Self)', *Theology and Sexuality*, 11 (1999), pp. 7–18.

divine reality of sheer grace and excessive giving that creates the possibility of mutuality and reciprocity, rather than mere exchange; they should be *catholic* in that they must be caught up in the project of the whole church; and they are *apostolic* in that they are not private affairs but are conducted within a community that understands itself as being under the authority of a tradition and in constant danger of betraying it. Due humility is therefore required in assessing the morality of any relationship. Neither Rudy nor Stuart addresses the issue of marriage head-on but it is evident that neither of them can regard marriage as a heterosexual relationship since, by queer definition, heterosexuality does not exist. They would seem to be arguing that moral, that is, ecclesially focused, sexual relationships that build up the body of Christ are what marriage is about.

Eugene Rogers

Eugene Rogers does address the marriage issue from a queer perspective. Rogers argues that marriage mirrors God's act in choosing humanity as his own. He notes that the covenant that God makes with Israel and with the church is non-biological in emphasis. In the case of the church it is represented by Paul as an act 'against nature' (Rom. 11:24), exactly the same phrase that he applies to same-sex relations in Romans 1, in the grafting of the Gentiles on to the olive tree of salvation.[59] God's choosing, then, is one that subverts notions of what is natural, which is perhaps why Paul utilises the language of adoption for salvation as well. What is marriage? For Rogers it is 'a community practice of asceticism for the whole person', 'a communal structure that frees the body to become as a means of sanctification'.[60] It is an ascetic practice by which God takes human desire up into the life of the triune God (which can in itself be understood as a form of marriage) and enables it to mirror at least partially the love between Christ and the church. Monasticism does this as well but in a different manner. Both monasticism and marriage involve

---

[59] Eugene F. Rogers, *Sexuality and the Christian Body: Their Way into the Triune God* (Oxford and Malden, MA: Blackwell, 1999), p. 64.

[60] Rogers, *Sexuality and the Christian Body*, pp. 70–1.

living with others over an extended period of time and being
transformed by them; both involve centring the body in the
process of sanctification; and both result in a hospitality towards
the stranger. In marriage this is often manifest in the welcoming
of a child (but can take other forms) and in monasticism it is
manifest in direct service to the community. Monasticism is a
direct witness to the fact that all human desire reaches its *telos* in
God. Marriage is an indirect working-out of this truth. So
marriage is not about the satisfaction of sexual desire, as
modernity would have it. It is about self-denial and discipline; it
is a moulding of one's desires and body into the life of God.
Marriage is therefore, in one sense, shorthand for Christian
discipleship. As Rogers notes, 'if marriage is the very form of
Christ's relation to the Father, marriage is the state of every
human being who takes on Christ's identity in baptism',[61] and

> The family resemblance by which same-sex unions deserve to
> be called marriages is the same resemblance by which
> Christians justify calling opposite-sex unions marriages: their
> resemblance to the marriage of Christ and the Church.[62]

It is worth pointing out that this marriage 'queers' gender
beautifully, for Christ's bride is both male and female. Marriage
then is the mirroring of God's election which is, in its turn, a
marriage. The Trinity is a perpetual wedding feast, the love of
the two, witnessed to and supported by the third, together
forming a community of love. To shut people out of marriage
on the grounds of the gender of their partner is not only to miss
the point of baptism. It is also to deprive them of self-denial, of
an ascetic practice in which God transforms them.

Marriage as Queer Practice

We are getting glimpses here from queer theology of what
marriage after homosexuality and heterosexuality might mean;
marriage, as Adrian Thatcher has put it, 'after modernity'.[63] It

---

[61] Rogers, *Sexuality and the Christian Body*, pp. 83–4.
[62] Rogers, *Sexuality and the Christian Body*, p. 211.
[63] Adrian Thatcher, *Marriage after Modernity: Christian Marriage in Postmodern Times* (Sheffield: Sheffield Academic Press, 1999).

is a determinedly unromantic relationship, ecclesial in orientation, ascetic in practice and expectation and one in which gender is destabilised and subverted. Marriage, in other words, as queer practice.

17

Single-Sex Marriage?
A Rite for Blessing Friendship in Traditional Christianity[1]

Alan Bray

John Boswell's final work as a professor of history at Yale provides an inevitable starting point for this chapter. In 1994 his *Same-Sex Unions in Premodern Europe* appeared and was met by a storm of debate and protest in the media and popular press as well as among academics. The controversial thesis of his book was that a ritual traditional among Greek Christians entitled the *adelphopoiesis* – literally a rite for the 'making of brothers' or 'sisters' – had functioned in the past as what in contemporary terms we would today recognise as a homosexual marriage, a thesis that indirectly was addressed to the recognition of homosexual partnerships today.[2] The surprised readers of *The New York Times* awoke to discover that 'Amid the debate about whether Christianity *should* bless unions between homosexuals, Boswell contends that it already has.' John Boswell's book was intended to be provocative and fully succeeded in that, but as reactions cooled two major objections to the way Boswell handled his evidence stood out clearly, both of which are right. One is that the expected ideals of the rite would not have comprehended sexual intercourse. The other is that his thesis disguises the fact that the rite did not preclude

---

[1] This chapter first appeared in *Theology and Sexuality*, 13 (September 2000). Permission to reproduce it here is gratefully acknowledged.

[2] (New York: Villard Books, 1994), subsequently republished as *The Marriage of Likeness: Same-Sex Unions in Premodern Europe* (London: HarperCollins, 1995 and Fontana, 1996).

the individuals involved also being married. Yet the matter will not rest confidently there, for the problem that remains is that an unqualified rejection of John Boswell's thesis in these terms is itself open to the same kind of criticism as the thesis itself. It reduces the range of what we recognise today as being sexual to the narrow question of sexual intercourse and it glosses over the historical disparity that in the past marriage has been one, as it is not in modern society, among several forms of what one might call voluntary kinship: kinship created not by blood but by ritual or a promise. The claim that the relationships blessed by this rite were sexual and akin to marriage *and* the claim that they were not both involve an unsettling degree of anachronism.

This chapter is directed to that problem. It consists of some reflections on the rite that among the inhabitants of the Latin West corresponded to John Boswell's Greek rite, characterised by them in the same language of kinship as in the Greek East but also more simply in that of friendship. In contrast to John Boswell, I have attempted to define how this rite might be understood in historical rather than contemporary terms and then – from that vantage point outside contemporary culture – to consider how that understanding might or might not illuminate the possible liturgical recognition of friendship today.

Since John Boswell published his *Same-Sex Unions in Premodern Europe* two major studies have appeared of the phenomenon that in the Latin West corresponded to his Greek rite. One of these is the symposium edited by the eminent medievalist Elizabeth A. R. Brown in the journal *Traditio* that responded directly to John Boswell's thesis.[3] The other is Pierre Chaplais' *Piers Gaveston: Edward II's Adoptive Brother*,[4] which appeared at the same point as John Boswell's book. While both represent major contributions they are strikingly cursory in their treatment of the specifically theological and liturgical issues raised, and it is to these issues that this chapter is directed.

---

[3] Elizabeth A.R. Brown, 'Ritual Brotherhood in Ancient and Medieval Europe: A Symposium', *Traditio*, 52 (1997), pp. 261–381.

[4] Pierre Chaplais, *Piers Gaveston: Edward II's Adoptive Brother* (Oxford: Clarendon Press, 1994).

Liturgists and Social Historians – A Missing Conversation?

In doing this I hope to direct attention also to a wider issue. It is odd how little historians have used the church's liturgy as a source for social history, tending rather to regard liturgical study as a specialism of ecclesiastical historians. Equally striking perhaps is how reluctant the new 'historicist' literary critics have been to draw on what to many of the inhabitants of the past appear to have been the most contested and symbolically significant literary texts of their age: the public liturgies of the church. The reason I suspect is partly a prejudice derived from systematic theologians, who have tended to regard liturgical study as a second-order activity. It is that prejudice that I suspect has found its way into the robust world of social historians and the new historicist literary critics; and a broader intention in this study is to press the case for the ways that social history and liturgical study can mutually illuminate each other, when brought together in ways that respect the distinctive methodology of each.

The potential for this, I would suggest, lies in grasping the primary theological role that liturgy has played in reconciling what one might call theological with pastoral imperatives. Some centuries further on, those 'pastoral imperatives' may well be the very history the social historian is seeking to recover; but to find the traces left of this history in the liturgies of the past the social historian has to take seriously the other side of the equation also: the theological imperatives that the liturgists of the past were seeking to reconcile and something of the theological algebra in which that reconciliation was expressed. If that is a contribution the study of liturgy could make to social history, in return social history can provide a tool that can map the liturgies of the past in close detail against the pastoral concerns they were designed to meet and in doing so address one of the recurring issues in liturgical study. Liturgists have always been characteristically wary of setting out the outlines of their concerns in a form distinct from the liturgies they have created, and that careful historical mapping of the theological against the pastoral can help towards recovering the unspoken design in their work – the liturgist as protagonist and theologian.

The Form of the Rite

In the discussion below I first assess the evidence for the form of the rite in the Latin West corresponding to the *adelphopoiesis* and then turn to the theology that it appears to represent. The necessary starting point is a difficult passage in Giraldus de Barri's *Topographica Hibernica*. This is not a sober and objective work but a piece of propaganda, intended to justify to its audience in Catholic Europe the invasion of Ireland by the Anglo-Norman army under Henry II in 1171. As evidence for Irish society a work of propaganda such as this is hardly reliable. Its value as historical evidence is rather I would suggest its indirect ability to preserve evidence of the values and prejudices of the *audience* that Giraldus was seeking to manipulate. In the course of this work, Giraldus describes a ritual confirming friendship which its audience could be expected in this way to recognise and value, or, rather, to recognise as here debased by the blood that, according to Giraldus, among the Irish follows its treacherously pious beginning:

> *Inter alia multa artis iniquae figmenta, hoc unum habent tanquam praecipuum argumentum. Sub religionis et pacis obtentu ad sacrum aliquem locum conveniunt, cum eo quem oppetere cupiunt. Primo compaternitatis foedera jungunt: deinde ter circa ecclesiam se invicem portant: postmodum ecclesiam intrantes, coram altari reliquiis sanctorum appositis, sacramentis mulitfarie praestitis, demum missae celebratione, et orationibus sacerdotum, tanquam desponsatione quadam indissolubiliter foederantur. Ad ultimum vero, ad majorem amicitiae confirmationem, et quasi negotii consumationem, sanguinem sponte ad hoc fusum uterque alterius bibit. Hoc autem de ritu gentilium adhuc habent, qui sanguine in firmandis foederibus uti solent. O quoties in ipso desponsationis hujus articulo, a viris sanguinum et dolosis tam dolose et inique funditur sanguis, ut alteruter penitus maneat exsanguis! O quoties eadem hora et incontinenti vel sequitur vel praevenit, vel etiam inaudito more sanguinolentum divortium ipsam interrumpit desponsationem.*

Among the many other deceits of their perverse ways, this one is particularly instructive. Under the appearance of piety and peace, they come together in some holy place with the man with whom they are eager to be united. First they join in covenants of spiritual brotherhood. Then they carry each other three times around the church. Then going into the church, before the altar and in the presence of relics of the saints, many oaths are made. Finally with a celebration of the mass and the prayers of priests they are joined indissolubly as if by a betrothal. But at the end as greater confirmation of their friendship and to conclude the proceedings each drinks the other's blood: this they retain from the custom of the pagans, who use blood in the sealing of oaths. How often, at this very moment of a betrothal, blood is shed by these violent and deceitful men so deceitfully and perversely that one or the other remains drained of blood! How often in that very improper hour does a bloody divorce follow, precede or even in an unheard-of-way interrupt the betrothal.[5]

What Giraldus is doing here I think is this. Giraldus' satire first attributes to this ritual all the proprieties to hand that could confirm the friendship created by ritual kinship; and he does this so comprehensively that each of the forms of ritual kinship that he knew his audience would value find their place. The first is that established by baptism. These vows, he tells his audience, are vows of *compaternitas. Compaternitas* was the spiritual brotherhood established at baptism between, among others, the sponsors of a child and its natural parents, relations which figured more significantly as the specifically social consequences of baptism than any subsequent tie to the child. The second that he invokes is that established by a betrothal. The vows, he goes on to assure his soon to be scandalised audience, are moreover given the force of a *desponsatio*: an agreement to a marriage. In the twelfth century a betrothal – a *desponsatio* – might precede the marriage itself by several years; but when it was solemnised at the church door, where the rite of baptism also began, its binding terms established kinship relations that stood with those created by marriage or a baptism. But in Giraldus' awesome composite there is no baby and no bride, for the third form of ritual kinship implied by Giraldus that leaves

---

[5] Bodleian Library/Laud Manuscripts/720/folio 224v. I have given the collated transcription in J. S. Brewer, James F. Dimock and G. F. Warner (eds.), *Giraldi Cambrensis Opera*, Vol. 5 (Rolls Series; 8 vols., 1861–91; London, 1867), p. 167. Rubric: '*De argumento nequitiae et novo desponsationis genere*'.

its trace in this account is the ritual brotherhood of the kind that
K. B. McFarlane pointed to some years ago: ritual brotherhood
created directly by vows of sworn brotherhood and without the
symbolic instrumentality of the child or the marriage.[6] The heady
mix in Giraldus' description invokes the spiritual kinship of *compaternitas*, the binding force of a betrothal and the liturgical form of
sworn brotherhood – a form whose culmination in this account is
the eucharist.

Giraldus then aims his blow. After a beginning that could not
have confirmed friendship in more solemn terms the pagan
addition proves disastrous. The blood of the pagan rite stimulates the blood-lust of the participants, and the ritual ends not
in friendship but in violence and murder. The drawing at the
opening in the Bodleian manuscript of two men fighting to
the death makes Giraldus' point. But the historical evidence
the passage contains lies not in what he has to say about the
Irish but in the evidence he indirectly preserves of the form of
a ritual that he knew his readers in Catholic Europe would
recognise and value. The force of Giraldus' satire depends on
familiarity with the rituals he is invoking and his audience's
acceptance of their legitimacy. The implication of this passage
from Giraldus' *Topographica Hibernica* is that his readers in Latin
Catholic Europe knew that the ceremony of 'sworn' brotherhood ended with a celebration of the mass, and this
knowledge prepares them to be all the more scandalised by the
blood that (according to Giraldus) all too often then follows
among the Irish.

That this is the right way to read the historical evidence in
this account is supported by the direct evidence of a letter
addressed on 14 July 1411 to the King of France, Charles VI, by
the sons of Duke Louis of Orléans, which the fifteenth-century
historian Juvénal des Ursins included in his *Histoire de Charles
VI*. It fills out the terse phrase '*en leglise de Saint Martin de
Harefleu*' ('in the church of St Martin at Harfleur') used in the
document that McFarlane edited of the compact of brotherhood in arms between Nicholas Molyneux and John Winter,
two esquires in the army of Henry V, also made in France in the

[6] K. B. McFarlane, 'A Business-Partnership in War and Administration,
1421–1445', *English Historical Review*, 78 (1963), pp. 290–310.

church at Harfleur almost to the day just ten years later on 12 July 1421. This letter[7] gives a detailed description of the rite by which their father had become the ritual 'brother' of his cousin Duke Jean of Burgundy on 20 November 1407 when, as in the ritual indirectly implied by Giraldus' account, they had made their communions together in a votive mass for this purpose. The ritual as Juvénal des Ursins summarises it is that

> *le dimanche vingtiesme jour de novembre monseigneur de Berry, et autres seigneurs assemblerent lesdits seigneurs d'Orleans et de Bourgongne, ils oüyrent tous la messe ensemble, et receurent le corps de Nostre Seigneur. Et prealablement jurerent bon amour et fraternité par ensemble.*

on Sunday the 20 November the Lord de Berry and other lords assembled together, and the said Lords of Orléans and of Burgundy heard the mass together and received the Body of Our Lord; and before doing this they swore true love and brotherhood together.

The unusual value of this letter lies in the stress it places on the customary and familiar nature of the rite followed in 1407, a point its writers press in their letter because of the infamy of the subsequent murder of their father by the servants of Duke Jean. As they put it, their father and Duke Jean during the ritual in 1407 had made

> *plusieurs grandes et solemnelles promesses, en tel cas accoustumées ... par especiales convenances sur ce faites*

many grand and solemn promises of the kind as are customary in such a situation ... by the special conventions recognised in such a matter.

Both of these pieces of evidence point, in the first case indirectly and in the second directly, to the same conclusion: that in the churches of Catholic Europe from at least the end of the twelfth century until the beginning of the fifteenth, the mass provided a familiar culmination for the creation of ritual 'brothers', a ritual completed in their taking holy communion together.

[7] In MM. Michaud and Poujoulat (eds.), *Nouvelle Collection des Mémoires* (Series I, Vol. 2; Lyon and Paris: Guyot Frères, 1851), pp. 456–64.

Was the rite employed by women as well as men? Each of these accounts depicts the rite as being used between men, but their terms do not explicitly exclude its use by women. The *adelphopoiesis* (and its Slavonic equivalent) did comprehend women, and the same was the case with the *compaternitas* to which Giraldus refers. Also as I describe below the implicit theology of the rite was not restricted to men. Women tend always to be less visible in medieval records, and an assumption that the rite in the Latin West necessarily excluded women would be an argument from silence. Whether *in practice* it comprehended women is a different matter.

A eucharistic practice such as this should not surprise us. In her classic study *Corpus Christi: The Eucharist in Late Medieval Culture* Miri Rubin has described how, in the eleventh and twelfth centuries, the eucharist was refigured as a symbol at the centre of the secular world about it, becoming incorporated into its forms of life, shaping them and in turn being shaped by them.[8] The ritual evident in these accounts was part of that process.

The ritual we can glimpse in these documents seems very probably to have been the form in which the fourteenth-century English king Edward II became the ritual brother of his friend Piers Gaveston. The arguments for a ritual brotherhood between them that have been put forward by Pierre Chaplais are based on the chronicle of the civil war years of Edward's reign among the Cottonian manuscripts in the British Library. This is how it describes Edward and Gaveston's first meeting:[9]

> *filius regis intuens, in eum tantum protinus amorem iniccit quod cum eo fraternitatis fedus iniit, et pre ceteris mortalibus indissolubile dileccionis vinculum secum elegit et firm[i]ter disposuit innodare.*

when the king's son gazed upon him, he straight away felt so much love that he entered into a covenant of brotherhood with him and chose and firmly resolved to bind himself to him, in an unbreakable bond of love before all men.

---

[8] M. Rubin, *Corpus Christi: The Eucharist in Late Medieval Culture* (2 vols.; Cambridge: Cambridge University Press, 1991).

[9] I have given Chaplais' transcription at p. 13 of his book, rather than that of George L. Haskins in 'A Chronicle of the Civil Wars of Edward II', *Speculum*, 14 (1939), p. 75.

The precision of the term '*fraternitatis fedus*' ('covenant of brotherhood') in this account corresponds to the '*compaternitatis foedera*' (the 'covenants of spiritual brotherhood') that Giraldus invokes, and the *Vita Edwardi Secundi* is equally explicit about the formal character of their friendship and characterises it in the language of fraternal adoption.[10] This is taken from the passage that follows its account of Gaveston's murder by Edward's opponents.

> *Occiderunt enim magnum comitem quem rex adoptauerat in fratrem, quem rex dilexit ut filium, quem rex habuit in socium et amicum.*

For they put to death a great earl whom the King had adopted as brother, whom the King loved as a son, whom the King regarded as friend and ally.

The *Annales Paulini* composed among the cathedral clergy at St Paul's uses the same term.

> *Rex quidem adoptivi fratris sui Petri de Gavastone personam exulare seu honorem ejus minuendum non potuit sustinere.*

Indeed the King could not bring himself to send his adoptive brother into exile or diminish his honour.[11]

The chronicles do not describe the form in which Edward and Gaveston swore their *fraternitatis fedus*, but that of their oaths together in 1307 at the time of Gaveston's first exile (at Edward I's command) is described in the memorandum in the close rolls[12] as having been taken 'upon God's body' and upon the relics and makes it probable that their earlier oaths also took the eucharistic form that Juvénal des Ursins was later to regard as customary. This phrase in the close rolls follows closely the 'oath sworn on the precious blood of Jesus Christ' of Juvénal des Ursins and Giraldus' 'in the presence of relics of the saints'.

---

[10] N. Denholm-Young (ed.), *Vita Edwardi Secundi* (London: Thomas Nelson & Sons, 1957), pp. 7, 17, 28.

[11] In William Stubbs (ed.), *Chronicles of the Reigns of Edward I and Edward II* (Rolls Series, 2 vols.; London, 1882), I, p. 263.

[12] *Calendar of the Close Rolls Edward I*, Vol. 5, *1302–1307* (London: HMSO, 1908), p. 526.

Assessing the Motives for the Rite

It is not I think persuasive to characterise in narrowly defined terms the motives for the relationships being created by this rite. One could take, as an example of an attempt to do this, the characterisation by the American historian Brent Shaw in the *Traditio* symposium:

> artificial brotherhoods were formed for the purposes of protection, defense, and armed aggression in a disintegrated social order in which the threat of violence and physical force was a real and ever-present danger ... I suggest that this institution was more frequently found ... inside state structures characterized by less formal or less 'rationalized' relationships of amity ... connected with the prevalence of primal forms of social organization in the face of the weakness of effective central state power.[13]

Was the ritual I have described, for example, employed to *force* individuals to make peace with each other, when their violent conflict was disrupting good order or they themselves were seeking to conclude a dispute? In some instances this seems to have been the case. The circumstances of the sworn brotherhood of the Dukes of Burgundy and Orléans would fit that description; but the details elsewhere belie so neat a generalisation. Such a characterisation fits neither the friendship of Nicholas Molyneux and John Winter nor that of Edward II and Piers Gaveston. The covenant between Nicholas Molyneux and John Winter concluded in the church of St Martin at Harfleur clearly was not the resolution of a dispute of this kind: in their agreement they recorded that they were prompted to become brothers in arms by the desire to augment the love and fraternity *already* growing between them ('*Premierement pour acroistre et augmenter lamour et fraternite qui est piera en commencee entre ledit Molyneux et Winter*'), and through their agreement they formed a close partnership that was to last throughout their lives. An ecclesiastical setting was apparently as appropriate for creating a brotherhood of this kind as for settling a

---

[13] Brent D. Shaw, 'Ritual Brotherhood in Roman and Post-Roman Society', *Traditio*, 52 (1997), pp. 329, 350 and 354.

dispute. The same is true of the ritual brotherhood of Edward
II and Piers Gaveston. If Edward II had been seeking a sworn
brotherhood to resolve a dispute he would have sought it
among the magnates who were threatening him and not in an
intimate who was ready to act for him like Piers Gaveston.

A reading of the use of the rite solely to settle disputes would
also require one to disregard the explicit terms used by both
Giraldus and the sons of the murdered Duke Louis of Orléans:
in the one case the ritual being described takes place when the
two men *desire* to come together in it – 'they come together in
some holy place with the man with whom they are eager to be
united' ('*ad sacrum aliquem locum conveniunt, cum eo quem oppetere
cupiunt*') – and in the other the term employed is 'true brotherhood and company of arms' ('*vraye fraternité et compagnée
d'armes*'): substantially the same term as the '*freres darmes*'
('brothers in arms') used in the agreement of Nicholas
Molyneux and John Winter. The 'special conventions recognised in such a matter' are not those for settling a dispute but
those for creating ritual brothers:

> *jurerent et promirent solemnellement vraye fraternité et compagnée
> d'armes ensemble, par especiales convenances sur ce faites.*

> they swore and solemnly promised true brotherhood and
> company of arms together, by the special conventions recog-
> nised in such a matter.[14]

Brent Shaw is rather here voicing the programmatic view of
the English nineteenth-century constitutional historians that, as
Pollock and Maitland put it in 1898, 'Step by step, as the power
of the State waxes ... kindred wanes'.[15] Where the friendship
created by kinship had obtruded on their accounts, its presence
was glossed over as a form of 'bastard feudalism' obstructing
the onward march of the royal administration. A figure like
Piers Gaveston, who was an intimate royal friend, clearly does
not fit Brent Shaw's characterisation. Neither do the careers of
Nicholas Molyneux and John Winter, who acted together in

[14] Michaud and Poujoulat, *Nouvelle Collection des Mémoires*, p. 457.
[15] Sir Frederick Pollock and Frederic William Maitland, *The History of English
Law before the Time of Edward I* (Cambridge: Cambridge University Press, 1898),
p. 1.

administering the household of the Regent of France, the Duke of Bedford. If there was an onward march of the king's rule of the kind nineteenth-century English historians believed they could trace, two sworn brothers like Nicholas Molyneux and John Winter were not its unruly opponents: they were part of it. That onward march – leading in their view to the constitutional settlement of English history – was the theme of the writings of the Victorian constitutional historians, but their historical framework was to be inherited by more recent historians such as Brent Shaw without the political programme it had been created to buttress; and Brent Shaw in his paper then dismisses evidence that conflicts with this view on *a priori* grounds as 'an exception', 'singular', 'occasional' – or simply as 'irregular'.[16]

A characterisation imposed from outside like this offers an impoverished view of history, that at root the historian's sources are just plain *facts* and that once the historian has concluded what they are really about he or she is then able to assemble the reliable sources and dispose of the rest as mere rhetoric – as an exception or something irregular. In such a view there is no place for the apprehension that the sources may in themselves be conceptually difficult, untranslatable directly into modern terms. A characterisation like that of Brent Shaw – essentially one in terms of violence – imposes a coherence on the material that is achieved only at the expense of taking one part of the evidence and discarding another; and similar problems arise when any other broad characterisation is attributed by the historian from above, whether in terms of commercial profit (as K. B. McFarlane suggested) or in erotic terms as John Boswell proposed.

In contrast it is striking how little use has been made in unravelling this conundrum of the evidence implicit in the form of the rite itself, to see it as it were from within. In Chaplais' book the ecclesiastical setting for ritual brotherhood is dealt with summarily and by a cursory hypothesis.

In pagan societies, the adoption ceremony sometimes included a ritual in which each of the two prospective brothers opened a vein and gave his partner some of his

---

[16] Shaw, 'Ritual Brotherhood', pp. 340, 351, 353.

blood to drink, or a mixture of the two bloods was drunk by
both; thus they could truly say that they were 'brothers of one
blood'. The same ritual is known to have been occasionally
observed by Christians, although it seems to have been more
usual for them to take part in a communion service in which
the two partners shared the same host.[17]

The study of the *adelphopoiesis* by Claudia Rapp in the *Traditio*
symposium had a firm grasp on the place the *adelphopoiesis*
occupied in Byzantine society, as well as on the analogous role
of the various forms of ritual kinship that I shall come to in a
moment.[18] But Claudia Rapp excluded in her paper any
discussion of the detail of the liturgy itself beyond the bare fact
of its use and is as brusque as Pierre Chaplais.

> In secular society ... the practice of ritual brotherhood was
> taken for granted and supported by the church, which
> sanctioned it through a ritual. ... By the twelfth century, the
> church authorities began to view with a critical eye
> the *adelphopoiesis* relations that involved laymen and declared
> that they were categorically forbidden by the church. ... But
> these ecclesiastical authorities still refrained from threat-
> ening any form of punishment. And the inclusion of the
> office in the *euchologia* shows that, despite their disapproval,
> the ritual continued to be practiced even into post-Byzantine
> times.[19]

It is striking how curiously featureless these passages are. *Why*
did Latin Christians regard the eucharist as significant, in the
context of ritual brotherhood (or sisterhood if this was
the case)? Why does the *adelphopoiesis* take the particular form
one sees in the liturgical collections – this form rather than any
other? The arbitrariness in Pierre Chaplais' hypothesis, almost

[17] Chaplais, *Piers Gaveston*, p. 33.
[18] Something that was pointed out by Evelyne Patlagean in her seminal
paper 'Christianization and Ritual Kinship in the Byzantine Area', in Robert
Forster and Orest Ranum (eds.), *Ritual, Religion, and the Sacred: Selections from
the Annales, Economies, Sociétés, Civilisations* (Baltimore: Johns Hopkins
University Press, 1982), pp. 81–94 (translated from *Annales, E. S. C.* 33 (May
–June 1978), pp. 625–36).
[19] Claudia Rapp, 'Ritual Brotherhood in Byzantium', *Traditio*, 52 (1997), pp.
319–26 (319 and 323).

the casualness, of the transition from one ritual practice to another tacitly shares the ecclesiology in the passage from Claudia Rapp that identifies the 'church' not with Pierre Chaplais' potentially still pagan Christians but with the 'ecclesiastical authorities'. Although neither Claudia Rapp nor Pierre Chaplais is explicit on the point, both are adopting here a view of 'popular' religion that takes it as axiomatic that 'popular' religion will necessarily lack the definition that canon lawyers and systematic theologians give to official religion, a view that renders popular religion as something necessarily featureless and – ultimately – unintelligible, the assumption Peter Brown has accurately characterised as a 'two-tiered' view of religion. Popular belief 'with so static and potentially undifferentiated a model' as he puts it in *The Cult of the Saints* 'can only show itself as a monotonous continuity'.[20]

Elizabeth A. R. Brown was more aware of these dangers in her paper on Western medieval Europe in the *Traditio* symposium, which analysed in detail the religious terms employed in descriptions by contemporary observers that fill in the silence of the Latin liturgical collections, where a liturgical practice of this kind without a specific office would be unlikely to appear. While the summary of her conclusions is similarly featureless – 'the absence of fraternal ceremonial from the liturgy is closely related to ... the lack of prohibitions, ecclesiastical and secular, against the bond' – she adds also an alternative possibility: 'On the other hand, the Western church certainly tolerated *and, arguably, moulded* the institution, which flourished as a useful spiritual, political, and economic mechanism.'[21] It is that suggestion I propose now to pursue here.

Society – Defining the Family

The guide I would suggest is the combination of different kinds of kinship terminology in Giraldus' awesome composite and

---

[20] Peter Brown, *The Cult of the Saints: Its Rise and Function in Latin Christianity* (London: SCM Press, 1981), pp. 12–22: quotations from pp. 19 and 21.

[21] Elizabeth A. R. Brown 'Ritual Brotherhood in Western Medieval Europe', pp. 357–81, quotations at pp. 358 and 375. The emphasis is mine.

the theological implications that raised. For the later historian to attempt with determined pedantry to undo the connections being made would be to miss the point that that confusion corresponds with precision to the texture of the social life in which they figured – although from a modern viewpoint this is by no means self-evident and needs some commentary. That the 'family' can be defined in several different ways – in terms of blood relations for example, but also as a common household, or in terms of marriage – tends now to be a technical point of interest only to sociologists and anthropologists, as in modern society these different definitions coincide closely. The family living together in the same household is conventionally the group of parents and their children linked by blood or marriage. In the past, as Jean-Louis Flandrin has pointed out, these definitions often did not coincide so nearly.[22]

One major cause of this mismatch was the many forms of what one might call 'voluntary' kinship, kinship created not by blood but by ritual or a promise. The difficulty for the modern viewer lies in that modern society recognises only one such 'voluntary' kinship, in marriage: in the past others have subsisted alongside it; and their aggregate effect was that (in England at least until well into the seventeenth century) an individual lived in effect in a potential plurality of families. He or she could be part of one family in terms of blood relations and simultaneously part of another in terms of the ritual kinship created by betrothal or marriage, by baptism, or as here by 'sworn' brotherhood (or sisterhood). The relations this created did not obliterate the boundaries of families; 'spiritual' kinship remained distinct from that created by birth or marriage, and there is no evidence that sworn kinship extended to others beyond those who made the promises that created it. But the cumulative effect of such a multiplicity of forms of 'voluntary' kinship was to embed the family within a wider and encompassing network of *friendship*; and when friendship is

---

[22] Jean-Louis Flandrin, *Familles: parenté, maison, sexualité dans l'ancienne société* (Paris: Librairie Hachette, 1976); translated by Richard Southern as *Families in Former Times* (Cambridge: Cambridge University Press, 1979), pp. 4–10.

given a formal and objective character by ritual and oath it is indistinguishable in its workings from kinship. Fostering and adoption further extended that interlocking network between households, and within it was placed the family in our contemporary and more limited sense of a group of parents and their children. Sworn kinship was one of the threads out of which that fabric was made. That network is peculiarly difficult to see from the vantage point of a modern historian. Its presence was created by those very mismatches that modern society lacks; where all definitions of the family are perceived to delineate the same group and no kinship is perceived to be, in the strict sense of the word, artificial.

Theology – The Shape of the Liturgy

There is though a 'but' to be added and one that points away from the social context of the rite and towards its implicit theology. If I am reading these sources correctly the rite does not then appear as an unreserved endorsement of the relationship being created. Neither Giraldus nor Juvénal des Ursins implies that the vows of sworn brotherhood were part of the mass: in both of these pieces of evidence, the mass rather follows the vows. No doubt Juvénal des Ursins was voicing a widely held view when he describes the ritual brotherhood of the Dukes of Orléans and Burgundy as '*sermentées et jurées sur le precieux corps de Jesus-Christ*' ('an oath sworn on the precious blood of Jesus Christ'),[23] but that is to gloss in a broad expression the insistent detail that the vows were not made within the mass. 'The Lords of Orléans and of Burgundy heard the mass together and received the Body of Our Lord; and *before doing this* they swore true love and brotherhood together.' The same detail appears again in Giraldus' account: '*Finally* with a celebration of the mass and the prayers of priests they are joined indissolubly as if by a betrothal.' In the evidence provided by Juvénal des Ursins and Giraldus alike, the mass is not the setting for the vows of sworn brotherhood but rather follows, as their culmination. In the careful proprieties of

---

[23] Michaud and Poujoulat, *Nouvelle Collection des Mémoires*, p. 456.

Giraldus' account, the separation in time is accompanied by a symbolic separation in space, between door and altar. '*Postmodum ecclesiam intrantes ...*' ('Then going into the church ...'). Giraldus' tell-tale phrase indicates what would have been self-evident to his audience. A betrothal was made at the church door. It was there that the rites of baptism began. It was there also, at the church door, that the vows of sworn kinship were exchanged, with the participants only then receiving holy communion together in the mass within that followed.

It is not difficult to see the reason for that reserve. To what end might this friendship be put? In the eighteenth-century Enlightenment, Immanuel Kant was to place the moral basis of friendship in an undifferentiated moral benevolence; and the civil society that began to emerge in England towards the end of the seventeenth century was an accurate expression of that view. In the traditional society of this chapter friendship was rather ultimately inalienable from the particular loyalties in which it was begun, and the ambiguities of that stance were the point on which its ethics turned. Fidelity in such a context easily gave rise to suspicions that were ever to hand of collusion and self-advancement. The point is that the church in the Latin West did not respond to this uncertainty by legislating for the diverse motives that could prompt sworn friendship. The answer it found was a distinctively liturgical solution. Its dilemma might well have been solved of course by relegating these vows to the secular world pure and simple. But as the historian John Bossy has argued, the eucharist of traditional Christians before and after the Reformation divide was recognised as restoring defective human relations in the society about it, and its 'social miracle' as he terms it was the work of kinship and friendship: the peace that was friendship, not peace as the opposite of war or the effect of victory.[24] Its solution lay in an Augustinian view of grace, that necessarily works in a world of defective human relations, and the eucharistic ritual of this paper provided a liturgical form that

[24] John Bossy, 'The Mass as a Social Institution 1200–1700', *Past and Present*, 100 (August 1983), pp. 29–61; *Christianity in the West 1400–1700* (Oxford: Oxford University Press, 1985); *Peace in the Post-Reformation* (Cambridge: Cambridge University Press, 1998).

allowed the church to respond with integrity to the potential for good in the vows being exchanged, without being compromised by the potential for misuse that inevitably accompanied them. Its theology was that of the grace imparted by the eucharist that could, with human co-operation, lead the promises towards the ideal to which they pointed. Its shape was that of the eucharistic action: in its transformation of the sacrifice for friends offered at the altar into the universal sacramental sign that it then offered in communion.

That implicit theology emerges most clearly from the comparison one can make between the *adelphopoiesis* and its Slavonic equivalent the *pobratimstvo*, which represented a response to the same dilemma but from within its own distinctively Byzantine milieu. Westerners had no difficulty in recognising it as the sworn kinship of the Latin West.[25] From at least the fourteenth century, the Franciscan friars in Dalmatia were employing a rite for creating sworn brothers among Latin Catholics – an *ordo ad fratres faciendum* – that corresponded to the *pobratimstvo* familiar among their neighbours that incorporated at least one of its prayers, in a Latin translation.[26] In the troubled history of their canon law one can see in explicit terms the same reservation with which Catholic Europe regarded its Western counterpart. It could lead, warned a twelfth-century Greek ecclesiastic, to 'many sins'; and Greek canon law has variously attempted to restrict the rite or to preclude its use altogether; although apparently with limited success judging by its continuing inclusion in the liturgical collections and its surviving use.[27] The *adelphopoiesis* and its Slavonic equivalent are characteristic products of their theological milieu, although they addressed the same fundamental dilemma as the eucharistic rite developed in the West.

Each was designed to negotiate the dangers of mutual appropriation present when church and world come together and did so by recognising the good in the vows exchanged as

---

[25] Brown, *Cult of the Saints*, p. 361.

[26] O. Antonin Zaninović OP, 'Dva Latinska spomenika o sklapanju pobratimstva u Dalmaciji', *Zbornik za narodni život I običaje južnih Slavena*, 45 (1971), pp. 713–24. I am grateful to Dr Wendy Bracewell for her drawing this article to my attention and for her translation of the paper for me.

[27] Rapp, 'Ritual Brotherhood in Byzantium', p. 323.

something still incomplete, as a potential; but while the Western form expressed this in a theology of grace shaped in distinctively eucharistic terms, the *adelphopoiesis* and *pobratimstvo* employed rather a distinctive Greek theology of praise. The differing responses to sworn brotherhood and sisterhood lie in what might at first seem merely a technical detail. In the *adelphopoiesis* (and its Slav equivalent the *pobratimstvo*) the bread and wine are not consecrated by the priest but are rather brought to the liturgy *already* consecrated (and the *ordo ad fratres faciendum* employed by Latin Catholics in Dalmatia evidently adopted the same device). In Catholic and Orthodox theology alike, when the bread and wine in the eucharist are taken, blessed, and broken by the priest they are *changed* into the body and blood of Christ. In that sense the *adelphopoiesis* and its Slavonic equivalent are not strictly eucharistic. Their shape is rather a distinctively Greek liturgy of praise. Characteristically the prayers of the *adelphopoiesis* and the *pobratimstvo* open with the praise of God as creator, as king, and as saviour and place the blessing of the participants that follows in that context.

> Lord God almighty who created man in his own image and likeness and gave him eternal life ...
> Lord our God, who has granted our petitions for our salvation ...
> Lord our God, you are the perfecter of love and teacher of the world and saviour of all ... [28]

Such a blessing – strictly a 'blessing' of God – places the *adelphopoiesis* and *pobratimstvo* with the rites for a betrothal, for the cutting of a boy's hair or beard, the prayers for rain, first fruits, or the blessing of seed corn that are also found in the manuscripts that contain the *adelphopoiesis* or its Slavonic equivalent: things that have a natural integrity and potential of their own, to which the believer responds in praise of their

---

[28] From the Slavonic *Euchologion Sinaiticum* translated by Constance Woods, *Communio*, 22 (Summer, 1995), pp. 316–42. Comparable passages from Boswell's translation of the *adelphopoiesis* (pp. 295 and 296): 'Forasmuch as Thou, O Lord and Ruler, art merciful and loving, who didst establish humankind after thine image and likeness ...'; 'O Lord Our God, who didst grant unto us all those things necessary for salvation ...'.

Creator.[29] The one views the potential good in the promises of ritual friendship, as it were from below, in a world of defective human relations; the other from above, from the viewpoint of the integrity of creation. This distinction is akin to that detected by historical liturgists in the differing rites for marriage in Greek and Latin Christianity, a Latin rite shaped from the eleventh century by the exchange of promises and a Greek liturgy preserving an older liturgical tradition that locates the liturgical action in a prayer of praise. In the one case this has been described as the support and clothing of a promise, whereas in the other it is the celebration and receiving of a gift.[30]

The differing response created a different trajectory. The point I think is this. Praise must be spoken, and a distinctive office emerged in Byzantine Christianity for the creation of ritual brotherhood and sisterhood and with it a canon law that sought to legislate explicitly for its ambiguities. In the West that development was eluded by its incorporation within the existing structures of the eucharist. The indirect effect has been to make the friendship of the Latin West far less visible to the historian than its Byzantine counterpart, but both were part of a phenomenon that once comprehended Greek and Latin Christianity alike.

Can the Past Speak to Today's Church?

Does this history have anything to say to the liturgical recognition of friendship today? As this chapter has been intended to demonstrate, there can be no simple passage from the one to the other. The value in recovering its history lies rather, I would suggest, at a more fundamental level: in its ability to raise radical questions about the terms in which this debate is being

---

[29] For example, in Barberini MS 336 in the Vatican Library: Anselm Strittmatter, 'The "Barberinum S. Marci" of Jacques Goar: Barberinianus graecus 336', *Ephemerides Liturgicae*, Anno 47 (NS 7) (1933), pp. 329–67, and the *Euchologion Sinaiticum* which Archimandrite Ephrem discusses in his review of John Boswell's book in *Sourozh*, 59 (February 1995), pp. 50–55 at p. 52.

[30] Michael Vasey, 'The Family and the Liturgy', in Stephen C. Barton (ed.), *The Family in Theological Perspective* (Edinburgh: T&T Clark, 1996), pp. 169–85.

conducted, and it arguably does so in at least two fundamental respects. The first is about the kind of ethical question at issue. Are sexual ethics an adequate framework in which to consider the ethical issues involved? In this study I have argued that the historical context for the past eucharistic rite it describes was a society in which the individual lived in effect in a potential plurality of 'families', one in terms of blood relations but others also in terms of the kinship established through baptism or the eucharist, and that their effect was to embed the family within a wider and encompassing network of formal friendship. The ethical question at issue in this rite lay in the role the relationships being blessed could then play more widely, beyond the individuals immediately involved. The past social context for the rite is irrecoverable, but that kind of ethical question is of more universal application, and the contemporary question it raises is whether homosexual partnerships today could also be considered within a framework of that kind.

There are reasons for believing that this may be possible. It is as a result of defining the question in terms such as these that the Evangelical Church in Germany (with which the Church of England is linked through the Meissen Agreement) authorised a service of blessing addressed not to the homosexual partnership as a lifestyle but to its ethical role. It is also of course in these terms that civil governments are viewing the recognition of single-sex partnerships, where what is at issue is the burden of social welfare they are recognised to assume – not questions of sexuality. A framework of this kind would raise questions such as the following. What kind of role do homosexual partnerships play in bearing the responsibilities of society more widely? In what sense are they – or could they be – drawn into the existing families of the two friends, as a loving uncle or aunt or as a support to the old? To address the question in these terms is to ask genuine questions that are not as yet easily answered, nor are they addressed exclusively either to the church or to homosexual couples, but they could provide a coherent framework in which this debate as a whole could be viewed. Questions like this are firmly within an orthodox framework and recognise both the place that the family has occupied in Christian belief and the complementarity of the sexes within the natural order at its heart. They represent an approach that does not put these at stake as the price for a pastoral response to the actual ethical role that is (or could be) played by homosexual friendships. Nor do they require an abandonment of traditional Christian belief about sexual chastity.

But if the first question raised is about ethics, the second is about prayer – and liturgy. Would the church be compromised by a service of blessing, even if one directed to the responsibilities carried by homosexual partnerships within society more widely? The form that question takes is distinctively modern, but the question itself is not. One cannot directly translate the church's reservations about the sworn friendship of the past into modern terms, but they touched on the dangers of mutual appropriation that are always present when church and world meet. I have argued in this chapter that the shape of the rite I have described was a form that allowed the church to recognise the potential for good in the relationships being blessed while confounding those dangers. Could this be the case also today with homosexual partnerships? The question raised by this history is less, to my mind, the possible revival of an ancient liturgical practice than whether a solution of the same kind may be possible in response to the questions raised by homosexual friendship today.

Here too there may be grounds for believing that this is possible. Archbishop Rowan Williams has recently suggested that an appropriate liturgical form for the recognition of homosexual friendship may be the offering of the eucharist for the couple's intentions and their blessing in the course of it but without any exchange of vows or rings within the eucharist itself. There could also be others, and the *adelphopoiesis* suggests a solution in terms of a different kind. The liturgical assembly, as Michael Vasey once put it, is a primary place where theology – the demanding task of understanding and responding to God – is done; and a radical question posed by the long and largely forgotten history of the liturgical recognition of friendship is this. Does the solution to the stalled and destructive debate over homosexual friendship within the church lie in finding a way of praying aright?

PART 7

Ending Marriage:
Roman Catholic Perspectives

Introduction

Parts 7 and 8 present complementary perspectives on the ending of marriages by means of a declaration of nullity or divorce, and the possibility of remarriage. There are impressive parallels between the two sections. Each section opens up contemporary thinking about ending marriage from within a recognised church, Roman Catholic and Church of England. Each section contains a clear statement of official teaching and practice in those churches. And each section includes constructive criticisms of the official positions taken.

In Part 7 Paul Robbins draws on his experience as Assistant to the Judicial Vicar, Metropolitan Tribunal of Liverpool, England. Scarcely anyone is better placed to describe the grounds for declaring invalid marriages that have been solemnized in the Roman Catholic Church. These grounds are not generally known outside that church: even among Roman Catholics there is widespread ignorance about them. Robbins explains that the church has always acknowledged that there are occasions when a marriage is not formed after a wedding ceremony. He draws on biblical teaching, official documents from Vatican II onwards, and on revised canon law, and outlines the several grounds on the basis of which defective consent is recognised and allowed to lead to a declaration of nullity.

Robbins provides an informed and contemporary account of developing Roman Catholic teaching which is both valuable in its own right and an informative background to other papers in this section. Three Roman Catholic theologians (all of whom have written renowned books on the subject), from three different countries, address the pastoral and theological problems arising from the operation of the annulment process. One obvious pastoral problem is the plight of those Catholics who are divorced and who remarry, yet whose first marriages are unable to be declared invalid. Cathy Molloy brings liberation theology to the 'impasse' between official teaching and the bitter pain of felt rejection by the church, endured by such people. She charts some developments in recent marital theology and argues that the church has not pondered the implications of these changes. Many Irish Catholics whose marriages break down report that the church often makes matters worse, and treats them and their pain unjustly and demeaningly. Catholics who remarry may find themselves torn between two communions, that of the eucharist, from which they are excluded, and the communion of their new marriage. The 'scandal' that would, allegedly, be caused by any apparent softening of the church's teaching on indissolubility, has been replaced by another, actual, scandal – that of the excessively harsh and rigid treatment of Christians whose marriages have failed. Liberation theology begins with people's suffering, and looks for liberation from oppression. Emphases on *praxis*, on hermeneutics, and on the experience of salvation, are said to lead to different conclusions, not least to the possible discovery of God's grace in the love for a new partner.

Timothy Buckley indicates how the Roman Catholic Church might resolve the painful tension between maintaining fidelity to her own teaching on the indissolubility of marriage and at the same time allowing the redeeming presence of Christ to touch more efficaciously the lives of those affected by marital breakdown. Buckley shows, perhaps surprisingly to some people, that the Catholic Church has always sought to find pastoral solutions to the problem of marital dissolution: indeed the extension of the nullity process in the late twentieth century is one such example. He notes there are two conflicting definitions of marriage in the *Catechism of the Catholic Church* and warns against simplistic appeals to authority in order to resolve continuing problems in the church's teaching. Too much stress has been placed on obtaining a declaration of nullity, however, and attention to the practice of the Orthodox Church would help release Rome from the 'trap' of supposing that marriage nullity was the only way of dissolving the marital bond. Central to Orthodox practice is the conviction that there is no human situation that places itself beyond the redeeming presence of Christ.

Margaret Farley undertakes a theological and philosophical analysis of the nature of our deepest personal commitments and applies this to the problem of the theological legitimacy of our breaking them. Farley notes the continuing impasse within the Roman Catholic Church between many moral theologians and official teaching, and identifies an underlying issue. We all want our marriages to last, but they remain fragile and the sense of marriage as an institution no longer has the power to keep us in them. The Christian doctrines of 'original sin' and of 'human nature', appropriately expressed, can help us to understand why marriages fail. But Farley notices an element within this teaching, so often negatively deployed, which throws new light on the problem of justifying divorce: the limitations of human nature extend to the scope of human choice, restricting our freedom. If a marriage becomes intolerable, choosing it to be tolerable cannot make it so. There remain many resources within Christian theology, faith and liturgy which assist us in our limitations, but these too are tainted by sexism in the church, and must pass through a 'clarifying critique'.

The commitment of marriage has an intention of permanence. If the church acknowledges divorce does it not undermine the church's witness to its own teaching about the lifelong commitment that marriage requires? Farley brings to the dilemma her work on personal commitments, showing that the generic grounds for being released from commitments can apply to marital commitments also. A commitment no longer binds when it has become impossible to keep, when it no longer fulfils any of the purposes it was meant to serve, and when another obligation comes into conflict with the first obligation, and the second overrides the first. While obligations remain to former spouses, arguments forbidding divorced persons to remarry are shown to be weak. There are 'faithful ways of ending marriages' and 'faithful possibilities of beginning again'.

18

Marriage Nullity in the Catholic Church: Not Every Wedding Produces a Marriage

Paul Robbins

The aim of this chapter is to explain in summary form the underlying principles of marriage nullity. This is followed by a brief introduction to the grounds in Catholic canon law by which consent to marriage can be declared to have been invalid.[1] As a starting point and because the grounds for nullity flow from the nature of marriage, it is necessary to agree a common understanding of Christian marriage, particularly with regard to its permanent nature, since a declaration of nullity can appear to negate this property of marriage.

The Source of the Church's Teaching on the Permanence of Marriage

The Christian churches believe in and teach the permanence of marriage. Christ's teaching 'what God has united, no one can divide'[2] is a powerful statement of the intervention of God in the lives of those who come together in marriage. Jesus does not see marriage merely as something arising from a woman and a man agreeing to form a community of life together. He sees it as a part of God's plan. He talks of something God has

---

[1] Limitations of space mean this chapter can focus only on the invalidating effects of defective consent. It is not possible to explain the procedures that might lead to a declaration of nullity, nor how a marriage might be invalid because of a defect of form or the presence of an impediment.

[2] Mk 10:9.

united. It follows from this that the bond is permanent. God has created that bond and so no one can break it. At the same time, it has been recognised through the ages that there are occasions when a marriage is not formed after a wedding ceremony. An obvious example of this occurs when one of the parties is bound by marriage promises made to another who is still alive.

When two people exchange marriage promises we assume that a permanent unbreakable marriage bond is formed. Thus, there is a general presumption that every wedding produces a marriage. This has been formulated in law in our different churches. As an example of this, the 1983 Catholic Code of Canon Law says: 'Marriage enjoys the favour of the law. Consequently, in doubt the validity of a marriage must be upheld until the contrary is proven.'[3]

Marriage nullity, by which a marriage is declared invalid, simply recognises that all weddings do not produce a marriage. The canon law of the Catholic Church, supported by the jurisprudence that has been formulated through the work of the church's tribunals, recognises that many broken marriages were never in fact true marriages. Thus, nullity recognises the absence of a true marriage. It does not bring a marriage to an end.

Christian Teaching regarding the Nature of Marriage

Only a very brief summary of Catholic teaching can be outlined here. In the documents of the Second Vatican Council, the concept of marriage as covenant is found.[4] The word 'covenant' was used in the Old Testament to describe the relationship between God and his chosen people. It was expressed in the declaration: 'You will be my people and I will be your God.'[5] There was an understanding between God and his people that

[3] Canon 1060. This is an English translation of the Latin text of Canon 1060 of the *Codex Iuris Canonici* (Vatican: Libreria Editrice Vaticana, 1983), subsequently referred to as 'CIC 1983'.
[4] See Vatican II, Pastoral Constitution *Gaudium et spes*, Acta Apostolicae Sedis 58 (1966) 1025-115, n. 48.
[5] Jer. 7:23.

he would watch over them provided they kept his laws. God so loved the world that he sent his only Son. With the coming of Jesus, a new covenant is formed which is linked to the old. Jesus, through his death on the cross, reconciled God to his people by the gift of himself – the supreme act of love. Now, in the new covenant, believers are asked by God to 'love one another as I have loved you'.[6]

Saint Paul tells us that this new covenant is the example of love to be copied by married couples. In the letter to the Ephesians, he presents God's message according to the customs of the time. He tells husbands to love their wives 'just as Christ loved the church and sacrificed himself for her'; in other words, to make a gift of their whole selves. He also tells wives to submit to their husbands, which again is an expression of self-gift.[7] Jesus gave his life for the church. It was a total unreserved gift of himself and is the supreme example of how Christians should approach marriage: the giving of one's life to another person for his or her good.

Pope Paul VI described the characteristic features of married love as fully human, total, faithful, exclusive and creative of life and says that this is achieved through the mutual gift of the husband and wife to one another.[8] Herein lies the essence of the marital relationship and what distinguishes it from all other relationships. The marital relationship is unique in that it constitutes the unreserved gift of one person to another and the acceptance of that gift by the other, for the well-being of each and, if God wills, the forming of new life in children. One rite of the wedding ceremony asks the couple: 'Are you ready, freely and *without reservation*, to give yourselves to each other in marriage?' In Catholic doctrine at least, marriage has two objectives: the well-being of the couple and the procreation and upbringing of children.[9] The first of these is self-evident. Unless they simply want the experience of a glamorous wedding, most

---

[6] Jn 13:34.

[7] Eph. 5:21–25.

[8] Paul VI, Encyclical Letter, *Humanae vitae*, 29 July 1968, Acta Apostolicae Sedis 60 (1968) 489–96, nn. 8–9.

[9] See Canon 1055, CIC 1983, which repeats the teaching of *Gaudium et spes*, n. 48.

people marry because they believe life will have greater value within marriage than if they remained single.

The nature of marriage as a gift of one person to another without reservation and the reciprocal acceptance of that gift also finds expression in Pope John Paul II's Apostolic Exhortation *Familiaris consortio*. He makes reference to the physical gift of a man and a woman to one another in marriage and says this sexual act is:

> by no means something purely biological, but concerns the innermost being of the human person as such. It is realised in a truly human way only if it is an integral part of the love by which a man and a woman commit themselves totally until death. The total physical self-giving would be a lie if it were not the sign and fruit of a total self-giving, in which the whole person, including the temporal dimension, is present.[10]

The Concept of Nullity

A declaration of marriage nullity, often referred to as 'an annulment', may be defined as 'a pronouncement by the competent authority that, at the time of the wedding, there was some defect defined by law that prevented the marriage from coming into existence'. This declaration is made by means of a decree. Note that nullity reveals the truth that a marriage was never formed. It does not change that truth, which was determined on the wedding day. A declaration of nullity does not make a marriage invalid; it declares it invalid. Either a true marriage was formed on the wedding day, or it was not.[11]

If the law is successfully to determine whether or not a marriage is formed, it has first to recognise how a marriage is

---

[10] John Paul II, Apostolic Exhortation, *Familiaris consortio,* 22 November 1981, Acta Apostolicae Sedis 74 (1982) 81–191, n. 11.

[11] The notion that a marriage may not be formed on the wedding day can be difficult to grasp. A marriage is a living relationship of two people, but it is often not easily distinguished from other relationships. We seek to make a distinction by signs such as exchanging wedding rings, issuing a certificate, having a public ceremony and adopting the same last name. These signs assist our belief that a marriage has begun, but they do not determine the existence of the marriage. The belief held by everybody on the wedding day and thereafter is shown to have been false if the marriage is later declared invalid.

created. We are all familiar with the phrase 'consent makes a marriage'. Catholic canon law provides a definition of how a marriage is formed. At first, it might appear too simple in relation to the underlying reality of two people, who, over a period of time, grow together in a relationship of love and make a permanent commitment to one another. Nevertheless, the canon contains all the elements that are essential in law for the validity (in the eyes of the Catholic Church) of a marriage, and hence is fundamental to an understanding of marriage nullity. The relevant canon states: 'A marriage is brought into being by the lawfully manifested consent of persons who are legally capable.'[12]

The three essential elements contained in this statement are, first, *consent*, which is the basis upon which a marriage is brought into existence; that is, each party agreeing to enter marriage with the other by an act of the will. Second, this consent must be *lawfully manifested*; that is, given or expressed in a way that the law determines. If it is not, the marriage may be invalid. And third, it can be given only by people who are *legally capable* of giving that consent; in other words, who are not prevented by impediment. The focus of this chapter is an explanation of how consent, the first of these, might be invalid.

Marital Consent and Grounds for Nullity

In the wedding ceremony the bride and groom say: 'I take you to be my lawful wedded wife/husband.' This is the moment of consent. This is the moment when the marriage begins. In this act, two things are presumed: that the intention of each spouse actually conforms to what is being said and that each is capable of giving valid consent to marriage. A serious defect of intention or lack of capacity would render invalid that person's consent. The possible grounds for nullity based on defective consent are set out below.

1. *Ignorance* In order that two people enter marriage validly, it is required in Catholic canon law that the parties know what they are doing. However, the level of knowledge for validity is

---

[12] Canon 1057, §1, CIC 1983.

absolutely basic. The law states: 'it is necessary that the contracting parties be at least not ignorant of the fact that marriage is a permanent partnership between a man and a woman, ordered to the procreation of children through some form of sexual co-operation'.[13] It can still happen, even today, that a person will be a party to a wedding ceremony without having any realistic knowledge of how children are procreated. Anyone who thinks that holding hands and kissing will result in children being born would probably be able to receive a declaration of nullity under the heading of this ground of ignorance.

2. *Lack of the use of reason*[14] This differs from the previous ground. In each situation, the person did not know what he or she was doing. However, under the first ground, a person normally capable of rational thought was ignorant of basic knowledge regarding marriage. The ground now being considered concerns those who give consent whilst of unsound mind, to the extent that the person is incapable of knowing what is happening. As it is the moment of consent that is important, this incapacity might be temporary.[15] A person's use of reason could be affected by drugs, abuse of alcohol, some temporary illness, fainting, delirium, an epileptic fit, or even excessive sleepiness. Although these might render the person's consent invalid, they are more likely to prevent consent being given at all, since the affected person will probably not be capable of expressing the words of consent. The most likely outcome in most of these circumstances is that consent would be delayed until the person recovered from the fit or faint.

3. *Lack of due discretion*[16] This is the most commonly cited ground for nullity. From the earliest years of intelligent life each of us makes thousands of decisions every day. All of these decisions involve an intricate process of thought, evaluation and judgement. Take, for example, the decision to buy a pair of shoes. It consists of many elements: are they the right colour, price, shape, style, fabric, size or comfort? Can I return them if

---

[13] Canon 1096, CIC 1983.

[14] Canon 1095, 1°, CIC 1983.

[15] It is beyond the scope of this chapter to examine in more detail the situation of a marriage in which one of the parties might be judged permanently to lack the use of reason.

[16] Canon 1095, 2°, CIC 1983.

I decide I have made a bad purchase? This example illustrates something of the complexity of thought and evaluative processes involved in making decisions. It is not difficult to see that the more insignificant the decision, the less is the need to give time to thinking about, evaluating and judging the advantages and disadvantages of the decision. On a scale of important decisions in life, buying a pair of shoes does not rate highly. For many people, the decision to marry would be very close to, if not at the top of, such a scale. It is after all a decision with lifelong consequences. It is not something that can be rectified easily if a mistake is made. As a decision with such grave consequences, the extent of thought, evaluation and judgement that accompanies the decision must be proportionately greater than that required for more mundane decisions.

Hence, a person proposing to enter a marriage covenant must have a minimal knowledge and awareness of the nature of that covenant, the rights and obligations attached to it and have evaluated to some limited extent how it might be lived out with the proposed spouse. Valid consent to enter a marriage covenant with another person can only be given after due discernment. Thus, there will be some period of time prior to the wedding for internal evaluation of the decision to marry and all that that entails. Put very simply, each party to a marriage should have some knowledge of what is required and have begun to picture himself or herself in that role of husband or wife to the proposed spouse. Such a person would possess 'due discretionary judgement'. The ground for nullity is usually termed simply: 'lack of due discretion'.

Hence, if a true marriage is to be formed it is apparent that the evaluation process[17] for marriage should focus on three things: the proposed spouse as a suitable person with whom I might live out the marriage promises; myself, including my fitness and desire to give myself in marriage; and my understanding of marriage, including the requirements of permanence, fidelity, openness to children and the need to play my part in building a partnership of the whole of life.

---

[17] For the majority of people, this process would be merely a matter of common sense. What is required here is no more than the natural process of evaluation before acting on any major decision.

To prove invalidity, it is required that there was a grave lack of discretionary judgement. Examples of those who might be said to be lacking in due discretion are:

- The man who begins an affair in the courtship and continues it into the marriage because he did not appreciate the importance of fidelity in marriage. His father was known to have had a long-term extramarital relationship.
- The woman of happily married parents who is so infatuated with the man she proposes to marry that she is either blind to his serious faults or assumes he will change them when he is married.
- The man who regularly enjoys his nights out with 'the lads' and his hobby of football and expects to continue these activities without limitation after marriage.
- The single mother who is so insecure that, desperate for love and affection, she enters marriage with a man who is a most unsuitable father figure for her child.
- The man who expects to retain control of his earnings, giving an inadequate amount to his wife for the upkeep of the family and home whilst retaining the balance to finance his new cars and frequently changing hobbies.
- The woman who lost her father at a young age and marries a man who is considerably older than her and to whom she does not feel sexually attracted.
- The man who belittles his wife in company and continues to flirt with other women in a manner offensive to his wife.
- The woman who prefers to take advice from and discuss with her mother the tensions and problems in the marriage without first making any attempt to resolve them with her husband.
- The man who 'does the honourable thing' when his girlfriend becomes pregnant and marriage has not been contemplated by either prior to the pregnancy being discovered.
- The woman on the rebound, who marries another soon after her previous fiancé ended their relationship.
- The woman or man who persistently puts furtherance of a career before spouse and/or family.

All of these examples express in one way or another a limitation in the gift of self that is the essence of the marriage covenant. They are also manifestations, perhaps just temporarily, of flaws of character, at least as far as capacity to give marital consent is concerned.

4. *Inability to fulfil the essential obligations of marriage*[18] A simple principle has formed the basis for an important ground for nullity. The principle can be stated as 'nobody is bound to the impossible'. Applied to marriage, if a person is not able to fulfil the promises made on the wedding day because of causes of a psychological nature, he or she can be said not to be bound by them. In practice, it is usually the other partner who applies for a declaration of nullity.

The general principle for this ground is that each party should be capable of acting in a manner compatible with the nature of marriage. Hence, there are implications for nullity when either party consistently acts in a manner that might be contrary to the nature of marriage as a partnership seeking the well-being of each spouse.[19] For example, any sexual problems that are contrary to the nature of marriage may give cause for considering nullity under this ground. One example would include non-consummation[20] due to psychological causes.[21] Another would arise from one party being seriously confused about his or her sexual orientation or identity. Also, any personality disorder, which by definition is grounded in the psyche, can be invalidating if it results in a union that seriously undermines the well-being of either spouse or that of the children. Obvious examples of this are unions in which one of the

---

[18] Canon 1095, 3°, CIC 1983.

[19] This is not negating the term 'for better, for worse' in the marriage promises. A distinction has to be made between the formation of a marriage that subsequently turns sour and the failure to form a true marriage from the beginning. The marriage promises relate to the future. When a couple promise to marry 'for better, for worse', they are stating that their commitment to each other is binding even if the quality of their partnership of life should deteriorate. A true marriage is created by the formation of a partnership that fosters the well-being of both parties. Hence, such potential has to be present at the beginning. A marriage that does not have that potential will be lacking in something essential to its nature.

[20] It is the reason for, and not the fact of, non-consummation that can render a marriage invalid.

[21] The impediment of impotence covers non-consummation for physical reasons.

spouses consistently or seriously abuses the other or the children. The same is true of certain mental illnesses or dependencies (drink, drugs, etc.). Sometimes, dependencies in themselves arise from other psychological problems. For example, a man who becomes dependent on drink during the marriage might well have started drinking as an escape from, say, the responsibilities of fatherhood. Of course, the minor imperfections present in everyone's personality would not in themselves render a marriage invalid.

There is always an important distinction to be made between circumstances that render a marriage invalid and those that simply make it difficult. The latter would not of themselves provide grounds for nullity. However, there is also a need to discern the difference between a couple struggling with a successful union and a couple who have simply resorted to living together when the marriage has all but failed.

5. *Error and fraud*[22] Two types of error will invalidate a marriage. The first is error of person. If my intention is to marry Andrea, and the bride lifts her veil at the end of the ceremony to reveal Andrea's twin sister, the marriage can be declared invalid. I made a mistake by giving my consent to the wrong person.

The second type of error that invalidates consent concerns error of a quality of a person. However, the possibility of the marriage then being declared invalid depends upon whether or not that quality was 'directly and principally intended'. The invalidating nature of this error can be better understood by recognising that a quality that is so intended is, perhaps only in the mind of the other, an integral and essential part of the person who has that quality. Thus, the quality is so important that the marriage would not be taking place without it. So, a man might claim: 'I married you because I believed I was the father of the child you were carrying. I would not otherwise have married you.' Some other qualities that might provide opportunities for the use of this ground are: absence of a serious disease or illness, lack of virginity, religious belief, relationship to a certain person or ownership of certain assets. It does not matter how frivolous the quality might appear.

[22] Canons 1097 and 1098, CIC 1983.

Provided it was directly and principally intended by the erring person, the marriage would be invalid. In practice, the test here is the effect on the marriage when the error is discovered. The discovery of an error regarding a quality that was directly and principally intended might be expected to have a seriously detrimental effect on the future success of the marriage.

Fraud in marriage has a similar effect to error. If a person resorts to fraud in order to trap the spouse into marriage, nullity might later be claimed. The subject matter of the fraud has to be of such importance that its discovery has a seriously disruptive effect on the partnership of conjugal life. For example, if one party did not reveal a criminal record for fear that the other would not continue with wedding plans, nullity might later be claimed if, when the criminal record came to light, the revelation resulted in serious disruption to the marriage. Without such serious disruption, it is assumed that the subject matter of the fraud was not essential to the parties coming together in marriage and so is not invalidating.

6. *Simulation*[23] Grounds for nullity may also arise from a defect in the intention of one of the parties. For valid consent, it is required that each spouse intends to enter a partnership appropriate to marriage, including openness to children, fidelity and permanence. If what is willed on the wedding day is not marriage with its essential elements or properties, that person's consent may be invalid.

Simulation is 'total' when marriage itself is excluded from the intention of the simulating party, or it is 'partial' when marriage is intended but some element such as fidelity, children or permanence is excluded. Total simulation occurs when the simulating party has, at the time of the wedding ceremony, something other than marriage in his or her mind. Thus, the simulating party does not mean the words spoken during the wedding. It is usually possible to identify some motive other than marriage for participation in the wedding. An example might be a desire to acquire a new civilian status such as British citizenship. One symptom of the more obvious cases of total simulation is the brevity of the common life after

---

[23] Canon 1101, CIC 1983.

the wedding. However, many years of common life does not rule out the possibility that simulation occurred.

The nullity heading of partial simulation concerns only a particular aspect of marriage. The ground most frequently encountered concerns an intention by one or both parties to exclude children from the marriage. The Catholic Church, at least, does not accept that a marriage is formed in such circumstances. Nevertheless, many true marriages are naturally childless and others do not produce children for many different reasons. Hence, in any case in which an intention against children is alleged, great care is needed in interpreting the facts. In particular, it has to be possible to say that such refusal was the result of a defective intention on the wedding day, as opposed to something arising from circumstances that occurred in the marriage itself.

The matter is potentially quite difficult since, besides partial simulation, the denial of the right to sexual acts generative of children (non-contracepted intercourse) might suggest other grounds for nullity. For example, a man who simply does not want the responsibility of fatherhood might have failed to make a proper evaluation of the nature of marriage and there are seemingly many marriages that fail after the birth of the first child. The same might be said if either party saw the furtherance of a career, individual interests, or three overseas holidays a year as a higher priority than parenthood. Also, a woman who refuses to have children because of fear of the pain of childbirth might be deemed unable to assume the essential obligations of marriage. This is not to say that a marriage involving any of these people could not turn out to be happy and apparently blessed by God. However, should any of them fail, there might be grounds for declaring such marriages to have been invalid.

Partial simulation can also be argued when one of the parties does not accept the permanent aspect of the marriage covenant. This would occur when one party reserved the right to end the marriage at will and then considered himself or herself free to enter a new marriage. Again, care is needed. Is it possible to distinguish a genuine intention at the time of the wedding to end the marriage at will from the practical reality that seeking a civil divorce is usually sensible after a failed marriage?

There would also be partial simulation if the element of fidelity in marriage was excluded from the consent of one of the parties. This would occur when the person was open to the possibility of having sexual relations with others, if the opportunity arose.

7. *Conditional consent*[24] The essence of marriage is an unreserved gift of one spouse to the other. Recognising this, the law makes specific provision when one or both parties attempt to impose conditions on consent. The law says that a marriage cannot be validly contracted if one of the spouses imposes a condition concerning the future. Such a condition implicitly places a reservation on the gift of self. An example of such a condition might be: 'I will marry you only on the condition that if the marriage fails you will be entitled to no more than £100,000 of my fortune.'

It is, however, possible to enter marriage when the condition concerns the past or present. The following condition could, therefore, be possible: 'I will marry you only on the condition that I am the father of the child you are carrying.' The validity of the consent will depend on the condition being satisfied at the time of exchanging consent. If it was later shown that the condition was not satisfied at that time, the marriage can be declared invalid. When it is not possible to verify the condition at the time of the wedding, the couple might be advised to wait until such time as it was verified. This might present difficulties in some cases; for example, when the condition is dependent upon verifying the paternity of a child not yet born.

8. *Force or fear*[25] This ground concerns those who see marriage as their only option when under the influence of some force or of grave fear inflicted *from outside*, such as a threat of physical harm should the wedding not take place. This has to be distinguished from those who see marriage as the only option because of a set of circumstances, such as the woman being pregnant. In these situations, people are usually reacting to a moral or social obligation and the pressure to marry comes from within themselves and might give rise to an allegation of nullity on other grounds. The ground of force or fear would

[24] Canon 1102, CIC 1983.
[25] Canon 1103, CIC 1983.

not apply in such circumstances, unless there was some outside force such as the girl's father threatening to kill the boy if he did not marry her. However, it suffices for the boy to believe that the father will kill him, whether or not the father would actually do so.

Also possible under this ground is what is known as reverential fear. This occurs when parents compel a child to marry against his or her will. Usually the child is so dependent on the parents, perhaps both financially and emotionally, that breaking away from home to escape the pressure is not possible. This might occur in arranged marriages or perhaps cultures in which it is not acceptable to be a single parent.

Conclusion

This chapter is only a brief introduction to the grounds for nullity in Catholic canon law. The challenge to many is in recognising that simply because two people have performed a wedding ceremony they have not necessarily formed a marriage. How do we discern 'what God has united' from a union that has never been a part of God's plan? When a partnership of the whole of life, formed by the joining together of two people by means of a mutual unreserved gift of self, has never been created after a wedding, is it appropriate to assume it is God-united and so incapable of division? The reality is that many so-called marriages fail and the root of that failure can be traced back to the wedding day. The possibility that a marriage was never formed cannot be ignored.

19

Theology and Reality: Impasse or New Horizons?

Cathy Molloy

Instability is regarded as one of the chief characteristics of modern marriage. Among the main reasons is the ongoing change in the self-understanding and status of women in virtually all cultures and societies which is radically changing the face of marriage. The desire to live marriage as a partnership of equals, whether in terms of fulfilment within the relationship, or of opportunities for employment outside the home, is profoundly affecting families, and the emerging reality is that women are more likely than men to initiate divorce. The institution of marriage, whether Christian or otherwise, is adapting slowly to the changing situation. This chapter presents some of the recent developments in the theology of marriage alongside voices of Roman Catholics who are faced with the impasse regarding remarriage in the absence of annulment. It is suggested that some insights of liberation theology have an important bearing on the issue and could provide new directions in the ongoing attempts to deal with it.

In a 1999 national study the Creighton University Center for Marriage and Family notes that changes in religious, marital and familial structures in the United States are dramatic and are 'creating contexts and concerns and needs that earlier generations never encountered'.[1] The research shows a relationship between religion and marriage and indicates that religion can impact both marital stability and satisfaction, and

---

[1] Creighton University Center for Marriage and Family, *Ministry to Interchurch Marriages, A National Study* (Nebraska: Creighton University, 1999), p. 9.

that marriage can impact the choice, practice and experience of religion. In the Roman Catholic Church there is widespread decrease in faith expressed in committed participation in church. There is now recognition that baptism no longer presumes faith, and so there is growing unease with the current position held in canon law that a valid marriage contract cannot exist between baptised persons without its being a sacrament.[2]

Theology

From an almost exclusive consideration of marriage as institution, described as a *contract*, the major shift in Roman Catholic theology at Vatican II which now sees it described as a *covenant* – an intimate partnership between two persons – continues to have far-reaching effects. Teaching that emphasised what marriage was *for* now focuses on what marriage *is* in itself. The centrality of love in marriage is reflected in the Vatican Council II document *Gaudium et spes*. Its description of marriage as 'a community of love', an 'intimate partnership of conjugal life and love' based in a 'conjugal covenant of irrevocable personal consent',[3] strongly expresses the change in thinking and attitude that now regards marriage as a personal reality.

Several factors are reflected in the developing theology: the fruits of the return to biblical sources characteristic of Vatican II, e.g., the notion of covenant and the retrieval of the Song of Songs; developments in the human sciences; and insights from the experience of married people. In theology there is new awareness of what marriage is, and what it could and should be. Consequently there is also new awareness of what marriage is not, and what it should not be. Alongside this is the important fact that many people having failed or been failed in their marriage want to try again and seek to have their new union at

[2] Canon 1055.2. *The Code of Canon Law* (London: Collins Liturgical Publications, 1983), p. 189.

[3] *Gaudium et spes*, para. 48, in Austin Flannery, OP (ed.), *Vatican Council II: The Conciliar and Post Conciliar Documents* (new revd edn; Collegeville: Liturgical Press, 1984), p. 950.

least recognised and blessed by the church, if not actually solemnised, or celebrated in church. Whether they go about this by way of divorce and remarriage or by way of annulment and subsequent marriage, the aim would appear the same.

Areas of Significant Development in Theology of Marriage

Personal love

In addressing the question of personal love in the marriage relationship, in the immediate aftermath of *Gaudium et spes*, Karl Rahner's contribution to the developing theology has been significant. He believes this love should be considered in its own distinctive nature.[4]

Rahner sees marriage as a sign of personal love at the physical and social level before it is a sacrament. His understanding of this love of husband and wife for one another (in all its aspects) as from, of, and oriented to God, as acquiring fresh roots through grace and uniting the whole of humanity, overcomes the physical/spiritual divide that is so characteristic of talk of love in the Christian tradition. For Rahner, love of God and love of neighbour mutually condition one another. Creation is God's self-communication, and God is primarily recognisable in personal interrelationships. Because it is God's love that sustains creation, gives humans life and love, and draws all to God through it, then the love between two people can lead them to reach each other at the deepest level of their being. The personal love which manifests itself in marriage is salvific through its source in the love of God, and intends God not only in the transcendent but in the nearness in which God's self is revealed – as the innermost mystery and life of the human person. In short Rahner is saying what we hear so often – where love is, there is God. At some fundamental level people know this. We *can know* what this is. Many couples know this, at least sometimes and to some degree, through the experience of

---

[4] Karl Rahner, 'Marriage as a Sacrament', *Theological Investigations*, X (New York: Herder & Herder, and Darton, Longman & Todd, 1973), pp. 199–221.

their life together, and perhaps especially through their experience of sexual love as the expression of their desire for unity. Those writing of the love described in the Song of Songs as the 'flame of Yahweh'[5] knew this.

The wide significance of Rahner's contribution is based in his belief that all of creation is 'graced', i.e., animated by God's own self-communication. All human love, therefore, in so far as it is a going out of self and a reaching towards another, is a reaching for God, and even a making present of God's love in our world. Implicit here is that sexual love also belongs in God's love and is of itself sacramental. Although he assumes children to be the natural fruit of this love, Rahner does not suggest that its purpose is other than to draw humans to their Creator and to one another. A welcome aspect of this understanding is that love need not be split into categories, that God is present in all love. It may be that theologians will turn again to Rahner in trying to come to the truth of love in the many human relationships that are not marriage and are yet waiting to be included in the human view of God's saving love.[6]

Sexual love as sacramental: The retrieval of the Song of Songs

From their various perspectives theologians such as Phyllis Trible, Theodore Mackin, Michael Lawler and Jack Dominian have advanced theological reflection on the explicitly sexual aspects of marital love. The Song of Songs is a significant text for all of them. Trible discusses the mutuality of love which 'knows the goodness of sex and hence knows not sexism'.[7] Mackin talks of sexual desire, sexual passion and pleasure as included in our understanding of Christian marriage as sacramental, as a place of God's encounter with men and women, and as a means to

---

[5] Song 8:7, *The Jerusalem Bible, Popular Edition* (London: Darton, Longman & Todd, 1974), p. 874.

[6] See Cathy Molloy, *Marriage: Theology and Reality* (Dublin: Columba Novalis, 1996), ch. 3, for a discussion of Rahner as a bridge between Vatican II and modern theology.

[7] Phyllis Trible, 'Depatriarchalizing in Biblical Interpretation', *Journal of American Academy of Religion*, 41 (1973), pp. 30–48.

holiness.[8] The articulation of these has given theology access to
new ways of including what was so often excluded from teaching
on Christian marriage.[9] The almost exclusive, centuries-old,
appropriation of the Song of Songs by the mystics and those
who allegorised it is redressed by its retrieval for those whose
story it primarily and properly is – ordinary men and women
whose love for one another is also particularly graced by God,
and no less special for being bodily expressed.[10]

Consummation

Consummation is an essential factor in the indissolubility of
sacramental marriage in Roman Catholic tradition and
practice. A personalist approach to consummation can be seen
for example in Karl Lehmann's contribution to the papers of
the 1977 International Theological Commission (theologians
appointed by the Holy See to study aspects of marriage).[11]
Lehmann reiterates that consent and consummation make
marriage indissoluble and then goes on to open up the
meaning of consummation in personal terms. He recognises
that the intimate sharing of life is what gives its integral
meaning to sexual intimacy, and that it is here that conjugal
consent is 'verified, sealed and comes to fruition'.[12] Kevin Kelly
also rejects an excessively physical interpretation of being two
'in one flesh'. While not denying the importance of the act of
intercourse he understands consummation to mean two
persons becoming one in a very real sense. The marriage is
consummated when the couple experience themselves as a
couple. This is a *de facto* recognition that marriage does not

[8] Theodore Mackin, *The Marital Sacrament* (New York: Paulist Press, 1989),
pp. 42–5.
[9] Michael Lawler, *Marriage and Sacrament* (Minnesota: Liturgical Press,
1993), p. 101.
[10] See Molloy, *Marriage*, pp. 29–32, for more detailed discussion of this
point.
[11] Karl Lehmann, 'The Sacramentality of Christian Marriage', in R. Malone
and J. Connery (eds.), *Contemporary Perspectives on Christian Marriage* (Chicago:
Loyola University Press, 1984).
[12] Lehmann, 'The Sacramentality of Christian Marriage', p. 111.

simply come into being by the exchange of consent followed by sexual intercourse.[13]

In the Protestant tradition Karl Barth approaches indissolubility from a perspective which may be helpful for us today.[14] The 'divine command' is the decisive factor, a marriage rooted in a choice of love made under and according to God's command, and lived in correspondence with the same command, cannot be dissolved. This marriage rests not just on the command of God but on God's calling and gift. Can anyone vouch for such a marriage? Can anyone have the conviction that they are obedient to the command? For Barth, no purely human action can be a guarantee of the divine joining that makes marriage permanent and indissoluble. Nothing from the most passionate *eros* to the blessing by a priest, not pronouncement nor consummation, nothing in human hands or consciousness can do this. Certain positive indicators may lead people to think they have such a marriage but they may be deceived. A standing in a marriage constituted by God can only be a standing in faith. A marriage without divine basis is radically dissoluble since there is no real union in God's judgement which cannot be known but only suspected, on the basis of 'certain terrible indications', and these too might be false. Barth believes people must be content to have provisional comfort only in this matter and not to receive the real thing at which they aim – the awareness that their marriage has been constituted by God.

Mention of 'certain terrible indications' recalls that there is a lacuna in relation to conflict and violence in much contemporary marital theology. Rosemary Haughton's unforgettable reference to a theology of marriage 'shattered by experience',[15] and the work of numerous women theologians have been very plainly showing the way, and still seem not to have been taken seriously in official church teaching and writing on marriage and family. Could clear teaching on what marriage *is*, be

[13] Kevin Kelly, *Divorce and Second Marriage* (London: Chapman, 1996), pp. 34–6.

[14] Karl Barth, *Church Dogmatics*, Vol. 3 (Edinburgh: T&T Clark, 1961), pp. 207–8.

[15] Rosemary Haughton, 'Marriage in Women's New Consciousness', in W. Roberts (ed.), *Commitment to Partnership* (New York: Paulist Press, 1987), p. 149.

accompanied by equally clear teaching on what marriage is *not?* Could the enunciating of the kind of relationship and the behaviours that exemplify Christian marriage sometimes be accompanied by enunciation of some of the more common behaviours in relationship that are a travesty of Christian marriage? The reluctance to spell things out, regarding violent and abusive marital relationships, is striking.

What women have been saying about this for a long time is being echoed by at least some men in the church. A group of Irish Jesuits notes that 'there can be a link between a traditional theology which effectively values women as second-class citizens and a culture which translates this evaluation into violent behaviour'.[16] A group of American male religious notes that 'There is the ambivalence in Christianity towards women, alongside the almost unconditional value and sanctity of the stable family unit which has, in many ways, contributed to a culture of male dominance and, unwittingly to a toleration of violence against women.'[17]

The Experience of Marital Breakdown in Relation to the Church

From within the Irish Catholic Church context, I want to consider some of the problems of marriage breakdown from the perspective of some of those whose experience it is. Statistics, however necessary in giving a picture of the general, put the particular at a remove. However many they are, and however the reality is, or is not, faced up to by our church, particular women and men and children are suffering the consequences. It is never simply a question of breakdown of marriage, of the possible remedy that annulment may provide, or the fact that Roman Catholic canon law or Christian theology is moving in this or that direction. Real people are in

[16] Brian Lennon, SJ, Gerry O'Hanlon, SJ, Bill Toner, SJ, Frank Sammon, SJ, *Women in the Church, An Issue of Solidarity* (Dublin: Jesuit Centre for Faith and Justice, 1995), p. 12.
[17] Gerry O'Hanlon, SJ, 'Women, Violence and the Response of Male Religious', in J. Habte (ed.), *Shalom Strategy* (Silversprings, MD: CMSM (Conference of Major Superiors of Men), 1996), p. 155.

real situations of real pain. As church, for the most part, we have stood by and failed to show even a minimum level of concern that might be expected of a Christian community. Clergy, religious and lay members of the church together share the responsibility for this.

How do some people experience their relationship to the church in the context of marriage breakdown? In a report circulated by a sub-committee of the Dublin Diocesan Women's Forum, people record that their difficulties are compounded rather than helped by the church.[18] They feel angry and alienated and have no sense that the church shares their pain. Re-integration of their lives takes place apart from the church, which is experienced as unsympathetic. They report the experience of rejection – 'the church doesn't want to know us any more, and we feel sad and lonely'. Because of exclusion from the sacraments, these people see themselves in a 'limbo' situation. They bear the rejection of a failed marriage and they experience rejection by the church. 'The biggest harm is to extinguish hope.'

In Northern Ireland, where people have suffered so much because of the political situation, the Forum for Catholic Women reports the same experience of rejection, alienation and abandonment by the church they believe in, and want and need to belong to so much. Individual stories about how people have experienced the annulment tribunal make pathetic listening as they recount long years of waiting for their case to be heard, and their very real sense of injustice at the hands of our church which is otherwise ready to preach to the world about justice. Justice within the church should be as important as the seeking of justice for whatever group. These people feel they are the forgotten ones, the marginalised. And we do well to remember that these are the voices of those who have begun to speak. This injustice within our church is compounded by the fact that too many people have no voice. They have neither the possibility nor the capacity to become involved in lengthy, and costly, and complex procedures, due to lack of money or education, or emotional or psychological strength or stamina, or, most often, a combination of all these factors.

[18] The reports of the Dublin Diocesan Women's Forum and of the Forum for Catholic Women (Belfast) are unpublished to date.

Impasse

In *Familiaris consortio*, Pope John Paul II calls for the ecclesial community to support such people, to give them much respect, solidarity, understanding and practical help.[19] For far too many of them the experience is as described above. It has been noted that 'the priests, the bishops, and the Pope may well utilize a vocabulary of *service* at the same time they continue to have behaviour patterns of *power*'.[20] Alongside this is the genuine difficulty of many people, cited in the papers of the International Theological Commission, in 'accepting current church discipline that tolerates the common life of a union after divorce but requires that sexual intercourse be excluded'.[21]

Where a new union, or remarriage, is concerned people find it a heavy burden to be asked, or expected, to make a choice between two kinds of communion. There is the communion that is vital to Christian life, participation in the union of love between Christ and the church, which is signified and effected by the eucharist, and which their state and condition of life is said to objectively contradict.[22] And there is the communion that is participation in the union of love between the partners, which is signified and effected by sexual intercourse. Both kinds of communion can be occasions of graced experience. If God's love is present in all love, is it right to seek to split that love, to divide and subdivide it? Could it be that in some instances, rather than contradicting the union of love between Christ and the church, couples who have divorced and remarried might rather be contributing to the sign of that love in the church and in the world?

The 'special pastoral reason' for not admitting the divorced and remarried to the eucharist, that 'the faithful would be led into error and confusion regarding the Church's teaching about the indissolubility of marriage',[23] may not be so obviously

---

[19] John Paul II, *Familiaris consortio* (London: Catholic Truth Society, 1981), para. 84, p. 159.

[20] Remy Parent, *A Church of the Baptized* (New York: Paulist Press, 1987), p. 83.

[21] Wilhelm Ernst, in Malone and Connery, *Contemporary Perspectives*, p. 88.

[22] John Paul II, *Familiaris consortio*, para. 84.

[23] John Paul II, *Familiaris consortio*, para. 84.

applicable to today. With wider education, and the many new means of providing it, might not the faithful be capable of discerning some of the subtler points of the teaching? Might they not be able to distinguish, as the faithful in the Orthodox Church are deemed capable of doing, between a first marriage and a subsequent blessing of a marriage after divorce and the requirements of the church have been met? It may be that this is already happening and that, almost twenty years later, the question of scandal (meaning here attitudes or behaviour that may be obstacles to faith and lead others to do wrong) is seen more in terms of the scandal of exclusion than of a lax approach to marriage. Many faithful people find it difficult, even impossible, to understand and accept what they see as excessively rigid and harsh treatment of people in second unions alongside the acceptance and welcome afforded sometimes to people who may be involved in serious exploitation of their fellow human beings. Education for this scandal is needed too.

Referring to the current situation regarding marriage, divorce and the Catholic Church as one of impasse, is not thereby to oppose the ideal of marriage as indissoluble. It is, however, to name the reality that now exists, and to recognise the growing credibility gap within and outside the church. The negative public image afforded to the annulment procedure may not be wholly justified. However, until there is an end to much of the secrecy surrounding it, and a more obvious transparency in terms of how judgements are arrived at, it will remain an unsatisfactory way to deal with marriage breakdown.

The absolute ban on remarriage in church would not have to be compromised by offering some welcome, or asking God's blessing on couples in second unions who sincerely desire to belong fully and actively to their parish community. In many cases all the signs are that God's blessing is already there, and some formal recognition of this could be the basis for a strengthening of their family bonds. One can only imagine the new life it would bring to the church as a whole. The fact that the exclusion of so many from the eucharist is a *de facto* exclusion of their children also is another reason for seriously reconsidering the discipline. Assurances that they are part of the church ring hollow when accompanied by the ongoing exclusion from the eucharist, which many experience as rejection however it is expressed.

Timothy Buckley speaks plainly of the difficulty of many clergy who, when faced with 'the anomalies and injustices of the system', have to admit that it is unsatisfactory and inadequate in the face of the pressing pastoral needs.[24] The well-documented attempt of the three German bishops of the Upper Rhine Province in 1993 to address the issue gave short-lived hope of a way forward, drawing on some aspects of the practice of the Orthodox Church.[25] However, simply to adopt the Orthodox discipline would not be the answer. Orthodox theologians too have expressed unease, noting an urgent need of the Orthodox Church 'to review its thought and practice of marriage and divorce today'. There is also a warning against 'official laxity' in reference to the gap between doctrine and practice.[26]

New Horizons?

'The Pope can say what he likes. I have my experience and I know what I know', commented one woman. In his chapter on Dialectic in *Method in Theology*, Bernard Lonergan discusses the notion of horizons at some length.[27] The horizon is the limit of one's field of vision. As you move about it recedes in front or closes in behind, so for different standpoints there are different horizons. Further for each different standpoint and horizon there are different visions of the totality of visible objects. Beyond the horizon are the objects that for the moment cannot be seen and within the horizon lie the objects that can now be seen. Are there horizons that cannot be transcended? Exploring horizons raises many questions about how our theology of marriage has been formulated and how it will be formulated in the future, and underlies the obvious importance

---

[24] Timothy Buckley, *What binds Marriage?* (London: Chapman, 1997), p. 117.

[25] Full text is reproduced in Kelly, *Divorce*, pp. 90–117.

[26] See, e.g., T. Stylianopolous, 'Marriage in the New Testament', *Greek Orthodox Theological Review*, 34:4 (1989), p. 345; and P. L'Huillier, 'The Indissolubility of Marriage in Orthodox Law and Practice', *St Vladimir's Theological Quarterly*, 32:3 (1988), p. 220.

[27] For what follows see Bernard Lonergan, *Method in Theology* (London: Darton, Longman & Todd, 1972), pp. 237–44.

of having women as well as men, married as well as celibate
theologians, engage in theological research. Could a broad-
ening of the horizon, e.g., to include some of the insights of
liberation theology, shed light on our thinking about marriage
and offer new ways to proceed?

Liberation theology

Some characteristics of liberation theology are its orientation
towards the poor and oppressed, its emphasis on *praxis* in the
light of the Word of God, its hermeneutics – scripture read as a
narrative of liberation – and its understanding of the nature of
salvation.[28]

This method in theology sets out to interpret and to change
the situation of those suffering intolerable material conditions
of poverty, injustice and oppression in Latin America – literally
matters of life and death. Without diminishing the urgency of
that context, I suggest that some of its insights may be of help
in addressing the experiences described in this chapter. The
poor, in the situation under consideration, include those who
experience themselves as discarded, unacceptable by the
church, on the edge or excluded, or perhaps tolerated, because
of their marital situation. In many cases their existential
situation, and its inherent conflict, leads them to experiences
of oppression, and alienation, within the church, often
compounded by material poverty. People whose relationship of
love with their new partner, and perhaps also children, is
precisely where they experience the love of God in their lives,
find that it is precisely this that precludes them from being full
participants in the church. What they experience as life-giving,
and would like to be celebrated in their faith community, is at
best tolerated among the people of God, and sometimes not
even that.

Biblical hermeneutics

In *The Liberation of Theology*, Juan Luis Segundo notes that

---

[28] Alister McGrath, *Christian Theology* (Oxford: Blackwell, 1994), pp. 105–7.

'oppression usually does not reveal itself in barefaced fashion; it hides and hallows itself behind ideologies that obscure what is really happening in concrete human reality'.[29] But God's revelation shows up in a different light when God's people find themselves in different historical situations. For Segundo the Bible is not the discourse of a universal God to a universal human being, and 'partiality is justified because we must find, and designate as the word of God, that *part* of divine revelation which *today* in the light of our concrete historical situation is most useful for the liberation to which God summons us'. He speaks of those who 'tend to muzzle the word of God by trying to make one particular portion of Scripture the word of God, not only for certain particular moments and situations, but also for all situations and all moments'. Wilhelm Ernst, of the International Theological Commission, refers to the right of the church to look again at scripture and its own teaching in the light of the faith of the time, as instanced in the past by the Pauline and Petrine privileges. I think they are saying the same thing.[30]

Liberation and salvation

The relationship between liberation and salvation is central to liberation theology. *Gaudium et spes* speaks about the relationship between temporal, earthly progress and the growth of the Kingdom.[31] The one is said to be of 'vital concern' to the other, in so far as it can contribute to the better ordering of human society. Gustavo Gutiérrez affirms the 'global character of the gratuitous gift of God's love'.[32] This affects all areas of human life. We can and should distinguish between the natural and supernatural, but they are ultimately unified. There is only one actual order of salvation, not one of the history of grace and a separate history of nature. Christ brings us liberation

---

[29] For what follows see Juan Luis Segundo, *The Liberation of Theology* (Maryknoll, NY Orbis Books, 1976), pp. 27–34.

[30] Wilhelm Ernst, 'Marriage as Institution', in Malone and Connery, *Contemporary Perspectives*, p. 88.

[31] *Gaudium et spes*, 39, in Austin Flannery, OP (ed.), *Vatican Council II: The Conciliar and Post Conciliar Documents*, p. 938.

[32] Gustavo Gutiérrez, *A Theology of Liberation* (London: SCM Press, 1974), p. 177.

from sin, the ultimate root of all disruption of friendship and of all injustice and oppression, to a sharing in the life of God. Salvation is the completion of liberation, communion with God and communion with one another. Gutiérrez points out that the Kingdom of God is not reducible to human history or human progress, but without historical liberative events there would be no growth in the Kingdom. God's saving power is revealed through saving actions in history and through human events. Liberation includes every dimension of humanity, and salvation embraces all human reality, transforming it, leading it to its fullness in Christ. The focus is on the presence of grace (accepted or rejected) in everyone.

Where is grace in this perspective? Simple questions direct the answer. Where is God to be encountered by human beings today? Where is God to be encountered among the groups who are marginalised by their churches? Does salvation begin now in our liberating, graced experiences? For some, perhaps many, their salvation begins through their refinding of their self-esteem, of their capacity to go beyond self in loving a new partner, in loving and caring for the children of that union. This is not to imply that salvation can ever be complete in this life, but a question remains, do we co-operate with grace or do we block it? Of course we block grace by our personal sin, but it may be true also that, as church, we block grace by some of our structures or laws for dealing with internal problems, or particular applications of those laws or structures. It may be that, in some instances, it is dis-grace rather than grace that is pushing people to the margins and leading to the kinds of experiences reported in this chapter. What might happen if we were to begin theological reflection from the perspective of those who are presently outsiders?

Utopia

How might the concept of utopia help? A dictionary definition of utopia is 'an imagined perfect place or state of things'. Utopia for Gutiérrez is characterised by its rootedness in present historical reality.[33] The deficiencies of the existing

[33] Gutiérrez, *A Theology of Liberation*, pp. 232–9.

order and their denouncing are largely the reason for the emergence of a utopia. But utopia announces what is not yet, but will be. It is the field of creative imagination which proposes the alternative values to those rejected. Utopia moves forward into the future. In between is the time for building – the historical *praxis*. But, according to Gutiérrez, if utopia does not lead to action in the present it is an evasion of reality. A rejection will be authentic and profound only if it is made within the very act of creating more human living conditions. Gutiérrez contrasts this with ideology which he sees as masking adequate and scientific knowledge of reality, and spontaneously fulfilling a function of preservation of the established order. It tends to dogmatise all that has fallen under its influence. Political action, science and faith do not escape this danger. I ask whether our theology of marriage escapes this danger?

From the developments we have seen, something is trying to emerge, some way of dealing with the impasse, which would more closely approach the truth of who we are as a community of followers of Jesus today. A way is struggling to emerge which respects our understanding of marriage as an indissoluble relationship, and that would recognise, at the same time, that we get things wrong sometimes. It is not always so clear that what God has joined, and what we think God has joined (as expressed by those who operate the annulment tribunals, or who exercise control over who may or may not remarry in church), is the same in all instances. Something is trying to emerge that is a more accurate representation of the love God has shown us in Jesus Christ, reflective of the justice, compassion, and mercy, and forgiveness we believe in, and hope for, in our understanding of salvation. In this understanding utopia is not an unrealistic, unfounded, way of approaching things.

Conclusion

Reflecting on the developing theology of marriage, on some articulated experiences of marriage breakdown within the church, and on some insights of liberation theology, what might be a way forward? Holding to a utopia grounded in present reality, could we creatively imagine and bring to being a celebration of commitment, a blessing and a welcoming of new unions, subject to the kind of process that the German bishops envisaged, alongside renewed efforts at education, support, reconciliation, and so on? For greater integrity there is need to reiterate our aspirations towards the ideals of marriage and at the same time to acknowledge and articulate what is unsaid, unacknowledged, in the present situation. To many the present situation seems only to propose the ideal to the extent of a seeming denial of the real. Might we hope for a real expression of the kind of solidarity that John Paul II calls for in *Christifideles laici*, which goes beyond a 'feeling of vague compassion, or shallow distress at the misfortunes of so many people', to 'a *firm and persevering determination* to commit oneself to the *common good*, that is to say, to the good of all and of each individual because *we are all really responsible for all*'?[34]

The present situation of widespread exclusion, far from strengthening marriage, may be contributing, not insignificantly, to its weakening. Undoubtedly it is weakening the church and we are deprived of many good people, resulting in what may be a refusal of grace within the whole people of God.

Change of course involves risk. We can only imagine what might be the positive result, for the whole Church, and indeed wider society, of including the divorced and remarried who sincerely want to participate fully. Given what we know from other disciplines of the benefits of reasonable family life, with support and welcome from the church community, it could prove transformative.

Liberation theology is a way of doing theology that is a challenge to the Christian churches, but much more it is a gift – the possibility of looking and acting in a new way. Some of its insights, such as the connection between liberation and salvation, considered alongside the developing theology and pastoral practice of marriage, have much to offer in regard to the present impasse.

---

[34] John Paul II, *Christifideles laici* (London: Catholic Truth Society, 1988), para. 42 (author's emphasis).

20

Faithful and Free:
Marriage in the Catholic Church

Timothy J. Buckley

Pastoral Solutions to Pastoral Problems

At the time when I began to think seriously about the
preparation of this chapter I was caught up in a correspondence battle in *The Catholic Herald*. For those of you not
acquainted with this publication, let me explain that it is one of
a number of Catholic weeklies in Britain. A friend alerted me to
a short item in the 'Home News' section of the edition of 4
February 2000, in which I was being accused of having
'erroneous' and 'distorted' views. The background to all this
was a study day for people involved in marriage and family life
ministry in the Diocese of Menevia in September 1999. Fr
Lewis, an advocate for his diocesan marriage tribunal, had read
a report of the day, which correctly stated that I am convinced
that 'the theology of marriage, particularly that of the *bond*'
needs to be re-examined. Fr Lewis, drawing his own conclusions, accused me of asking 'that the Catholic Church should
look again at its teaching on the permanence of the marriage
bond'. He added: 'It does no-one any good to present the
infallible teaching of the Church as being in need of
re-examination.'

I carefully examined that original article and his subsequent
letters and I became convinced that Fr Lewis had not read my
book, *What binds Marriage?*,[1] or anything else I have written on

---

[1] Timothy J. Buckley, *What binds Marriage?* (London: Chapman, 1997).

the subject. I mention this because I believe that we must be willing to listen to one another and study the arguments if we are to have a fruitful debate on this or any other subject. None of us has the total picture nor does any of us have all the answers. However, a particular difficulty in the Catholic community is the tendency in certain theological circles to try to close a discussion with an appeal to authority. Of course this was precisely what Fr Lewis sought to do by asserting that the matter had been infallibly defined.

I responded to him by pointing out that I have been 'at pains to distinguish between what is the consistent and undeniable teaching of the Church and what remains open to dispute'. I only ask whether, in trying to defend the fundamental belief in the sanctity of marriage, legal systems or pastoral strategies have evolved in our different traditions, which neither successfully defend this tenet of belief nor promote other fundamental gospel imperatives. I think I can confidently predict that the kind of issues which beset us in the Catholic Church are not too far removed from those which challenge most Christian traditions, albeit that they may approach these matters from very different angles.

In her chapter (see Ch. 21) Margaret Farley argues convincingly that the time has come for Catholic theology and pastoral practice to recognise that divorce is not in itself incompatible with the gospel. I have much sympathy with what she says. There remain in the Catholic community, as in many other Christian communities, large numbers of people who feel abandoned over this question. Yet the extraordinary fact is that the Catholic Church has in fact countenanced divorce throughout its history. This may come as a surprise to many of you, even the Catholics, but an examination of the tradition reveals that the church has found a way of accepting the dissolution of the bond of marriage in many situations. It has reserved its absolute prohibition on divorce only to consummated sacramental marriages. It is not so much that the church would issue a writ of divorce: rather it has accepted that a new situation – for example a new marriage bond or the solemn vows of religion – effectively dissolves the original bond. This has nothing to do with the practice of annulment. I will explain the basis of these positions later. For now it is enough to realise that the church has consistently sought pastoral solutions to pastoral problems, yet at the same time has tried to hold the line and defend its fundamental belief in the sanctity and permanence of marriage.

I suggest that similar situations exist in almost all our church communities. The Bishop of Winchester honestly reflects on the struggles within the Church of England (see Ch. 22), which are compounded by the fact that it is the Established Church. May I say that I believe the teaching document produced by the Anglican House of Bishops (1999) is excellent.[2] I think the bishops have succeeded in focusing on the heart of the Christian tradition about marriage, while showing a genuine concern and understanding for the kind of problems which beset so many in contemporary society. If Synod eventually accepts the kind of direction they have given, new pastoral options similar to those recommended by some theologians in the Catholic Church for use in the internal forum of an individual's conscience, may become the norm.

Before moving to reflect on what further options there might be in the face of the complex pastoral situation today, I would like to make a plea for those who, like me, have sought to find a way forward in this field. Belief in the sanctity and permanence of marriage is not incompatible with seeking justice and peace for those for whom marriage has ended in breakdown and disappointment. I believe it is God's plan that people be bonded in peaceful and faithful relationships, and that the united family is the ideal setting in which to bring up children. Jesus himself took us back to the teaching of Genesis (Mt. 19:4–5). At the same time, we have to grapple with the paradox of a Kingdom, already established, yet still awaiting fulfilment. Christ is risen, yet much remains to be redeemed. I believe that the Lord's loving presence can reach into every broken situation and redeem it.

Modern society presents us with an altogether new set of circumstances in the field of human relationships and of marriage itself. In *Marriage after Modernity*[3] Adrian Thatcher has

---

[2] *Marriage: A teaching document from the House of Bishops of the Church of England* (London: Church House Publishing, 1999).

[3] Adrian Thatcher, *Marriage after Modernity: Christian Marriage in Postmodern Times* (Sheffield: Sheffield Academic Press, 1999).

examined the current trends in detail, and although some of us may not be comfortable with what is happening, there is no point in burying our heads in the sand and wishing it were otherwise. Jesus did not live in ideal circumstances either, but always he was pointing us towards a more fulfilling way of living. His responses to people's relationship problems, including the breakdown of marriage, are no exception. Every author who writes on this subject analyses the scripture texts and seeks to unravel them in the hope of understanding the Lord's will for contemporary men and women. Thus in my own study of the problem I sought to understand the meaning of the key scriptural references on divorce and match them against Jesus' teaching as a whole.[4] As a result of the advances in scriptural scholarship during the last century we are in a better position than ever to realise that the picture is more complex than some theologians from earlier generations would have us believe. One thing which I find particularly frustrating is the suggestion that there has been some kind of unbroken tradition from apostolic times, and that it is unacceptable that we should be asking questions about matters which were satisfactorily solved from the very beginning. Even a superficial look at the different strands of opinion in the early church and throughout the Patristic period confounds such a theory. For those with the time and the interest, Theodore Mackin, in his monumental study of the question,[5] explores this complex history in detail. At one point he comments:

> The modern student may be surprised to find that the first one thousand years of Christian history would go by before unanimity would be established even in the Western, Latin sector of the Church – not to mention that the disagreement between Latin West on the one hand and the Orthodox East on the other would become permanent.

---

[4] Buckley, *What binds Marriage?*, pp. 29–40.
[5] Theodore Mackin, SJ, *Divorce and Remarriage* (New York: Paulist Press, 1984), p. 114.

The Bond in Catholic Theology

Undoubtedly one of the most significant influences on Catholic theology was the interpretation of Paul's directive to the Corinthians (1 Cor. 7:10–16). Here Paul permits separation if it is the result of one of the partners converting to Christianity and the non-believer insists on leaving. Interestingly his reason was that it is better for people to live in peace. Eventually the conclusion was reached that this did open the way to the possibility of another union and the dissolution of the original bond. Theologically it was deduced that there is a substantial difference between the bond created between two baptised Christians, which is understood to be a sacrament, and that which results from any other relationship. Only the former was understood to constitute the bond to which the Lord was referring when he said: 'What God has joined together, let no one separate' (Mt. 19:6).

Much of the legislation now holding sway in the Catholic community and redounding on many of those in broken marriages, paradoxically, was the result of pastoral initiatives, which sought to resolve the problem of broken marriages. In his correspondence with me an exasperated Fr Lewis challenged me in this way:

> The question is really very simple. Is the Pope's teaching that a ratified and consummated sacramental marriage between two baptised Christians is indissoluble right or wrong?

> I look forward to Fr Buckley's clear and unequivocal endorsement of the Holy Father's words.[6]

You will notice two things: firstly the appeal to authority; secondly the complicated formula that was put before me. I replied that I had 'no difficulty in giving my assent' to the Pope, but I went on to point out that far from being simple, the statement is actually very complicated. It is the formula found in article 1640 of the *Catechism of the Catholic Church*,[7] and the church has had to adopt it precisely because of this history.

---

[6] *The Catholic Herald*, 25 February 2000, p. 7.
[7] *Catechism of the Catholic Church* (London: Chapman, 1994).

Ironically the 'unequivocal' teaching is to be found in article 1614 of the *Catechism*, which states:

> In his preaching Jesus unequivocally taught the original meaning of the union of man and woman as the Creator willed it from the beginning: permission given by Moses to divorce one's wife was a concession to the hardness of hearts. The matrimonial union of man and woman is indissoluble: God himself has determined it: 'what therefore God has joined together, let no man put asunder.'

You will note that there are no exceptions suggested here and the teaching is about marriage *per se*, not sacramental marriage or marriage 'in the Lord'. There is a real difficulty here in the use of language because you end up arguing that marriage is indissoluble, but that some marriages are more indissoluble than others.

These two conflicting definitions of the bond of marriage in the *Catechism of the Catholic Church* express the dilemma which faces the whole of the Christian community. There is an underlying belief in the sanctity and permanence of marriage which is clear in Jesus' teaching, yet there remains the problem that in practice marriages do fail. What is peculiar about the Catholic position is that alongside the long and complicated history of seeking pastoral solutions wherever possible, there is the added dimension of a medieval theological system, which sought to define every aspect of our relationship with God and his creation in clear and absolute terms.[8] Hinging its defence of the indissolubility of marriage in this specific way the Catholic Church has concluded that it does not have the power to dissolve such marriages. Thus article 1640 of the *Catechism* goes on to say that 'the Church does not have the power to contravene this disposition of divine wisdom'. Not surprisingly then in the letter already cited Fr Lewis quoted the Pope's address in January 2000 to the Roman Rota,[9] when he elaborated on this point.

---

[8] For a discussion of the Scholastic definition of the bond see Buckley, *What binds Marriage?*, pp. 54–6.

[9] The Rota is the special Tribunal which sits in Rome, mainly as a Court of Appeal for the local tribunals in the dioceses around the world.

There is an increasingly widespread idea that the Roman Pontiff's power, being the vicarious exercise of Christ's divine power,[...] could be extended in some cases also to the dissolution of ratified and consummated marriages. In view of the doubts and anxieties this idea could cause, it is necessary to reaffirm that a ratified and consummated sacramental marriage can never be dissolved, not even by the power of the Roman Pontiff. The opposite assertion would imply the thesis that there is no absolutely indissoluble marriage, which would be contrary to what the Church has taught and still teaches about the indissolubility of the marital bond.

Annulments

I hope that this short explanation of the Catholic tradition may help to explain why the annulment process has come to play such a prominent part in our pastoral response to the problem of marital breakdown. Once you have trapped yourself into this kind of theological reasoning, the only escape is to establish that for whatever reason the bond never actually existed. Thus the original union may be declared null and void and the partners are free to enter into a new, hopefully valid, relationship. There are good reasons why historically both the church and the state have retained this option. Clearly there are times when people have entered marriage under false pretences or under duress. In such circumstances there can be no free giving of oneself to another and it is surely unarguable that society and the church should be able to free people from any obligations, thought to have been undertaken in such circumstances. The difficulty for the Catholic Church is that, because this is the only official option in a great many situations, the process may appear – indeed may become – somewhat contrived. Undoubtedly the Pope has been deeply concerned about this for a long time: hence his determined addresses to the Roman Rota each January. These notwithstanding, there remains an enormous problem on the ground. Again I do not wish to rehearse arguments that I have explored before both in my book and in subsequent articles.[10] Suffice it to say that the experiences of both priests and people in this field are varied and may depend very much on geographical location as well as theological understanding.

After the Second Vatican Council the grounds for annulling a marriage were extended to include a host of psychological factors. These were largely the fruit of advances in modern psychology which have helped us to understand better our own psycho-sexual make-up as well as the dynamics which affect our relationships. Canon lawyers and theologians rightly seized the initiative and in the revised Code of Canon Law they were included under the following generic clauses: 'those who suffer from a grave lack of discretionary judgement concerning the essential matrimonial rights and obligations to be mutually given and accepted'; and 'those who, because of causes of a psychological nature, are unable to assume the essential obligations of marriage'.[11]

Again I will not explore this question in detail because I have dealt with it elsewhere,[12] but the further question has to be asked: Is this the best forum in which to be using such an analysis? Some will argue that a lawyer with sufficient determination can establish grounds for annulment in virtually any case presented to him. You simply have to start from the conviction that the seeds of the destruction of the marriage must have been inherent from the very beginning. Of course it is this scenario which the Pope greatly fears.

In fairness to the Catholic community, the decision in some parts of the world – most notably the English-speaking – to pursue this process with a will, has been a genuine attempt to respond in a practical way to the crises in many people's lives. The most remarkable recent example of a local church

---

[10] Timothy J. Buckley, 'Caring for the Remarried', *Priests and People*, 9:8, 9 (August–September 1995), pp. 325–30; 'Second Marriage: An opportunity for Spiritual Growth', *The Way*, 37:4 (October 1997), pp. 314–24; 'Second Marriage: Complications in the Catholic Church', *The Way*, 37:4 (October 1997), pp. 325–33; 'English Catholics and Divorce', in Michael P. Hornsby-Smith (ed.), *Catholics in England 1950–2000: Historical and Sociological Perspectives* (London: Cassell, 1999), pp. 199–218; 'Defining the bond of marriage', *INTAMS Review*, 5:2 (1999), pp. 187–90.

[11] *The Code of Canon Law* (London: Collins, 1983), Canon 1095.

[12] See Buckley, *What binds Marriage?*, pp. 160–3.

reaching out in this area was brought to my attention recently. Bishop Kenneth Untener of Saginaw in the USA, to mark the Millennium Jubilee Year, decided to do all he could in his diocese to release people who found themselves in so-called irregular marriage situations. Accordingly he has sought to streamline the annulment process by having forty lay people trained as advocates and offering the service free of charge. He is quoted as saying: 'This is the year when we should find every way possible for people to get right with their church. And one of the main reasons people don't feel right about the church is the problems they have with divorce. I want people to find healing in the church.'[13] In December 1999 he sent a taped message to all 111 parishes in the diocese in which he said: 'In the Diocese of Saginaw, nudged along by the spirit of the year 2000, we have simplified the procedures [...] We have trained lay people who can personally walk through it with each person. We have also eliminated all fees or contributions associated with this journey. It's a free trip home.'[14] I have not heard any follow-up to this, but the article reporting this plan did acknowledge that in the past 'Vatican officials have criticised dioceses in the United States for issuing more annulments than any other country'. The bishop is said to have argued that 'he is not breaking any rules – only making sure that church laws are used to benefit as many Catholics as possible'.

Obviously the Saginaw tribunal cannot guarantee the granting of an annulment to every petitioner, but clearly the signal is being sent out that every case will be treated with great sympathy and the expectation is that the vast majority will be granted. I do not anticipate Rome will respond kindly to this initiative, but I can understand why it has emerged. For my part I think it is another illustration of the trap the Catholic Church has created for itself, and I still believe another, a better way could be found to address this problem.

---

[13] David Crumm, 'Bishop's plan will benefit divorced Catholics', *Detroit Free Press* (9 November 1999), p. 7A.

[14] Crumm, 'Bishop's plan', p. 7A.

The Redeeming Presence of Christ

Some years ago the German Redemptorist Fr Bernard Häring –
who can certainly be counted among the leading moral
theologians of the twentieth century – addressed the problem
of divorce and remarriage in the Catholic Church. He entitled
his short treatise *No Way Out?*[15] Like us today he examined the
complexity of the situation in Catholic jurisprudence and
pastoral practice and concluded that there must be a way of
liberating people from the anomalies and injustices that arise
out of the present dispensation. I treasure the fact that towards
the end of his life I was able to discuss my work with Bernard
Häring. I took heart from the fact that in his last letter to me,
after the publication of my book, he urged me to continue to
work in the field. Not everyone agrees with Häring, but he did
us a great service by pointing the debate in the direction of the
Orthodox East. Of course it would be simplistic to imagine that
all our traditions could readily incorporate the theology of
oikonomia,[16] but I am convinced that it is when we are in
dialogue with one another that we are most likely to discern the
way forward.

Pope John Paul II has spoken eloquently about his hopes of
reunion with the East as a Millennium project. Their discipline
in this whole area is very different from those not only of the
Catholic Church, but also many of the Reformed churches. In
any future dialogue with the East a key element will surely be
the treatment of the divorced and remarried. If we believe that
they have simply been too liberal or misinterpreted the
exception clauses in Matthew,[17] then we may have misunderstood the whole basis of their approach. My eyes were opened
when, towards the end of my research, I interviewed the Greek
Orthodox Archbishop Gregorios of Thyateira and Great
Britain.[18] It was then that I discovered that the *oikonomia* of the
East was not a process applied to pastoral problems, like
the annulment process, but their whole way of theologising

---

[15] Bernard Häring, *No Way Out? Pastoral Care of the Divorced and Remarried*
(Middlegreen, Slough: St Paul Publications, 1989).

[16] For a definition, see Buckley, *What binds Marriage?*, pp. 125–6.

[17] Mt. 5:32 and 19:9.

[18] See Buckley, *What binds Marriage?*, pp. 174–6.

about God's saving presence in Christ. He challenged me to consider whether there are situations into which the saving presence of Christ cannot reach. For me that is the crux of the matter. Are we to say that in spite of our best efforts there will remain people who are beyond the sacramental ministry of the church because their marriage situations cannot be regularised? And for Catholics this affects not only marriage but also admission to the sacraments of reconciliation and the eucharist. This obtains no matter how contrite they are or how careful they have been to ensure justice among all those who may have been hurt as a result of a previous marriage breaking down.

There is a gut feeling among many of us that this simply cannot be what the Lord wants. Let me quote the late Cardinal Hume, addressing the Pope on behalf of the English bishops, when they visited Rome in autumn 1997:

> In this work of reconciliation we are continually confronted, as pastors, with the situation of those in an 'irregular union' for whom there is no perceived possibility of canonical regularisation. We must maintain the clear and consistent teaching of the Church concerning marriage. We must also act pastorally toward those in this situation whether Catholics already or seeking full communion in the Church. In this century especially, the relationship between membership of the Church and reception of Holy Communion has been affirmed and appreciated. It is not surprising that, despite reassurances, those who are not permitted to receive Holy Communion find themselves estranged from the family of the Church gathered for the Mass. We are conscious of your deep concern for these couples and their families and your invitation 'to help them experience the charity of Christ ... to trust in God's mercy ... and to find concrete ways of conversion and participation in the life of the community of the Church' (24 January 1997). We are anxious to receive encouragement from you to explore every possible avenue by which we may address this important and sensitive aspect of our pastoral ministry.[19]

Cardinal Hume was always sensitive and diplomatic in these

---

[19] *Briefing*, 27:11 (20 November 1997), p. 8.

delicate areas of pastoral concern, but you do not have to read between the lines to realise that there is a deep sense of dissatisfaction with the *status quo*. Yet even as I record this I can hear the voices of those who want clear direction, crying out: 'That is all very well, but what in practice do you propose to put in place of the present system?'

Let me go back to Bernard Häring. Towards the end of his life he wrote a couple of books about his own personal experience of the church and of his work as a moral theologian and spiritual guide.[20] Undoubtedly he was greatly influenced by his experiences during the Second World War. As a member of the medical corps in the German army he found ways of ministering both to the military and civilian populations and indeed across the religious divide. Once the war was over and he was invited to pursue the study of moral theology he set himself to challenge the rigorous moral teaching that had shaped his own formation and that still dominated so much Catholic teaching. In this he was to be a true son of his founder, Saint Alphonsus Liguori, who had waged war against the strict Jansenistic approach, which dominated much of the moral understanding of the eighteenth century. It should be noted too that after those wartime experiences Häring became totally committed to the ecumenical cause. He remained in dialogue with other traditions and other religions to his dying day. That first period of theological work and reflection culminated in his three volumes, *The Law of Christ*,[21] and in his contribution as an expert at the Second Vatican Council. In *The Law of Christ* he sought to move Christian moral thinking away from a rigid legalistic mentality to the recognition that laws make sense only when they are caught up in the supreme law of the gospel: love of God and of neighbour.

At the Council he played a major part in compiling the text of the final document, *Gaudium et spes*,[22] and particularly the articles on Marriage and Family Life (46–52). At last the church

---

[20] Bernard Häring, *My Witness for the Church* (New York: Paulist Press, 1992); *My Hope for the Church* (Alton: Redemptorist Publications, 1999).

[21] Bernard Häring, *The Law of Christ* (3 vols.; Cork: Mercier, 1963–67).

[22] Austin Flannery (ed.), *Vatican Council II: The Conciliar and Post Conciliar Documents* (2 vols.; Collegeville: Liturgical Press, 1984 and Leominster: Fowler Wright Books, 1987), I, pp. 903–1014.

was to begin to put the emphasis on marriage as a covenant, caught up in God's covenant love for his people, rather than on the nature of the contract and the exchange of rights and obligations. This was part of a whole process whereby Häring was searching for ways of freeing people to realise that fidelity in any walk of life is achieved not by our own human efforts, but by exposing ourselves to the gracious and loving presence of the Lord. When he came to rewrite his moral theology in the 1970s, he would entitle the three volumes: *Free and Faithful in Christ*.[23] The title says everything about the direction in which Häring was moving. He had become more and more convinced that the gospel message was one of liberation for human beings weighed down by oppression in its many forms, including sin. It is no secret that in his later years he became increasingly frustrated with what he regarded as the dictatorial attitude of Rome and the Roman Congregations. He had seen enough in his life to realise the dangers of trying to impose one's will on other human beings. He realised that the moral life could be lived only when the person acknowledges that Jesus is Lord and seeks to live in the power of the Spirit. He realised that Jesus calls us to follow him in fidelity, which in turn calls for a free response on our part. No one can force us to be faithful. In his own day Jesus called many to follow him; some did, others refused, few remained totally faithful throughout. And so it has continued down through the centuries.

This is the point to leave this discussion, with the emphasis on the redeeming presence of Christ. Readers will have noted the tension between compassion at the plight of individuals and the struggle of the teaching church to proclaim and maintain the truth. I want to assert unequivocally the sanctity and permanence of marriage and the importance of family life, along with other Christians. At the same time we are very conscious of the inadequacies of the Christian community's response down through the centuries as it has sought to find ways of defending these truths, while not abandoning those for whom they have proved impossible to live. The gospel is full of paradoxes and in this field we are confronted by many; but at the heart of them

---

[23] Bernard Häring, *Free and Faithful in Christ* (3 vols.; Slough: St Paul Publications, 1979).

all is how we understand the redeeming presence of Christ. The Catholic theology of the bond is something to which I can give my consent, but whose existence in any given situation I can never definitively prove. Faced with such sadness in so many people's lives, and amidst so much uncertainty, I am fearful of demanding of people more than they may be able to carry, and Jesus did warn about imposing burdens (Mt. 23:4).

In this Millennium Year the Catholic Church has highlighted the notion of Jubilee, seeing in Jesus the one who truly cancels the debt and sets us free. In this context many voices have been raised on behalf of those trapped in seemingly intractable relationship problems. There is a heartfelt conviction that there remains a way for them to remain faithful without being burdened with the extraordinary vocation of celibacy. We are caught up in a great mystery and there is much that we will never fully know or understand. I think we have to be humble and trusting. It is here that I find the Orthodox way so appealing. They too stand firm on their belief in the sanctity and indissolubility of sacramental marriage, but faced with a broken relationship, with a situation which badly needs redeeming, they find a way forward. They do not compromise their fundamental beliefs, but recognising the graciousness of God, they entrust the situation to the Lord, seeking justice and peace for all concerned. If I understand *oikonomia* correctly in this situation, they stop trying to theologise, but rather throw themselves on the mercy of God. That seems to me to be very close to the gospel.

21

Marriage, Divorce and Personal Commitments

Margaret A. Farley

The particular topic I will address in this chapter is the significance of interpersonal commitment for marriage and the implications of marital commitment for our ethical evaluations of divorce and the second marriages that may follow divorce.[1] I have addressed this topic before, but in the almost ten years since my last effort,[2] the questions have become more, not less, urgent. Partly, this is because of the continuing escalation of numbers of divorces in Western society, not only in general in the society but specifically among members of the Christian churches. And partly, it is because there has been little success in adjudicating the differences between, on one hand, stands taken by church leaders, and, on the other hand, the perspectives of many theologians, Christian ethicists, and canonists. This latter is especially true in my own tradition, that of the Roman Catholic Church.

The Situation

In 1992 I noted that while an avalanche of theological literature was published in the 1960s and 1970s addressing

---

[1] My discussion of marriage and divorce is limited here to heterosexual marriage, but I believe that much of what I say has meaning also for considerations of same-sex marriage.

[2] See Margaret A. Farley, 'The Concept of Commitment as Applied to Marriage and Divorce', *Canon Law Society of America Proceedings*, 54 (1992), pp. 87–97. See also my previous essays, 'Divorce and Remarriage: A Moral Perspective', in William P. Roberts (ed.), *Divorce and Remarriage* (Kansas City, MO: Sheed & Ward, 1990), pp. 107–27; 'Divorce, Remarriage, and Pastoral Practice', in Charles E. Curran (ed.), *Moral Theology: Challenges for the Future* (Mahwah, NJ: Paulist Press, 1990), pp. 213–39.

divorce and remarriage in the Roman Catholic Church, this outpouring fell off markedly and almost disappeared in the 1980s and early 1990s. Some important biblical, historical and canonical studies continued during these years, but they were met with little general interest and much less urgency of concern. The majority of Roman Catholic moral theologians, for example, had resolved in their own minds the questions raised out of the contemporary experience of co-believers, and most of the interesting ideas seemed to be already on the table. Moreover, significant pastoral solutions to concrete situations of anguish and pain seemed to have been found by the mid-1970s.

There remained, however, serious disagreements between many Catholic moral theologians and official church leaders on certain issues. Significant changes had indeed taken place in the institutional church's interpretation and application of the law regarding divorce and remarriage. Vatican II, for example, had provided a new articulation of the meaning of Christian marriage and a new emphasis on pastoral approaches to difficult situations. In its aftermath, the bases for marriage annulments were broadened; exceptions to laws regarding divorce were expanded under the 'Pauline privilege' and the power of 'Papal dissolution';[3] and an appeal to the 'internal forum' of individual conscience became effective as a way to allow many Catholics in stable second marriages to return to the sacraments. Yet a serious impasse continued to exist between the opinions of moral theologians and the teachings of the church hierarchy regarding the indissolubility of genuinely valid sacramental

---

[3] The Pauline privilege is based on 1 Cor. 7:15 where Paul allows that if a convert to the Christian faith is confronted with great hostility and even enmity from a non-Christian spouse, 'in these circumstances the brother or sister is not tied'. This exception applies when two unbaptised persons marry; one of them is subsequently baptised; and the unbaptised spouse 'departs'. In this case, divorce is acceptable, and the baptised person may even remarry. See J. P. Beal, J. A. Coriden, T. J. Green (eds.), *New Commentary on the Code of Canon Law* (New York: Paulist Press, 2000), pp. 1365–70. Papal power of dissolution refers to the Pope's power to dissolve a marriage in specific cases. Beal et. al., *New Commentary*, pp. 1372–5.

marriages.[4] The failure to bring these positions closer together has gradually eroded much of the optimism in the Roman Catholic community regarding a just and peaceful resolution to the problems it faces in this area of its life.

In the 1990s pressures grew to pull back from earlier pastoral responses to troubling situations and issues. Criticisms from all sides were levelled at the introduction of more flexible procedures in the work of marriage tribunals; official pronouncements multiplied, prohibiting the return of divorced and remarried Roman Catholics to a sharing in the eucharist; and while pastoral ministries to the divorced and remarried grew, they were frustrated by the tensions in Roman Catholic approaches to the canonical and sacramental issues involved. Hence, during the 1990s, the avalanche of theological writings on these matters began again and continues unabated.[5] The Catholic hierarchy has produced significant statements as well, primarily but not solely reiterating a restrictive traditional position.[6] It would not be accurate to

---

[4] For a short history of this period and its developments in official Catholic Church teachings, see Farley, 'Divorce, Remarriage, and Pastoral Practice', pp. 224–6.

[5] For publications available in English, see, e.g., Bernard Häring, *No Way Out? Pastoral Care of the Divorced and Remarried* (Middlegreen, Slough: St Paul Publications, 1991); Pierre Hegy and Joseph Martos (eds.), *Catholic Divorce: The Deception of Annulments* (New York: Continuum, 2000); Kenneth R. Himes and James A. Coriden, 'Pastoral Care of the Divorced and Remarried', *Theological Studies*, 57 (March 1996), pp. 97–123; Kevin T. Kelly, *Divorce and Second Marriage: Facing the Challenge* (rev. edn; London: Geoffrey Chapman, 1996); Ladislas Örsy, 'Marriage Annulments: An Interview with Ladislas Örsy', *America*, 177 (4 Oct. 1997), pp. 10–18; James A. Schmeiser, 'Reception of the Eucharist by Divorced and Remarried Catholics', *Liturgical Ministry*, 5 (Winter 1996), pp. 10–21. A spate of publications on the family have also been relevant to the questions of divorce and remarriage. See, e.g., Margaret A. Farley, 'Family', in Judith A. Dwyer (ed.), *The New Dictionary of Catholic Social Thought* (Collegeville, MN: The Liturgical Press, 1994), pp. 371–81; Lisa Sowle Cahill and Dietmar Mieth (eds.), *The Family, Concilium* 1995/4 (Maryknoll, NY: Orbis Books, 1995); Anne Carr and Mary Stewart Van Leewen (eds.), *Religion, Feminism, and the Family* (Louisville, KY: Westminster John Knox, 1996); Mary Anne Foley, 'Toward an Ecclesiology of the "Domestic Church"', *Église et Théologie*, 27 (1996), pp. 351–73.

[6] See, e.g., the now famous initiative by three German bishops (suggesting a more flexible approach to individual cases): Bishop Karl Lehmann, Archbishop Oskar Saier, Bishop Walter Kasper, 'Pastoral Ministry: The Divorced and Remarried', *Origins*, 23 (10 March 1994), pp. 670–6; and the

place all theologians on one side of the issue and all church leaders on the other, though to some extent the major struggle is between a majority of theologians and key church officials.

The Problem

But what is to be done to mediate these positions? The problem does not seem resolvable simply by either relativising or absolutising past norms. There are in place good initiatives (as other chapters in this volume attest) for healing old wounds and strengthening new ties, and we have come a long way in our discernment of the moral imperatives before us. Yet the need for insight, for wisdom that will serve freedom and hope, remains; and some promise of this lies in persevering with efforts to adjudicate between conflicting views. To this end, let me try to assess the problem anew, stepping back for a moment from the well-known arguments and counter-arguments.

Debates until now have tended to focus on juridical, moral and ontological interpretations of the bond that marriage entails. All of these elements are intrinsic to the problem, and they must continue to be addressed. Suppose we ask first, however, why the problem as a whole is so important to us – in the Roman Catholic Church and in all the Christian churches. Why do we care so much that marriages are fragile, or that divorce and remarriage seem inevitable, even though they may not be our best remedy for the vulnerability of marriage itself? A number of answers can be given to this question, and their rich complexity is not captured by simple statements that something is right or wrong, or that certain patterns of

---

Vatican response: Cardinal Joseph Ratzinger, 'Reception of Communion: Divorced-and-Remarried Catholics', *Origins*, 24 (27 Oct. 1994), pp. 337, 339–40; and the bishops' response in turn: Bishop Karl Lehmann, Archbishop Oskar Saier, Bishop Walter Kasper, 'Response to the Vatican Letter', *Origins*, 24 (27 Oct. 1994), pp. 341–4. See also the firm reiteration of a traditional position by John Paul II, 'The Ratified and Consummated Sacramental Marriage', *Origins*, 29 (10 Feb. 2000), pp. 553–5. A variety of statements have also been published by individual bishops, e.g., Bishop Sean O'Malley, 'An Annulment is Not a Divorce', *Origins*, 27 (19 June 1997), pp. 65–8. Most recently (on 24 June 2000), the Vatican, through its Pontifical Council for Legislative Texts, reaffirmed the traditional ban on communion for divorced persons who have remarried (reported in *The New York Times*, 6 July 2000).

behaviour fit (or do not fit) an assumed pattern of Christian life. For example, Christians by and large believe that it is God's intention that marriage should be 'for life'. We also recognise that it is not only God's desire and intention that are at stake, but our own. When we reach a point in a relationship where we want to share our life with another individual, marriage (at least in some form) looks like our best option. The very nature of this love moves us to want to sustain it for ever; our happiness seems to lead in this direction. And many of us still think that building a family is among the greatest of human enterprises. We also recognise the need for stability not only in our own lives but also in the societies on which we depend. And we still believe in the distinctiveness and importance of the bond of marriage as part of the fabric of the life of the church. Marriage, then, with permanence as one of its essential elements, is what God wants and we want and need – whether for ourselves or for others.

And yet it does not seem to work. The promises we make do not always hold; the desires we experience are not always fulfilled; the wholeness our love seeks is often elusive; the families we try to build are often fragmented and troubled; the stability we count on all too often disappears under our feet; and there is among us too much suffering and pain. Some analysts tell us that this is because ours is an era of radical individualism; we are not able to take responsibility for one another in the way past generations have done. Or ours is a hopelessly hedonistic culture, lost to the forms of discipline that human life requires. Or we belong to a sadly anxious and alienated set of generations, disturbed by too much war and death, too much ambiguous progress and change, too much expectation with too little wisdom about how to achieve what we yearn for and expect.

But maybe the explanation is both simpler than all of this, and at the same time more complex. What if our troubles regarding marriage and family are the consequence of real incapacities – not all of our own making, but part of our share in the 'human condition'? The kinds of incapacities we experience may be yet another manifestation of 'original sin', the primary consequence of which is not disordered lust (as many of our Christian predecessors thought) but our 'almost inability' to live together? Whether one interprets 'original sin' in fairly literal terms (its consequences passed on from one generation to another, in a humanity still broken even though redeemed) or in terms of a social context (in which we are weakened by one another's failings as much as we are strengthened by one another's virtue),[7] the struggle 'to live together' goes on, century after century, among peoples, nations, religions, classes. It goes on, too, in our most intimate lives, our most intimate relationships, especially when what is at stake is genuinely sharing our lives together on a day-to-day basis.

Our incapacities to sustain marriage and family are dramatically revealed at this point in our history for particular reasons. In the past, the 'institution' of marriage sustained the relationship between partners in a marriage, and, when necessary, it covered over the fragility and sometimes even terror of the relationship. (It did not matter so much whether husbands and wives, for example, loved one another or got along well with one another. If they did not, they could spend their time in other circles of men or women in which each could find strength, companionship, and even solace.) Society, the church, culture, almost every other institution worked to maintain the *institution* of marriage because it served their aims. The goal was largely social utility, whether for the sake of the empire, the tribe, the nation, or the church. In turn, marriage as institution could for centuries on end sustain (or circumvent) marriage as relationship, and it could stabilise the intergenerational family that was most frequently formed. Today there is, in a sense, no recognisable 'institution' of marriage,[8] no institution that can be assumed to do for intimate relations what the marriage institution of the past could do.

What will, then, hold marriage as a relationship? What will hold the relationships that form our marriages? Not presently a strong and unquestioned institution, not the love itself, not the

---

[7] See, e.g., the interpretation of 'original sin' offered in Karl Rahner, *Foundations of Christian Faith* (trans. William V. Dych; New York: The Seabury Press, 1978), pp. 106–15. It can be argued, of course, that when this concept applies to social context, then the interpretations of individualism, hedonism, etc., as the source of our problem may prevail.

[8] I am not implying that the sea changes in family structures are a bad thing. They are simply a fact of life.

sanctioned 'laws' of marriage, not even the children born of marriage. Love is notoriously fickle, waxing and waning in ways we cannot always control. And all the laws proclaimed, even reinforced by sanctions, do not save us from our inabilities to live together in peace and in joy. Children do hold us to one another and to them, but we have massive evidence that they alone cannot save our marriages.

We need not, however, appeal to doctrines of original sin in the sense of 'brokenness' or 'fall', to understand all of this. We can also appeal to a theology of human nature, a theology of essentially human possibilities and limitations. One of the things revealed to us in our present experience of so much powerlessness before the unravelling of a given marriage is that the efficaciousness of our free choice is limited. If freedom is our power of self-determination; if it is our capacity to take hold of ourselves by ratifying or refusing to identify with our own spontaneous desires, loves, judgements, obligations; then it is indeed the capacity to fashion ourselves according to the self we choose.[9] Yet sheer free choice – the 'grit your teeth and do it' sort of choice – is so limited. We want to remain loving and faithful, peaceful and strong, utterly self-forgetful and devoted, in a relationship of marriage. This may be easily said, but not so easily done. If life with a particular other becomes intolerable – as it can become – it will not be made tolerable simply by choosing it so, not by controlling the other or even by controlling one's own self. Freedom may be our noblest feature, that by which we determine our own destiny in some kind of ultimate sense. Yet it has limited power to shape our own inner selves or our relationships with others.

In the face of limitation and powerlessness, what is there in the Christian tradition to strengthen us, to help us fashion our freedom and love? We have symbols and images, beliefs and convictions, memories and hopes: and what do they yield? Understandings of 'covenant', of 'sacrament', of Christian

[9] I am obviously not addressing here the complex issues of whether we are free in any way, or whether we even have (or are) 'selves'. In a forthcoming book on *The Experience of Free Choice* I intend to take up these questions, but for now I only assume certain interpretations of our experience – ones, however, that I believe resonate with ordinary experience, whether or not they stand up in systematic theories.

agape and unconditional fidelity; metaphors of Christ in relation to the church, and 'two in one flesh'; interpretations of gender complementarity and the church as family. We have theologies of sexuality and friendship and embodiment and justice. In so far as we make all of these resources our own – elements in our faith, informers of our hope, reinforcements of our love – they do help us to sustain our choices and to remain loyal to our intentions. Yet these particular elements in our tradition have themselves come upon hard times, and not only because of our infidelities. As ideas, images, theological construals, they no longer offer sure remedies for our weaknesses of mind and heart, or sure bridges for our limited freedom. Even when lodged in genuinely sacramental realities, they do not by themselves solve our present inability to sustain our marriages in the ways we have wanted to sustain them. And why not? Or why not, at least as much as they have done so for other generations in the Christian community?

A justifiable 'hermeneutic of suspicion' has undercut for us, as well it should, the past power of many of these notions in our traditions. We have learned, for example, that covenants were all too often, in the biblical tradition, between unequals; Christ's relation to the church has been all too often translated into gender-assigned roles; 'two in one flesh' covered over the frequent loss of identity and violation of an individual's (usually a woman's) own humanhood; myths of marriage and friendship sometimes became 'cheap grace'; the church's history regarding sexuality is so greatly flawed; and so on. All of these images and ideas may be retrievable, but not without passing through a clarifying critique.

So, where shall we go? Where is grace in all of this? How does grace 'work' in these aspects of our lives? How does 'sacramental grace' function, and how can it be recognised and nurtured? One place we might look is to the nature of the commitment that is at the heart of marriage. Probing its experience and its meaning may shed light on the ways of sustaining marriage as well as the ways of letting it go.

The Marriage Commitment: Making, Keeping, Changing

Like any other explicit, expressed, interpersonal commitment, marriage involves the giving of one's word.[10] But what do we give when we give our word, and why do we give it? First, giving our word has to do with an intention of action not only in the present but in the future. In the case of marriage, we give our word regarding interior actions (of respect, love, trust, and so forth) and exterior actions (regarding a way of sharing a life together), promising these actions on into the future, indeed (at least in the Christian tradition) until we die. We do not simply predict our actions in the future, nor only resolve to do them. To give our word means, fundamentally, to give to another a claim over ourselves, a claim on our doing and being what we have promised.

What happens, then, when we make a commitment (including a commitment in marriage) is that we enter a new form of relationship. We 'send' (from the Latin, *mittere*) our word into another; we 'place' ourselves in the other to whom we give our word. Frequently in human affairs we try to concretise this, express it and symbolise it, by making the 'word' tangible. For example, we sign our name on contracts; we give rings as signs of our word and ourselves; we exchange gifts to signal the exchange of our promises. And why do we do this? Precisely because our loves, our intentions, are fragile. Commitment in the human community implies a state of affairs in which there is doubt about our future actions; it implies the possibility of failure to do in the future what we intend in the present; it is necessary for those who recognise both their brokenness and the sheer limits of their freedom to determine, in some final way, their own future. The primary purpose, then, of interpersonal and social commitments is to provide some reliability of expectation regarding the actions of free persons whose wills are shakable.[11] Commitments give us

---

[10] I adapt here an analysis of 'commitment' made at much greater length in my *Personal Commitments: Beginning, Keeping, Changing* (San Francisco: Harper, 1986), especially ch. 2.

[11] When God makes promises to us, enters into covenant with us, it is not because God's will is shakable, but because God wants to give us a claim on God, and wants us to know thereby (as best we can understand) the sort of unconditional love that is God's for us.

grounds for counting on one another, even on ourselves. The purpose of promising is both to assure the other of the future we promise and to strengthen ourselves in our intentions for the future. It does so because to give our word is to undertake a new obligation for which there will be sanctions should we fail in fulfilling it (we stand to lose the 'word' we have given, to lose our reputation or our goods, even our happiness and sometimes perhaps even our salvation). By committing ourselves we give, as it were, a new law to ourselves; we bind ourselves by the claim we give to another. We do so not because we must, but because this is what we want to do. We want to be held to what we most truly want to do and be. The 'word' we give now calls to us from the one who holds it, the one to whom we have entrusted it. What commitment means, then, and what it entails, is a new relation in the *present*, a relation of binding and being bound, giving and being claimed; but the commitment points to the *future*. In the present, a new relationship begins, and it is what moves into the future.[12]

This is true of all human commitments, but there are elements specific to the commitment to marry that are extremely important to our understanding of it and to our gaining any light on what it means and how it can be lived. For example, the commitment to marry is essentially mutual: two liberties meet, two words are given, two claims are yielded and held. Moreover, marriage involves a commitment to more than one person. At least in a Christian construal of what marriage is, a commitment is made not only to one's partner but to God and to a community of persons (to the church and to the wider society). In addition, while a commitment to marry is made to persons, its content includes a commitment to a certain framework of life in relation to persons. That is, while those who marry commit themselves to love one another, they do so by committing themselves to whatever is understood as the 'institution' of marriage.[13] 'Framework', of course, has more

---

[12] Our free choice cannot 'settle' ahead of time our future. But it can influence our future. It can change our reality in the present, change our relationships in the present, so that what we do in the future can – depending on what we do and under what circumstances – be accurately described as 'faithfulness', or 'betrayal'.

[13] Despite the fact that we have so little of the 'institution' left, there remains some content to what 'marriage' means.

than one level of meaning in this context. There is a level at which 'marriage' is a framework that structures a relationship into some generic form (for example, most generic understandings of marriage include the element of permanence). There is also a level where framework means a certain cultural or religious model of marriage (as, for example, when it includes sexual exclusivity, and either a hierarchical structure or one of equality between spouses). And finally there is a level of framework which is the particular structure implied or already worked out by particular participants in a given relationship of marriage (as, for example, the ways in which they will share their possessions, relate to one another's families, and educate their children).

In our own culture, and certainly in the Christian tradition, an intention of permanence is included in the marital commitment. Given massive historical changes in social contexts, some of the reasons for incorporating the element of permanence in the framework of marriage have changed, though many remain the same. The importance of interpersonal reasons has grown (as we have seen), and institutional reasons receded. Yet there have always been reasons for permanence that are intrinsic to the marital relationship itself and reasons of social utility beyond the relationship. Love itself can want to give its whole future, to bind itself irrevocably to the one loved and to express itself in this way. It may also be argued that sexuality is best served in a context of permanent commitment, where it has a chance of being nurtured and integrated into the whole of one's personality and one's primary relationship. Further, an intention of (and commitment to) permanence is for the good of children and the good of the church (in which marriage can function as a way of Christian life and a sign of God's presence).

Yet here we meet the heart of a problem. If an intention of permanence is intrinsic to the meaning of Christian marriage, and if marriage as a commitment is self-obligating, is it ever justifiable to end a marriage short of the death of one's spouse? Can the claim given to another in the commitment of marriage ever be released? This is the central moral question for both divorce and remarriage. And behind this, perhaps, lies the further question: If a marital commitment to permanence cannot be released, should such a commitment reasonably be made in a time when our ability to sustain it seems so compromised? Or if we come to understand more fully what is needed in order to live our commitments 'to the end', will we thereby learn better not only how to sustain them but also how, if finally necessary, to let them go?

Divorce

We are used to acknowledging release from a marriage obligation when it can be determined that some basic flaw marked the original marrying – a flaw in the procedure, a lack of full consent, a situation of unfreedom of any kind (whether physical, psychological, or moral). This kind of 'release' is, of course, not really a release from an obligation but a recognition that no marriage obligation was ever truly undertaken; the marriage did not really, validly, take place. The much more difficult question is whether the obligation intrinsic to a genuinely valid, Christian (especially a sacramental) marriage can ever be ended without betrayal, without the unjustified and unjustifiable violation of a claim that was once yielded to another.

My own position is that a marriage commitment is subject to release on the same ultimate grounds that any extremely serious, nearly unconditional, permanent commitment may cease to bind.[14] This implies that there can indeed be situations in which too much has changed – one or both partners have changed, the relationship has changed, the original reason for the commitment seems altogether gone. The point of a permanent commitment, of course, is to bind those who make it in spite of any changes that may come. But can it always hold? Can it hold absolutely, in the face of radical and unexpected change? My answer: sometimes it cannot. Sometimes the obligation must be released, and the commitment can be justifiably changed.

To understand situations such as these, it is useful to look at the generic grounds for discerning when a commitment no

[14] See *Personal Commitments*, ch. 7. I do not want to imply that there can be no absolute commitments, unconditionally binding no matter what. But marriage is not one of them.

longer obligates.[15] Three grounds are defensible, it seems to me, and they can be applied in the context of marriage and divorce. A commitment no longer binds when (1) it becomes *impossible* to keep; (2) it no longer fulfils any of the *purposes* it was meant to serve; (3) another obligation comes into *conflict* with the first obligation, and the second is judged to *override* the first. Only one of these conditions needs to be in place (though often more than one characterises the situation) in order to justify a release from the commitment-obligation. It is sometimes extremely difficult to discern when such conditions actually come to be, but that they do and that they can be identified, even in relation to marriage, seems to me to be without doubt. Some brief observations regarding each of these conditions may help to make this clear.

First, then, when it truly becomes *impossible* to sustain a marriage relationship, the obligation to do so is released. Impossibility, especially physical impossibility, has long been accepted as a general justifying reason for release from the obligation of a promise. The kind of impossibility that is relevant for marriage commitments is not, of course, physical but psychological or moral.[16] Hence, recognising it is less like perceiving an incontrovertible fact than like making a judgement or even a decision. Still, examples can be given – of irremediable rupture in a relationship, or utter helplessness in the face of violence, or inability to go on in a relationship that threatens one's very identity as a person; and it seems true that a threshold of genuine impossibility does exist. We do know of situations in which what was once love is now seemingly irreversible bitterness and hatred, so that to remain together threatens utter destruction to the partners themselves and to

---

[15] I provide a fuller description of these generic reasons or conditions in ch. 7 of *Personal Commitments*. I have also discussed in more detail the adaptation of these in the context of marital commitment and divorce in the essays cited in note 2 above.

[16] There is not space in this chapter to include a discussion of what I have elsewhere called the 'way of fidelity'. That is, I can only assume here the kind of effort, wisdom, etc., that is necessary to prevent the point of 'impossibility' being reached. For this more positive treatment, see *Personal Commitments*, ch. 4. There as here, however, I acknowledge that circumstances can emerge, whether with or without anyone's culpability, when nonetheless it becomes genuinely impossible to sustain a commitment-obligation.

others. We know of situations where some aspects of the relationship may still survive but others prove so contradictory to marriage that at least one partner can no longer sustain it (as, for example, in a situation of relentless domestic violence). Or apathy and despair can burden a person and a relationship to a degree that, without drastic change, one is convinced one will, as a person, die. Or it may even happen that a new love arises, and it becomes too late to 'turn back' (whatever one should have done about refusing this path in the first instance).

Second, a marriage commitment may reach a point where it has *completely lost its purpose*, its whole *raison d'être*, its intrinsic meaning. It is meant, for example, to serve love and life for spouses, for family, for society, for God. In order to do this it includes a commitment, as we have seen, to a 'framework' for loving. But if the framework becomes a threat to the very love it is to serve, if it weakens it or contradicts it or blocks it, then the very commitment to love may require that the commitment to marriage as a framework must come to an end. Of course, marriage has multiple meanings and purposes, but it may be, in some circumstances, that *all* of these are undermined by the marriage itself (or some are so gravely undermined as to jeopardise them all). If so, the obligation to the marriage commitment is released.

Third, if another obligation *conflicts* with and *takes priority over* the commitment to marriage, then the marriage bond may be released. Given the seriousness of the commitment to marry, there are not many other obligations that can supersede it. It is, after all, made with the kind of unconditionality that is meant to override other claims almost without exception. Yet there may be times when other fundamental obligations do take priority – fundamental obligations to God, to children, to society, even to one's spouse (when, for example, commitment to the well-being of the spouse conflicts with continued commitment to relationship within the framework of marriage). It is also possible for a fundamental obligation to one's own self to justify ending a marriage (not because love of self takes priority over love of another, but because no relationship should be sustained that entails, for example, the complete physical or psychological destruction of a person, including oneself).

When under certain conditions a marriage commitment ceases to bind, are there no obligations (human and Christian) that remain in relation to one's spouse? Clearly there are. Though commitment to a framework for loving is not completely unconditional or absolute, there are unconditional requirements within it. For example, there is never any justification to stop loving someone altogether – not a marriage partner any more than a stranger or even an enemy. When it is no longer possible or morally good to love someone within the framework of marriage, it is still possible that we love that individual at least with the love that is universally due all persons. It may even be that an obligation to a particular love is required, one that is in *some* way faithful to the relationship that once existed. But let me turn briefly to what remains perhaps the most difficult question, especially in the Roman Catholic tradition. That is, when the commitment to marriage no longer binds as such, when a true divorce is morally justified, is it also justifiable to remarry?

Remarriage

The traditional Roman Catholic position has been and is that even if an end must come to a marriage in the sense of separation from shared 'bed and board', there remains nonetheless an obligation not to remarry. The reason for this, of course, lies ultimately in a conviction that the original marriage in some sense continues to exist. Against the position I have just outlined (wherein the original marriage may no longer exist) are serious arguments such as: (1) Christian sacramental marriage, unlike other commitments, is under the command of God and the interpretation of that command by Jesus Christ. Hence, the indissolubility of marriage remains absolute. (2) The 'framework' or institution of marriage is under the governance of the church. There is, therefore, a special stipulation included in the marriage commitment whereby there will always be a juridical 'remainder'. Even if every other aspect of the commitment becomes impossible or meaningless or in conflict with a greater obligation, this much of the marriage commitment still holds. (3) A commitment to marriage, with valid consent and sexual consummation, changes the partners in their very being. No longer are they bound only legally or morally, but they are ontologically bound in an irreversible way.

I have elsewhere addressed these arguments, and I can here only summarise my responses to them.[17] Regarding the first, biblical scholars seem to me to have shown effectively the exegetical difficulties of using New Testament texts to settle the question of an absolute requirement of indissolubility in marriage.[18] Regarding the second, a purely ecclesiastical juridical basis has never been given as the incontestable and absolute ground for indissolubility (human laws can be changed, or exceptions can be developed).[19] Even the third argument, regarding the ontological union of spouses, is difficult to maintain with traditional warrants. Despite escalating language regarding the 'two in one flesh' image (in terms of an 'ultimate gift' of spouses to one another, or the 'nuptial meaning' of the body[20]), any concept of fusion between persons risks ignoring the realities of individual persons, and rests too often on symbols of purity/defilement that can no longer be sustained. Moreover, appeals to ontological union fail to acknowledge the limits of human freedom (as I have tried to outline them earlier in this chapter).

This said, I am nonetheless inclined to acknowledge that some kind of bond of being is effected through marriage, and even that it remains in some form when the marriage commitment has come to an end. When two persons commit themselves to one another in the profound form of marrying; when they share their lives together for whatever period of time; they *are* somehow changed, united, in their beings. There are many ways in which this change continues, no matter what. After the marriage has ended, what remains may even include a 'bodily' bonding (now experienced positively or negatively) as a result of the sexual relationship that once was part of the marriage. There may also remain a spiritual bonding (positively or negatively experienced) as a result of months or years of shared history. If the marriage resulted in children, former spouses will be held together for years in the ongoing project of

---

[17] See essays cited in note 2.

[18] See, e.g., Mary Rose D'Angelo, 'Remarriage and the Divorce Sayings Attributed to Jesus', in Roberts, *Divorce and Remarriage*, pp. 78–106.

[19] See, e.g., John T. Noonan, *Power to Dissolve* (Cambridge, MA: The Belknap Press of Harvard University Press, 1972).

[20] See, e.g., the many writings of John Paul II on marriage.

parenting. In any case, the lives of two persons once married to one another are for ever qualified by the experience of that marriage. The depth of what remains admits of degrees, but something remains.

But does what remains disallow a second marriage? My own opinion is that it does not. Whatever ongoing obligation a residual bond entails, it need not include a prohibition of remarriage, any more than the ongoing union between spouses after one of them has died prohibits a second marriage on the part of the one who still lives.

Context, Conclusion and Ongoing Task

What, then, have I been trying to suggest in all that I have said thus far? First, I have based my considerations on the conviction that it is important to continue trying to adjudicate conflicts within the Christian community on issues of divorce and remarriage. Second, I have suggested that this ongoing effort may be helped by an alternative interpretation of the causes of the widespread breakdown of marriage – an interpretation that takes into account the limits of human freedom and the incapacities endemic to the 'human condition', historically and culturally shaped. Third, I have turned to an analysis of the marriage commitment in order to determine its elements, obligations, and the possibilities of its release.

My underlying interest in all of this has been the question of 'how grace works'. Christians believe that the grace of God is available in and through Christian marriage. The evidence of failed marriages suggests that this grace is not automatically effective. We need to learn how to (or we need the grace to) access it, nurture it, discern its ways. Our questions expand, then, to an exploration of how grace works in our loves, our incapacities, our promises, our ordinary efforts to live out our lives together, and even in our failures. I have not, in this chapter, probed the question of the 'ways of fidelity',[21] though this is of the utmost, indeed primary, importance. I have tried

[21] Though were I to do so, I would attempt to adapt chs. 4, 5 and 8 of my *Personal Commitments* in a way comparable to my adaptation of ch. 7 in this chapter.

only to ask about the faithful ways of ending marriages and the faithful possibilities of beginning again. In so far as we gain wisdom on all of these questions we shall find a healing word which may both strengthen marriages and, when it is necessary, ease the pain of their ending. Grace, I want to argue, can extend in all of these directions.

PART 8

Ending Marriage:
Anglican Perspectives

Introduction

Part 8 is the second of two consecutive sections to consider theological and pastoral questions surrounding divorce and remarriage, this time from an Anglican, specifically Church of England, perspective. The chapters that follow are arranged in three pairs. In the first pair Michael Scott-Joynt describes the content of two recent publications of the House of Bishops of the Church of England, one a teaching document on marriage, the other a discussion document on marriage in church after divorce. His chapter also provides a description of the historical and social circumstances surrounding the two documents, and explains something of the bishops' purposes in issuing them. As Chair of the working party which produced one of them, he is uniquely qualified to provide an insider's view of 'official' Church of England thinking on these matters at the present time. Bishop Michael also describes the initial reception of the documents, and hazards his own view of what the longer-term responses to the documents are likely to be.

Timothy Woods reflects on some of the awkward dilemmas which the situation, addressed by these two documents, poses for pastoral practice. Woods recalls being required by canon law to marry a couple, both of whom were not previously married and had children from previous relationships. He was, however, prevented from officiating at the marriage of another couple, where the bridegroom had been formerly married, and whose former wife had had an affair within ten weeks of their wedding. These cases highlight theological and pastoral difficulties entailed by the Church of England's present 'confused' policy about remarriage. Behind these anomalies Woods finds

373

further contradictions. One is the incompatibility between a 'patriarchal' church which delights in making pronouncements and enforcing disciplines, and a broad church which encompasses difference. Another incompatibility lies in people's perceptions of the church's alternative faces, at once affirming and welcoming, while at the same time judging and excluding. Woods asks what inferences people might draw from these appearances about the operational understanding of God that they presuppose, and urges that a 'communal' or relational understanding of marriage must replace a 'contractual' one before these dilemmas can be resolved.

The second pair of chapters consists of two highly original essays on ecclesiastical law, both of which have direct consequences for understanding the Church of England's teaching and practice regarding divorce and remarriage, and on the status of divorced and remarried people within it. The relation between civil and ecclesiastical law shows wide variation in the nations of Christendom. In England this relationship follows a model that has today become rare; and an examination of it, as it affects valid, legal marriage, yields gains for a theological understanding of civil society. Far from adopting a 'two kingdoms' or 'two spheres' approach to church and state, the tradition of 'Christian England' assumed a near identity between them. The two essays analyse this relationship and draw conclusions which will clearly influence the debate in the Church of England, and shed light on discussions among Anglicans and Episcopalians elsewhere. Augur Pearce tests how far, with regard to matrimonial law, nation and church have continued to coalesce or to become distinct. Examining various debates in marriage law from the Reformation onwards, he shows that the national Parliament has never formally disclaimed its responsibility to express the Christian conscience of the nation. As Pearce wryly observes, such a position 'gives significant support to those ... who hold themselves loyal members of the English church, and yet find the law of the land more easily reconcilable with their consciences than the pronouncements of bishops and synods'.

Jacqueline Humphreys' and Simon J. Taylor's chapter focuses directly on the contribution of civil law to the ecclesial and theological understanding of marital indissolubility. They show how the Church of England has *de facto* accepted civil control over the entry of people into marriage, their exit from marriage, and subsequent re-entry into further marriage. That church has no self-contained law of marriage, and its canon law describing marriage depends on civil law for its interpretation. At the Reformation, the monarch became the highest authority for church law in England. When Parliament legislated against informal marriage in 1753, it claimed jurisdiction over the conditions of entry into marriage, and the Church of England was obliged to recognise this. In the cases of prohibited degrees and the recognition of nullity the church amended its canons in order to conform to civil law. Indeed it has no account of the validity of marriage different to that provided by the civil law.

The Church of England is bound to recognise marriages it does not perform. Actually, in common with other churches, it does not perform marriages at all, as its liturgies attest, but witnesses and blesses them. Humphreys and Taylor scrutinise a recent 'teaching document' (see Ch. 22) of the House of Bishops and conclude that the bishops do not think Christian marriage is 'qualitatively different' to other marriages. This position is consistent with the belief that marriage is 'a gift of God in creation'. The church, then, does not add *ex opere operato* anything to a marriage by performing a ceremony. The church has submitted to Parliament in its growing control of the exit from marriage. The ecclesiastical courts were divested by Parliament of responsibility for marriage and divorce in 1857. But the church is obliged to recognise marriages which it has not conducted, and these include remarriages. Neither does the conscience clause, which exempts clergy from the obligation to perform second marriages, allow the church to fail to recognise them.

On grounds of consistency, then, Humphreys and Taylor argue that the church's canonical teaching that marriage is a lifelong union does not support the doctrine that marriage is ontologically indissoluble. However, indissolubility remains as a moral imperative, and continuing commitments to children and to one's former spouse indicate that a former marriage does not completely end. Humphreys and Taylor argue that the Church of England's marital theology could, and should, learn from its legal heritage. It should recognise, as civil law does, that marriages end, and it should not insist on a 'quasi-juridical assessment of who should be entitled to remarry in church'. This would greatly free up the church to develop its ministry in supporting marriages and helping divorced and divorcing couples.

The final pair of chapters, while they belong to church history and to biblical theology, are also able to contribute to the eventual resolution of contemporary Anglican angst over remarriage. Cordelia Moyse's authoritative study of the Mothers' Union leads her to conclude that for most of its history, it made an 'idol' of a precept which had no place in its founding documents, 'the sanctity of marriage'. As this 'ideology' took hold, Moyse shows how the intense conservatism of the Mothers' Union led it to oppose divorce reforms. Its determination to exclude divorced women from its membership nearly resulted in its demise as a world-wide organisation and as a voice for marriage and Christian family life in the British Isles. Only in the late 1960s did that organisation withdraw its opposition to divorce on the ground of irretrievable breakdown, and subsequently revert to its original purpose: supporting family life. Moyse acutely observes that, having made this change, the organisation became free from its self-imposed burden of imposing on others a particular view of marriage, and free for 'promoting conditions favourable to stable family life'. Moyse's chapter provides a fascinating glimpse into the internal struggles of a conservative organisation resisting change, and then embracing it. Readers may both detect a familiar dynamic in the events she describes, and hope for a similar movement among comparable conservative power groups and organisations in the churches in the present century.

Greg Forster provides an historical and contextual approach to the remarriage of divorced people. Drawing on extra-biblical sources roughly contemporary with Jesus, Forster concentrates not simply on the words Jesus used in his teaching about marriage and divorce in Mark 10 and Matthew 19, but on why Jesus said what he did. The Gospels enable us to glimpse the empathic, insightful character of Jesus ('the good shepherd'), and this in turn enables us to see how, given conventional Jewish law at the time, he takes the side of divorced women and regards routine legal procedure as incitement to adultery (Jesus the Rabbi). Once Jesus is understood less as a legislator, and more as an 'ethical teacher', his teaching on divorce can be understood less as a legalistic prescription, and more as an invitation to his hearers to let their attitudes and practices be shaped by the way God acts. When contemporary followers of Jesus, Forster powerfully suggests, are true to the spirit of his teaching, they will both affirm lifelong marriage, and admit that marriages break down. When this happens, they will want to ensure that divorce is equitably managed, and remarriage considered, not least as a feasible means of human support. Nonetheless, in the face of the high incidence of divorce, it may also be necessary to become counter-cultural in proposing alternatives to divorce and doing more to support marriage. This, too, is to follow Christ.

22

Marriage, Marriage after Divorce and the Church of England: Seeking Coherent Teaching and Consistent Practice

Michael Scott-Joynt

Introduction

In September 1999 the House of Bishops of the Church of England published *Marriage: A teaching document from the House of Bishops of the Church of England*;[1] and in January 2000 *Marriage in Church after Divorce: a discussion document from a Working Party*,[2] which I chaired. The latter was initiated by a resolution of the Church of England's General Synod in November 1994; the former was first envisaged as a preface to it, before it was decided to develop it as an independent publication to establish a context for the latter and for other work in hand in support of marriage.

Such a beginning already suggests that I may be something of an 'odd person out' in this Conference – a position underlined and signified by my presence today in uniform! I am a bishop called both to discern and to grow into and to express the church's teaching for the sake of both church and public. This means that the primary community within which I work at these

---

[1] *Marriage: A teaching document from the House of Bishops of the Church of England* (London: Church House Publishing, 1999).

[2] *Marriage in Church after Divorce: a discussion document from a Working Party* (London: Church House Publishing, 2000).

questions, by study both of Christian and of other faith, and of secular writing, and by prayer and reflection, discussion and argument, and to which in the end I owe both accountability and allegiance, is not the academy. In my case it is the Church of England and its House of Bishops, the Diocese of Winchester, the Anglican Communion and a network of ecumenical relationships; this is the context in which I am seeking to discern and to represent the mind of the church and, ultimately, the mind of Christ, in and for the situation in which we live today.

In what follows I shall summarise the content of the two papers that I have just mentioned, setting them in two contexts: that of the Church of England (the Anglican Church of this country) and of the churches in England more widely; and in what I perceive and experience to be the wider social and political context in which marriage is today undertaken and practised, studied and discussed, in England. In the hope of further illuminating both contexts, I shall reflect on the reactions to the two documents in the media and in the church, from the necessarily partial (in at least two senses!) viewpoint of an official spokesperson at the sharp end of these reactions and of responding to them. And I shall speculate, less than half-way through the consultation period within the Church of England on *Marriage in Church after Divorce*, about what may be the main reactions to, and even the Church of England's eventual verdicts upon, this latest attempt to seek 'coherent teaching and consistent practice'. By then you may see why it was that, when it was announced in 1996 that I was to chair the latest Working Party on this classically knotty set of questions, and I received a generous note of good wishes from Bishop Kenneth Skelton, who as Bishop of Lichfield had chaired the group that produced in 1978 the last major Church of England Report upon them, *Marriage and the Church's Task*,[3] his postcard also included the words 'poisoned' and 'chalice'!

The Background

The Church of England's interest in marriage, and its responsibility for marriages in England, remains considerable.

---

[3] *Marriage and the Church's Task* (London: CIO Publishing, 1978).

Through its clergy and its churches it was responsible in 1996 (the last year for which figures are available) for 27% of all marriages in England, for 41% of marriages which were the first marriage for both parties, and for 65% of all marriages with a religious ceremony.[4] In English law anyone who has not been previously married, and who is seeking to marry someone (of the opposite sex) who likewise has not been previously married, has a right to marriage in their parish church according to the rites and ceremonies of the Church of England. But since divorce became a possibility in English law in 1857, parishioners, clergy and the church itself have wrestled with the difficulties inherent in establishing 'coherent teaching and consistent practice' concerning marriage in church after divorce. Through the same period the constitutional position of the Church of England, including the presence of its two archbishops and twenty-four of its bishops in the Upper House of Parliament (the House of Lords), has also kept the Church of England closely engaged with political reactions to the question 'whither marriage?' in English society. It has been in a position to seek to influence the development of the law of divorce – most recently in the passage of the Family Law Act 1996, some of whose more controversial provisions, most of which had the support of bishops in the Upper House, have been put on ice by the present Government. *Marriage in Church after Divorce* lists and summarises this 'wrestling' on the part of the Church of England, in a series of reports since 1966.[5]

The Working Party responsible for that document began its work in 1996 and reported to the House of Bishops of the Church of England in the autumn of 1998; but its report was not published by the House until January 2000. It is instructive, both concerning the Church of England and concerning the society in which it is set, to consider the reasons for this delay before looking at the content of the document and its proposals, and at the House of Bishops' *Marriage* which preceded it and in the light of which it should be read.

[4] Office for National Statistics, 1999.
[5] *Marriage in Church after Divorce*, pp. 1–9.

Irrespective of what the document actually said, would it lead to the portrayal of the Church of England as 'soft', vacillating and in retreat around marriage? And this, at a time when it was active with others, and especially with the Roman Catholic Church in England and Wales, in seeking to stiffen and give content to the still-new Government's expressed intentions to be supportive of marriage? And as the millennium approached? How might the 'Charles and Camilla' story be running at the time of the report's publication whenever that might be? How might the General Synod treat this set of issues on which there was admittedly a range of conviction and opinion in the church, and how would its reactions be reported in the Press, when the divisions and ill-feeling over the decision to ordain women were still fresh in the memory, and those around same-sex relationships were a matter of everyday experience not least to bishops and their postbags? In the event, the House of Bishops first looked to strengthen the argumentation in the report for the theology of marriage in which it is based; and then judged that it should produce a teaching document on marriage which could both stand by itself as an appropriate statement of the House, and provide a context for *Marriage in Church after Divorce* which would be published after a suitable interval.

In a moment I shall offer a summary of each of these two documents; but before doing so, I want to note some of the characteristics of contemporary English society, and not least of its media, as they may relate to marriage and to Christian (indeed to more generally religious) speaking about it. I can attempt only an impressionistic, and a necessarily personal, summary. Among these characteristics I think of a priority for choice and satisfaction, rather than for acceptance and restraint; an impatience with the past, and with any kind of authority or 'authority-figures'; and fear of, and hostility to the commitment of, marriage based in a sometimes politically motivated extrapolation of bad experience of marriage so that this is seen as the norm. 'As long as it does no harm' has widely become the only constraint admitted upon behaviour. The recognised grounds for public policy are the expressed desires or the short-term needs of individuals, or the welfare of children, rather than people's long-term development and maturing, the 'health' of the estate of marriage or the 'good' of supporting it.

Advertising and the media reflect, encourage and recruit to
this culture. They depict cohabitation, promiscuity, adultery
and under-age sexual activity as not just normal (because for so
many they are) but as mature and desirable; and what product
will be sold today by linking it to restraint in matters sexual?! In
this culture, and so for journalists and producers working
within it, affected by it but also shaping it, Christian reference-
points, indeed those of any major faith, are profoundly foreign,
even in principle unacceptable: whether Bible or other sacred
text, tradition, belief and practice down the centuries and
across the contemporary world. Christianity, or any major
religious faith (and they are often lumped together, with more
than a hint of denigration, as 'institutional religion'), is
manifestly not modern, and so must have had its day. So a
clearly stated, politically incorrect, Christian position is often
perceived and described as 'bigotry'; its secularist competitor is
not, even when stated with some violence and with little
attempt to understand what it opposes. And neither the Church
of England, nor any other church, nor any other faith, fits in its
structures and practices the paradigms of Cabinet, Parliament
and political parties, nor of a public limited company, nor of
any other organisation with which journalists are familiar. But
in the Church of England at any rate, there are single-issue
campaigners of the sort that journalists recognise and with
whom they know how to deal.

Marriage: A Teaching Document

Marriage: A teaching document is presented with a brief preface
over the signatures of the Archbishops of Canterbury and York,
and then in seventeen pages of text of which the first word is
'God'. The first seven of these pages seek to describe the
character and significance of marriage for those who marry and
for society, attractively presenting the Christian understanding
expressed in the Marriage Services of the *Book of Common Prayer*
and the *Alternative Service Book*. Marriage is a pattern that God
has given in creation; it reflects and enters into the love that is
the character of God the Holy Trinity; it is deeply rooted in
human beings' social instincts; and through marriage a man
and a woman may learn love together over the course of their
lives. Such growth in love needs the practices and disciplines of

marriage; sexual intercourse properly belongs within marriage exclusively; by marriage a new unit of society is created, so that the weakening of marriage has serious implications for the mutual belonging and care that is exercised within the community at large. The making of promises in public and before God, in a setting of prayer and of listening to his promises to us, is liberating; both because it focuses our intentions, and because it calls on a community of well-wishers to support our intentions as a couple, and claims God's faithful love to support our own weak resolve to be faithful.

The bishops seek to be understanding and gentle about the challenges that face those approaching marriage, and that lead many today to judge that they can think about lifelong commitment only once they are living together – a course which they do not, however, recommend; and they go on to speak of the church's approach to marriage breakdown, and about the possibility of a further marriage after divorce. The document does not minimise 'the disaster of a broken marriage' for all concerned, noting both that promises have been broken in attitudes the partners have taken and in ways they have treated each other, and that contemporary society imposes heavy burdens on marriage. And while it agrees that all Christians believe that marriage is 'indissoluble' in the sense that the promises are made unconditionally for life, the bishops' document stands with what it declares to be the teaching both of scripture and of the reformers of the Church of England that a marriage can 'die', and that a second marriage in the lifetime of a former partner is a possibility. It is, though, not only for the intending partners to such a marriage, but for the church itself, to decide whether it should be solemnised in an act of worship – because the church has to safeguard the understanding of marriage as a lifelong vocation. So a further marriage after a divorce is always 'an exceptional act'; and in considering its response to a request for such a marriage, the church will be concerned that the person who has been married before has significantly recovered emotional stability, and gained sufficient understanding of how the first marriage 'came to grief'; and it will seek to avoid 'suspicion that the new marriage consecrates an old infidelity'.

The bishops' document ends with two short appendices: 'What does the Church have to say to a couple who are living together without being married?', and 'What does the Church have to say to someone whose marriage has broken down?'

Marriage: A teaching document was published, and with another bishop I shared in presenting it to the Press and to the broadcasting media, on 20 September 1999. On 5 September a national broadsheet newspaper had published a disturbingly well-informed if somewhat tendentious account both of this document and of the report eventually published in January 2000, and of the discussions in the House of Bishops that had led to their separation in time. And in the following week the news broke that the wife of a recently appointed suffragan bishop was leaving him for another, also married, clergyman. While many in the church welcomed both the bishops' initiative and the content and style of the document, others both in the church and in the media found it too didactic and academic, too long, too short, too simple, either too sensitive or not sensitive enough to contemporary feelings and experience, and in danger of undermining its intentions by attending to the realities of marital breakdown and of cohabitation and to the possibility of a further marriage. And of course some simply disagreed with its denial that marriage is 'indissoluble' in the sense that a divorce decree is ineffective and a subsequent marriage invalid in the eyes of God.

Marriage in Church after Divorce

Marriage in Church after Divorce is necessarily a more substantial document. Its initial 'Note by the House of Bishops' makes explicit reference to their earlier document, recommending its reading in full as background to this report which was issued as a consultation document to dioceses; the church is asked to consider it, and to report conclusions, reactions and advice to the House of Bishops by 31 March 2001. It will then be for the House to decide how to proceed, and what recommendations to bring to the Church of England's General Synod. Specifically, the church's councils are asked: 'Do you accept the principle (approved by the General Synod in 1981) that there are circumstances in which a divorced person may be married in church during the lifetime of a former spouse?'

While accepting this principle, the Working Party 'holds

steadfastly' to the view that marriage is a gift of God in creation and a means of grace, and that it should always be undertaken as a lifelong commitment. It reviews, as it was asked to do, present practice in the Church of England and the stages and reforms through which it has developed, noting that those who look to the Church of England for its ministry in this field have good reasons for finding our present practice contradictory in principle and simply unfair, because uneven and unpredictable, in their experience. Diocesan bishops' guidelines on marriage in church after divorce vary from diocese to diocese, in many cases quite significantly. Practice also varies from parish to parish within any diocese, because it is for the parish priest to decide whether she or he will solemnize any marriage after divorce, or a particular marriage, or allow the parish church to be used for such a service. In some dioceses such marriages are clearly discouraged, with the clergy encouraged rather to consider a Service of Prayer and Dedication after a civil marriage; in others further marriage in church is not at all uncommon – and in 1996 some 10% of all marriages in the Church of England and the Church in Wales involved a divorced person with a former spouse still living.[6] Some dioceses encourage clergy to consult their bishop about every request that they consider, and two or three have carefully designed structures for this consultation; others do not. Most keep no records of requests made to clergy and of their outcome; and no statistics of this sort are at present available for the Church of England as a whole.

The Working Party explores a number of options, both in the experience of the Church of England and of other parts of the Anglican Communion, and in the practices of contemporary ecumenical partners, Roman Catholic, Protestant and Orthodox. It proposes what it believes to be a workable way forward for the Church of England consonant with its history and its decisions over the last thirty years, its convictions about marriage and its opportunities and responsibilities within English society – a way forward which, it believes, holds out some real hope that coherent teaching and consistent practice can be largely achieved across the Church of England.

[6] Office for National Statistics, 1999.

It proposes that the church should provide a common procedure authorising incumbents, where they see fit, to officiate at the further marriage of divorced people with a former spouse still living. Believing that broad consistency of practice across the country is desirable, it proposes a set of pastoral criteria, principles and procedures building on the draft Guidelines produced by the House of Bishops in 1985. It encourages clergy to be both pastoral and rigorous in applying these, so as to ensure that there is no presumption that couples have an automatic entitlement to be married in church in such circumstances; and it advises bishops to design systems which will enable clergy always to consult them, whether directly or through an adviser acting on their behalf. It recognises that clergy will need education and training if they are to fulfil these requirements appropriately. Proper statistics of further marriages should be kept in each diocese. Services of Prayer and Dedication after civil marriage should remain available.

In making these proposals, the Working Party has accepted the church's judgement in the 1980s that the Church of England should not seek to establish a system of diocesan or regional tribunals to investigate the background to requests for marriage in church after divorce. More controversially (and some would say, fatally), it not only leaves the decision in any particular case to the parish priest; but it does not propose any attempt to remove the parish priest's freedom to refuse altogether to solemnize such marriages or to allow the parish church to be used for them – out of respect for her or his conscientious judgement.

Initial Responses

When *Marriage in Church after Divorce* was published, and I spent a day presenting it to the media and responding to their enquiries, it felt to me as if the Report might have been published not in January 2000 but soon after the death of Archbishop Geoffrey Fisher in 1972 – or even soon after his retirement in 1961! Perhaps this was something that I should have anticipated, because a 1955 address of his, to a group of 'city men', had been republished and widely circulated late in

1999![7] It seemed to me that the journalists and broadcasters who were questioning me had paid a great deal of attention to those, inside and outside the Church of England, who disliked the developments of the last twenty-five to thirty years from which I and my colleagues had been asked to begin our work. By the same token, they seem to have listened hardly at all to those for whom these developments were the atmosphere in which they had been glad to live for so many years!

Other initial reactions to *Marriage in Church after Divorce* may be pointers to the character of the responses to it that will emerge as dioceses and parishes work on it through this year (2000) and until next March (2001). But before I end by risking a forecast of some of these, I want to say something about the current political context in the United Kingdom, and particularly in England, concerning marriage. As I suggested earlier, in the first years of the present New Labour Government (May 1997 on) the churches were hopeful that the Government would prove explicitly supportive of marriage, both in fiscal and other legislative provision and more generally in its language and perceived stance. But the Green Paper *Supporting Families*,[8] published in the autumn of 1998, while generally welcomed by the Board for Social Responsibility of the Church of England, was seen by it as 'weakened by its ambivalence in relation to marriage'. *Supporting Families* states that 'Marriage is still the surest foundation for raising children and remains the choice of the majority of people in Britain. We want to strengthen the institution of marriage to help more marriages succeed.'[9] But there is then no further mention of marriage until the following revealing paragraph:

> This Government believes that marriage provides a strong foundation for stable relationships. This does not mean trying to make people marry, or criticising or penalising people who choose not to. We do not believe that Government should interfere in people's lives in that way.

---

[7] Archbishop Geoffrey Fisher, *Problems of Marriage and Divorce* (Sutton, Surrey: Belmont House Publishing, 1999).

[8] *Supporting Families: A consultation document* (Stationery Office Group Ltd, 1998).

[9] *Supporting Families*, p. 4, para. 8.

But we do share the belief of the majority of people that marriage provides the most reliable framework for raising children.

Here is an explicit denial of any responsibility to support marriage for itself, as 'fundamental to human flourishing',[10] a stance consistently confirmed since then by the Government's refusal, as it has dismissively put it, to 'preach about marriage' and to contemplate any 'discrimination' (I use the word advisedly) between marriage on the one hand and 'stable relationships', whether same-sex or heterosexual, on the other.

Future Directions

How will *Marriage in Church after Divorce* be received by the Church of England? Many people, including many clergy and bishops, find it a conservative document offering little more than practices and guidelines with which they are already familiar; though the 'little more' is admittedly the explicit authorisation of marriage in church after divorce for couples whose situation falls within certain guidelines where hitherto such marriages were officially, in most dioceses at any rate, discouraged. This constituency may question details of the guidelines, and perhaps still more the requirement that the bishop should be consulted, directly or through an adviser of his appointment, in every case; but it will welcome the Report and its proposals even if without much excitement. Some, though, may question whether this is the right moment for the Church of England to risk being depicted as 'soft on marriage and marriage-breakdown', however unjust such a depiction might be.

Some will argue against our proposal that decisions in these matters should continue to lie with the parish priest, on the ground that the discrimination between one couple and another, inherent in such decisions, is fraught with difficulties especially in small communities, or that too much clergy time will be taken by the demands of this ministry. Some see the

---

[10] Response by the Church of England Board for Social Responsibility to *Supporting Families*, March 1999, p. 2.

proposed guidelines as unworkable. Some will again argue for
the alternative of a nullity procedure along the lines of that
practised by the Roman Catholic Church. Some have never
agreed with the 1981 resolution of the General Synod 'that
there are circumstances in which a divorced person may be
married in church during the lifetime of a former partner'; of
these, some believe that a divorce decree is ineffective and a
subsequent marriage invalid, and so adulterous, in the eyes of
God; others continue to think it right to defend marriage by
limiting the church's practice, in cases of marriage after
divorce, to Services after Civil Marriage.

It will be said, too, that we have fought shy of the only
proposal that could pave the way for 'coherent teaching and
consistent practice' in the Church of England: the removal
(which would require Parliamentary legislation) of the
conscientious right of the parish priest to refuse to conduct
the marriage of a divorced person whose spouse is still living,
or to allow the church for which she or he is responsible to
be used for such a service. Such a step, though, would entail
the Church of England becoming very much less 'broad' a
church than it is; though this very 'breadth' may prove the
reason, in the end, why the proposals of *Marriage in Church
after Divorce* may not be accepted – or why, if accepted, they
do not prove to make for 'coherent teaching and consistent
practice'!

I have already quoted from the teaching document, *Marriage*,
the stipulation that 'a further marriage after divorce is an
exceptional act'.[11] The emphasis on its exceptional character
has recently been underlined by Richard B. Hays.[12] Hays argues
that 'the church must reaffirm its historic teaching that, since
marriage is a covenant before God, divorce is therefore flatly
contrary to God's will, save in certain extraordinary circumstances'; and he asks 'how can we enable our marriages to resist
the corrosive cultural influences that make divorce seem
inevitable?' I too am sensitive to the danger that any attempt,
even one of the kind for which I now have a large responsibility,

---

[11] *Marriage*, p. 18.
[12] Richard B. Hays, *The Moral Vision of the New Testament* (Edinburgh: T&T
Clark, 1997), pp. 372, 374.

to make more coherent and consistent the church's teaching and practice around the marriage of divorced people, will have the effect of softening still further people's will to persevere in marriage. Will it make us still more accepting of marriage breakdown and divorce as griefs to be anticipated, with lifelong marriage becoming increasingly a counter-cultural exception rather than the norm?

So should the church retreat from this particular front line (of marriage breakdown), just when – even, because – increasing numbers of people today, and among them increasing numbers of Christians, find themselves on it to their own great distress and damage. To ask the question in this sharp form, must also be to answer 'no', especially from the standpoint, history and responsibilities of the Church of England; though I recognise that the paths, to which I believe that we have to be committed, are hazardous.

Marriage is a first-order issue for Christian doctrine and practice, and the church must be committed to its support, defence and advocacy. Marriage is of crucial importance both for society and for the maturing and fulfilment, the flourishing, of individuals. Marital breakdown and separation, if not divorce, among Christians, and the church's positions around further marriage after divorce, have demonstrably been issues for the church since the formation of the Gospels, and in every church all over the world. As many people today are divorced, and therefore many of those seeking to marry are divorced, the church cannot escape the range of questions that all this poses to its evangelism, apologetic and pastoral care. It follows, I judge, that the churches, and among them the Church of England, have to keep considering marriage in church after divorce. We have to discover ways of representing, even in our present culture and in the face of much that appears in the print and broadcasting media that are a part of it, God's gift of lifelong faithful marriage, and at the same time God's character to forgive those whose marriages come to grief and who seek his forgiveness. There is no alternative to wrestling with the inherent tensions between these two, God's gift and God's character, for Christian teaching and practice.

23

Contract or Communion?
A Dilemma for the Church of England

Timothy J. Woods

I am an Anglican priest, appreciative of the intellectual rigour of much debate within the Anglican Communion, and of the diversity of tradition and practice that characterises it. However, I find myself increasingly ill-at-ease with the inconsistencies and mixed messages that we as a church seem to be promulgating, by what we do as much as by what we say.

In March 2000, a dozen Anglican curates in a post-ordination training group met to discuss the pastoral implications of divorce and remarriage. The speaker asked them to divide into two groups, and then for each individual to write down what they believed the essence of marriage to be with a view to discussing their responses. Both groups concluded that marriage is basically a legal contract, albeit one that could be sanctified through the church. Concepts of covenant and communion were not mentioned at any point in either group's discussion.

The Church of England is confused, not simply about the possibility of remarriage after divorce, but about the essence and nature of marriage itself. As an established church, it is caught between two tendencies. On the one hand, there seems to be a desire to make patriarchal pronouncements, as if the church could continue to sustain a role as the nation's moral guardian in a postmodern era. On the other hand, the very diversity which characterises the church in its theology and pastoral praxis militates against the positing of a particular doctrinal or dogmatic stance. As long as the church remains established, there is bound to be a tendency towards legalism, because the church operates in both the local and national community as a legal entity rather than as a free association of worshippers. The continued existence of the Church of England is still bound up with its statutory role.

From the premodern into the modern era, the tension between being moral guardian and having a richly diverse character has been sustainable because the Church of England has operated within a national context that has taken as normative an ethical base that is broadly Christian. For example, the availability of education for all sectors of society, and the rise of a comprehensive health service have taken place in a social framework founded on essentially Christian assumptions. One such assumption is that all persons are equal before God. However, the advent of the postmodern era, in which there appear to be very few agreed absolutes, and where the individual is regarded as sovereign, has exposed the Church of England's inability to claim that it speaks with authority. If the postmodern world appears muddled to the church, no less does the church seem muddled to the wider world.

Contradictions

Robert and Diana came to see me a few years ago with a view to getting married, in church. Robert was an officer in the Royal Navy, and his first marriage had broken up within ten weeks, because his wife had begun an affair with another man as soon as he went back to sea. Following the 1957 Act of Convocation, the Church of England does not permit remarriage in church, and even though the first marriage had ended several years before the beginning of the new relationship, and even though there were no children involved, the only way that Robert could remarry in the eyes of the church would be if his former spouse died.

This year, I officiated at the marriage of Susan and Michael. Neither had been previously married, and so, under the canon law of the church, I was obliged to conduct their marriage within their parish church. Yet each of the parties already had two children by previous long-term relationships. Those relationships consisted in long-term cohabitation, and in Scotland would have been regarded as common law marriage in each case. For all that I knew, the new relationship may have caused the breakdown of the old ones, and morally might have been considered to be adulterous. Even if that were the case, I would still have had a statutory obligation to officiate at this marriage.

In so far as clergy have toed the line, and refused marriage in church to divorcees, is it the case that we have presented divorce as an unforgivable sin, from the point of view of the couple? To do so would be to contradict Jesus' teaching reported in Mark 3:28–29.

On the other hand, where clergy have been obliged to conduct marriages despite anxieties regarding the children of previous relationships, or the nature of the present relationship, is there not a danger of giving the impression that marriage will provide the solution or cure for all relational difficulties? All too often, children brought to a new marital relationship are treated almost as though they were appendages belonging somehow to one or other party. By assuming that children accept the new parental relationship, the church downplays their significance in the survival of that relationship. Yet, in Adrian Thatcher's words: 'The "reality" of children's experience cannot be detached from an adequate theology of marriage.'[1] Thatcher argues that the suffering experience of children should become determinative. But a church which obliges clergy to conduct marriages for the unmarried, and refuses remarriage for the divorced, can take no proper account of the children already born to either or both parties, nor of the part they will play in the blossoming or otherwise of the new relationship.

The surrounding legalities help to give both clergy and laypeople the impression that the essence of marriage is a contract. A contract is 'an agreement enforceable at law between two or more persons whereby rights are acquired by one or more to certain acts or forbearances on the part of the other or others'.[2] In short it consists of a static arrangement, which allows new possibilities to be pursued. But to focus on the

---

[1] Adrian Thatcher, *Marriage after Modernity: Christian Marriage in Postmodern Times* (Sheffield: Sheffield Academic Press, 1999), p. 152.

[2] Kenneth Smith and Dennis J. Keenan, *English Law* (3rd edn; London: Pitman, 1969), p. 91.

contract is to risk losing sight of the dynamic life of the relationship itself, and divorce becomes simply breach of a contract, rather than also the painful possibility that relationships sometimes have to change or be superseded. The healing that Robert needed after the shock and pain of the premature breakdown of his first marriage was most likely to be found in learning to trust a new partner to the point where he could remarry. To turn Robert and Diana away was to deny them an opportunity to be healed, and in effect to declare that God had withdrawn his blessing from them, for good.

Recognising that remarriage continues to present the Church of England with a problem, the House of Bishops set up a Working Party, which recently produced the report *Marriage in Church after Divorce: a discussion document from a Working Party*. The unanimous conclusion of the Working Party was that 'the Church should provide a common procedure authorizing incumbents, where they see fit, to officiate at the further marriage of divorced people with a former spouse still living'.[3] Appropriate pastoral criteria, principles and procedures will need to be established in order to enable this change to take place, and the 1957 Act of Convocation will need to be revoked in order to change the legal framework.

However, in its attempt to reach out to those wishing to remarry after divorce, the report allows for clergy who conscientiously object to further marriage in church to be able to opt out of any new provisions. Just as those who objected to the ordination of women to priesthood were permitted to maintain an 'alternative integrity', so the church is about to enshrine a second 'alternative integrity' in the matter of remarriage after divorce.

Under the law as it now stands, in relation to the residence qualifications necessary for a marriage to take place, the opportunity to be remarried in church will continue to be dependent on geography. In many areas this is the case at present, because significant numbers of clergy in probably all dioceses of the Church of England are prepared to ignore the Act of

[3] House of Bishops of the Church of England, *Marriage in Church after Divorce: a discussion document from a Working Party* (London: Church House Publishing, 2000), p. 45, para. 8.1.

Convocation within their own parishes, while others are not. The recommendations of the working party will simply have the effect of authorising what is happening anyway. Remarriage after divorce looks set to remain a postcode lottery, unless it becomes possible to relax residence qualifications for marriage. Confusion about remarriage seems likely to prolong this extraordinary geographical injustice for as long as the church remains unable to reach a consensus about the nature of marriage itself. A practical implication of this confusion will be that significant numbers of requests for remarriage will continue to be diverted to the Free Churches. The House of Bishops' report states that, in 1996, 62% of all marriages in Methodist churches involved at least one divorced person.[4] The equivalent figure for the United Reformed Church was 64%.[5]

Some Possible Theological Implications

Marriage is one of the opportunities that the church has to meet with, and assist, people who are not regular worshippers. As a result of its long established history, many people who do not attend church at all as a rule will identify themselves as Church of England, and will use the Anglican tradition for baptism, marriage and funeral services. An aspect of the discussion about remarriage that seems to have been missed in *Marriage in Church after Divorce* is the potential impact upon those who wish to marry or remarry for their understanding of the nature of God. The way in which the church deals with moral and ethical questions will suggest to those who stand on or beyond the fringe of the church what sort of God we worship, and what the character of God's love is likely to be. (It is true of course that many regular worshippers struggle to identify a clear doctrine of God within the church's teaching!)

A dogmatic stance on the matter of marriage betrays a legalistic view of God's moral demands. The patriarchal church effectively represents a perception of God as remote and judgmental, requiring that his (*sic*) creation accords with a

---

[4] *Marriage in Church after Divorce*, p. 31, para. 5.2.
[5] *Marriage in Church after Divorce*, p. 33, para. 5.4.

pre-ordained plan. God's love and acceptance thus become conditional on human compliance, actual or intended. Confronted with the patriarchal institution, couples such as Robert and Diana find themselves rejected and confused, unable to receive through the church the forgiveness and healing that they need in order to make their new relationship blossom and grow. God as Monad, presented by the patriarchal church, demands an unattainable perfection, and remarriage is not therefore a viable option. At a point of need, the church turns them away, and presents God as unapproachable. Discovery that in another parish the clergy might have ignored the rules and married them anyway could help to present God as not simply inaccessible, but fickle!

Part of the crisis faced by marriage itself is that it has been associated for too long with patriarchy. For all that the practice of formalising or solemnizing marriage had the effect of providing a modicum of protection to women and children in the premodern and early modern era, the patriarchal character and expectations of society have allowed marriage to provide legitimised space for oppression. When the church signals its unwillingness to remarry, it does so not because it is challenging patriarchy but because in itself it is patriarchal. Those desiring to remarry after divorce may find themselves in a position where, having 'failed' in a first marriage riddled with patriarchal expectations, they wish to enter a new relationship founded in mutuality. Yet the church that proclaims a gospel rhetoric of love and radical equality of persons will not accept them.

Adrian Thatcher insists that Christian marriage can and must be redeemed by breaking with patriarchy. He argues that 'the loving communion on which [Christian marriage] is founded is the communion of the Trinitarian God, and the invitation to share in it is given by the self-giving of the Trinitarian God in the Person of Christ'.[6] Just as marriage has to be disentangled from patriarchy, so it is the case that the church must disentangle its presentation of the gospel from patriarchal conceptualisations of God. John Zizioulas, writing from an Orthodox perspective, insists that the church is not simply an

---

[6] Thatcher, *Marriage after Modernity*, p. 293.

institution but a way of being, and that members of the church become 'images of God', not by their own efforts, but by taking on God's way of relationship, God's communion with the world.[7] He claims that 'The being of God is a relational being: without the concept of communion, it would not be possible to speak of the being of God ... It would be unthinkable to speak of the "one God" before speaking of the God who is "communion", that is to say, of the Holy Trinity.'[8]

A Trinitarian model of God enables the church to emphasise the relational rather than the legalistic, and, instead of presenting a set of static dogmas as the foundation for marriage, to engage with couples in a journey of exploration into mutual hope. From the church's point of view, the emphasis on the legal framework has made the business of processing requests for marriage very manageable. In an era where good management, understood as control, appears essential in a fast-changing culture, it is tempting to maintain such a straightforward approach. Yet a better management of our theological heritage would lead the church to reckon with marriage as in essence *relational rather than contractual,* and therefore more rather than less inclined to be complex and messy.

Zizioulas reflects that 'The eucharist was not the act of a pre-existing Church; it was an event constitutive of the being of the Church, enabling the Church to be.'[9] The church, then, is communion, reflecting the Trinitarian view that God's essence is to be found in the communion of Persons. The eucharistic celebration at the heart of the church's life properly allows for forgiveness and the healing of relationships as a part of the sharing one with another in the Body of Christ. Forgiveness and healing are instruments for growth and development of persons in relationship, and contribute to the dynamic life of the eucharistic community. In addressing the question of remarriage, a Trinitarian approach will help couples to find healing in the process of exploring a new relationship. To tell

[7] John D. Zizioulas, *Being as Communion* (London: Darton, Longman & Todd, 1985), p. 15.

[8] Zizioulas, *Being as Communion,* p. 17.

[9] Zizioulas, *Being as Communion,* p. 21.

Robert that he may be remarried in church is to help him leave his first marriage behind, and to enter a new commitment freely, with a sense of being embraced by the active love of God.

To seek remarriage is to hope that the new start will lead to better experience of relationship than the first marriage allowed. At this point on the couple's journey, the church can draw on the model of communion as the ground for marriage, and there is the opportunity to present the new start as of a different order from the patriarchal context that may have damaged the earlier experience. If marriage can be presented as essentially communion rather than contract, it becomes possible to speak of the children of previous relationships inclusively. One of the difficulties with a contract approach is that the focus of the marriage is narrowed to the arrangements between the couple, and children who represent an enduring reality from past relationships become automatically peripheral to the new one. The contract focus implies that children are part of the baggage of the past.

This is a problem, whether the parties to the marriage have been married before or not. However, when the church is prepared to allow for marriage between parents who have not previously married, like Michael and Susan, there is perhaps a greater danger of giving couples desiring remarriage a set of distorted ideas. In the first place, there is considerable evidence that children hold themselves responsible for marriage breakdown, and frequently bear a sense of irrational guilt into adulthood. The church effectively underscores that guilt if it will not honour a fresh start for either of the parties. Although a sense of guilt may remain, a Trinitarian focus on communion as the heart of marriage offers the possibility of including children of previous relationships. Preparation for remarriage would then embrace the children, and look at their place in the dynamic life of the evolving new relationship in such a way that they experience healing and forgiveness.

To shift an understanding of marriage towards an emphasis on communion is to raise questions about how relationships evolve, and what insights the church can bring to bear for persons committing themselves to new relationships. No longer need the church highlight the legal constraints or demands, because that is not what couples need to help their marriage develop and grow. While a legal framework still has a value, a communion approach offers the possibility that the church could facilitate marriage as a process, rather than aiming only to conduct its inaugural ceremony. The Church of England offers guidelines to help the deepening of commitment and understanding in new relationships through organisations like FLAME (Family Life and Marriage Education) which frequently form part of a diocese's structure. This approach tends to promote a Trinitarian view of marriage, and provides a method by which couples seeking remarriage can be equipped to make a fresh start. It is not clear to what extent parishes or clergy make use of these or similar resources as they prepare couples for marriage, and it seems probable that the availability of good marriage preparation is itself a postcode lottery.

Marriage, Establishment and Evangelism

The offering of guidelines for the encouraging and enabling of new relationships suggests a larger question, because requests for marriage represent rare opportunities for systematic engagement between the church and a culture which is increasingly secularised. Given the steadily falling attendance at regular worship in most traditions, and the rise in average age of congregations, it is perhaps strange that church weddings remain as popular as they are.[10] If the church is perceived as capable of making more of a marriage ceremony than alternative civil forms, how may the opportunity be used to present the valuable insights of Christian tradition to couples who bear no particular allegiance to a faith community?

It is important to consider what the guidelines may be for the encounter between the gospel and the world. Is it clear what the church is aiming to do when offering a Christian framework for marriage to those who do not otherwise identify themselves with the corporate life of the Body of Christ? If marriage is crudely understood as a tool for evangelism, then the age distribution of most congregations seems to indicate that the

---

[10] Grace Davie, *Religion in Britain since 1945* (Oxford: Blackwell, 1994), p. 121.

tool is not being used very effectively! At times, the church appears to be locked into a mindset that suggests firstly that the goal of evangelism is to fill empty pews, and secondly that all that needs to be done is to find the right formula and revival will ensue. Partly because of its place as an established church, and partly because of the patriarchal culture in which it is steeped, the Church of England has been ill-equipped to address the social and economic context of a postmodern era.

The questions about remarriage illustrate the problem well. On the one hand the church has failed to bring to bear any consistent theological approach in its attempts to address the sexual and feminist revolutions that have profoundly affected the ways in which contemporary culture understands marriage. Even talk of sacramentality, for all its value, fails to resonate in a society which is losing any consensus on where to look for truth, or for God. On the other hand, the church has failed to engage consistently with the fast-moving socio-political context in which it exists. The support for the Jubilee 2000 Campaign among Anglicans and members of other Christian traditions has been striking and effective. But in thinking through the handling of marriage and remarriage, there has, for example, been a reluctance to hear the stories of women in violent relationships, or to recognise the effect of consistent abuse on children. Perhaps this is because the church has treated marriage as though it were its own territory, but the voices of those who are marginalised by distorted and abusive relationships are only just being heard.

Conclusion

As an established institution, the Church of England is inherently patriarchal. Yet there is a wide diversity of practice among its parishes, many clergy and congregations challenging historical assumptions by their inclusiveness and their readiness to embrace the casualties of broken relationships. In the search for an adequate and appropriate response to requests for remarriage, the bishops would do well to consult with church leaders of other traditions where remarriage is commonplace, and to listen to their experience in the search for a theologically consistent approach. Among those traditions will be the voices of other churches within the Anglican Communion, who have already wrestled with some of the theological and practical questions that beset us. On the wider horizon, it will be essential for the church as an institution to consider more critically how its dogma and doctrine are being understood in a changing, secularised social context. What we are saying, or think we are saying, will not necessarily be heard in the way we expect in the postmodern era. In the light of all this, what are the guidelines for the encounter between the gospel and the world? Is there a sense in which the question of remarriage is the tip of an iceberg, representing the urgency with which the church will have to change direction in its engagement with the wider community?

Is there also a danger that the church is approaching the whole debate about marriage from the wrong end? Is it possible that bishops and theologians have a tendency to indulge in cerebral reflection on their own long experience and the learned works of past generations, whereas an incarnational approach to the subject would be soaked in the passion of young people seeking relationship? In a church whose regular worshippers are predominantly of late middle age or older,[11] there may be a significant risk of ignoring the views and expectations of those most likely to be requesting marriage. At any rate, despite the report of the bishops' Working Party, divorce looks set to remain an irredeemable sin in the Church of England for the time being – but only in certain parishes!

[11] Davie, *Religion in Britain*, p. 121.

24

The Christian Claims of the English Law of Marriage

C. C. A. Pearce

One Law or Two?

Many who speak of the English church distinguish 'the law' of that church from the law of the land. Marriage lends itself particularly well to such a dichotomy, and we hear a good deal about what 'canon law' does or does not allow parish clergy to do, and what 'the state' has done beyond what ecclesiastical opinion can accept. The heirs of the Oxford Movement, the vanguard in the campaign for 'spiritual independence', proved extremely successful in shifting popular perceptions and official terminology; the fruits of their work appear in the language of many modern writers on ecclesiastical law.

Yet there remains a real question how far such a distinction makes sense in the context of English public religion. Sociologically, the Church of England is far from coterminous with the nation. Theologically, at least to many people, it could never be the nation 'wearing its spiritual hat'. But the law is a different matter. There was clearly a time when the English law of religion did regard the national church as exactly that – another way of saying 'Christian England'. And despite the efforts of the Tractarians – despite the great compromise of 1919, whereby religious legislation, though still passed with parliamentary authority, was to be 'framed' by a body representative only of active churchgoers – despite nearly a century of Measures drafted by believers in the Church of England as a distinct society – there is strong evidence that the law's basic attitude has remained unchanged.

This chapter is not intended to debate the rights and wrongs of such a situation. My concern is only to ask how far the English law of marriage shows such a situation to exist. But even that limited question is not entirely academic. Because if the English law of marriage is still treated as the law of Christian England – and thus the only law that the Church of England possesses – that implies certain claims for its Christian provenance. It asserts that Parliament, in making this law, remains (as Richard Hooker put it) 'a court not so merely temporal as it might meddle with nothing but only leather and wool';[1] and it gives significant support to those – now or in the future – who hold themselves loyal members of the English church, and yet find the law of the land more easily reconcilable with their consciences than the pronouncements of bishops and synods.

This chapter will therefore address two questions. Looking at certain significant debates on marriage legislation, it will ask how far parliamentarians accepted the theologically neutral role ascribed to them by the doctrine of separate spheres for 'church' and 'state'. And more seriously still, it will ask whether Parliament has adopted such a role, by creating or recognising a separate matrimonial 'law of the church'.

The Christian Commonwealth and the Reformation

In sixteenth-century England the medieval notion of the 'Christian commonwealth' had won firm hold; organs of the one society worked together to further God's will for that society. The law affecting 'spirituals' was no less part of the law of the land for emanating from different sources and being applied in separate courts.

England's assertion of ecclesiastical autonomy from the 1530s did not challenge this unity of civil and Christian communities. What it challenged was Gregory VII's idea that government in spiritual and temporal fields must necessarily be distinct, since spiritual government required holy orders. The passing of the Tudor reforming statutes was itself the clearest

---

[1] Richard Hooker, *Of the Lawes of Ecclesiastical Polity*, Book VIII, ch. 6, para. 11 (*Works*, ed. John Keble, Oxford, 1888, Vol. III, p. 409).

statement that Gregory's principle was no more. English princes might have no interest in preaching the Word or administering the sacraments, but they had a great interest in ecclesiastical jurisdiction.

In many ways the charter of England's ecclesiastical autonomy was the preamble to the Ecclesiastical Licences Act 1533. This located the source of both spiritual and temporal law in ordinary legislation (laws 'devised made and ordained within the realm'), or in the adoption of foreign rules into the common custom of the realm (through reception by the people of England 'at their own free liberty').

This had two logical implications for the canons made by the clerical convocations: one was that unless these restated existing law, they would bind nobody but clerics. The other was that even in relation to the clergy they were void if inconsistent with general common law or with statute.[2]

The Reformation thus redefined the authority of the law governing 'spirituals'. But it left much substantive law unchanged, and left the episcopal courts with their accustomed business. These continued dispensing justice *pro salute animae*, specialists applying rules still derived largely from the Western *jus commune*.

Sir Edward Coke's expression for the law commonly administered in these courts, of which Westminster Hall took no regular cognisance, was 'the King's ecclesiastical law'.[3] But it *was* 'the King's'. King's Bench justices would not only confine it within its proper scope and support it by temporal sanctions; they would also work it out for themselves if they had to, and recognise the right and duty of diocesan judges to interpret and apply the indigenous common law.[4] As it was put succinctly in a decision of 1945, 'The law is one, though jurisdiction as to its enforcement is divided.'[5]

---

[2] *Middleton v. Crofts* (1736) 2 Atk 650; Submission of the Clergy Act 1533, s.3.
[3] *Caudrey's* case (1591) 5 Co Rep 1a.
[4] *Carter v. Crawley* (1680) T Raym 496; *Shotter v. Friend* (1690) 2 Salk 547.
[5] *A.-G. v. Dean & Chapter of Ripon* [1945] Ch 239.

Marriage Law after the Reformation

The formation and validity of marriage, the obligations accompanying the marriage bond and the remedies for breach of those obligations all remained after the Reformation within the competence of the episcopal judicial hierarchy and governed largely by 'the King's ecclesiastical law'. As the Garbett Commission pointed out in 1947,[6] little in this field was of indigenous origin and there would have been remarkably little English marriage law but for the adoption of the *jus commune*. This was so even though matters *affected* by marriage often belonged in Westminster Hall.

Yet here as in any other branch of law, statute was paramount. Episcopal tribunals accepted England's early departures from medieval law – the repeal of canons on priestly celibacy;[7] the claim of the marital dispensing power for the King in Parliament and their delegates;[8] and the implied assertion of parliamentary authority to dissolve the marriage bond in accordance with the Matthaean exception.[9] They later accepted likewise a major departure in marriage formation, when Lord Hardwicke's Act rendered void the clandestine marriages until then only irregular.[10]

One group alone asserted a 'law of the church' on marriage different from that enforced and followed in the courts of the land. These were the Roman Catholics, acknowledging only the jurisdiction of their own hierarchy and the marital decrees of the Council of Trent.

---

[6] *The Canon Law of the Church of England, being the Report of the Archbishops' Commission on Canon Law* (London: SPCK, 1947).

[7] Clergy Marriage Act 1548.

[8] Ecclesiastical Licences Act 1533, preamble.

[9] A claim implied in the passing of personal divorce Acts since the seventeenth century. See also stat. 32 Hen. VIII c.38 (1540), excluding impediments to marriage 'without the levitical degrees' other than those arising from 'God's law'. It is doubtful whether this Act was intended to abolish any impediment previously recognised; see *Hill v. Good* (1696) 1 Mod 254.

[10] Marriage Act 1753. The fact that this Act recognised the marriages of Jews only if conformable to Jewish custom meant that the episcopal courts could quite properly find themselves receiving evidence and ruling on what Jewish custom required; *Lindo v. Belisario* (1795) 1 Hag Con 216.

The Matrimonial Causes Act 1857

So we come to 1857, when much of these courts' matrimonial jurisdiction[11] was transferred to a new tribunal in Westminster Hall. On this court was also conferred the power to dissolve the marriage bond in adultery cases, hitherto exercised by Parliament itself using personal bill procedure. Neither of these developments altered the substantive law. Nor – to most people – did they sever the union of English and Christian rules on marriage. Archbishop Sumner himself voted for the Act following a learned parliamentary discussion of the Matthaean exception. The high-church Viscount Cecil looked back eighty years later and remarked that 'most people believe the 1857 change was in accordance with the Christian rule'.[12]

Yet the Act's practical effect was considerable, in that divorce ceased to be confined to the rich and well-informed. This happened to coincide with an era of biblical scholarship in which some took the 'Matthaean exception' to be a compiler's gloss, while others questioned its sanction for remarriage. The Act accordingly contained a compromise between respect for the conscientious scruples of clerics and the right of parishioners to contract any lawful marriage in their local church.[13] While an incumbent might decline to officiate personally for a 'guilty party', he could not in that event refuse the use of the church building to another minister prepared to take his place.

In 1857 the clerical convocations had recently resumed business and Tractarian thinking was rife. Following the *Gorham* judgement there was already some enthusiasm for

---

[11] The moral jurisdiction to punish adultery remained unaffected, though obsolescent; so did the power to dispense from publication of banns.

[12] 19 July 1937, 106 *Hansard (Lords)* col. 574.

[13] The authority from which a *prima facie* duty of parish clergy to solemnize the lawful marriage of parishioners, both by licence and *a fortiori* after banns, is derived is *Argar v. Holdsworth* (1758) 2 Lee 515; although the duty has since been affirmed by implication in the 1857 and subsequent Acts, as well as by the House of Lords in *Thompson v. Dibdin* [1912] AC 533. Recent doubts as to whether a duty to solemnize after banns was indeed to be deduced from the original judgment of Lee, D. A. rest upon the doubtful premise that a common licence could ever be thought to *command*, rather than permit, solemnization. See, e.g., Michael G. Smith, 'An interpretation of *Argar v. Holdsworth*' (1998) 5 Ecc LJ 34.

distinguishing the 'law of the church' from one 'imposed by the state'. Still it was only a minority who saw in the marriage legislation any reason to make such a distinction, equating the 'law of the church' with the scruples of the exempted incumbents.

The Deceased Wife's Sister's Marriage Act 1907

Fifty years of acrimony between high churchmen and common lawyers had passed by the time that the next significant reform was made. The convocations were a great deal more vocal in 1907, and the economic demise of the civilian profession had passed the torch of church legal scholarship largely to Tractarian incumbents, learned in the *jus commune* but not faced with English realities through experience of actual judicial business. Both inside and outside Parliament, during the progress of the Deceased Wife's Sister's Marriage Bill, a view was in evidence that the church had, and would retain, its own 'law' on marital capacity.

Part of the argument was that the degrees of affinity impeding marriage, based on Archbishop Parker's table, were incorporated into a canon – a spiritual matter which convocation should decide. To the common lawyer this was unconvincing; if the canon had any authority over the marriages of laymen, it was because it expressed rules adopted into the common law, which Parliament could change.[14]

There was also a more directly theological dispute: some considered the 'one-flesh' doctrine of marriage to make a spouse's sister into one's own, with whom any marriage would be incestuous. Such a literal extrapolation of Christ's words did not commend itself to all theologians.

Some conservative Christians opposed the legislation root and branch; consistently with the view that the marriage law of church and nation were one, and should remain so. Others contended that the 'law of the church' would remain unaffected by the Bill – a belief to which the draftsman's words

[14] The rule in question was also to be found in an Act of Parliament – 28 Hen. VIII c.7 (1536) – which itself declared such marriages 'contrary to the laws of God'.

that marriages authorised by it should be valid 'as a civil contract' certainly contributed.

Archbishop Davidson and his supporters adopted the second tactic, moving four consequential amendments: one to make the marriages in question valid only if solemnized without church rites; another to preserve disciplinary sanctions against a minister who himself married under the Act; another to enable even laypeople who did so to be refused communion and Christian burial; and another to extend the 'conscience clause' – which, as initially drawn, followed the 1857 wording – to allow a minister to refuse the use of his church altogether.

The sanctions against laypeople, proposed by Lord Robert Cecil, fell in the House of Commons, as did Davidson's proposal in the Lords to make church solemnization invalid.[15] Davidson's other two amendments passed. The imposition of a double standard for clergy and laity, although open to weighty objections of principle pointed out by Lord Courtney of Penrith, was already a legal commonplace thanks to the power of the convocations to bind the clergy by canon; and government counsel against 'interfering with the discipline of the church over its own servants' was followed.[16]

Of particular interest, given the later history, is how the 'conscience clause' came to be extended, allowing a clergyman's scruples to prevail over parishioners' rights. The mood in the Commons was against this, and the Lords amendment might well have been reversed but for the pressure to pass the Bill – a private member's initiative – by the end of the session. Several members spoke defending the 'common law right of Englishmen', which could not be expected to bow to the scruples of clergy who neither were, nor represented, the English church as a whole. But, advising concession of the point, Sir Brampton Gurdon predicted – with some justice – that 'in two or three years people will have forgotten that these

---

[15] 7 June 1907, *Hansard (Commons)* col. 1423; 23 August 1907, *Hansard (Lords)* col. 1265.

[16] 26 August 1907, *Hansard (Lords)* cols. 6–9 (Lord Courtney, Lord Tweedmouth). (The issues raised by rules affecting only the clergy are beyond the scope of this chapter.)

marriages were ever forbidden', and that the conscience clause would be seldom invoked.[17]

The successful amendments were therefore inconclusive on the principle whether there could be – as Cecil and Davidson suggested – a 'law of the church' for laypeople distinct from that of the land. The strongest denial of this came from Lord James of Hereford:

> It is said that the law of the church is what we now have to follow. But this which is termed 'the law of the church' springs from the decision of a diocesan synod. The opinions expressed by councils of the pre-reformed church are not recognised as law in this country.... They may instruct us ... but are no more to be tolerated as having the effect of law than the opinions of convocation. Guided by my own conscience, and seeking such guidance as will assist me, I protest against this country, blessed with the results of the great Reformation, going back to the opinions of the early bishops and learned men of narrow views for rules as to what is right and wrong for the social life of today.... There can be no law in this matter but the law of Parliament.[18]

The Bishop of London replied: 'What is the good of the church if in every case it is considered almost an impertinence for the church to have a different standard from that of the world?'[19] But Lord James was not denying the need for the church to live by Christian standards. What he denied was that it was for ecclesiastical professionals to set them. The clergy could point to ideals, as part of their task of preaching the Word; but it was not for them alone to decide how far such ideals should find legal expression. His appeal in the passage just quoted to the 'results of the great Reformation', 'guided by my own conscience and seeking such guidance as will assist me', was the declaration of an educated English Protestant, asserting the right of every Christian to form faith-based judgements and of Christian legislators to base their conduct accordingly.

---

[17] 7 June 1907, *Hansard (Commons)* cols. 1498, 1501–54; 27 August, cols. 413–14 (Lord Robert Cecil, White, Napier, Essex, Sir Brampton Gurdon).
[18] 20 August 1907, *Hansard (Lords)* col. 366.
[19] *Hansard (Lords)* col. 386.

Lord Robert Cecil (perhaps surprisingly) admitted that an Act could change the ecclesiastical law in this field, asserting interestingly that any Bill so intended should properly be a government Bill. But he took his stand on the words 'as a civil contract' to deny that *this* Bill would have any such effect.[20] Ultimately Parliament failed to define these words; but an opportunity soon arose for the courts to do so.

I need not tell the full saga of *Bannister v. Thompson*, the case in which a minister, considering the parties to a marriage legitimised by the 1907 Act to be 'open and notorious evil livers' and refusing them communion (despite the rejection of Cecil's clause to enable this), was disciplined for acting unlawfully.[21] It is enough to quote from the speech of Lord Ashbourne when the case was finally decided by the House of Lords:

> The effect of [the Act] was to make such a marriage lawful for all purposes, entitled to be recognised as such within the realm or without, and that without stint or qualification.... The words 'as a civil contract' ... may have been inserted to relieve the clergy from the obligation of performing or aiding the marriage, *but they cannot make duality in marriage.*[22]

The Matrimonial Causes Act 1937 and the 'Conscience Clause'

It was in the year of Edward VIII's abdication that A. P. Herbert secured a Second Reading for what was to become the Matrimonial Causes Act 1937. The Church Assembly, responsible for framing legislation on 'any matter concerning the Church of England' and expressing an opinion on any matter of religious or public concern, was then seventeen years old, and Parliament had, with occasional exceptions, got out of the habit of acting directly to regulate public religion. Many who had not been prepared to identify the clerical convocations with 'the church' felt differently about a body with lay

---

[20] 7 June 1907, *Hansard (Commons)* cols. 1016–18.

[21] See Bruce S. Bennett, '*Bannister v. Thompson* and Afterwards – The Church of England and the Deceased Wife's Sister's Marriage Act', *Journal of Ecclesiastical History*, 49 (1998), p. 668.

[22] *Thompson v. Dibdin* [1912] AC 533 at 543 (author's emphasis).

participation, even though this only represented active conformists and was debarred from directly pronouncing on theology.

Many Parliamentarians therefore distinguished between the proposal to permit divorce and remarriage on grounds of cruelty, desertion and insanity, and the discipline of the Church of England, which they professed not to touch. Alan Herbert himself quoted a Church Union booklet dividing 'the moral standards which the Church of England must impose upon its own members' from those which 'a largely secularised state can force upon its citizens as such'.[23] The archbishops' benevolent neutrality toward the Bill was based on their understanding that existing church discipline would be unaffected.

Yet there was very little in the Bill itself to support such assumptions. Herbert's 'conscience clause' effectively extended the 1907 compromise both to the new grounds of divorce and to divorces for adultery possible since 1857, so that henceforth the use of a parish church might be refused in any of these situations.[24] On Third Reading in the Lords, Viscount Cecil claimed this as 'a clear admission' of 'division between the law of the church and the law of the state'.[25] But it will be recalled that the House of Commons had shown no such intention in approving the 1907 provision itself; and that the *Thompson* judgement had rejected the very construction of the 1907 wording that Cecil wished to put on its 1937 equivalent. Further, the 1937 wording permitting remarriage did not even use the 1907 'civil contract' terminology. Cecil's logic required an identification of the clergy with the church which Bishop Hensley Henson said was 'news to him'.[26] Bishop Whittingham

---

[23] 20 November 1936, *Hansard (Commons)* col. 2083. Liberals regarded this extension as a compromise acceptable in the interest of securing the Bill; see *Modern Churchman* editorial, April 1936.

[24] The clause was enacted as Matrimonial Causes Act 1937, s.11, and thereby inserted as a new s.184(2) in the Supreme Court of Judicature (Consolidation) Act 1925.

[25] 19 July 1937, *Hansard (Lords)* col. 578.

[26] *Hansard (Lords)* col. 588. There were, anyhow, theologically contentious marriages which the 'conscience clause' did not cover, such as those of persons whose former marriage had been annulled for subsequent refusal to consummate – a ground almost as controversial in some quarters as divorce. The 'clause' initially extended to remarriage following judicial presumption of death; but seems to do so no longer, following redrafting in 1973.

of St Edmundsbury and Ipswich challenged Cecil's suggestion that the laws of church and state were diverging. He continued: 'I disagree also with the Archbishop's urging that the Bill is against the law of the church. No doubt it depends in part upon your conception of what the government of the church really is ... all proceedings in the past with regard to the law of matrimony have been laws of the church and of Parliament too'. [27]

Extra-Parliamentary Moves in the 1930s for a 'Church Marriage Discipline'

The passage of Herbert's Bill was accompanied by debates on marriage discipline in the convocations. Some years earlier these had described remarriage as 'sinful, even if not conventionally immoral', and demanded 'liberty for the church to discipline her own members as necessary for the vindication of her own law'.[28] In 1937 the northern bishops approved regulations governing the 'readmission' of married divorcees to communion, and the next year the southern bishops adopted similar regulations as 'guidance in the exercise of their pastoral responsibility'. In June 1938 resolutions against church remarriage were adopted in both provinces.[29]

To Tractarians, these resolutions restated and defined the 'marriage law' they had always believed 'the church' to have. They were also not without practical effect: Bruce Bennett reports[30] that some parish clergy did in fact apply the convocations' eucharistic 'discipline'. Episcopal discretion and patronage were also used to enforce the church remarriage resolutions indirectly; common licences were refused and, in

---

[27] *Hansard (Lords)* col. 582.

[28] Convocation of Canterbury, 1910, 1914; Arthur R. Winnett, *Divorce and Remarriage in Anglicanism* (London: Macmillan, 1958).

[29] *York Journal of Convocation* (January 1937), pp. 49–52; *Chronicle of Convocation* (June 1938), p. 384.

[30] Bruce Bennett, 'The Church of England and the Law of Divorce since 1857 – Marriage Discipline, Ecclesiastical Law and the Establishment', *Journal of Ecclesiastical History*, 45 (1994), p. 625.

Mervyn Stockwood's words, 'clergy who had the courage to stand by their legal rights often ... feared for their careers'.[31]

The fact that no parishioners vindicated their rights to communion through the courts[32] is of sociological significance, whether this shows willing submission to discipline, simple indifference, or a choice to worship elsewhere. But legally it says nothing at all. If canons did not bind the laity, much less did mere resolutions, whether styled 'Acts of Convocation' or not.[33] The law remained the law even if not invoked. Had parishioners proceeded against ministers refusing them communion, they would, like Bannister, have been entitled to succeed.

Parliament's Self-understanding in the 1937 Debate

If the 1937 conscience clause did not in fact recognise separate marriage laws of 'church' and 'state', and if the actions of the convocations cannot properly be regarded as 'law' at all, the question arises how far parliamentarians saw themselves during the debate as taking decisions for Christian England.

Of course there were members asserting that Parliament was not the place for 'spiritual' decisions.[34] A basis for episcopal neutrality was expressed with customary clarity by William Temple: 'The grounds on which the law of state and church should be determined are different, hence there may be a difference in the law itself.... There is a difference between what the state imposes under penalty and what the church summons her members to as an ideal.' [35]

Temple's words, though, had more in common with the continental Lutheran doctrine of the two regiments, than with Hooker's teaching on the goals common to the church and the

[31] Mervyn Stockwood, *Chanctonbury Ring – An Autobiography* (London: Hodder & Stoughton, 1982), p. 166.
[32] Refusal of communion without lawful cause is prohibited by the Sacrament Act 1547, s.8.
[33] Since 1970 the statements formerly termed Acts of Convocation have been styled Acts of Synod.
[34] E.g., Ernest Thurtle; 20 November 1936, *Hansard (Commons)* cols. 2116–17; 28 May 1937, cols. 631–32.
[35] 1 June 1937, *Hansard (Lords)* col. 782.

converted civil community. Few of Temple's contemporaries would have denied the distinction between ideals and legal requirements under penalty; but many refused to categorise the ideals in Jesus' teaching as in *any* sense 'law',[36] and considered exclusion from parochial ministrations to be as penal as imprisonment for bigamy.

Nor did all conservative churchmen accept the dichotomy which the episcopal leadership postulated. Commander Agnew, who had followed Temple's line on Second Reading, showed a change of heart at the Report stage: 'This state is still a Christian state ... I for one feel obliged ... to insert into our legislation the strongest and most powerful Christian bias that I can get put into it.'[37]

Furse of St Albans, another Christian legislator of the old school, believed in the same hardline 'standard' as the archbishops. But he felt obliged to do what he could to see that standard generally enforced: 'We come to this House summoned by His Majesty to give him counsel.'[38]

Christian thinking was also advanced in support for the Herbert Bill. The theological evidence before the Gorell Commission, whose recommendations Herbert was seeking to implement, had divided sharply between conservative and liberal, as did the Commission's Report:[39] the clerical canonist Edward Wood stood with Charles Gore and Cosmo Lang against William Inge, Hastings Rashdall and Herbert Hensley Henson.

It was argued that the Matthaean exception was not only authentic, but set a general precedent for exceptions to indissolubility. The 'one flesh' remarks attributed to Jesus could be explained as an ideal, in line with much of his other teaching, rather than a law to be enforced by his followers. It could be contended that the factual death of a marriage relationship was the sign that God himself, for whatever reason, had sundered those whom he had joined. And overlaying all such arguments

---

[36] Hastings Rashdall's 1910 sermon to this effect had been extremely influential; Winnett, *Divorce and Remarriage in Anglicanism.*

[37] 28 May 1937, *Hansard (Commons)* col. 605.

[38] 1 June 1937, *Hansard (Lords)* col. 762.

[39] *Report of the Royal Commission on Divorce and Matrimonial Causes*, London 1912 (Parliamentary Papers 1912/13, xviii 143).

of detail was the Liberal Christian conviction that no enforcement of rules could be as true to the spirit of Christ as relieving the hardship for which the existing law had to answer.

As a bishop in 1937, Hensley Henson considered it Parliament's place to make a Christian decision: 'If it were to go out that the law of England had parted company with Christian law, I think it would be a great disaster to the nation.... I believe ... that this bill if passed, so far from bringing the law into conflict ... would bring the law of England into deeper and truer harmony with [the law of Christ].'[40] Barnes of Birmingham objected to a Bill, harmonising marriage law with 'the opinion [of] the overwhelming majority of enlightened Christian people in this country', being treated as 'a concession to a semi-pagan community'.[41] Bishop Whittingham spoke of some remarriages as 'unions on which I am certain that God's blessing rests'.[42] Sir Francis Ackland's Commons speech in favour of the Second Reading reflected on the social background to Jesus' reported prohibition, and explained his vote by a conclusion on where 'the best religious opinion' lay.[43] Lionel Sorensen emphasised the sincerity of religious conviction which motivated the Bill's supporters.[44]

Herbert's final speech before the Third Reading vote made high claims for the altered marriage law:

I maintain with all solemnity and reverence that there is not a single word in this Bill of which [Christ, as a realist] would not approve.... In the finest sense of the word, this is a Christian Bill.[45]

Among active churchgoers of the time, these may have been minority views. They were certainly not the universal view in Parliament. But they do show that Parliament's failure to make any explicit change in the unity of English marriage law was not entirely by oversight.

[40] *Hansard (Lords)* col. 769.
[41] *Hansard (Lords)* cols. 812, 818.
[42] *Hansard (Lords)* col. 584.
[43] 20 November 1936, *Hansard (Commons)* cols. 2100–2.
[44] *Hansard (Commons)* col. 2104; 28 May 1937, cols. 585, 600.
[45] 28 May 1937, *Hansard (Commons)* col. 644; 1 June 1937, *Hansard (Lords)* cols. 738–39 (Viscount FitzAlan of Derwent).

Extra-Parliamentary Moves in the 1950s

Viscount Cecil, recognising the legal limitations of the 1937 convocation resolutions, did in fact introduce a draft Measure in the Church Assembly that autumn. N. P. Williams' counter-proposal, that the Assembly take its stand behind the convocations, carried the day. Nonetheless, another attempt to give the convocation view on marriage legal 'teeth' was made in the canon law revision project of the 1950s.

The draft canons annexed to the Garbett Report of 1947 contained a general provision (Canon 9) requiring the laity to submit to the canon law on pain of forfeiting ecclesiastical office and rights to ministrations. A specific prohibition (Canon 38) forbade the remarriage of a divorced person in church. The Report claimed that the 1937 'conscience clause' 'can only be an admission that the law of the church, unlike the civil law, does not recognise a divorce with the right of remarriage'.[46]

Nonetheless, the group of government lawyers advising on the revision project recognised immediately that a canon placing any new restriction on the laity would need the backing of an Act or Measure.[47] In Archbishop Fisher they found a prelate more willing to listen to legal advice than any predecessor since Tait. Their leading light, the Treasury Solicitor Sir Thomas Barnes, who continued to advise long after retirement from the Civil Service, held views contrasting sharply with the Garbett Commission, as evidenced by his 1957 comment on draft Canon 7, 'Of the Law of the Church of England'. 'The law of the Church of England is, like any other part of the law of England, to be found in the common law and in statutes in force from time to time, and it would seem unnecessary to state this.'[48]

In May 1956 both convocations accepted Barnes' group's advice that the attempt to pass enabling legislation for Canon

---

[46] *The Canon Law of the Church of England*, pp. 66–7.

[47] Such backing was indeed given for restrictions on ordination of remarried divorcees: Clergy (Ordination and Miscellaneous Provisions) Measure 1964, s.9, and Canon C4 para. 3.

[48] Fisher papers, Lambeth Palace Library, folio 196/73 ('Document K'); see also minutes of Steering Committee's Executive meeting, 23 July 1957, same vol.

38 would cause more difficulty with Parliament than it was worth.[49] Canon 9 shared the same fate two years later, having been shelved since 1953 and then tacked (with remarkably little discussion) onto Barnes' proposal to abandon Canons 7 and 8.

There remained a hardline majority opinion against remarriage, which found expression in the October 1957 republication as an 'Act of Convocation' of the Canterbury resolutions of the 1930s. But the relatively tame acquiescence in Barnes' advice showed that even hardliners were now prepared to rely upon moral persuasion rather than high claims for a separate 'church's law'.

Recent Legislative Developments

Very much less needs to be said about more recent changes in marriage law. While the General Synod has frequently *discussed* marriage issues at length, and the issue is back on the current agenda, only twice (during the 1980s) has it purported to legislate: rescinding the 1930s resolutions on admission to communion,[50] and modifying restrictions on ordination of the remarried.[51] Parliament's initial rejection – on theological grounds – of the latter Measure showed 'Christian nation' thinking to be not necessarily the ally of Liberal Christianity.

The general marriage law has seen four significant changes since 1937. Collusion between spouses ceased to be an absolute bar to divorce from 1963; the Divorce Reform Act 1969 introduced the concept of 'irretrievable breakdown'; the impediment of affinity was further narrowed in 1986; while the Family Law Act 1996 removes 'fault' entirely from divorce proceedings.

The second and third of these developments flowed substantially from archiepiscopal initiatives: the Mortimer and Seear Reports *Putting Asunder* (1964) and *No Just Cause* (1984). The initiative for the others lay elsewhere; but in none was 'church law' versus 'general law' a burning issue. The reason could be

---

[49] *York Journal of Convocation* (May 1956), pp. 60–63; *Chronicle of Convocation* (May 1956), pp. 49–50, 81.
[50] 13 *General Synod Report of Proceedings* 606.
[51] Clergy Ordination Measure 1990.

found in *Putting Asunder*, whose principal author[52] was a veteran of the Garbett Commission. Refining Temple's 1937 approach, this asserted that

> The state's matrimonial law is not a translation of the teaching of Jesus into legal terms, but an allowance of that hardness of heart of which Jesus took account. It is not to be judged by the standard of the church's own law and pastoral discipline. The church must advise the state resting on premises enjoying wide acknowledgment in the nation as a whole.[53]

In the debate on the 1986 Marriage (Prohibited Degrees of Relationship) Bill, Bishop Walker of Ely reiterated this view, appealing 'to that honest Anglican tradition whereby Christian thinkers, attempting to think about the world, have made use of all the understanding which Christian faith has to offer but yet have not seen themselves as having to "treat the world tyrannously as though it were the church"'.[54]

Yet *Putting Asunder*'s assumption of the existence of 'the church's own law and pastoral discipline' was difficult to reconcile with the history of the 'conscience clause', the unequivocal ruling of the House of Lords in *Thompson* and the abandonment of the remarriage canon.

Nor did the recent Acts change matters. Both the divorce Acts left the 'conscience clause' where it is today, in a form substantially unchanged from the 1937 wording.[55] The 1986 Act provided in similar terms for the newly-authorised affinous marriages, while at the same time envisaging active co-operation from the episcopate in facilitating such marriages in church.[56]

The General Synod could of course change the position tomorrow if it were confident of parliamentary approval for the necessary Measure; but it is interesting to compare the caution

---

[52] Robert Mortimer, Bishop of Exeter.

[53] *Putting Asunder – the Report of the Archbishop of Canterbury's Group on Divorce Law* (London: 1966), p. 12.

[54] 9 December 1985, *Hansard (Lords)* col. 50.

[55] Matrimonial Causes Act 1965, s.8(2).

[56] Marriage (Prohibited Degrees of Relationship) Act 1986, insertions into Marriage Act 1949 (new s.5A and sub-sections in s.16).

displayed in the recent 'discussion document'[57] with that counselled by Sir Thomas Barnes in 1956.

So far as the laity of the Church of England is concerned, I suggest it would be fairer to say that what we have from bishops and synods is guidance as to how the choices given by the law should be made: guidance that carries weight on account of the learning, experience and sincerity of its authors, but ultimately guidance to be weighed by each Christian individual against all the other factors that inform conscientious decision. And one such factor is the national conscience as expressed in Parliament, which once asserted the nation's fundamental Christianity[58] and – however individual members may understand their role – has never yet formally disclaimed it.

[57] *Marriage in Church after Divorce: A discussion document from a Working Party* (London: Church House Publishing, 2000).

[58] Ecclesiastical Licences Act 1533, s.13.

25

Mystical Union: Legal and Theological Perspectives on Marriage

Jacqueline Humphreys and Simon J. Taylor

Introduction

This chapter argues that the theology of the Church of England regarding marriage is dependent upon the changing civil law of marriage and divorce. Since Lord Hardwicke's Act, which abolished informal marriage, and implicitly since the Reformation, the church has accepted civil control over the beginnings and endings of marriage. This leads us to question the understanding of marriage as ontologically indissoluble. The Church of England is in a unique position as the church by law established. However, the Anglican experience raises important issues for other Christian churches. The 'mystical union' in the title is taken from the Anglican marriage liturgy. Such a union is only properly understood when both the legal and theological aspects of marriage are examined. It may, therefore, be taken as a metaphor for the relationship of the two perspectives that we bring to this subject.

Marriage in English Law

There is no full definition of marriage within the civil law of England.[1] It is not the practice of a common law jurisdiction to

---

[1] Judicial pronouncements, and the rubric in the *Book of Common Prayer* (as set out in the Schedule to the Act of Uniformity 1662), do not amount to a theory or 'doctrine' of marriage within civil law.

provide definitions and doctrines. The civil law of marriage in effect deals with two questions: 'How do people become married?' and 'What does it mean for people to be married?' It is only in answering those two questions that English law defines marriage.

In contrast, the canon law of the Church of England provides a clear definition of marriage in Canon B30(1):

> The Church of England affirms, according to our Lord's teaching, that marriage is in its nature a union permanent and life-long, for better for worse, till death them do part, of one man with one woman, to the exclusion of all others on either side, for the procreation and nurture of children, for the hallowing and right direction of the natural instincts and affections, and for the mutual society, help and comfort which the one ought to have of the other, both in prosperity and adversity.

In seeking to answer the first of the two questions identified above, the church is dependent entirely upon the civil law as we shall show. When considering what it means to be married, the canons have little to say beyond this assertion of indissolubility in Canon B30.[2] It is also worth noting that canons only bind clergy, not laity.[3] The church's teaching on what it means to be married must be found outside its law (see below).

Historical Background

At the Reformation the King became the highest authority for church law in England. Canon law only remained law so far as it was not repugnant to royal prerogative, common law or statute.[4] The Queen in Parliament remains the highest authority for church law, although from 1919 the framing of

---

[2] *The Canons of the Church of England* (6th edn; London: Church House Publishing, 2000), p. 51.

[3] See Norman Doe, *The Legal Framework of the Church of England: A Critical Study in a Comparative Context* (Oxford: Clarendon Press, 1996), p. 18.

[4] Submission of Clergy Act 1533 (25 Hen. VIII c. 19), repealed under Mary I but reinstated by Elizabeth I by the Act of Supremacy (1558). The effect of this statute upon matters of worship and doctrine has been limited by the Church of England (Worship and Doctrine) Measure 1974.

much church legislation has been delegated to the church's own governing bodies.[5] Previously, Parliament legislated directly for the church, thus church law and civil law were distinguishable only by content, not by form or authority. It is therefore not possible to speak of a self-contained Anglican law of marriage, separate from the civil law. The church may only make its own rules about marriage so far as the civil law permits it to do so.

Prior to 1753 the law governing entry into marriage was essentially the pre-Reformation canon law.[6] A marriage was formed either by the exchanging of words of present intent to marry, or by the exchange of words of future intent to marry followed by consummation. Marriages could therefore be entered into not only publicly with proper formalities, but also informally or even secretly. The church disapproved of clandestine marriages, but did not challenge their validity.[7] An injunction to solemnize the marriage properly often formed part of the sentence of an ecclesiastical court that had already decided in favour of the existence of an informal marriage.[8]

Lord Hardwicke's Marriage Act 1753[9] outlawed clandestine marriage in England.[10] For the first time in English law specific formalities were required for a valid marriage. These formalities were the rites and procedural requirements of the Church

---

[5] By the Church of England Assembly (Powers) Act 1919, and the Synodical Government Measure 1962.

[6] It did not, on the whole, fall foul of the Submission of Clergy Act. The ecclesiastical courts, now regarded as part of the King's court system, retained jurisdiction over marriage.

[7] In 1200 Archbishop Hubert Walter introduced the requirement of triple publication of banns before marriage, and in 1215 this custom was extended by Innocent III to the whole of Christendom. See Joseph Jackson, *The Formation and Annulment of Marriage* (London: Butterworths, 1969), p. 14.

[8] Jackson, *The Formation and Annulment of Marriage*, p. 13.

[9] 26 Geo. II c.33.

[10] The Council of Trent (1545–1563) ruled that, for the Roman Catholic Church, valid marriages had to take place in the presence of a priest and two other witnesses, essentially outlawing clandestine marriage in the Catholic world. Therefore, from the Reformation until 1753, 'the law of marriage presents the paradoxical case in which the English Church clung to a part of the medieval Roman Canon Law which the Roman Catholic Church itself discarded' (R. H. Helmholz, *Roman Canon Law in Reformation England* (Cambridge: Cambridge University Press, 1990), p. 69).

of England, with exemptions for Quakers and Jews only. The Church of England also no longer recognises informal marriage. Whatever controversy at the time,[11] the 1753 Act was enforced by the ecclesiastical courts and the church has not sought to reinstate informal marriage. The church has accepted that actions and words which in 1752 would have produced a valid, indissoluble marriage, from 1753 no longer do so.

Current English Civil Law

The current civil law continues to define the entry into marriage, and continues to provide that English marriages that do not comply with the civil rules are not valid marriages. Civil law regards a marriage as void, even when conducted under the correct formalities, if the parties are within the prohibited degrees of consanguinity and affinity;[12] where either is under 16;[13] where either is already lawfully married;[14] where they are not respectively male and female;[15] and where either is domiciled in England and Wales and also a party to a polygamous marriage conducted outside of England and Wales.[16] The compliance of Anglican clergy with these rules is required by the state. A priest is guilty of a criminal offence if he or she knowingly and wilfully permits a void marriage to take place, or

---

[11] According to O'Donovan, 'several [Members of Parliament] suggested that the cost of a licence deterred many of the poor from marrying in church and that those labourers mobile by trade would be prevented from marrying at all' (K. O'Donovan, *Sexual Divisions in Law* (London: Weidenfield & Nicolson, 1985), p. 45 cited in Brenda Hoggett and David Pearl, *The Family, Law and Society: Cases and Materials* (3rd edn; London: Butterworths, 1991), p. 31). The church made no protest about this aspect of the Act. Winnett records that 'the Church accepted the Act, the Bishops supporting the Chancellor in the Lords and the Ecclesiastical Courts subsequently enforcing its provisions' (Arthur Robert Winnett, *Divorce and Remarriage in Anglicanism* (London: Macmillan, 1958), p. 132).

[12] Marriage Act 1949, s.1 and Matrimonial Causes Act 1973, s.11(a)(i).

[13] Marriage Act 1949, s.2 and Matrimonial Causes Act 1973, s.11(a)(ii).

[14] Matrimonial Causes Act 1973, s.11(b).

[15] Matrimonial Causes Act 1973, s.11(c).

[16] Matrimonial Causes Act 1973, s.11(d).

knowingly and wilfully fails to comply with the proper formalities.[17]

The civil law also recognises that a marriage may be voidable, that is valid until either party challenges it successfully in the courts.[18] The grounds on which a marriage may be voided are:[19]

   (a) non-consummation due to the incapacity of either party;

   (b) non-consummation due to the wilful refusal of the respondent;

   (c) invalid consent;

   (d) either party was suffering from a mental disorder making them unfit for marriage;

   (e) the respondent was suffering from a communicable venereal disease;

   (f) the respondent was pregnant by someone other than the petitioner.

However, the granting of a nullity decree is not automatic and there are bars to relief. No nullity on grounds of invalid consent, mental disorder or venereal disease may be made three years after the marriage.[20] In any case the petitioner must be ignorant of the fact at the time of marriage,[21] and after discovering it must not have behaved so as to infer acceptance such that it would be unjust to the respondent to grant the decree.[22]

From a legal perspective, it is vital that there are definitive rules about whether a person is validly married, because of the

---

[17] See Marriage Act 1949, s.75. Indeed there are further requirements leading to civil and canonical penalties which do not void a marriage if not complied with. For example, the marriage of persons under 18 without their parents' consent, or conducting a marriage outside the hours of 8 a.m. to 6 p.m.

[18] For the development of the concept of voidable marriage in English law after the Reformation see Jackson, *The Formation and Annulment of Marriage*, p. 54.

[19] Matrimonial Causes Act 1973, s.12. The following list is an abbreviated paraphrase of this section.

[20] Matrimonial Causes Act 1973, s.13(2).

[21] Matrimonial Causes Act 1973, s.13(3).

[22] Matrimonial Causes Act 1973, s.13(1).

legal consequences of marriage.[23] For example, a widow's pension can only be paid to a widow. A person can only be convicted of bigamy if his or her first marriage is valid. Marital status is also relevant to inheritance and to financial settlements after separation.

Marriage in Anglican Theology

It cannot be stressed enough that Lord Hardwicke's Act places the entry into marriage clearly in the jurisdiction of the civil law by prescribing the formalities required for a valid marriage. Ironically, the formalities prescribed at first were those of the Church of England, but this should not be allowed to obscure the fact that, in limiting the required formularies to the church's rites, Parliament is claiming jurisdiction over the entry into marriage, not the church. The church has even altered its canons to keep in step with the civil law. Two examples of this must suffice.

The first concerns the law of prohibited degrees. At the Reformation the extended impediments present in Roman canon law, and the practice of granting dispensations from them, were consciously discarded and replaced with a table of kindred and affinity. However, the modern Canon B31, dealing with impediments to marriage, was amended following the Marriage (Prohibited Degrees of Relationship) Act 1986. This Act permits the marriage of a person to the parent, grandparent, child or grandchild of a former spouse, in certain defined circumstances.[24] The amendment of the canon to accommodate this Act shows the church was prepared not only to permit the civil law to define those able to contract marriage against the previous law of the church, but also to adapt its own law to the terms defined by the state.

---

[23] The vast majority of applications to the ecclesiastical courts in the medieval and early modern period were to prove the validity of a marriage, rather than to obtain a nullity or seek judicial separation. See Martin Ingram, *Church Courts, Sex and Marriage in England 1570–1640* (Cambridge: Cambridge University Press, 1987), pp. 171, 189.

[24] Prior to this Act such marriages were absolutely forbidden by both civil and canon law.

The law of nullity provides a second example of the church's submission to the civil law, albeit under protest. 'Wilful refusal to consummate' was a new basis for nullity, introduced by the 1937 Act. A report published in 1955 by a commission appointed by the archbishops indicated that they disapproved of this new ground, primarily because it introduced the concept of nullity arising from an event occurring after the marriage, rather than a defect at the time of the marriage.[25] It was not only logically wrong, but also outside the canonical tradition of nullity. However, despite registering disapproval, the commission recommended no amendment to the canons to prevent the remarriage of such persons in church. It did not recommend setting up church marriage tribunals, to establish whether a nullity could have been obtained on proper canonical grounds. It rather recommended that the church abide by the decisions of the civil courts, and try to educate the public and the legal professions not to seek divorce where a nullity decree would be appropriate.

The Church of England, therefore, has no account of the validity of marriage different to that provided by the civil law. The church is bound to accept the legality and validity of marriages it does not perform, and indeed may be excused from performing. The case of *R v. Dibdin*[26] provides an illustration of this. A clergyman sought to exclude from communion a couple who had been legally married in Canada at a time when their marriage would have been illegal in England. The wife was the sister of the husband's deceased first wife. However, by the time the clergyman sought to exclude them, their marriage could have been legally contracted in England.[27] The Court of Appeal held that persons whose marriage was permitted under civil law could not be regarded as 'notorious sinners' under canon

---

[25] *The Church and the Law of Nullity of Marriage: The Report of a Commission appointed by the Archbishops of Canterbury and York in 1949 at the request of the Convocations* (London: SPCK, 1955).

[26] [1909] P 57.

[27] Following the enactment of the Deceased Wife's Sister's Marriage Act 1907.

law and thus excluded from communion. The Master of the Rolls said:

> Marriage ... is one and the same thing whether the contract is made in church with religious vows superadded, or whether it is made in a Nonconformist chapel with religious ceremonies, or whether it is made before a consul abroad, or before a registrar, without any religious ceremonies. So far as I am aware the Established Church has never refused to recognise any marriage which by our law is valid as being otherwise than a good marriage for ecclesiastical purposes.[28]

In fact, the church has always recognised marriages conducted outside its rites. The ecclesiastical courts, before Lord Hardwicke's Act, deliberated over the validity or otherwise of informal marriages which by definition were not conducted by the church. Marriage, according to the *Alternative Service Book* (ASB), is 'a gift of God in creation',[29] and it is on this theological basis that the church has always recognised marriages conducted outside its jurisdiction, whether those of other religions or those that are purely secular. Article XXV of the Thirty-nine Articles refuses to count marriage as a sacrament of the same nature as baptism and the eucharist because it has not 'any visible sign or ceremony ordained of God'.[30] That is to say, there is no specific form by which a marriage may be known. Rather, the church recognises many ways in which a valid marriage can be contracted. Lord Hardwicke's Marriage Act, and the civil control of entry into marriage it established, simply falls under this rubric.

In fact, marriage is not something that the church 'does' at all. Rather it witnesses and blesses the marriage of two people who marry each other. The ASB marriage service begins, 'We have come together in the presence of God, to *witness* the

---

[28] [1909] P 57, p. 109.

[29] The *Alternative Service Book 1980* (Oxford: Oxford University Press, 1980), p. 288. The *Book of Common Prayer* (BCP) has the more prosaic description of marriage as 'instituted of God in the time of man's innocence' (p. 189).

[30] The Article leaves open the possibility that it may be a sacrament that is not like those of baptism and the eucharist.

marriage of N and N, to *ask his blessing on them*, and to share in their joy.'[31] The model for this is Jesus' presence at a wedding in Cana.[32] Jesus certainly contributed to the joy of the feast, but his presence at the wedding adds nothing to the marriage *as a marriage*. The *Book of Common Prayer* describes Jesus' having 'adorned and beautified' the wedding at Cana with his presence, and a Church of England Working Party suggests that 'the Church's presence at a marriage ... *elevates* it'.[33] Yet the Working Party stresses that 'this does not make the Church a *primary actor* in the exchange of vows'. There is nothing magical about a church wedding that somehow leaves the couple 'more married' than if they had entered into marriage elsewhere.

All this has led to some anxiety among Anglicans as to what is distinctive about Christian marriage. A recent document from the House of Bishops of the Church of England describes three ways in which 'Christian marriage' is distinctive. The first sees the issue as one of understanding. The bishops recognise the reality and success of unbelievers' marriages, but say that

> it is important that those who marry know the full extent of what they are doing. And Christians believe that that requires an understanding of the love that God has shown mankind in Christ, a love which marriage is called to reflect. Those who understand God's love to them will understand their own love as a part of God's work in the world, and will be better equipped for what they undertake.[34]

Here the bishops locate the distinctiveness of Christian marriage in a particular understanding of marriage. Thus a Christian marriage is one in which at least one of the partners has an understanding of marriage that is informed by the

---

[31] ASB, p. 288 (emphasis added). In this respect the ASB is superior to the BCP's rather misleading statement that 'we are gathered here ... to *join* this Man and this Woman in holy Matrimony' (BCP, p. 189). The extent to which God can be said to have 'joined together' the couple is clearly dependent upon their consent and the vows they have made to one another.

[32] Jn 2:1–11.

[33] *Marriage in Church after Divorce: a discussion document from a Working Party commissioned by the House of Bishops of the Church of England* (London: Church House Publishing, 2000), p. 15.

[34] *Marriage: a teaching document from the House of Bishops of the Church of England* (London: Church House Publishing, 1999), p. 12.

Christian teaching. Any marriage can, therefore, become a Christian marriage by the conversion of one of the partners.

Secondly, the bishops interpret the description of marriage as a 'sacrament' to mean that 'the pledged relation of husband and wife is a sign of the pledge of love that Christ has for his Church'.[35] Again, it seems any marriage can be such a sign, if the partners choose to see it as such.

Finally, the bishops locate the distinctiveness of Christian marriage in the context in which it is begun. Thus the bishops say that 'the grace of God in the Holy Spirit is given to all who enter marriage in the conscious desire to hear his call, seeking his strength to live together as they have promised. This is why marriage in the context of worship . . . is an important ministry of the Church.'[36] Here the 'Christian' element of marriage could be seen as the liturgical context in which it begins. Yet the document will not permit so stark an interpretation. Rather, the context of worship is an intercession for the grace of God to be given to the couple. This request is made especially at the start of a marriage, but it is a request that must be repeated throughout the marriage.

Christian marriage is, therefore, only relatively distinct from other marriages. It is not qualitatively different, but is about the understanding of marriage that the couple has. Primarily this understanding of marriage is concerned about what it means to live as a married couple. The beginning of marriage, though important, is not the focus of this understanding so much as the continuing relationship.

Two things must be said at this juncture. First, a better understanding of marriage does not necessarily lead to a more 'successful' marriage, however defined. There is a slight hint of this in the teaching document, but it is a temptation to be resisted. Secondly, we want to reject the idea that only those marriages begun in a liturgical ceremony can be Christian marriages. There is nothing about the church ceremony that is essential for a fully valid marriage, however desirable such

[35] *Marriage*, p. 13. The bishops are careful to note that, in accordance with Article XXV, 'the term [sacrament] does not have exactly the same sense as when it is applied to the two "sacraments of the gospel", baptism and the eucharist'.

[36] *Marriage*, p. 13.

ceremonies may be. Christian marriage cannot be reduced to a liturgical origin, nor can those marriages that were begun outside such a context be regarded as somehow imperfect, invalid or deficient. For the Church of England, control of the entry into marriage lies with the civil law. This, we have suggested, is part of the church's vision of marriage as a gift of God in creation. That Christians may wish to take a particular approach to how the married life is to be lived is of no consequence to this.

Indissolubility in English Law

Obtaining a divorce

Since the Reformation English divorce law has been gradually changing from the indissolubilist position of the pre-Reformation church to the radical view of divorce in the Family Law Act 1996, which is yet to come into force.

The canon law applied by the ecclesiastical courts after the Reformation remained essentially unchanged until 1857. The ecclesiastical courts could annul a marriage and provide for divorce *a mensa et thoro*, the equivalent of modern judicial separation, which does not allow subsequent remarriage.[37] Parliament became the forum for the development of divorce. From 1670 Parliament began to grant divorces which allowed the parties to remarry.[38] Such divorces were expensive, and effectively restricted to the upper classes. Only 317 parliamentary divorces were obtained from 1670 to 1857.[39]

During the periods when legal divorce was difficult people organised their separations in other ways, taking more or less

---

[37] See Jackson, *The Formation and Annulment of Marriage*, p. 32.

[38] Lord Ross' case, cited in Jackson, *The Formation and Annulment of Marriage*, p. 38. For the history of parliamentary divorce see Winnett, *Divorce and Remarriage in Anglicanism*, pp. 116, 128–30, 134, 183; Jackson, *The Formation and Annulment of Marriage*, pp. 34–40 and *Rayden and Jackson's Law and Practice in Divorce and Family Matters*, Vol. 1 (15th edn; London: Butterworths, 1988), p. 7.

[39] *Rayden and Jackson*, p. 7. Of these, only four petitions were by wives. For a chronological distribution, see Winnett, *Divorce and Remarriage in Anglicanism*, p. 129.

notice of the law. Three forms of separation are considered here. First, parties could simply separate, without seeking a formal order from the courts. This could be by agreement, or against the wishes of one of the parties. With clandestine marriage, and limited record keeping, it was not difficult for a person to move to a new area and remarry.[40] Unsurprisingly, 'there is good reason to believe that thousands, perhaps tens of thousands, of marriages in eighteenth-century England were in fact bigamous'.[41] In some areas of the country, marriage customs existed, which regulated the day-to-day life of many people, despite having no status as formal law. Handfasting was a tradition of exchanging promises before witnesses that lasted only a year and a day, unless the woman became pregnant, when the vows became binding.[42] Jumping the broom allowed a couple to live together with the woman keeping her name, property and rights over her children.[43] These traditions often also permitted informal separation. However, these customs were outside the *law* of marriage. If disputes about such situations came before the ecclesiastical courts, the existence of the marriage would be judged under canon law, and the court could punish the parties for fornication or bigamy where appropriate.

Second, the practice of wife-selling grew up from the sixteenth century.[44] The terms of the contracts of sale varied, but were used to attempt to avoid the legal consequences of the subsisting first marriage, such as the wife's right to dower,[45] the husband's liability for the wife's debts and his right to take

---

[40] This would have been rather easier for a man than a woman, not least because a pregnant woman would be more conspicuous than her partner. Houlbrooke suggests that women were presented to the court for punishment for sexual incontinence 'simply because they had just left, or just arrived in, the area of a court's jurisdiction by themselves' (Ralph Houlbrooke, *Church Courts and the People during the English Reformation* (Oxford: Oxford University Press, 1979), pp. 76–7).

[41] Lawrence Stone, *Broken Lives: Separation and Divorce in England 1660–1858* (Oxford: Oxford University Press, 1993), p. 22.

[42] Stephen Parker, *Informal Marriage, Cohabitation and the Law, 1750–1989* (Basingstoke: Macmillan, 1990), p. 18.

[43] Parker, *Informal Marriage*, p. 24.

[44] See Stone, *Broken Lives*, p. 18.

[45] The inheritance of one-third of the husband's estate upon his death.

her property and money. Stone says that 'these wife-sales were merely a public method of divorce by mutual consent, a development of what had long been customary procedure among the poor, that is to extract a bribe from a wife's lover in return for not prosecuting him in the church courts'.[46]

Third, separation by private deed became common among the propertied classes in the eighteenth century. These deeds could provide for maintenance for the wife, together with an indemnity for the husband against her debts, and make provision for the care of children. These deeds could declare that the wife had the right to act as a single woman, important to enable her to hold property and support herself. Such a declaration was considered binding in the common law courts by 1800.[47]

The Matrimonial Causes Act 1857 set up the legal framework for divorce that lasted until 1969. The matrimonial jurisdiction of the ecclesiastical courts was abolished and replaced by a civil Court of Divorce and Matrimonial Causes.[48] At first a divorce could only be obtained on the basis of adultery for the husband and 'aggravated' adultery for the wife.[49] It could be refused if the petitioner's behaviour 'did not measure up to the requirements of the law'[50] and connivance, condonation and collusion were absolute bars to obtaining divorce.

The Divorce Reform Act 1969 fundamentally altered the grounds for divorce, and provides the basis for the present law under the Matrimonial Causes Act 1973. The sole ground for divorce is that the marriage has broken down irretrievably, proven by one of five facts: adultery, unreasonable behaviour, desertion, two years' separation with consent, or five years' separation.[51] The bars to divorce were abolished save that a petition

[46] Stone, *Broken Lives*, p. 19.
[47] See Stone, *Broken Lives*, p. 19.
[48] Matrimonial Causes Act 1857, 20 and 21 Vict. ch. 85. This court is the forerunner of the modern Family Division of the High Court. The new court had the same jurisdiction as, and was bound to decide cases upon the same principles as, the old ecclesiastical courts, save in so far as changed by statute.
[49] I.e., adultery combined with incest, rape, bigamy, sodomy, bestiality, or cruelty. A wife could finally petition on the grounds of adultery alone following the Matrimonial Causes Act 1923.
[50] *Rayden and Jackson*, p. 8.
[51] See Matrimonial Causes Act 1973, s.1(2).

on the ground of five years' separation can be refused if the respondent would suffer grave financial or other hardship.[52]

The present law enables both spouses to apply for financial relief after divorce, and gives the court wide discretion to enable it to act more or less justly with regard to the financial consequences of the breakdown of the marriage.[53] The law is concerned to ensure that despite the dissolution of the marriage the parties meet their ongoing obligations towards each other and their children. While the status of marriage is dissoluble, the financial obligations towards one's former spouse may not be, and one's obligations towards one's children rarely are.[54]

The ethos of practice in family law today is to promote a conciliatory approach to proceedings wherever possible. The majority of divorces are undefended, and most divorcing couples organise their financial situation and make arrangements for their children with little or no involvement by solicitors. An interdisciplinary approach to family law problems is promoted at a governmental level, and acted upon at a local level. The legal approach to the breakdown of relationships has changed fundamentally over the past thirty years. As Penny Mansfield says,

> those who ... supported divorce reform [in 1969] were positive about divorce, arguing that more people should be given a second chance of finding marital happiness. Three decades later, with greater experience of divorce, we have a better understanding of the complex nature of marital breakdown, in particular its impact on the couple and their children. By 1995, the aim of reform was to prevent marital breakdown, discourage hasty divorce and to minimise discord for the children.[55]

---

[52] Matrimonial Causes Act 1973, s.10. In practice, the petitioner usually makes sufficient financial provision so that no hardship occurs, thus permitting the divorce to proceed.

[53] Under the Matrimonial Causes Act 1973 (as amended).

[54] The Child Support Act 1991 prevents a 'clean break' with respect to financial provision for children.

[55] Penny Mansfield, 'From Divorce Prevention to Marriage Support', in Rt Hon. Lord Justice Thorpe and Elizabeth Clarke (eds.), *No Fault or Flaw: The Future of the Family Law Act 1996* (Bristol: Family Law, 2000), p. 30.

This conciliatory approach was further developed by the Family Law Act 1996. However, Part II of this Act, containing 'one of the most radical and far-reaching reforms'[56] to divorce law this century, has not yet come into effect and seems unlikely ever to do so.[57]

Indissolubility in Anglican Theology

It should be apparent that with civil control over the entry into marriage goes civil control over the end of marriage. John Keble argued that the 1857 Matrimonial Causes Act would establish a state law of marriage differing from the ecclesiastical law and questioned Parliament's right to do so:

> Neither is Parliament free to ordain, nor the Church to obey, anything which affects Holy Matrimony as it is a spiritual and supernatural ordinance. Least of all may we give up, to the State or any created Power, that which is the very token and mark to distinguish the marriages which are blessed in heaven from those which are merely agreed upon earth; viz. their absolute Indissolubility.[58]

Keble was, however, too late in this protestation. Civil control over marriage had already been established by Lord Hardwicke's Act over a century earlier.

The Church of England is bound to recognise marriages that are conducted outside its formularies. This includes marriages that follow divorce. Provision was made for those who, like Keble, object to, as they saw it, the removal of the notion of indissolubility from marriage by the 1857 Act. This took the form of a 'clergy conscience clause'. The clergy were exempted from their obligation to marry all their parishioners where a party to a proposed marriage was a divorcee whose former

[56] Janet Walker, 'Wither the Family Law Act, Part II?', in Thorpe and Clarke, *No Fault or Flaw*, p. 3.
[57] It was due to come into effect in March 2000.
[58] John Keble, *Sequel of the Argument against immediately repealing the Laws which treat the Nuptial Bond as indissoluble* (London: Parkers, 1857), p. 217. Keble's distinction between marriages 'blessed in heaven' and those 'merely agreed upon earth' may represent an attempt to distinguish between Christian and non-Christian marriages.

spouse was still living.[59] The Matrimonial Causes Act 1857 permitted a clergyman to refuse to solemnize the remarriage of a respondent to a successful divorce petition founded on his or her adultery.[60] The exception was enlarged in 1937 when the grounds for divorce were extended. Now all divorcees can be excluded and a priest no longer has to make his or her church available for another to perform the marriage.[61] Within this exemption the church has made rules about when such remarriage should be allowed to take place in church. These regulations are contained in an Act of Convocation from 1957, as amended in 1982 and 1985.[62] The conscience clause does not allow the church to question the *validity* of marriages after divorce. The church can refuse to solemnize such marriages, but is nevertheless required to recognise them *as marriages*.[63]

---

[59] Under *Argar v. Holdsworth* (1758) 2 Lee 515, an Anglican clergyman is under a positive duty to marry all his parishioners, irrespective of their faith or lack of it. For a detailed view that this case does not justify the imposition of such a duty see Doe, *The Legal Framework of the Church of England*, pp. 358–68. However, see Mark Hill, *Ecclesiastical Law* (London: Butterworths, 1995), p. 305, who argues that even if *Argar v. Holdsworth* was misunderstood, 'the passage of time and the unqualified acceptance of such a right (and corresponding duty on the priest) makes it highly likely that a customary right (and duty) has evolved in any event'. For the church's understanding of its position, see *An Honourable Estate: The Doctrine of Marriage according to English Law and the Obligation of the Church to marry all parishioners who are not divorced* (Report of a Working Party established by the Standing Committee of the General Synod of the Church of England) (London: Church House Publishing, 1988).

[60] Under the 1857 Act, any minister who refused such a wedding was required to make their church available for the marriage to be conducted by another minister who held the bishop's licence. Some bishops, such as Bishop Wilberforce of Oxford, refused to issue licences for the marriage of divorced persons. (There is even one report of Wilberforce withdrawing the licence from a curate who performed such a marriage.) Clergy, since they cannot by law be required to conduct such marriages, are subject to the canons and lesser legislation of the church, including rules made by the bishop of the diocese in which they minister. Effectively the Acts of 1857 and 1937 pass the decision as to whether a divorced person be allowed to marry in church to the church itself. See Winnett, *Divorce and Remarriage in Anglicanism*, pp. 188–92, 230–3.

[61] The exemption can presently be found in the Matrimonial Causes Act 1965, s.8(2).

[62] See *The Canons of the Church of England*, pp. 192–3. An Act of Convocation has moral, but not legal, force.

[63] This point was seen by some in the debate over the 1857 Act. Winnett records that the Bishop of Salisbury opposed the conscience clause 'on the grounds that what was the teaching of the Church was made to appear a mere

Indeed, it would have been odd were the church not to recognise such marriages. From 1753 until 1836, those who obtained a divorce by Act of Parliament could only be remarried according to the rites of the Church of England, unless they were Quakers or Jews. There was, therefore, a legal entitlement for divorced persons to be married in church until the 1857 Act brought divorce within reach of those unable to fund an Act of Parliament.

Many Anglicans have found the 1857 Act and its successors to be a direct challenge to the understanding of marriage as indissoluble. This was Keble's argument and has been a major motivation of resistance to the remarriage of divorced persons in church ever since. We contend that this shows a mistaken view of the indissolubility of marriage. We suggest that, whatever else it may be, marriage is not indissoluble in the sense of persisting until the death of one of the partners, regardless of other circumstances. The basis for this assertion is precisely the recognition of marriages of divorced persons which is required of the church and which the church has always given. If a person's second marriage is recognised as valid while their former partner still lives, then this implies that the former marriage has been dissolved. Canon B30 cannot therefore be regarded as asserting an ontological indissolubility. The recent Working Party commissioned by the House of Bishops recognises that 'it can be said in a literal sense of two living people that they *were* married and are *no longer* married'.[64] However else the indissolubility of marriage is understood, it cannot be as an ontological statement. The 'conscience clause'

---

matter of moral scruple on the part of the clergy' (Winnett, *Divorce and Remarriage in Anglicanism*, p. 144). Bishop Wilberforce of Oxford is reported to have said that he would prefer no such immunity for the clergy rather than the clause be passed as it was.

[64] *Marriage in Church after Divorce*, p. 12. However, this recognition is followed by the addition, in parentheses, of the suggestion that 'it needs pastoral discernment to determine whether a relationship still exists or not in a particular case. In an age of comparatively straightforward divorce proceedings which may still favour speedy divorce, a decree from a court may not be the last word on the matter' (pp. 12–13). This is a patent absurdity to the extent that it suggests that two people who have been through the entirety of juridical divorce proceeding and have been granted a divorce by the court may in some meaningful sense be described as 'married'.

allows a member of the clergy to maintain a personal belief in the ontological indissolubility of marriage. Nonetheless, the Church of England is formally committed to the position that marriages can be, and are, dissolved by the civil courts. Indeed, if Canon B30 is understood to dispute this, it is invalid under the Submission of the Clergy Act 1533.

This is not to say that it is meaningless to describe marriage as indissoluble. Indissolubility may still remain as a moral imperative, an ideal and as the intention of those entering into marriage. Canon B30 must be interpreted in this way. There is little doubt that a lifelong loving marriage can provide a more fulfilling relationship for the couple and a more stable nurturing environment for their children. The present civil law of divorce recognises both the indissolubility and dissolubility of marriage. Its recognition of the latter is clear from the fact that it permits divorce. Its recognition of the former consists in the fact that the parties are regarded as having ongoing commitments and obligations to one another and, especially, to their children. The church could learn much from this approach, both theologically and pastorally. It would do well to follow the civil law in accepting the reality of divorce (something we have argued it already does at least implicitly), and to drop its current insistence on a quasi-judicial assessment of who should be entitled to remarry in church (which is a crude recapitulation of the work of the courts). This would leave it free to develop its ministry in supporting marriages and helping divorced and divorcing couples with the practical, emotional and spiritual consequences of divorce, something the civil law cannot effectively do.

An earlier Church of England Working Party counselled that the church should continue to marry all those who are not divorced and who request the church's blessing upon their marriage. 'For centuries, the Church of England has willingly offered Christian ministry to all who are prepared to receive it. Marrying people is one aspect of this ministry. To alter this would suggest that the church is no longer willing or able to carry forward its mission. It would represent a serious loss of nerve.'[65] This ministry of marrying people, we have argued, is

[65] *An Honourable Estate*, p. 77.

limited to witnessing and asking for the blessing of marriages. Since the church recognises the marriages of divorced people, its continued refusal to witness and ask for the blessing of such marriages is in danger of shirking the church's mission in this respect. To the extent that the church refuses to witness such marriages it is engaging in ostrich-like behaviour inconsistent with its recognition of their legality. To refuse to ask for God's blessing on such marriages is in danger of being an attempt to restrain God's grace.[66]

Conclusion

In our introduction we suggested that the relationship of law and theology might be understood as a 'mystical union'. Since the 1857 Act, this union has been undermined by a misguided theological opposition to the existence of divorce. We propose that the recognition of divorce would allow the church to pursue a pastoral mission that is in greater contact with the reality of the people it seeks to serve. It would also begin to heal the breach between theology and law that has been so destructive to the church's mission, and allow the church to provide better marriage support services that complement the approach of the civil law. The legal and theological framework for this still exists, as we have attempted to show. Unless the church's official teaching accepts these realities, the church will become increasingly irrelevant in matters of marriage and divorce.

---

[66] Indeed, the church has offered services of blessing after civil marriage since the 1970s (*Marriage in Church after Divorce*, p. 41). *Marriage in Church after Divorce* recommends that the church permit such marriages be solemnized in church. We would, however, take issue with the necessity of the eight 'pastoral criteria' that it suggests be applied in each case as a qualification for entry into marriage in church.

26

Idolatry and Pragmatism: The Sanctity of Marriage and the Mothers' Union 1876–1976

Cordelia Moyse

The 'Idol' of 'the Sanctity of Marriage'

No study of the Church of England and its attitude to divorce in the twentieth century is complete without listening to the voice of the Mothers' Union.[1] It was by far the largest lay organisation and its first object for most of its history was 'to uphold the sanctity of marriage'.[2] While it saw itself as 'the handmaid' of the church, its views on marriage were not simply a reflection of official church thinking. Clinging to a literal belief in Jesus' words against divorce, the MU made an idol of 'the sanctity of marriage'. This idol required a pure membership and opposition to all divorce. To a society and church seeking to make sense of marital breakdown, the MU became an increasingly irrelevant organisation. It could only be released from its bondage to a false idol when churches across the Anglican Communion, no longer finding it useful to the mission of the

---

[1] Hereafter referred to as 'the MU'.

[2] It existed in most parishes in Britain at some time in the twentieth century. At its peak in the British Isles, membership for England, Wales and Ireland in 1938 was 538,016. In 1995 the figure for the above countries including Scotland was 145,980. The MU took as its administrative units those of the church: the parish, the deanery and the diocese. The MU existed under the authority of the archbishops, bishops and, at the branch level, that of the incumbent. Clergy wives were the natural leaders of the organisation at local and national level due to their knowledge and influence within the church.

church, questioned its purpose.[3] Spurred on primarily by the
fear of extinction, the MU readily embraced the 'relational'
view of marriage promoted by such church reports as *Putting
Asunder*, in 1966, and *Marriage, Divorce and the Church* in 1971.[4]

It is important to note, however, that the now synonymous
association of the MU and marriage did not exist in its early
years. Mary Sumner's purpose in forming the MU in 1876 was
to equip mothers for 'one of the greatest and most important
professions in the world'.[5] Her society combined practical
child-care advice and training with Christian teaching and
prayer. Only in 1892, fifteen years after its founding, did the
organisation make upholding 'the sanctity of marriage' its first
object.[6] In a pamphlet promoting the new object Sumner wrote
that the church and the home were the two divine institutions
of the world, with the latter founded on faithful marriage. She
saw marriage as the foundation of a nation's life and the source
of its morality and she believed it was being attacked by the
rising demand for increased divorce facilities. 'No words [about
divorce] can be plainer than those of our Lord Jesus Christ
Himself', she wrote. 'What therefore God hath joined together,
let no man put asunder.'[7]

The new object had no immediate effect on membership
qualifications or on MU activity. Full membership was simply
open to married women who were mothers.[8] Nevertheless
the concept of witness, which would later be used in the
construction of the idolatrous ideology of 'sanctity of

[3] *New Dimensions: The Report of the Bishop of Willesden's Commission on the Objects
and Policies of The Mothers' Union* (London: SPCK, 1972), para. 342.

[4] *Putting Asunder: A Divorce Law for Contemporary Society, The Report of a Group
appointed by the Archbishop of Canterbury in January 1964* (London: SPCK, 1966);
*Marriage, Divorce and the Church, The Report of the Commission on the Christian
Doctrine of Marriage* (London: SPCK, 1971).

[5] Quoted in Olive Parker, *For the Family's Sake: A History of the Mothers' Union
1876–1976* (London: Mowbray, 1975), p. 5.

[6] 29 February 1892, Winchester Diocesan Council Minute Book, p. 39,
145M85/C2/1/1, Hampshire Record Office, Winchester. The idea that the
quality of family life depended on the married life of parents had been present
at least as early as 1887. See Violet B. Lancaster, *A Short History of the Mothers'
Union* (MU, 1958), p. 42.

[7] Mrs Sumner, *First Object of the Mothers' Union, To Uphold the Sanctity of
Marriage* (MU, nd).

[8] Other women could join as associates. See Lancaster, *A Short History*, p. 19.

marriage', was already present. For the MU, 'to witness' did not mean that one merely testified to one's beliefs, but that one had to 'walk the talk' by living them out in one's daily life. While 'the sanctity of marriage' remained undefined in the constitution at this time, in its literature the MU explicitly instructed members on how to embody their belief in the first object. As wives they were given practical advice on fulfilling their domestic duties and how to avoid giving their husbands any cause for grievance. As mothers they were to teach their children by word and action what marriage should be, so that they, in their turn, could set up Christian homes.[9] Nevertheless not all members had a full understanding of what was meant by 'the sanctity of marriage'. This was clear when in 1898 a request to include the word 'indissolubility' in the first object was refused on the ground that the phrase 'the sanctity of marriage' implicitly contained that idea.[10]

An Anti-Divorce Society

Yet early in the twentieth century when demand for divorce reform was growing in size and respectability, the MU decisively established its credentials as an anti-divorce society. Faced by what it saw as a threat to a divine institution, the MU increasingly came to see itself as the guardian of marriage for the nation.[11] It therefore set about changing itself in two significant ways. The first was by widening its field of action. Instead of just concerning itself with ministering to and supporting its membership in personally upholding its objects, the MU began to campaign and influence parliamentary legislation

---

[9] *Mothers' Union Journal*, April 1898, pp. 26–8; July 1898, pp. 63–4; January 1899, pp. 14–15. For a rare example of use of the word 'indissoluble' see *Mothers in Council* (the journal for the educated and higher class membership), October 1896, p. 199.

[10] 13 May 1898, Central Council Minutes (CCM), I, p. 59, MU Archives, Mary Sumner House, London.

[11] While the Royal Commission on Marriage and Divorce (1909-12) was sitting, a speaker voiced the opinion that the 1857 Divorce Bill had passed when the MU had not existed and asked whether 'God had raised up the MU for such a time as this?' *Mothers in Council*, July 1911, vol. XXI, p. 184.

concerning marriage and family life of the nation. Asserting in 1910 that the proposed extension of divorce facilities was not merely a political question but a domestic and religious one, the MU entered the world of politics. By so doing it hoped it would stop the attack on marriage at its source.[12] Taking on a representational role for mothers further necessitated the MU adopting new methods of working. For example, it presented both qualitative and quantitative evidence against divorce reform to the Royal Commission on Divorce and Matrimonial Causes in 1910.[13]

The basis of the MU's opposition to the extension of divorce jurisdiction and the granting of divorce for matrimonial offences beyond adultery was unequivocally stated in 1910 and remained substantially the same until the end of the 1960s.[14] Interestingly it was based primarily on a utilitarian rather than a theological view of marriage despite the claim that its views on divorce were grounded in the Bible and the Prayer Book.[15] At the heart of the MU resistance to divorce reform was the belief that the 1857 Divorce Act had brought misery to many; that it had undermined marriage by encouraging people to enter it recklessly; and that it had increased the number of broken homes and fuelled sexual immorality. Divorce was even condemned for producing 'poisonous literature' such as Thomas Hardy's novel *Jude the Obscure*, which was seen as denigrating marriage.[16] On the few occasions when the MU did condemn divorce on the ground of Jesus' teaching in Mark's Gospel, no reference was made to then current biblical scholarship. Such engagement with biblical criticism would have strengthened the MU's case as the so-called Matthaean exception, which did permit divorce on the ground of adultery, was considered a later addition to

---

[12] *The Mothers' Union Handbook and Central Report 1910*, p. 42.

[13] *Royal Commission on Divorce and Matrimonial Causes, Cd. 6479 Parliamentary Papers, 1912–13*, XIX, qq16886–17170. Hereafter referred to as *RC 1912–13*.

[14] *RC 1912–13*, qq16886–17170. *Extracts from the Report 1951–55 of the Royal Commission on Marriage and Divorce with Notes for Mothers' Union Speakers* (MU, nd).

[15] *RC 1912–13*, qq16939–40.

[16] Mrs Sumner, *Poisonous Literature: Its Alarming Increase* (MU, nd); Mrs Sumner, *Divorce: A National Danger* (MU, nd).

that Gospel.[17] As a result of its views, the MU was not even prepared to consider improving the law, let alone extending access to it. In its ideal world the 1857 Act would be repealed. The only remedy for marital difficulties the MU thought compatible with Christian teaching on marriage was separation, which took women out of physical danger but did not break the bond of marriage.[18]

The second way the MU forged its identity as an anti-divorce society was through the creation of membership rules which explicitly excluded women who had been divorced. In an age of rising divorce it was no longer enough for members to testify that divorce was socially evil and against divine law. They had to reject divorce as a solution to their own marital problems, however great. It was this understanding of 'witness' that forced the MU to embark on a series of constitutional changes. It was only in 1912, thirty-six years after its formation, that the constitution stated for the first time that 'divorce must be regarded as a disqualification for membership'.[19] Oddly though this did not mean that existing members understood that they could not divorce or be divorced after joining. In 1918 the Central Council, the governing body of the world-wide organisation, passed a resolution that 'any person, already belonging to the MU who passes through the Divorce Court ceases *ipso facto* to be a member'. This blanket condemnation was by no means uncontroversial in an era when every divorce petition required an innocent and guilty party. So uncharitable was this ruling that when the vote to confirm it was taken a quarter of the Council voted against it![20]

Having defined who could witness to 'the sanctity of marriage', the MU embarked on defining what the phrase actually meant at a time when even divorce reformers and writers such as Lord Buckmaster, Sir Arthur Conan Doyle and Dr Marie Stopes were using the phrase. By a large majority the Central Council adopted the first part of the 1920 Lambeth

---

[17] Sumner, *Divorce.* For a discussion of the Matthaean exception see Cordelia Moyse, 'Marriage and Divorce Law Reform in England and Wales 1909–1937' (unpublished PhD thesis, Cambridge University, 1996), pp. 143–4.
[18] *RC 1912–13*, qq16918;16962.
[19] Six members voted against its inclusion. 6 June 1912, CCM, IV, p. 61.
[20] 4 June 1918, CCM, V, p. 76; 16–17 June 1919, CCM, V, pp. 168–71.

Conference resolution which described marriage as 'a lifelong and indissoluble union'. This was the first time that sanctity had been officially defined in this way and even though Mary Sumner's own daughter claimed that the resolution accorded with her now deceased mother's understanding of the nature of marriage, some members remained unconvinced and resigned from office.[21] The prohibition of all divorcees was finally written in stone when, in 1926, the MU was granted its royal charter.[22]

Whereas the application of a narrow definition of 'witness' was accomplished relatively smoothly, the MU's mission to resist legislation designed to extend divorce facilities was much more problematic. By the 1920s, as a result of its great success and popularity, the MU had become the unofficial Church of England's women's organisation. Yet it found itself pursuing a different strategy regarding opposition to divorce reform to that of the church hierarchy. Both Davidson and Lang, when Archbishop of Canterbury, were prepared to be pragmatic in their tactics. By contrast the declared intention of the MU was a principled opposition to all divorce legislation.[23] Archbishop Davidson adopted a strategy of attempting to head off comprehensive legislation by supporting attempts to remove the obvious injustices of the law such as the high cost of divorce which made it unobtainable to working-class people and the inequality between men and women in regard to obtaining divorce on the ground of adultery. With this strategy in mind he wrote to Mrs Barclay, the Central President, to stop the MU

[21] 1–2 December 1920, CCM, V, pp. 266–71. For examples of resignations see: 15 December 1920, Executive Minutes (EM), VIII, p. 256; 13 January 1921, EM, VIII, p. 262, MU Archives.

[22] The Central Council initially wanted to bar women who had married a divorced man even after the death of his former wife. This was overturned by the Executive. 1 December 1925, CCM, VI, pp. 106–7; 14 January 1926, EM, X, p. 107. This hard line contrasted with the treatment of members who fell short of maintaining 'the sanctity of marriage' in other ways. Women separated from their husbands could become members. While unmarried mothers could not belong, if they later married and wanted to be members they could because 'the sin' was committed before admission.

[23] It did not oppose the Matrimonial Causes Bill in 1923 because it did not want to oppose a bill designed simply to end the sexual double standard in divorce. 13 March 1923, CCM, VI, p. 147.

446 *Celebrating Christian Marriage*

campaigning against Lord Gorell's bill in 1921. It was only with extreme reluctance that she agreed to his request.[24]

A 'Pure' Membership

A. P. Herbert's divorce bill in 1936 presented further difficulties for the MU as it was designed to end the collusion and farce taking place in south coast hotels which all agreed was bringing the law into disrepute. Some members of the Central Council wanted to support the parts of the bill that made the law 'a little more decent and wholesome' for people outside the MU, while condemning those clauses that increased facilities for divorce. While it was unfortunate for the long-term credibility of the organisation that their arguments failed to win the day, at the time the most immediate problem for the MU was that by campaigning against the bill it appeared again to be out of line with the church.[25] The action of Lang, the most senior churchman, abstaining on an issue on which the MU was expending great energy in resisting caused great pain to the organisation.[26] Mrs Woods, the Central President, was so worried by the appearance of disloyalty that she sought Lang's backing for a letter to every member explaining the legitimacy of MU policy.[27] In the light of the church's equivocal lead on the matter, the MU's claim that it was witnessing to the teaching of the church looked decidedly shaky. The ability of some church leaders, such as Bishop Henson of Durham, to respond to the social need for divorce while believing in the ideal of marriage as lifelong was beyond the MU at this time.

The concept of witnessing to 'the sanctity of marriage'

[24] 17 March 1921, EM, VIII, pp. 282–3. *The Workers' Paper*, August 1921, p. 143.

[25] The resolution that passed stated 'that while there are some clauses ... the MU would not oppose, the Central Council feel compelled to record the opposition of the Mothers' Union to the Bill as a whole because of the clauses it contains which increase the grounds for divorce'. This was carried with two voting against and some abstentions. 2–3 December 1936, CCM, X, pp. 397–405.

[26] 24 June 1937, 5 *Hansard H.L.Deb.* 105, cols. 743–51; 19 July 1937, *Hansard H.L. Deb.* 106, cols. 572–73.

[27] 14 January 1937, EM, XII, p. 271; 11 February 1937, EM, XII, p. 274. *The Workers' Paper*, August 1937, pp. 158–9.

through the purity of its membership came under increasing attack from the late 1930s because of developments in the pastoral ministry of the church. Before then its exclusive membership qualifications could be seen as mirroring the church's own witness to 'the sanctity of marriage'. For at the same time the MU had been constructing a pure membership, the church had been curtailing the right of divorcees to marry in church.[28] Yet in the minds of some people a decision by the church in 1938 seemed to open up a clear gap between the MU's attitude to its members and that of the church on the matter of divorce. For while church policy was to exclude remarried divorcees from holy communion it would allow their readmission under certain circumstances with episcopal sanction. By so doing the church showed that remarried divorcees were not beyond its pastoral reach and could be full members.[29]

This development in the pastoral and reconciling ministry of the church made the MU vulnerable to two criticisms. The first was that its membership rules, unlike those of the church, made no distinction between divorced and remarried women. All were excluded. The decisions of convocation in the late 1930s made it clear that for the church the problem was not divorce *per se* but remarriage. This raised the question why divorced women could not belong to the MU. The second criticism was that the church allowed penitent divorcees who had remarried access to the sacrament with the consent of the bishop while a mere church society would not in any circumstances let a remarried woman be a member. What lay at the heart of the criticism was the very success of the MU. Parish clergy disliked the divisions caused in their parishes by divorcees not being admitted to what was often *the* only women's society. Many male clergy must also have resented a lay women's organisation seeming to set itself apart from, if not in opposition to, the priesthood. The result was in effect an open season on the MU within the church. Clergy accused it of being unchristian, uncharitable, pharisaical and

---

[28] Moyse, 'Marriage and Divorce Law Reform', p. 156.
[29] Moyse, 'Marriage and Divorce Law Reform', pp. 186–90. See also Appendix 9, *Marriage, Divorce and the Church.*

bigoted.[30] The advocates of change within the organisation were no less harsh. The Diocesan President of Salisbury likened the MU's resistance to change to a 'hardening of the arteries' which could only ultimately result in death.[31]

In response the MU attempted to downplay its own importance. Rightly it presented itself as an organisation set up for a limited purpose and one that never intended to become *the* Church of England women's society.[32] Its mission to witness to 'the sanctity of marriage' through the purity of its membership, it argued, had only become exclusive as divorce had become more common among Christians. The MU claimed its exclusiveness was simply comparable to that of an order of celibate priests in a church which admitted married clergy. It did not exclude divorcees because they had committed an unforgivable sin, but because they could no longer witness to the first object.[33] Yet the hard-line, dare one say 'macho', image of the MU was embraced by the organisation. This was especially true in the 1950s when Mrs Fisher was Central President and her husband, Geoffrey Fisher, was Archbishop of Canterbury. The MU was encouraged to see its role as providing the strict witness to the doctrine of indissoluble marriage that the church had reaffirmed in 1938 but which the church could not maintain when exercising a national pastoral ministry.[34] Archbishop Fisher grandly described the MU as 'the Church's commando unit' on marriage. Unfortunately, as a clerical opponent of the MU's exclusiveness wrote to Fisher, a 'commando unit' left 'a trail of wounded and broken spirits in its wake'.[35]

In the end, however, the irresistible force for change came not from within the Church of England but from elsewhere in

---

[30] See letter from the Revd N. S. Power to Mrs Fisher, 18 September 1952, and letter from the Revd Edward Ashford, 29 July 1952, MU/CO/001/65, MU Archives; 7 January 1955, *The Church of England Newspaper*, p. 7.

[31] 3–4 December 1947, CCM, XIII, p. 31.

[32] 3–4 December 1947, CCM, XIII, p. 32. Cathleen Llewellyn-Davies, *Membership of the Mothers' Union. How to answer some questions* (MU, nd) p. 4.

[33] Letter to Mrs Knight, 12 April 1954, MU/CO/001/65.

[34] 24–25 November 1954, CCM, XIV, pp. 454–5.

[35] Draft of Fisher's speech, 10 June 1952 and the Revd Edward Ashford's letter, 22 July 1952, Geoffrey Fisher Papers, vol. 105, pp. 316; 324, Lambeth Palace Library, London.

the Anglican Communion. Throughout its history the MU had grappled with how to witness to its understanding of 'the sanctity of marriage' in different parts of the Communion. It had successfully maintained a general uniformity of membership rules despite operating in cultures shaped by other faiths. Often its solution to perceived cultural difference was to allow so-called 'native' branches to adopt less demanding rules.[36] What made the challenge to the membership rules different in the 1960s from previous decades was that it came from white commonwealth countries and that the proposed changes were supported, if not initiated, by their church hierarchy. Autonomy in decision making lay at the heart of the demands for change. For the Canadian MU the change of church canons in Canada permitting divorcees to marry in church under certain conditions meant that its rules forbidding membership to divorcees isolated it from the church which it wished to serve. When the Canadian Dominion Council of the MU unilaterally widened its membership rules in 1967, it was automatically disaffiliated from the world-wide MU.[37] The New Zealand MU, frightened by the harsh treatment of Canada, then attempted to change from within the membership rules of the world-wide organisation.[38]

The World-Wide Council in July 1968 was dominated by New Zealand's proposals for changes in membership rules and the granting of autonomy.[39] New Zealand wanted admission to membership for divorced women who had not remarried and for those remarried women who had been readmitted to communion by their bishop. It did not propose to change the objects of the MU, just the membership qualifications. The heart of the debate in 1968 therefore focused on the relationship between membership criteria and the objects, namely, whether the MU could witness to 'the sanctity of marriage' if her members did not live out that belief in their own lives.

[36] See for example, 4 December 1913, CCM, IV, pp. 168–9; 8 March, 1934, EM, XII, p. 124.
[37] 5 October 1967, EM, XVIII, p. 16; 9 November 1967, EM, XVIII, pp. 20–1; 24–25 June 1970, CCM, XVIII, pp. 112–13.
[38] 23–24 July 1968, CCM, XVIII, pp. 47–8.
[39] From 1930 the MU followed the ten-year cycle of the Lambeth Conference and convened a world-wide conference.

In a long and passionate debate the diversity of experience of the delegates was evident. While for speakers from the British Isles the debate took place against a background of a rapidly declining membership, members from Africa and India talked of the difficulty of upholding monogamous marriage in societies where polygamy was common.[40] Yet a common theme was the relationship between the church and MU policy on divorce. Many delegates, whether for or against change, voiced concern at what they would tell their bishops when they got home.[41] In the end, however, the belief that only non-divorced women could witness to the sanctity of marriage remained secure. By 270 votes to 83 a resolution was carried 'that the qualifications for full membership in the Mothers' Union remain unchanged'.[42]

Signs of Hope

Yet the matter was not closed. At the end of the Council it was announced that a Commission was to be appointed to examine the MU's objects. It was charged with considering how the MU's witness '[could] be maintained and its work of strengthening Christian family life extended, [bearing] in mind that the life-long nature of marriage is the foundation of family life, and taking into account changes in civil and ecclesiastical law'.[43] The Anglo-Catholic Bishop of Willesden, Graham Leonard, was appointed chairman. The Commission of ten consisted of three MU members, two clergy, two lawyers and two distinguished non-MU lay women.[44] While the Commission was gathering its

[40] 23–24 July 1968, CCM, XVIII, pp. 38–9; 43–5. Between 1965 and 1971 membership in the British Isles declined from 425,582 to 334,081.

[41] 23–24 July 1968, CCM, XVIII, pp. 35; 48–9. Attempts were made by the Central President to discover the views of bishops. In some English dioceses the views of clergy were canvassed by members before the Council met. 27 April 1967, EM, XVII, pp. 308; 312.

[42] 23–24 July 1968, CCM, XVIII, p. 46. Of the speakers taking part in the debate, twenty-five were from Britain; ten were African; eight Australian; five from New Zealand; three West Indian; two Indian and one Canadian.

[43] 23–24 July 1968, CCM, XVIII, p. 57.

[44] The MU members were Mrs Quentin Edwards, Mrs Ian Norman and Mrs Richard Page. The non-MU members were: Colonel G. I. A. D. Draper, the Revd Anthony Duncan, Lady Gorell Barnes, Dr Margaret Hewitt, Mr E. G. Norman and the Revd Douglas Webster.

evidence neither the world nor the MU stood still. Further evidence of marginalisation of the MU and its mission in the church was provided by the continuing closure of branches as those members and clergy who wanted the MU to change felt they could wait no longer. There were, however, for the first time, signs of hope. The first was that the MU was open to new thinking on marriage; namely, the primary importance of the quality of the relationship that made a marriage. Unlike earlier periods the MU in the late 1960s did not resist divorce reform *per se*. Most surprisingly, it did not oppose basing divorce on the principle of irretrievable marital breakdown.[45] No doubt it was heavily influenced by the Archbishop of Canterbury's report, *Putting Asunder*, not least because some of its signatories were good friends of the MU.[46] By the 1960s it had to acknowledge that total opposition to divorce had not prevented an escalating divorce rate. It therefore embraced the Report's teaching that Christians could in good faith work to improve secular law as Jesus' teaching was about the true nature of marriage which transcends any legal system of rights and duties.[47]

Further evidence that opinion was moving was provided by the response of an MU committee set up to examine *Marriage, Divorce and the Church*, the report of the so-called Root Commission, published in 1971. This was the first church report to spend any time analysing marriage and marriage breakdown in terms of both couples' emotional needs and duties. Significantly the majority of the MU committee agreed that 'refusing relief to broken marriages or insisting that the empty form is a living reality does nothing to strengthen

[45] It had opposed this principle when it had been discussed by the Royal Commission on Marriage and Divorce in the 1950s. See *Extracts from the Report 1951–55 of the Royal Commission on Marriage and Divorce*, pp. 40–1.

[46] The Chairman of the Archbishop's Group, the Bishop of Exeter, had long been a supporter of the Mothers' Union, and the barrister, Quentin Edwards, was married to a member of the MU who sat on the Bishop of Willesden's Commission.

[47] Working with other women's groups it lobbied for an improvement in the financial position of divorced women especially those whom it considered would be the innocent victims of the new law, namely those who had been divorced against their will and were not guilty of any matrimonial offence. 27–28 November 1968, CCM, XVIII, p. 75; 16–17 July 1969, CCM, XVIII, p. 87.

marriage but can, indeed, bring the institution into general disrepute'.[48]

The second sign of hope, and perhaps the most critical sign that the MU would change by responding to the desire of many to build more nurturing and emotionally satisfying marital relationships, was a change in leadership. In 1970 Joanne Hallifax, Central President since 1962, stood down. Although the Commission had been set up during her term of office she did not believe that the MU could change its rules without sacrificing what she saw as its witness to the truth. For Hallifax, the purity of the membership was inextricably linked to its mission. She described the 1960s as a period when 'a new spirit of compassion' was competing with 'another insight which was unpopular and out of fashion – that Christian moral standards are founded on divine sanctions'.[49] By contrast the new President, Susan Varah, wife of the Revd Chad Varah, founder of the Samaritans, believed it right to 'witness to what we believe, [provided] we do it humbly, ever open to correction [by] the Holy Spirit'.[50]

But the publication in 1972 of *New Dimensions*, the Bishop of Willesden's Commission's findings, did not provide an immediate solution to the MU's dilemma.[51] While the Commissioners agreed that the MU needed to be more responsive to the changing needs of families, they disagreed about who was eligible to undertake that ministry.[52] The bishop in a minority of three believed that the MU had always stood for indissoluble marriage and wished to bring the MU into line with church discipline which did not exclude from the sacraments those who had divorced but not remarried. He proposed that divorced but not remarried women should be eligible for membership.[53] The majority report on the other hand, signed

---

[48] Joint Report of Northern and Southern Marriage Groups, April 1972, MU/CO/PRES/004/13, MU Archives.

[49] Statement to the Commission from the Central President, Mrs Ronald Hallifax, JP, MU/CO/003/03, MU Archives; 27 April 1967, EM, XVII, p. 307.

[50] Summing up by the Central President, 20–23 June 1972, CCM, XIX, p. 68.

[51] 22–23 June, CCM, XIX pp. 68–70.

[52] *New Dimensions*, Part III, paras. 1–18; Appendix G. The minority report was signed by the Chairman, the Revd Anthony Duncan and Dr Margaret Hewitt; the majority report by six including all the MU members. Lady Gorell Barnes signed a dissenting appendix.

[53] *New Dimensions*, Part I, paras. 298–306.

by six commissioners, proposed that membership be open to all who supported the objects regardless of their marital status. Nevertheless these signatories could not contemplate totally freeing the MU from the burden of its past and so recommended that there should be a 'tertiary order' for whose who wished to maintain the traditional purity of the MU's witness to 'the sanctity of marriage'.[54]

Supporting Family Life

Much to the Bishop of Willesden's disgust, after a year's discussion of *New Dimensions* in the dioceses, the Central Council in July 1973 accepted neither set of proposals. Although both groups of Commissioners supported five new objects for the organisation their proposed membership criteria showed that there was at best unease about remarried women testifying to the ideal of lifelong marriage. The MU, in contrast, boldly decided to completely destroy its traditional concept of witness and to have one form of membership open to all who could accept the new objects. Out went 'the sanctity of marriage' and in its place came the more modest object of upholding 'our Lord's teaching on the nature of marriage'.[55] By embracing all who wished to witness to 'the nature of marriage' the MU came into line with contemporary church thinking as expressed in *Putting Asunder* and the Root Commission report. The nature of true marriage was indissoluble but the MU recognised that not all people were able to achieve it. Unity in the new MU was to be maintained by adherence to the objects rather than to a narrow membership qualification.[56]

By abandoning the attempt to impose a particular view of marriage and witness on its world-wide membership, the MU was free to expend more energy on what had originally been its

---

[54] *New Dimensions*, Part I, paras. 348; 366–9.

[55] 2–6 July 1973, CCM, XIX, p. 148. In *New Dimensions* the proposed object had included the phrase 'the lifelong nature of the marriage vows as taught by the Church' but this was not contained in the final version (para. 255).

[56] Autonomous provinces could make membership qualifications which were stricter than the ones which were passed at the 1973 conference. 2–6 July 1973, CCM, XIX, pp. 150–2.

primary purpose: supporting family life. Now in addition to equipping parents to bring up their children, the MU aimed 'to promote conditions in society favourable to stable homes and happy childhood [and] to help those whose family life [had] met with adversity'.[57] These changes were not cosmetic. MU members are now to be found running Child Contact centres for divorced parents or in prison visitors' centres running crèches for the children of prisoners. No longer bound to oppose every recommendation to improve the working of divorce law, the MU engages in promoting conditions favourable to stable family life by canvassing its members on legal reforms and preparing detailed submissions to government departments.[58]

In 1973 the MU managed to bring to an end the tyranny of its self-imposed definition of witnessing to 'the sanctity of marriage' by which it had become enslaved. Perhaps surprisingly the MU's witness to the 'sanctity of marriage' was overturned by little theological debate and was accompanied by no major rift in the organisation.[59] This was because by the 1960s the MU's very existence was at stake. This was demonstrated when it was forced to choose between two features which made up its identity: its own definition of 'the sanctity of marriage' and its role as the 'handmaid' of the church. Its rigid membership criteria and total opposition to all divorce reform could make no contribution to an Anglican Communion which was reformulating the relationship between its doctrine and discipline nor to a society which was coming to see marriage more as an intimate partnership than a social institution. Recognising the danger of irrelevance the MU pragmatically chose to widen its remit. By so doing it came closer in spirit to its original purpose of the 1870s than it had for most of the twentieth century.

[57] 2–6 July 1973, CCM, XIX p. 148.
[58] See, for example, Comments from the Marriage Group of the MU on the Law Society's Discussion Paper 'A Better Way Out', 4 February 1980, MU/SC/OO6/11, MU Archives.
[59] For some members it was so significant that they wanted the MU to be wound up and a new organisation set up under the new rules. 31 delegates voted for this and 266 against. 2–6 July 1973, CCM, XIX, p. 161.

27

Why Was Jesus a Pastor to the Divorced? The Social Background to Mark 10 and Matthew 19

Greg Forster

Much has been written about *what* Jesus said in connection with divorce, especially about the meaning of the word *porneia*,[1] and the Hebrew behind it – *'erwath-dabhar* of Deuteronomy 24:1. I have come across less discussion about *how* and *why* Jesus said what he did. These questions are equally important in discovering what Jesus was trying to say about divorce against his own cultural setting. How big a factor in first-century Palestine was divorce?

It is not wrong to tease out the meaning of words. But I suspect that one point Jesus was making was that to worry at texts misses the point! I will compare the reports of Jesus' teaching on divorce with other references to relationships in the Gospels and with contemporary practice and thinking, so far as can be ascertained, in Judaism and among the Samaritans. I will ask what Jesus was trying to do within the social dynamics of his day, and whether that sheds light on our application of his teaching. I will suggest that Jesus was a teacher of ethics, and did not simply tell his followers what to do or how to apply the injunctions of the Torah using the correct procedures, but rather equipped them to think through for themselves how to deal with marital (and other) issues.[2]

In addition to the New Testament, my primary source has been the Mishnah, with glances at Philo, Josephus and the

[1] Mt. 5:32 and 19:9.
[2] This chapter develops points made in my *Healing Love's Wounds* (London: MarshallPickering, 1995).

more accessible of the Dead Sea Scrolls. My approach to the Gospels is fairly conservative, but not uncritical; I accept that the Mishnah has its roots in a time when Jews were responsible for their own local governance of Palestine, but contains later layers. Philo wrote near the time of Jesus, but is distant in space and thought. The scrolls too portray a Judaism contemporary with Jesus, even if the community which produced them cut itself off from mainstream Jewish life. Each source was written with a different purpose, which coloured the way it was written. The purpose and style of the material will filter some of the information I am trying to gain, but is itself part of the data by which I shall contrast Mark 10 with its social context. For instance, the Mishnah is in large part a record of case law, so to criticise it for being legalistic is unfair, but if we can see the attitudes behind the case law, or find evidence as to how often it was applied, then we are in business!

The Good Shepherd

Let me begin with two observations made by St John. 'Jesus himself did not trust himself to them because he understood them all, and because he did not need anyone to tip him off about anyone. *He himself understood what made someone tick*' (Jn 2:24–25).[3] Jesus was a shrewd observer of human nature. His dealings with people, individually and in crowds, reveal that. I believe it characterises his ministry and teaching about marriage, divorce and the people caught up in both. John also contrasts the 'generosity and integrity' (1:17) of his ministry with Mosaic law.

Now a specific text: 'Joseph, her husband, strictly law-observant though he was, did not want to stigmatise her. He was minded to divorce her on the quiet. While he was thinking this over an angel ... told him, "do not be afraid to take Mary as your wife"' (Mt. 1:19–20). John Robinson described study of Jesus' self-consciousness as 'the last tabu'[4] and I too feel that hesitancy. I wonder, however, whether we can legitimately see

---

[3] Many Bible quotations in this chapter have been translated by the author.
[4] John Robinson, *Twelve More New Testament Studies* (London: SCM Press, 1984), ch. 11.

here, and in occasions during his ministry, factors which shaped his thinking. Whatever scholars make of Matthew's infancy narratives, accusations were levelled at Jesus in his lifetime about his paternity (e.g., Jn 8:41, 48, or the hint in Mk 6:3 – 'son of Mary'). It was assumed, if not required, of an observant Jewish man that he should divorce a betrothed or new wife found not to be a virgin. Some explanation at least within the family would be circulated, to which Jesus at some stage became party. In Joseph's story of an angelic revelation we have the strongest of counterblasts to conventional Jewish morality.[5]

John supplements the synoptic accounts of Jesus' ministry with an early incident in which Jesus talks with a woman at a well in Samaria. Such an encounter surprised his followers (Jn 4:9, 27). Both he and she seem relaxed about it after her initial surprise that as a Jew he should speak to a Samaritan. Such an encounter could give rise to an accusation of adultery in strict Jewish circles, judging from *m.Ketubot* 1:8 (about a girl seen in conversation with a man in the street). The theological significance of John's story lies in Jesus' self-disclosure; the incidental detail includes the woman's relationships with husbands. John does not specifically say that she was divorced, and there is no explicit condemnation of her. The idea that divorce ended at least some of her marriages may be true, but is imported into the story by preachers who see Jesus as exposing her sins.[6] She would have been middle-aged, almost elderly by contemporary standards, kept as a drawer of water as much as a 'common law' wife, with no 'father's house' to turn to for support. It was to protect her from further distress that Jesus asked to speak with her 'husband', who might otherwise find 'something unseemly' in reports of her conversation with Jesus and dismiss her. His would be the initiative, for in Jewish and Samaritan law a wife did not have power to divorce her husband. Those who suggest that Jesus was exposing the 'sin' of her divorces have overlooked that. She might ask a court to compel a husband to

---

[5] *m.Ket.* 1:1–2. See G. J. Wenham and W. E. Heth, *Jesus and Divorce* (Carlisle: Paternoster, 1997), p. 232.

[6] E.g., A. C. Cornes (who heard the same sermons as I did as a student!), *Divorce and Remarriage* (London: Hodder & Stoughton, 1993), p. 390, misquoting Paula Clifford.

divorce her if he became unpleasantly ill or worked as a tanner.[7] As a Samaritan she possibly had the power to contest a divorce herself when it came to the Samaritan high priest.[8]

That at least is conventional wisdom about Jewish law at the time, but the law is not all. I see a possibility that a woman could buy herself out of a marriage.[9] Perhaps she was a termagant, and provoked her husbands to divorce her. (Such a possibility may lie behind Mk 10:12, though the words there imply that the wife takes the *legal* initiative.) The Rabbis recognised that a wife could play awkward in connection with divorce.[10] However, I do not think this applies here, though she may have been painted black by the husbands who had divorced her, even 'making her out to be an adulteress' (Mt. 5:32). In fact she joyfully tells her compatriots, 'He discussed with me all I ever did.' Is that the reaction of an exposed adulteress? John has not recorded all the conversation, but indicates how she had at last found someone who understood her and valued her and her life and thus brought her the 'living water' of respect. In wanting to talk with her man he had shown that understanding and was sorting out her future security, building on the present rather than undoing it.

In this I have made assumptions no greater than those in the conventional preachers' portrait. They reflect more truly the picture we have of Jesus' dealings with ordinary people, especially women, in the Gospels. Did what he heard of this woman's hurts at her loss of successive husbands colour what he later said about divorce? Towards the end of Jesus' ministry we find the incident recorded in John 8:1–11.[11] He is put on the spot by a group of Pharisees who have caught a woman in the act of adultery. The law says she should be stoned (as should the man whom they have apparently let escape). Would Jesus renege on the law, or sanction a death penalty in defiance of

---

[7] *m.Ket.* 7:9, 10.

[8] J. Bowman, *Samaritan Documents* (Pittsburgh: Pickwick Press, 1977), pp. 298–328. The relevant documents are not clear, and rather later than our period.

[9] *m.Git.* 7:5. 'Here are your divorce papers on condition that you give me 200 *zuz*' (post 70 CE).

[10] *m.Git.* 7:6 (post 70 CE).

[11] Stylistically it fits better at Lk. 21:38, as in the *f*13 family of manuscripts.

Roman authority? Would he condone her offence? The story of how he addressed her sin with gentle understanding, as well as outwitting his opponents, made such an impression on the early church that it would not go away, for all that it could be embarrassing. It encapsulated Jesus' pastoral touch, opening the way for a better future for her, though we do not hear the final outcome. All things being equal, she could expect to be divorced by her husband (or husband-to-be, but had he been in the crowd which sloped off as Jesus wrote on the ground, and what of her father, since in strict Rabbinic usage stoning was reserved for the betrothed?).[12] She was forbidden to marry her paramour.[13] Jesus' priority here is pastoral, defending someone who was in a weak position, both personally and structurally, in a male-dominated community.[14] His severe teaching over divorce needs to be interpreted in this light.

What Jesus wrote is a matter of speculation. R. Johanan b. Zakkai, who was Jesus' contemporary and as an old man rescued Rabbinic Judaism after 70 CE, is credited with abandoning the ordeal of the bitter waters (Num. 5:11–31) on the grounds that 'adulterers became many'.[15] The text he used to justify this was Hosea 4:14, where God declines to punish women ('daughters' as well as 'brides') for adultery because their menfolk are equally adulterous. Were Jesus and R. Johanan aware of each other's thinking?

Jesus – the Rabbi?

And so to Mark 10:1–12 and its related passages (Mt. 19:3–12; Mt. 5:32; Lk. 16:18): it is here that I want particularly to consider not just *what* Jesus said, but *how* and *why* he said it. The

---

[12] *m.San.* 7:4, see also *m.Ket.* 4:3, though Philo indicates a dispute, in Alexandria at least, as to how such cases should be rated – *De Spec. Leg.* III 72. He rated betrothal, which might last up to a year while the bride prepared, as a commitment as strong as marriage.

[13] *m.Yev.* 2:8, *m.Sot.* 5:1 – second century CE – though, if not spoken for, she could be betrothed by intercourse in certain circumstances; *m.Ket.* 4:4: *m.Kidd.* 1:1.

[14] E.g., 'She continues within the control of her father until she enters the control of her husband in marriage' (*m.Ket.* 4:5).

[15] *m.Sot.* 9:9.

pericope is set in Peraea, which was Herod Antipas' domain, near Jericho, where Herod had a winter palace. Since Tertullian, writers have noted that what Jesus was asked about was a touchy subject with Herod, and that John the Baptist had recently been beheaded in connection with Herod's divorce and remarriage within forbidden degrees. The Pharisees' choice of the geographic location to 'test' Jesus increases that significance. He had spoken on the subject before (the collection of his teaching in Mt. 5 touches on it; Lk. 16:18 is set earlier on the same journey).

Jesus' approach is in contrast with the Rabbis', whose concern was with correct procedures and the validity of bills of divorce. That seems the case by the time the Mishnah was compiled a century and more later. Perhaps the way Jesus cites their deduction from Deuteronomy 24:1 at Matthew 5:31 highlights their focus of attention in his day also. *Gittin,* the tractate on Divorce Documents, contains nine chapters and 75 sections. Of these only the last – 9:10 – refers to primary causes for a divorce. The rest deal with the correct form for a deed of divorce, who may write and witness it, how it may be delivered (even to the extent of deciding whether a paper thrown at a wife who is on the roof is valid if it reaches roof level and drifts down again), who may benefit from the financial arrangements if she is only betrothed or widowed while the divorce papers are being delivered, and how long she may continue to eat from Temple-sacrifices if she was married to a Cohen! This is case law, of course, and the modern equivalents go into similar details. With responsibilities for running society were not the Rabbis right to be concerned with details? As a modern Rabbi has pointed out to me, fair and transparent procedure protects people and is right and proper. But the medium had become the message. They tithed mint and cummin, and forgot the weightier principles of the law. The procedure had become the heart of a process. It was common enough for scriveners to write out pro-forma divorce papers for use 'off the shelf'.[16] Even when they do ask what is right,[17] it is to wonder how wide the implied permission for divorce extends in Deuteronomy

---

[16] *m.Git.* 3:2 – second century CE.
[17] *m.Git.* 9:10.

24:1. Is the stress on 'indecency' (*erwah*), or 'in anything' (*dabar*), or 'in his sight'?[18]

My impression from reading *m.Sotah and m.Ketubot* is that despite Shammai's strictures divorce by the husband was relatively straightforward so long as the woman's *ketubah* was paid to her. (One section suggests that if she confessed to adultery, she could still claim her *ketubah*.[19]) The reasons why a divorce might take place are far wider than adultery – if a man indicated on oath that his wife should not eat, or wear, certain things, for instance[20] – so long as *ketubah* is paid. (*Ketubah* is not quite bride-price, but more a surety against death or divorce guaranteeing the wife's maintenance. It could function as a disincentive to divorce.) If adultery were proven, the *ketubah* was forfeit. If there were no witnesses, the ordeal of the bitter waters (Num. 5:11–31) might be applied, and there was a specific flag-stone in the Temple fitted with a ring-handle so that soil from beneath it could be used in the ritual.[21] Is that a sign of frequency, or forethought?

What the Pharisees thought of in terms of routine legal procedure based on textual analysis, Jesus, in the graphic directness we have already seen, categorises as incitement to adultery. 'I tell you, everyone who dismisses his wife (apart from grounds of immorality) makes her suffer adultery, and whoever marries a divorced woman commits adultery' (Mt. 5:32). In terms of literary form, this section of the Sermon on the Mount reads very like a Mishnaic tractate. 'R. Such-a-one says XXX, but the Sages say YYY.' Jesus, or Matthew, could use the form, but the content was strikingly new. Matthew claims 'the people were amazed at his teaching, for he taught as someone with authority, and not like the scribes' (Mt. 7:29). He has cut through the legal formalities like a Gordian knot to expose how people are affected by this casual process. Some modern commentators hint at this point when they suggest that the phrase 'apart from grounds of immorality' means

---

[18] See *Sifre* Deut. 269 (quoted in J. Neusner, *The Rabbinic Traditions about the Pharisees before 70 CE*, Vol. 2 (Leiden: Brill, 1971), p. 37).

[19] *m.Sot.* 1:5, but contra 4:2.

[20] *m.Ket.* 7:2–5.

[21] *m.Sot.* 2:2.

something like 'forget that debate about *porneia* in Deuteronomy 24:1!'[22]

Matthew 5:32 is a difficult text and some manuscripts leave out the final clause. Perhaps it was difficult for those who copied Matthew's text to grasp the implications of Jesus' words, for the word adultery would not normally be used in connection with a woman who was not, or was no longer, married. Adultery offended the husband's rights and honour: it adulterated her for him. Jesus, however, is looking at the situation from the wife's point of view. If she has not been immoral she is being painted as such, since this would absolve the husband from repayment of the *ketubah*. (This is one interpretation of the difficult phrase 'makes her suffer adultery', i.e., 'makes her out to be an adulteress'.) More likely he means that she is forced into going out to look for a new husband, since *ketubot* might be difficult to recover. If she did not have a father's house to return to there was no support outside a family for a woman alone. Her rights and honour are infringed, and she is likely to have to act immorally to find maintenance, even though the traditional laws[23] specified payment of her *ketubah* for maintenance at the time of the divorce – if she had not committed some alleged marital offence. (How much of the Hillel/Shammai debate was about whether dowry had to be repaid, rather than permission to divorce?)

A similar saying is preserved at Luke 16:18. At first appearance this chapter is a random collection, but a common thread is that Jesus is speaking in support of the socially weak (or Luke has collated such teaching, which indicates how he saw a divorced woman). 'Everyone who dismisses his wife and marries another is committing adultery, and the man who marries someone divorced from her husband is committing adultery.' The emphasis is on remarriage as the act that is adulterous; in the first clause the offended party is the first wife; in the second the offended party is the first husband which would be more in accord with conventional wisdom at the time,

---

[22] Summarised in Wenham and Heth, *Jesus and Divorce*, p. 179. While I think this is the force of Jesus' point in Mt. 19, we ask a lot of the grammar of Mt. 5:32 to translate it that way!

[23] *m.Ket.* 4:2, 7–9; 7:1–5; *m.Sot.* 4:1–5 – first and second centuries CE.

except that he had explicitly surrendered his interest in her, unless what we have here is an extension of the Rabbinic rule that the adulterer cannot marry his mistress.[24]

I find it difficult to believe that Jesus was saying that some *metaphysical* bond still exists. Metaphysics was not a Hebrew way of thinking. That is why I am looking for some practical social effect that Jesus was trying to prevent. But he said many things out of keeping with contemporary thinking, so such a novel approach is possible.[25] I believe that Jesus is saying *moral* bonds still exist. The close personal obligations of marriage – and its economic implications connected with *ketubot* – cannot just be shrugged aside by the structurally more powerful party. The emotional bonds still exist, even if the divorcing party denies it. That may seem anachronistic, for the ancient world was less conscious of the psychological scars than we are, but Jesus' understanding of human feelings was out of his time, so such an interpretation is also possible.[26]

Jesus – the Ethical Teacher?

And what was Jesus' motive in talking like this? Was he acting as a legislator, saying to his followers 'Thou shalt not divorce', or was he using a parabolic way of teaching in order to bring out the enormity of divorce? – 'If you divorce and remarry you are as good as breaking one of the ten commandments, so don't think about it! Divorce is not just a simple legal procedure to get right, or pay the right amount for. It is a sin, because of what it does to the other people involved.' I take it in the latter way;[27]

---

[24] *m.Sot.* 5:1.

[25] Even Philo, whose milieu was partly Greek and who devotes a great deal of effort to interpreting Hebrew scriptures in term of Platonic Idealism, does not speak of any metaphysical or ideal reality that is marriage.

[26] Modern American Rabbis have seen in *m.Ket.* 5:6, which indicates how frequently different tradesmen should have intercourse with their wives, a recognition by the ancient Rabbis of women's sexual feelings and needs (E. J. Lipman, *The Mishnah, Oral Teachings of Judaism* (New York: W. W. Norton & Co., 1970)). See also 1 Cor. 7:3–5 – a less detailed parallel.

[27] Is the emphasis on remarriage as adultery an opposition to remarriage *per se*, or a means of discouraging easy divorce by saying 'You can't instantly pair off with someone else'? What evidence is there that Jesus might be thinking of an ontological marriage persisting beyond the phenomenological split?

Jesus gives his followers the moral choice to respond if they
have ears to hear. He acts as an ethicist, not a sergeant-major.

So, to return to Matthew 19 and Mark 10; in an area of mixed
population Rabbinic law restricting divorce procedure to the
man might be less dominant. Among Jews in Egypt it was not
strictly adhered to,[28] while even in *m.Git.* 2:5 a woman may write
her divorce papers! This weakens the argument that Mark
added the clause about a woman initiating divorce (10:12) for a
Roman audience. The way Matthew reports the question sets it
in the context of the debate between the houses of Shammai
and Hillel referred to in *m.Git.* 9:10. Hillel's followers argued
that divorce was permissible for a range of reasons. Shammaites
might well exaggerate this into 'any kind of reason'. The 'test'
could partly have been to get him to take sides.[29]

There may be a contrast between the words 'instruct' (*entello*)
and 'permit' (*epitrepho*). If that is intended, then in Mark Jesus
is asking what the law commands and the Pharisees defensively
quote the permissive legislation on which they based their
arguments. Jesus regards this as secondary to the creation
ordinance. In Matthew too, where the contrast is clearer, Jesus
points out that Moses did not *command* divorce, but *permitted* it
as a concession to human stubbornness, and then reminds
them of God's original plan.[30] In using Genesis 2 as definitive
Jesus is not simply capping one text with another. He appeals to
the way God made the world and the human race. He invites his
hearers to let their moral practice and attitudes be shaped by
the way God acts, just as he had invited people to consider
God's lilies in the field, or his rain falling on the just and on the
unjust, in order to shape their attitude to wealth or vengeance.

[28] L. H. Feldman, 'Palestinian and Diaspora Judaism in the First Century', in
H. Shanks (ed.), *Christianity and Rabbinic Judaism* (London: SPCK, 1993), p. 29.

[29] This was not the only dispute between the two 'houses' – it is just the one
Christians have been told most about! In *m.Sot.* 4:2 the Shammaites appear
more lenient to an accused wife, and in the dispute over grounds for divorce
they limit male freedom more severely.

[30] Malachi appears to have looked back to Gen. 2 in his plea for lifelong
loyalty in marriage (Mal. 2:15). Where Philo, the Rabbis and some Essenes do
cite a 'creation' command is in their expectation that every Jewish man would
marry. The command is to 'be fruitful and multiply' (Gen. 1:29). The houses
of Shammai and Hillel disputed as to whether two children, or two sons were
to be expected, and when divorce of a barren wife was permitted to attain this.

In other words he is working as an ethical teacher, training his hearers to look beyond proof-texts to principles with which to mould their conscience. He is teaching his followers, and any Pharisee who cares to listen, that the governing principle for shaping moral conduct is not a text, but God's character as seen in his works (Mt. 5:45, 48). One-to-one commitment and the rewards that stem from it are what God intended of marriage in creation, and this is the model for the new creation that the Messiah brings. That should be the governing principle both in interpreting the law for the age that is now (he tells the Pharisees), and for living in the age to come which begins from now for those 'to whom it is given'.

In neither Gospel does Jesus say that Moses was wrong to permit divorce. Since his teaching was already known the Pharisees' trick may have been to get him to set aside something in the law because of his views against divorce. What he does say is that divorce was a second best, allowed because of human recalcitrance, not God's original intention. That this might continue to be the case, even after the coming of the kingdom, seems to have been in Jesus' mind too, if (as I believe) the recognition that 'not everyone can take this saying' applies not to the disciples' words 'it is not a good thing to marry' (Mt. 19:10), but to his earlier equation of remarriage and adultery (Mt. 19:9). In his reference to eunuchs Jesus again shows sympathy with those ill-treated by people with power, and the high value he placed on self-sacrifice for his cause. Was he asking this sacrifice of all his divorced followers, or of a limited number to whom was given this gift of singleness? As so often he leaves the question open, inviting his followers to make their own moral decision over 'to whom is it given?' The good teacher teaches his disciples how to be his equal (Mt. 10:25; Lk. 6:40).

Matthew and Mark are describing the same incident, but there are differences, which come to a head with the final saying about divorce and remarriage. If they retold the event in terms appropriate to their audiences, Mark retains Jesus' striking insistence on lifelong commitment and Jesus' defence of a woman's rights when he said her husband could commit adultery 'against her'. Matthew meets the needs of a largely Jewish church in Western Syria, brought up on the Hillel/Shammai debate, by reporting the story in terms of that debate. He leaves out the verse about a woman initiating divorce since it was less relevant for them, and deals with what they would ask about – the duty (as per Shammai and Hillel) to divorce a wife on grounds of her immoral conduct (*porneia*)[31] and the wider permission the Hillelites felt to divorce on other grounds.

It is a mistake to think that Jesus only ever talked about a subject once, and that the relationship between 'parallel' texts is purely literary – one author cribbing off the other and making his own changes for theological motives. As an itinerant preacher Jesus faced the same questions and gave the same messages on different occasions (with at times the same old hecklers!). On one memorable occasion opposite Jericho he was heckled over divorce, and around that incident the two writers collated his teaching on the subject. The memories of each are perhaps prompted by what was relevant for his churches. Thus *both* accounts can be used to give a full picture of Jesus' teaching. They used the conventions of first-century biography, highlighting the character of their subject through his sayings.[32] This filtered the detailed ethical arguments.

So did Jesus allow divorce on the grounds of (the wife's) *porneia*, as only Matthew reports, twice? In the incident as Mark reports it there is no need for such an exception. His emphasis is that divorce is not a creation ordinance, nor part of God's best intentions for humankind. He reminds an audience for whom divorce was a source of prurient gossip that Jesus told them not even to contemplate it. An exception would weaken the point. Matthew's audience approached divorce differently; it had been a subject of theological debate, and they knew that

---

[31] There is a debate as to the meaning of *porneia*. Does use of this word (rather than *moicheia*) reflect a debate which Philo implies was going on in Judaism as to how some quasi-marital offences were to be classified (*De. Spec. Leg.* III, 72 on the seduction of a betrothed woman)? Does *porneia* here actually mean 'within forbidden degrees', as some recent commentators have argued? In this case Matthew merely clarifies what most Jews would take to be obvious. It is hardly an 'exception'.

[32] See R. A. Burridge, 'About People, by People, for People: Gospel Genre and Audiences', in R. Bauckham (ed.), *The Gospels for all Christians* (Edinburgh: T&T Clark, 1998; Grand Rapids, Eerdmans, 1998), p. 113. An even clearer example of Jesus as an ethical teacher is found in his reply to the man who wanted his inheritance. See Lk. 12:13–21.

there was an exception implied (and in Rabbinic teaching *required*) in the law. Where did Jesus stand in that debate? Matthew's account focuses on how Jesus handled the debate, and so his narrative at 19:9 answers the question he began with. He is saying 'actually both Hillel and Shammai got it wrong. Divorce was never God's primary intention – but when it comes to the crunch, Shammai was nearer the mark, though Moses did not *command* divorce even for *porneia.*' Divorce can never be a *mitsvah,* a religious duty. Jesus did recognise the limited 'Matthaean' exception, but taught that no one was bound to take it. That Paul allows another exception (1 Cor. 7:15) suggests that he knew Christ had permitted one.

But Jesus did not lightly accept that people would divorce, for all that it appears significantly common in his milieu. The casual disposal of another human being to whom one has been intimately related is not to be contemplated, and neither is the deliberate sundering of a relationship that fulfils God's plans in creation. Lightly to take on a woman so cast off is in fact connivance with the first husband's sin (if not cashing in on her *ketubah*!), and also tantamount to adultery.[33] Where the wife disposes of her husband she comes under the same criticism. The one party whom Jesus does not criticise is the divorced but otherwise chaste wife; with some sympathy he recognises (Mt. 5:32) that she is forced towards adultery to maintain herself. This was not the kind of treatment that God created people for! Jesus' motive in denouncing divorce was the protection of the weak in a system in which (at least in the hands of Hillel's followers, and Gentile cultures) cynical use of legal niceties cloaked abuse and ill-treatment.

And the Twenty-First Century?

If that was the spirit behind the letter of what Jesus said, we too should act on that motive, asking how we may go and do likewise. We should not insist on a fault-based divorce system on the basis of the Matthaean exception, if it was a concession not

---

[33] H. Danby reports that the Rabbis tried to prevent immediate remarriage, but had to recognise that it happened! See H. Danby (trans.), *The Mishnah* (Cambridge: Cambridge University Press, 1933), p. 297, note.

a principle, and Jesus worked at conciliation (Mt. 18:16). We should not harden our attitude to divorce because scholars narrow down the meaning of *porneia*. But in our society divorce is very common, though there is greater parity between spouses, and remarriage may not follow immediately. Is acceptance of divorce *equitably managed*, with the likelihood of remarriage as the most feasible means of human support, the least bad course of action when a marriage has become a means of abuse, and conciliation (Mt. 18:17) fails? Is divorce in the twenty-first century so casual and unjust that our response has to be as counter-cultural as Jesus', or do attempts at the support of marriage, such as described elsewhere in this book, fulfil his purpose for our time?

INDEX OF AUTHORS

469

Celebrating Christian Marriage

INDEX OF SUBJECTS

477